SWEDEN: Model for a World

Other books by Hudson Strode

NOW IN MEXICO

TIMELESS MEXICO

FINLAND FOREVER

SOUTH BY THUNDERBIRD

THE PAGEANT OF CUBA

THE STORY OF BERMUDA

IMMORTAL LYRICS: AN ANTHOLOGY OF ENGLISH LYRICS

SPRING HARVEST: AN ANTHOLOGY OF ALABAMA STORIES

HUDSON STRODE

SWEDEN

MODEL FOR A WORLD

NEW YORK

HARCOURT, BRACE AND COMPANY

For

NABOTH HEDIN

20896

CONTENTS

ix

FOREWORD

It was on a sunny afternoon in mid-Atlantic in June of 1937 that the idea to see Scandinavia came to me with compelling emphasis. I was on my way to England for a vacation-business trip, and I had just finished a slim volume called *Northern Summer* by a man with a strange name which I had never seen before, Gösta af Geijerstam. The narrator merely related with humor and zest the summer of an almost impecunious Scandinavian writer living with his wife and brood of five blond children on an island, Storevik, in a Norwegian fjord, with a view of "amber-colored mountains, marvelously luminous and clear." The children ran joyously naked about the fields and rocks, turning light biscuit-color in the sun. Though the family often had little to eat except fish and clabber, and sometimes only clabber, their life was exceedingly rich in imponderables.

It lifted the heart to read of such casualness about income, such exhilaration and satisfaction in elemental things like sunshine and water, reaping and fishing, a sheltering cottage and family love. Thoreau's words "that man is richest whose pleasures are the cheapest" came naturally to mind. I did not know then that the author's late father was one of Sweden's renowned writers, or that Sigrid Undset was a frequent visitor to Storevik and godmother to the baby girl. But I knew that if there were, in these discordant, grasping times, such refreshing families who enjoyed calm ecstasy in simple living, I wanted to see the land that bred them. As I closed the book and gazed beyond the deck rail at the blue-green sea, I determined to spend a year in Scandinavia, as soon as I could persuade my university to give me a leave of absence. For from desultory readings and Marquis Childs's *Sweden: The Middle Way,* I was already impressed by the enlightened manner in which the Northern Democracies handled social problems. And since I purposed some day to write a book on the emerging New South with its broadening horizons and mighty industrial expansion, I wanted to see wherein my section of the States might profit from the Scandinavian design for the general welfare.

In February, 1939, my wife and I sailed on the *Drottningholm* for Scandinavia. By the time the war began in September, we had traveled in almost every part of the four Northern Countries and I had eight packed composition books of notes and interviews. We had been to northern Norway by ship, to Finland's Arctic Ocean coast by bus, to the Russian border of southeast Finland, to the German border in Denmark. In Sweden we had traveled virtually everywhere except in the great northern territory known as Lapland.

When the Second World War began, Thérèse and I were in Helsinki, and because I had come to admire greatly the endurance and courage and accomplishments of the Finns, I was moved to write first a book about Finland,* which was published in March, 1941, on the anniversary of the bitter peace treaty with Soviet Russia after the Winter War. The following war years made such a change in the complexion of things that I temporarily laid aside my researches on Scandinavia. Then, before taking up the postponed work, in the summer of 1946 I returned to see how the Scandinavian people fared in the postwar period, to talk with new leaders, to visit places we had missed, and to check up on our enthusiastic impressions of 1939. It was my announced intention to write a book on Denmark, Norway, and Sweden together to be called *Three Stars to the North*. But the urges and shifts of authorship are not to be counted on and, as I proceeded with the chapters on Sweden, I found myself impelled to do a whole volume on Sweden alone. I purpose to write separate books on Denmark and Norway.

In beginning a book on one of the Scandinavian democracies, one is tempted to borrow Laurence Sterne's first sentence from *A Sentimental Journey* and write: "They order this matter better in"—Denmark, or Norway, or Sweden as the case may be.

"Well, if you will pardon me," Dr. Gunnar Heckscher, the well-known young professor of political science, once said to me, "Sweden is really twenty years ahead of the United States."

The statement was so direct and conclusive that I was somewhat taken aback. Dr. Heckscher was entertaining me in his rooms at

---

* *Finland Forever*, New York, Harcourt, Brace.

Uppsala University, where I had gone to interview him in 1939. I was the more impressed because I knew that he was well acquainted with the United States, having lectured at Princeton University for a year and having traveled the country from California to Virginia. I knew, too, that he was no Socialist, but one who had been consistent in voting the Conservative ticket.

In the months that followed, as I observed the Swedish way and looked with intense interest into various phases of Swedish life, Dr. Heckscher's challenging words echoed and re-echoed, begging denial or confirmation. On the whole, he was right. I came to look upon Sweden and the other Northern Democracies as something of a model which other nations might observe with profit.

Though the three Nordic peoples differ almost as much in temperament as the New Englander, the Middle-Westerner, and the Southerner, they are very close together in ideals, objectives, politics, integrity, and sense of values. So in this book when I say Swedish, the reader may in generalities be pleased to substitute the word Scandinavian. While this particular volume is devoted to Sweden alone, it is also in praise of Norway and Denmark, and indeed Denmark has more than often been the pioneer and leader in the advanced social consciousness of the Scandinavians. The physical differences in the countries are obvious. Norway towers over Sweden in the magnificence and splendor of its breathtaking scenery. And Sweden has little of that idyllic charm of Denmark's smiling countryside, filled with delightful, gay-hearted people. Neither so grandly impressive as Norway, nor so alluring as Denmark, Sweden is yet a country so well-ordered, so satisfying, so reassuring and admirable, that one gets that strange sense of peace that comes only when in the presence of one's superior.

"No sort of scientific teaching," wrote Dostoevski, "no kind of common interest, will teach men to share property and privilege with equal consideration for all. Everyone will think his share too small and then will be always envying, complaining, and attacking one another." Yet somehow, with a modicum of strife or bitterness, the Swedes have managed to achieve a harmonious, even-keeled commonwealth, where no man is denied his just rights, and where special merit usually does not go unrewarded. A country without slums or degrading poverty, with no illiteracy, with virtually no unemployment, and with excellent medical care provided for all at low cost and assurance of old age support, Sweden's standard of general culture and attractive living for the low income groups exceeds that of the United States in every particular except the possession of motor cars.

When I read a press release from Sweden dated January 6, 1949, announcing that "five hundred bathtubs a day were being produced at the Gustavsberg porcelain factory of the Swedish Cooperative Union," I thought of Queen Sophia and the march of time in the first half of this century. Today every laborer might have his own private bathtub, but when the mother of the present king took a bath, the people knew it and made a public pleasure. For there was no running hot water in the royal palace in her time. Twice a month liveried flunkies would go to the public bathing establishments for the queen's bath water, and citizens would gather in the street to cheer when the steaming tubs went by. "Oh, no, this wasn't so long ago," said the late Fröken Eva Fröberg, an old but energetic woman leader of Sweden's Conservative Party, who told me the story; "Sophia lived until 1913." "And," she added, "though 'clean' is the word for Sweden that foreign commentators never fail to stress, and though the Swedish reputation for cleanliness goes back into the centuries, all this fuss and fury about frequent deep-tub bathing is comparatively new."

The cooperative wholesale manufacture of bathtubs is hardly more than a bagatelle in the social advancement of Sweden, which has been so remarkable since the death of Queen Sophia. Investigators or mere discerning travelers who have journeyed extensively and observed daily living in foreign countries are agreed that no country in the world today has higher standards of living for the entire commonwealth than Sweden. Not only is this the opinion since World War II, in which Sweden managed to avoid direct involvement, but at the beginning of 1939 a visit to Sweden was like discovering a brave new world that one might hope for in some future age.

The old meaning of the word "proletariat" has disappeared in Sweden. The laboring class that corresponds to the proletariat in other countries is the best educated, best dressed, best mannered and most self-respecting laboring class I have ever observed. And nowhere is the common man closer to the aristocrat in looks, bearing, and behavior. The democratic Swedes as a rule are paradoxically aristocratic in attitude. They recognize and admire distinction, and in their five decades of mounting social advancement the Social Democratic leaders have not striven to pull down the upper classes, but only to uplift the lower classes.

"As a heart at ease flies into no extremes, but is ever on its center," Sweden is a country of few extremes except in good order, cleanliness, and general well-being—and then only extreme by contrast with the rest of the world. In this far northern country one may see a triumphant democracy affecting every aspect of national society and standing unpretentiously and entirely unself-consciously as a model on which to form a better world.

In making this statement I am not unmindful that Sweden is an almost completely homogeneous land—in the course of history she has never been invaded by any foreign power except her Danish cousins—and having only seven million inhabitants * virtually all of one blood and one religious faith (Lutheran) she does not have many of the problems that confront the United States. However, impressed by Childs's eye-opening book on Sweden, President Franklin D. Roosevelt sent a special mission to observe and report on the Swedish patterns. Great Britain's Socialist party leaders closely examined the Scandinavian Democracies before creating the new social services of their present Government. In some respects the British have gone beyond the Swedes and, say the Swedish key men, perhaps too fast, before the people are properly seasoned and prepared for some of the changes. In 1939 several prominent Swedish Labor party men said to me exactly or in effect: "Our message to America is patience. Human nature being what it is, reforms should come gradually through educational processes and not as rash gestures."

Although the title of this book contains the challenging phrase "Model for a World" that may incline some persons to bridle, it is not meant to imply that what is good for Scandinavia would be a workable good for all the peoples of the world today. Surely no discriminating reader will surmise that I advocate, on the one hand, that all nations plunge headlong into socialization or, on the other,

---

* There are some 6,000 Lapps and about 35,000 Finns in the far north.

that I recommend setting up new constitutional monarchies or even extending existing ones beyond their usefulness to the State and the general welfare. Naturally, I do not favor following the Swedes or the Danes or the Norwegians in all their ways. Swedes have their minus as well as their plus, which the perceptive will discern in the text. But in this age of social change, I do think that the leaders and the ordinary citizens of any nation, be it Canada, Uruguay, Spain, or Thailand, to say nothing of the United States, would profit by examining the agreeable Scandinavian compromise between capitalism and socialism to see what might prove constructive blessings to themselves.

The Swedes are somewhat embarrassed by so much praise and wonder from foreign observers. They protest vigorously that their country is no Utopia. But those who have really read Thomas More's conception of that ideal commonwealth would surely admit that, except for its dark months of winter, contemporary Sweden seems more desirable than the imaginary Utopia would have been with its regimentation and undoubted dullness. The Swedes have certainly not consciously tried to set up any Utopia; they have simply evolved a decent, purposeful, and abundant way of life, and proved the exciting fact that true democracy can work, and work well, and yet recognize distinctions. In talking with the head of the Youth Movement of the Social Democratic party whose father had been a labor agitator thirty years before, I was agreeably surprised when the young man said: "After all, education's chief goal is to give men the power of distinguishing what is first rate from what is not."

While the Swedish body politic has in no sense followed Rousseau with intentional awareness, it indeed seems to have worked on his theory that man is by nature good and that the social order can be made to express that goodness.

Like its own tall men, Sweden is a long, upstanding country, reaching almost a thousand miles from south to north, and at its widest no more than three hundred miles in breadth. The distance between its most northern and most southern limits approximates the mileage between London and Rome. In shape it resembles the state of California. With its 173,349 square miles, including its lakes, it is larger than California by about 15,000 square miles, and it is about three and a half times as extensive as England or Alabama.

One of the first things that strikes visitors happily is that there are not too many people in Sweden, but plenty of breathing space. The number of persons in Sweden—6,924,888 on January 1, 1949—is a little less than in California and almost 1,000,000 less than in the city of New York.

Though Sweden ranks fifth in area among the countries of Europe, it is seventeenth in population. In population density, there are only forty-three persons to a square mile, which may be compared to 470 in Great Britain and 700 in Belgium. And with some 96,000 lakes and 4,600 miles of seashore, claustrophobia is virtually an unknown psychosis.

A century ago almost eighty per cent of the Swedish people depended for a livelihood on agriculture and auxiliary occupations. As recently as 1870, persons who lived on farms composed a little more than seventy per cent of the population. With the revolutionary change from manual to machine production that swept Europe and the United States in the last quarter of the nineteenth century, the agricultural population declined, and by 1945 only thirty-one per cent of Sweden's people lived in rural districts.

Although one-seventh of Sweden lies above the Arctic Circle, because of the Gulf Stream the winters are not nearly as severe as might be expected. In Stockholm, the mean temperature in January, the coldest month, is about 28° F. The summers are generally delightful, and occasionally they can be quite warm; the Stockholm thermometers touched an unprecedented 95° F. one day in 1948.

The Swedes have long enjoyed a reputation for taking care of their natural resources. For decades a national forestry board has made it imperative that every felled tree be replaced by a young one. And no trees may be cut until the authorities mark them ready.

Sweden's economic soundness through the years is attested by the fact that the Nobel awards have remained close to $40,000 each in value ever since the first ones offered in 1901. In worst depression years they barely went below $30,000. In 1931 they were as high as $45,000, and in the postwar year of 1948 they amounted to $44,400. Virtually all the Nobel money is invested in Swedish securities, and the dividends remain much the same whether a Conservative or a Labor Government is in power.

Sweden's stability in economics may be compared to the dependability and incorruptibility of her law courts. From ancient times comes a favorite Swedish maxim: "Where law is obeyed, the country prospers." The Swedish laws are plainly worded, their meaning clear. Justice is not to be distorted by lawyers' tricks. The Swedish way of life is synonymous with "freedom based on law."

As a sympathetic observer, I have attempted in this book to give an informal account of the Swedish design for living; to portray, as it were, the image of Swedish democracy. Both in 1939 and 1946 I was interested in almost everything from consumers' cooperatives and old-age homes to glass-making and modern architecture, from opera and smörgåsbord to sports and prison reform. I count my friends among labor leaders and capitalists, farmers and factory workers, shop keepers and intellectuals, artists and landed gentry and some members of the royal family. Through the chapters I touch on various determinants by which Swedes steer their modern course. For instance, the Swedes' devotion to nature and the great out-of-doors has caused industry to be decentralized, with factories and workers' cottages set by lakes in deep woods, where industrial fatigue is minimized and any edges of economic hardships lose their sharpness.

I have endeavored to note the ruling motives of Sweden's aspirations, the quality of her ethics, and her theories and principles of taste. In other words, I have tried to set forth the means by which Sweden meets the challenge and exigencies of modern civilization. And in doing so, I unfold some of the particular delights of traveling through the land.

In attempting to present a living picture of democratic Sweden and the Swedes themselves, by no means do I describe all the places I have visited. I have selected only half a dozen significant provinces to write about, and I tell the story exactly as it happened to me personally when I visited them. I have left out descriptions of many memorable spots like the idyllic village of Gränna in Småland, at pear-blossom time undoubtedly the most charming of all the little towns in Sweden. Though I have visited more than three-score Swedish industries in operation and seen countless workers' homes from vestibule to kitchen, I have selected lesser-known industries like the Orrefors Glassworks to write about rather than the much-publicized Sandviken Steel Works, with its attractive, model housing arrangements for the employees scattered through the woods. In a few instances, however, I must plead guilty to repetition; but I repeat deliberately, because sometimes material used in one section may be needed for emphasis or at least as cross-reference in another. In all cases I have kept the Swedish spelling of their towns—for instance, Göteborg rather than the Anglicized Gothenburg—and I have followed the Swedish histories in using Gustav rather than Gustaf for the Christian name of kings and men. For variety and the reader's sake, I have arranged the order of the sections arbitrarily.

In endeavoring to give the flavor of Swedes at work and at home, I have recorded numerous verbatim conversations. I try to show the Swedes as they are in their daily routines, in the hope that the reader will get the feel of the country of which that urbane Czech Karel Čapek wrote consummately: "The wanderer in this strange land feels more of a man and a gentleman than anywhere else in the world."

HUDSON STRODE

Cherokee Road
Tuscaloosa, Alabama
July 14, 1949

A/B Flyg Trafik

Aerial view of center of Stockholm with Nordiska Museum on Djurgården Island in foreground and the Royal Palace in center of background. The water in the back is Lake Mälaren and all the other various bodies of water seen are inlets from the Baltic Sea.

Strode

The Orpheus Fountain of Carl Milles stands to one side of the façade of Ivar Tengbom's Concert House.

Svenska Turistföreningen

Stockholm's Town Hall, sometimes called "the most remarkable building since the Renaissance."

Poppel

A simple Stockholm apartment house built by the Swedish Housing Cooperative Society situated on Reymersholm Island in Lake Mälaren.

Loggia entrance before modern Chapel of the Holy Cross at the Forest Crematory, Stockholm, where a funeral including casket, cremation, and urn may be had for one hundred twenty-five dollars.

Poppel

H. P. Persson

Summer evening near Leksand, Dalarna.

Svenska Turistföreningen

The towers of the ancient city wall of Visby.

Coze

Typical young country girl from Värmland.

Afternoon coffee on a farmhouse veranda in Dalarna.

Köpman

Olander

Skiing by the light of Lapland's midnight sun.

A hiker pauses to sun his bare back amid the snows of Lapland.

T. Dahll

Bertil Norberg

Crown Prince Gustav Adolf (second from right) fishing on the Tärna Alv in Lapland.

Svenska Turistföreningen

King Gustav III, the eighteenth century patron of arts and letters, in the painting by Alexander Roslin at Gripsholm Castle.

Gullers

Some city kids on free vacation have finished their mugs of afternoon milk at Flaten Beach on the Baltic, and are now waiting for the bus to take them back to Stockholm.

Strode

Workmen's cottages at Gränna in pear blossom time.

The workmen's dwellings of the Cooperative Union on Kvarnholmen Island are all of the most modern type.

Svenska Turistföreningen

Bertil Norberg

Timber floating is a chief seasonal occupation in North Sweden.

S. Larson
Heurlin

Royal Swedish Airforce

Aerial view of the sixteenth century Castle of Vittskövle in Skåne, one of the handsomest strongholds still used as a private dwelling.

Top left—Trolleholm Castle built in the fourteenth century is home of Count Gustaf Trolle-Bonde.

Bottom left—One of the most graceful and home-like of the Skåne Castles is that of Vrams Gunnarstorp erected in 1632 in Dutch Renaissance style with sand-stone ornaments. It is particularly famous for its magnificent park with extraordinary boxwood hedges.

Jaerke

Interior of Malmö Municipal Theater, which can accommodate 2,200 spectators when back auditorium walls are lifted for standees.

The façade and courtyard of the modern Malmö Municipal Theater opened in 1944.

Jaerke

I

PLACES, PROVINCES, AND PHASES OF DAILY LIFE

I.

Stockholm, City of Space and Grace

Show me your city, and I will tell you what are the cultural aims of its population.

—ELIEL SAARINEN

FLIGHT AND REMEMBERING

I WAS ROUTED to fly to Scandinavia by way of Gander and return by Goose. But because a stubborn cloud squatted on the Nova Scotia airfield just as we were ready to leave New York and would not budge, our plane was forced to go farther north to Goose Bay in Labrador to refuel for the ocean hop. On my return I had to cancel a booked flight via Iceland which would have brought me back by Goose, and I flew from Prestwick in Scotland direct to Gander. It made no difference, because it was just as pleasant one way as the other.

In the upper air, after we rose from the Labrador runway at eleven o'clock at night and headed towards the Atlantic, all was smooth and contenting. The blanket-tucked passengers slept out most of the hours over the ocean. As I reclined in the long seat of the American Overseas airliner, I opened the drawn window curtains slightly and peered at the serene pale midnight sky. Looking up from within this miracle of winged locomotion, I thought of the smokehole at the top of a Laplander's tent of reindeer hides, through which he can nightly fix his gaze on the everlasting mystery of the firmament just as I was doing now. Though modern man had not changed the verities by his inventions, he had indeed accelerated time and telescoped distance. Stockholm was only a day and night distant from New York, with three generous stopovers along the way.

3

No such trip by regular airplane flights had been possible in 1939, when I had gone and returned by ocean liner. Both voyages by sea had turned out to be more exciting than those by air. We had sailed in an icy February on the steady old *Drottningholm,* and somewhere south of Greenland, Captain Ericson had turned north into the teeth of a terrific storm to rescue twenty Norwegian seal hunters, who had radioed distress but could not give their exact position. For two days and nights like the good Samaritan the Swedish-American liner searched the tempestuous sea for the lost men. Finally when hope was almost extinguished on both sides, we found the disabled little tub, and in a blinding hailstorm, with waves forty feet high, ship's officers and sailors volunteered to effect the most sensational rescue I have ever witnessed. When we returned to the States in the fall on the last regular run the *Gripsholm* was to make during the war, the passengers were required to sleep with life preservers within reaching distance, since the *Athenia* had been blown up a few weeks before. So both those extraordinary sea voyages had held hazards and excitements that by comparison made the swift trip through the thin air seem as calm as a pony-cart ride down a rural lane.

As our plane approached a rim of land in the other hemisphere and we advanced our watches six hours to make up for the difference in sun time, I was thinking of our first impression of Sweden the 1st of March in 1939. After that grim tempest-tossed trip, which made us three days late, Thérèse and I had found Göteborg bathed in brilliant sunshine and touched with intimations of spring. Green grass had ventured through the snow, and little round flowers called "golden balls" made bright pools of yellow under trees. Everything was extraordinarily clean. The sailors' district seemed all new with neat, comfortable houses. It was exciting to find no slums and see no squalor in a seaport of 300,000 inhabitants, where the harbor bustled with international shipping, and the greatest shipbuilding activity in Scandinavia was going full blast. There were space and light in the business sections. In some of the busiest streets parks extended along one side, and, where the snow had vanished, grassy lawns reached to the very edge of the pavement. In a splendid hilly park elegant, pink-cheeked old gentlemen, wearing Persian lamb caps and carrying sticks, briskly took their morning constitutionals, while under-school-age children, watched by nursemaids, played in winter snow or spring grass as the mood prompted.

An attractive young man, employed by the Swedish-American Line, came to meet us because of mutual friends and drove us about in his new Ford. He turned out to be a baron, who worked for his living, though he bore one of Sweden's oldest and noblest names. He was proud to point out manifestations of the admirable state of general welfare. We were struck by the modern architecture in hospitals and churches, in the engineering college and in primary schools, and in apartment houses for workers.

The seventeenth century and the second quarter of the twentieth had made the most impressive imprints on the city's atmosphere. The inner town, with its seventeenth-century buildings, is divided from the outer town by a moat, laid by Dutch engineers for the twenty-five-year-old King Gustavus Adolphus, who founded Göteborg in 1619. The focal point of the outer town is the modern Civic Center, Götaplatsen, one of the most arresting squares of our times, completed in 1935, with the modernistic Concert Hall, the new Municipal Theater, and the Art Museum, with Carl Milles's Poseidon Fountain before it. We were told of the personal pride of Göteborg's merchant princes and shipbuilders, who delighted in continued munificence to make their city ever more beautiful.

On the way to the young baron's home for luncheon, we stopped to see orchids, great glasshouses full of exquisite, rare specimens, as fine as any I had ever admired in Brazil or Colombia. Because of their exotic nature the orchids of the Botanical Gardens are a greater pride and joy to the citizen of Göteborg than the new Maritime Museum, with its modern lighting and superlative arrangement.

What impressed us as much as anything else that first morning in Sweden was the fact that Scandinavians are so very much like the better type of Americans. One feels at home with them at once, as one could never quite feel on first meeting Spaniards, Russians, Italians, Frenchmen, or Germans, or even the Irish.

Within our host's house, there was only one feature that was definitely different and Swedish, and we were to come across it in every Swedish home or apartment in which we were entertained. It was the open vestibule furnished with a mirror and a narrow dressing table set with silver-backed brush and comb, powder and what-not, for repairing one's toilet, after topcoats and hats had been removed, before being received by the hostess.

With the sun pouring in the high windows of the dining room over vases of narcissi and bright pots of azaleas, we had a delicious luncheon. When we were put on the Stockholm train, letters of introduction to friends in the capital were slipped into our hands, along with an airmail edition of the London *Times* and our seat reservations. So our March introduction to those far-northern latitudes could hardly have been more auspicious.

Our arrival at Stockholm that night, though in a snow flurry, was as cheering in its way as that at Göteborg had been; for at Hotel Stockholm we found a corner sitting room and bedroom waiting for us, with tulips, daffodils, and anemones, and sprigs of budding elm sent to my wife by Madeleine Hamilton, who had crossed on the *Drottningholm* with us.

The hotel is as noted for its absolute modernity as for its odd situation. It begins six stories up, occupying the two top floors of a handsome block-big office building, designed by Ivar Tengbom, one of Sweden's foremost architects of our time. All chaste white and silver and blue, with blond furniture and excellent low modern beds, its soundproof rooms, though smallish, are as comfortable as they are attractive. The charm and efficiency of its manager, Madame Arpi-Bertil, are known in London and New York; her taste and supervision extend to the design of the breakfast china and the manners of the porters and maids (who are each personally trained by her).

Our sitting room looked down upon the bare-branched treetops of King's Park that extends to the quay. The lights scattered through the park made it look as though the trees themselves were fitfully illuminated. A full moon shone on the thin blanket of new-fallen snow that covered the roofs and enhanced the cool beauty of the night. It was very cozy in the rooms and we went to bed with high anticipation of the Scandinavian year to follow.

Now on this July morning seven years later I was remembering that first happy day in Sweden, when the signal to fasten seat belts flashed. Our plane was coming down on Irish soil by the River Shannon which flowed through sun-drenched meadows decked with wild flowers. We stopped long enough at the international airport for a hearty roast-beef luncheon and a stretch of legs. Then we flew low straight across Ireland, the gray Irish Sea, and England's emerald middle. We dined above the North Sea, and then paused for a while at the Copenhagen Airport, bounded by the blue strait called Öresund and by scented fields stacked with new-cut hay and spotted with fluttering sea gulls.

As we rose from the field and flew up the watery strip of Öresund that divides Denmark from Sweden, the pink-lavender glow of a nine-o'clock sunset turned Copenhagen's copper spires to green-gold, while a half-moon silvered the Swedish plains of Skåne, with their moated castles and prosperous farms. Then came the somber woods with frequent lakes scattered among them like pewter platters of odd shapes. From the plane one could see that the electric lights of main streets of towns led invariably to a lake's edge.

Though the upper sky took on the deep bluish tinge of grapes, the vanished sun continued for a long time to make crayon-like streaks of flamingo pink on the horizon's pale gold rim. Then the northern twilight suffused everything with a soft bath of silver, and this was as close to darkness as comes the Swedish summer night.

"LOOK A LONG TIME"

When the gleam of Stockholm became visible, the pilot, my friend George Burgard, of Burma Flying Tiger fame, sent for me to come up to the cockpit. Water lay on either side the golden haze that was Sweden's capital. To the west, it was Lake Mälaren with its seventy miles' extent and its scores of verdant islands and multi-form peninsulas. To the east, it was the Baltic Sea, where the thousand little islands of the rock-ribbed Archipelago protect the city like a haphazard guard of honor twenty miles deep. And all about the luminosity, like attracted moths, trees surged from south and from north, filling the spaces that were not buildings or inlets or canals.

In the very heart of the city, the long thrusting arm of the Baltic and the capricious Lake Mälaren meet and divide and sub-divide the site of Stockholm into chunks of many shapes and sizes, making beauty out of diversity and offering excuse for quantities of picturesque bridges, great and small, high and low. Not even Venice is richer in bridges.

Some islands rise in sheer escarpments, and others lift themselves barely above the water's edge. But the webs of electrical illumination linked them all together in slender chains of flame-gold. Stockholm's shimmering incandescence reflected in the myriad waterways gave the scene redoubled loveliness. Numerous cities have exciting water fronts, but none I know have water before, behind, around, between, beneath; flowing here in natural curves, confined there in long, slender, man-made diagonals. With the exception of Rio de Janeiro, where mountains tumble dramatically into bays, Stockholm has more variety in contour than any other capital of the globe. By night, Rio is fantastically beautiful, with a palpable, sensual quality that can be disturbing. Stockholm's is perhaps a more satisfying beauty, for the multiplicity of its lights and waterways keep a certain decorum in creating enchantment and offer peace in the same breath with excitement.

When we landed at the Bromma Airport sometime before midnight, a Swedish friend came forward to meet me, bearing a message as precious as a jeweled key to the city. He had secured for me a front room at the Grand Hotel, where the view is unsurpassed by that of any hotel in Europe.

The room with the magic casement proved a reality. I turned off the lights, pulled back the dark velvet hangings, which had been drawn tight to shut out the white summer night, and feasted my eyes on a collection of the city's chief glories. My third-floor window looked direct to the the granite bridge called Norrbro, which joins the island of the Old Town with the richest segment of the mainland. Under the bridge the salty Baltic and the sweet water of Lake Mälaren meet and commingle in perpetual foam-flecked delight. The slender arm of the sea lay between me and that magnificent architectural pile, the Royal Palace, built early in the eighteenth century and designed by Sweden's greatest architect of all times, Nicodemus Tessin the Younger. Behind the palace rose the towers of three historic churches: St. Gertrud's, Storkyrkan (the cathedral), and Riddarholm, with its airy spire of iron lace and the tombs of most of Sweden's kings and queens.

High to the left and beyond this island known as "The City Between the Bridges" rose the cliffs of Söder, with villas along the top, and at sea level the docks marked for London, Hamburg, Antwerp, Riga. To the near right side of the swirling confluence of waters lay the square honoring Gustavus Adolphus, Sweden's greatest hero-king. There, facing his bronze replica on horseback, stood on opposite sides the Foreign Office and the Royal Opera House. Between the Opera and the hotel was the beginning of the flowering, tree-lined King's Park, once a royal promenade.

The little island between Gustavus Adolphus Square and the Royal Palace held the House of Parliament on its high embankment and down at the water's edge an out-of-doors cooperative café embowered in willows, with Carl Milles's famous statue, "The Sun Singer," facing the east and the harbor where both merchant ships and visiting foreign men-of-war docked. Directly beneath the hotel's front windows were moored three small white passenger steamers that plied the waters of the Archipelago. Farther along, beneath the quay that curved up the natural incline to the Opera, reposed the fishing boats of Stockholm old-timers, who still catch Baltic smelts in great round basket nets right under the King's walls.

In the middle distance, three bridges beyond the Norrbro, rose the noble silhouette of the Town Hall's tower, with its topping three gold crowns hanging like a cluster of stars in the pale, starless sky.

It was not merely the beauty of architecture and the historical associations or the variety of contours with their patterns of electrical illumination that accounted for the fascination and satisfaction of the scene. It was the unearthly quality of the midnight light from the heavens, which fell upon the solid and most rational capital city, like a faëry gossamer of white-blue transparency. The façades of stone and marble, the quay and the cobbled street glimmered dimly, as if possessing the properties of glowworms. Mystery and tenderness blended in the summer night.

With the sea gulls and civilians settled in sleep, the city lay wrapped in country-like stillness. The only stirring creatures to be seen were young sailors, winding down along the quay singly or in pairs or threes. They would pass the hotel on their way to the coral-colored naval headquarters on Skeppsholmen, the bridged island out of sight to the left beyond the National Art Museum. Occasionally one of them would swerve in his tracks, but who could say for sure whether the unsteadiness was due to strong drink and not, perhaps, to the night's romantic spell?

For in my third-floor window I was enjoying a gentle delirium myself. I recalled Rodin's last words to Carl Milles and felt justified. "Carl," Rodin had said, "whenever you see beauty, look a long time."

So I continued to look at Stockholm for a long time. And as I gazed across the dark silvery water to the old palace, I remembered the last time I had been within its courts. It was a time of anxiety, the second World War was only six days old. At the request of his Social-Democratic ministers, the King had called an extraordinary session of the Riksdag—the major attention of the Government was now perforce to be turned from social welfare to national defense. This was the first time since 1919 that a national emergency warranted such an event. The regular annual opening of Parliament occurs the first fortnight of January, and always at the Royal Palace, even though in this democratic country the king is never permitted to attend any of the subsequent sessions in the House of Parliament.

My Social-Democratic friend, Nils Horney, foreign editor of the Stockholm Labor paper, *Morgontidningen,* had secured for me a coveted seat in the press gallery at the opening of this extraordinary session on Saturday, September 9, 1939.

Horney and I arrived at the west entrance to the palace courtyard just as the King's gilded carriage was going out through another gateway, bearing His Majesty to attend a brief preliminary prayer service in the near-by Cathedral Storkyrkan. Within the palace we climbed a broad curving sweep of marble stairs between lines of the Royal Guardsmen, the cream of Swedish youth, dressed in Charles XII uniforms, with chamois-colored jackets, silver breastplates, and black tricornered hats trimmed with gold braid. Behind the guards along the stair-wall hung tapestries of deep blue and faded yellow. And the proud young men stood as motionless as the woven figures behind them, with their gun butts resting on the stair treads, bayonets at a sharp angle.

In a reception room, ladies-in-waiting stood by the windows, in black taffeta evening dresses with puffed sleeves, the regulation court costume of ladies of rank below princesses—a Swedish innovation of bygone days to prevent extravagance and feminine rivalry.

Gentlemen in broadcloth and gold braid were coming up, making noiseless gestures of clicking heels as they bent over the ladies' hands.

We were ushered through a series of rooms made into corridors of gold tooled leather screens, and then down a short flight of blue carpeted steps into the Hall of the Realm, where on the right rose a broad stage with a silver throne. The three hundred and eighty members of the Riksdag were already seated, and the thirty of us with press invitations sat in a two-rowed gallery along a side wall a few feet above the floor. My seat was in the upper row of the narrow gallery, second nearest the throne stage, and between those of my socialist friend and the Swedish woman correspondent of the *Christian Science Monitor*. As the personages arrived, my two companions identified them for me.

Over the back of the empty throne was draped an elaborate cloak of ermine with a long train of ruby-colored velvet, richly embroidered with small golden crowns. To the right of the throne stood a small square table covered with blue velvet embossed with more golden crowns, and on it lay the jeweled crown, which King Gustav V has never actually worn at any ceremony.* On the same table were other symbols of vanished regal power—an orb, a sceptre, and a horn with anointing oil. At a signal, two high officers entered and took their places at right and left just behind the throne. Eight other dignitaries came and ranged themselves at the back of the stage. Then the ladies of the court arrived, carrying their black trains over their white-gloved arms, and took their places according to official protocol in the gallery opposite that for the press. In a corner of the stage itself was a lower box where three ladies now entered. The first two were the top ladies-in-waiting, with names and titles centuries old, and a third, for whom the seat nearest the throne was reserved, was the wife of the Social-Democratic Prime Minister Per Albin Hansson; she had once been a lady's maid and a milliner. She was followed by wives of other members of the Government. Of the diplomats, the Norwegian ambassador with his wife entered first, followed by Madame Kollontay, the grand old ambassadress of Soviet Russia. Then came the German and French ministers and stood side by side. Following the last of the foreign diplomats came the Bishop of Stockholm

* See reign of King Gustav in Section III.

adorned with the pale-blue silk of the Order of the Seraphim. And last of the commoners came the commander of the Swedish armed forces, his breast gleaming with medals, though he had never led Swedish soldiers to war, Sweden having been at peace for a hundred and twenty-five years.

In an upper box above Mrs. Hansson and her companions now appeared three royal princesses: first, Sibylla, wife of the Crown Prince's eldest son, Prince Gustav Adolf; then Princess Ingeborg, Danish-born sister-in-law of the King and mother of the Crown Princess Martha of Norway and of the late Queen Astrid of the Belgians. Last, to the front seat of honor, came Crown Princess Louise, sister of England's Earl Mountbatten of Burma. All three ladies wore their court jewels and evening gowns in pale colors. As a hush fell upon the assembly, the princesses came to the front of their box, one by one, and each made three sweeping bows, two to the members of Parliament and the spectators, and one toward the empty throne.

Then came the hereditary princes of the royal house to occupy the six chairs on either side of the throne: the aged King's two aged brothers, Prince Carl and Prince Eugen, two of his grandsons, Prince Gustav Adolf and Prince Bertil, and then his sons, Prince Wilhelm and Crown Prince Gustav Adolf. Finally, the octogenarian monarch himself entered, spruce in military attire, and seated himself on the ermine-draped throne. When he rose to address his Labor-dominated Parliament which he saluted as "Swedish men and women," he began with the time-honored statement, "Sweden's relations with other powers are good."

The gravity of the world situation, the sadness for the inevitable suffering to come, and the alerting of Sweden to potential danger were all in the speech, and, most important, the country's determination to hold to a course of armed neutrality in keeping with national honor and dignity.

The pomp and ceremony seemed as anachronistic in these democratic days as the occasion was solemn and ominous. In September, 1939, one wondered if royalty in any guise would survive the new-lighted conflagration that might spread to the globe's far corners. While I doubted if the Social-Democrat at my side or any member of his party on the floor would deliberately abolish the royal symbols of Swedish nationality and tradition, if it lay in his power, yet in the imminent upheaval of a world war, the end to such things might naturally come about. I thought I might be witnessing one of the last acts of its kind in history. But now, seven years later, as I again looked out across the water to the splendidly proportioned palace that loomed so assuredly strong in the twilight of 1 A.M., the structure continued to symbolize Swedish balance and that "sweet reasonableness" that has attended all the remarkable advance in Scandinavian social ideals and practices.

BRIGHT IS THE MORNING

As Stockholm glimmers enchantingly on a summer's night, by day the city sparkles. The radiance of morning falling on the rippling waterways makes a scintillation that infiltrates the atmosphere, freshening marble, brick, and bronze, as well as foliage and complexions. Beneath the cloudless azure, the color tone of Stockholm seems champagne, chrome, and salmon, with roofs and towers of copper-green and russet, and water of aquamarine. In the distance the three gilded crowns poised above the Town Hall's tower suggest birds of golden plumage hovering in perpetual good omen.

The Swedish national colors, blue and yellow like the sky and the sun, fly from flag poles along the North Bridge and before the Parliament House. Immaculate white ships take on morning passengers departing for holiday destinations in the Archipelago. Business executives arrive by private motorboat from their summer places on the sea. Bicycles flash along in the sunshine, pedaled by bare-headed, fair-haired riders. Automobiles move swiftly, but noiselessly, for in Stockholm horns are outlawed. Despite the purposeful metropolitan activity, a pleasant quiet abides, for factories are forbidden to whistle, and Swedes are a soft-spoken people. Everything in sight shines with cleanliness, not a spot of grime or litter anywhere. The waste receptacles, enameled in light-blue and white, are so attractive and convenient they seem to invite contributions of newspapers and cigarette butts. A Swede would not think of leaving an orange peeling on the quay. A six-year-old child knows better than to discard a candy wrapper thoughtlessly. Civic pride in Stockholm begins with the youngsters, whose faces look as well washed as the city streets.

In this sparkling, prosperous city, so advanced in social welfare, yet graced with a patina of aristocratic tradition, one has an uncommon sense of well-being from his first waking in the morning. Part of the harmonious feeling comes from the spaciousness made by the waterways and the belts of greenery, and part from the politeness and self-respect and good looks of the well-dressed, healthy people on the streets. There is something in the air that says Stockholm is made for living, for the enjoyment of all its citizens, and not for mere getting and spending. As I go down a street scented with the fragrance of lime trees, I have the impression that right has triumphed in a beautiful world.

Postwar Stockholm differed from the capital of 1939 in only three noticeable respects. First, before apartment houses great solid rectangles of split birch-wood logs were piled almost a story high with consummate neatness, sometimes in the parkways, sometimes down the centers of boulevards. The novelty was due to war-begotten shortages in foreign coal. Second, a mighty building program was in full swing, not only in apartment houses, but in schools and extra bridges and a vast and most modern hospital. But the construction was chiefly at the city's edges and beyond into the fields and woodlands and outlying islands, where there would always be space and light and greenery and more than often a view of water.

Within the commercial center of the city the third innovation was portable gardens—modernistic white pottery tubs of blooming flowers set out in artistic arrangements in groups of threes or fives on sidewalks and at street corners. For the public's delectation yellow and bronze snapdragons flowered in public squares, pink and white cornflowers at boat landings, variegated asters at tram stations, blue delphinium at entrances to underground public toilets. At first I wondered if the growing flowers were for sale. But they were merely the city gardener's new conception for adding sweetness and light to business districts.

The commerce of Stockholm has always been beguiled of some of its material aspect by numerous small parks and squares. In the midst of the most busy section is pretty Berzelii Park, with flowering shrubs, benches for enjoying the band concerts, and a huge restaurant called Berns', with flower-bright balconies and with refreshment tables spreading out beneath venerable shade trees. Just east of the park and the Royal Dramatic Theater begins the fashionable shorefront boulevard, Strandvägen, which faces a blue bay, with private yachts and small passenger boats that go to Visby and Copenhagen. Where the shops on Strandvägen cease, foreign legations and expensive apartment houses begin, and the boulevard ends characteristically like so many Stockholm thoroughfares in an extensive park spotted with museums.

Within the city limits, besides the miles of waterways that make for healthy breathing, twenty-five hundred acres are given over to well-tended parks, which is all the more remarkable, since one may reach open country in a fifteen-minute bus ride, or the open sea in a half-hour by train. As civic pride goes hand in hand with the Swedish sense of personal rights and human dignity, so the rural heritage is implicit in the municipal arrangements. Walk in any direction for five minutes and one is bound to come upon trees or water or both together. For the islands are generally edged with green, the parks have little streams and fountains, and thirty-five wading pools for children are scattered about the city.

Stockholm's spaciousness is due not only to its God-given topography but, in great measure, to its enlightened municipal planners. Considerably more than a third of the city has been built since 1930. But by 1930 it was virtually impossible to find anything that might be truly designated as a slum. The Swede's inherent passion for orderliness and cleanliness makes the slum idea particularly abhorrent to him. Fully forty years ago the city began the clearing of unhygienic, dark, cramped tenements. The Administrative Council bought up large tracts of land in the suburbs and sold plots to home builders with ninety per cent credit on the entire cost of structure, land, and planting.* So the outskirts of Stockholm are really clusters of little garden cities, where individuality and variety are achieved more in the landscaping than in the style of cottage.

The new apartment houses, both privately owned and cooperative, are obviously designed practically for a practical people, with emphasis on space, light, and playgrounds. They are all painted in

* See section on Cooperative Housing.

gentle colors. No Stockholmer may indulge his caprice and paint a house "a color that cries." Freedom in this democratic land does not mean that one may offend the sensibilities of a neighborhood. A builder must submit his plans and his color scheme to a façade committee, which jealously guards the city's architectural harmony.* While the cream-colored apartment houses are sometimes criticized for their functional severity and their standard picture windows, monotony is broken by bright awnings of royal blue or rust or orange or chartreuse, as well as by profuse balconies with flower boxes.

MARKET SQUARE WITH MUSIC

The emphasis Swedes put on flowers as amenities of daily living, the stranger notes almost as quickly as he does the role that running water plays in enhancing the beauty of Stockholm's buildings.

The most memorable spot in Stockholm to exist without foreground or background of water is the square called Haymarket (Hötorget), just off King's Street, one of the busiest commercial thoroughfares in the city. But Hötorget has a fluidity all its own and abounds in color. It is a movable flower market, and under white canopies green vegetables are also sold and pink shrimp and silver-scaled fish. The counting and weighing and wrapping are done in the very shadow of Ivar Tengbom's porticoed Concert House to the unheard melody of Orpheus. For with lyre held aloft, the magnificent young God of Music stands on tiptoe in bronze splendor in the center of Carl Milles's most evocative fountain. The multi-statued group is set on a granite foundation before the last three of the ten towering, twelve-sided columns topped with modern adaptations of Corinthian capitals. As Orpheus eternally plucks his lyre, four dead youths and four dead maidens rise in wonderment from the nether world, drawn up by the lyric magic. They are long and slender figures, both male and female, narrow-hipped, small-buttocked. And they are ever in graceful motion in an ecstasy of listening, some with raised fists clenched against the sweetness and some with heads declined and hands hanging loose in surrender to the spell. The whole grouping has a marvelous sense of movement. The fingers of

* See section on Cooperative Housing.

Orpheus' right hand are so patently in the act of making music; the listening figures are so perceptibly ascending.

To me this Haymarket Square, where citizens have congregated for three hundred years, is an epitome of the good Swedish life. In the Concert House, besides the weekly programs of the State-subsidized symphony orchestra and those of foreign artists, the gala ceremony at which the king hands out the golden Nobel medals is held each December, and here the Swedish Cooperative Union holds it annual sessions. Across the square on the west is the great cooperative department store P.U.B., where working people and others can buy good clothes and attractive house furnishings at moderate prices. For some tourists the many-storied P.U.B. holds more interest than the Milles statue, because Greta Garbo once sold hats there. In any case fortuitously Haymarket Square commemorates these two great living Swedish artists Milles and Garbo.

The ten stone steps that extend the full width of the Concert House's façade have their summer quota of sun-seekers, who sit absorbing the rays, while enjoying the kaleidoscopic movement in the square.

The flower market spread out between the two landmarks, the Concert House and the department store, scents the morning air with a blend of garden-fresh perfume. The stands are closely packed and laden with simple meadow flowers and cultivated blossoms, all at extraordinarily low prices: lilies and roses and enormous sweet peas, marigolds and cornflowers, gladioli and tiny linnaeas, named for the great botanist Linnaeus.

As I rambled about the square in full summer, I kept thinking of my first sight of Hötorget on a sunny March 11th in 1939, and how surprised my wife was to find in these northerly latitudes this open place with half an acre of cut flowers and potted plants set up on tables on the snowless stones. Thérèse had bought a large armful of white tulips and yellow Dutch iris and the first sprays of pear blossoms to come in that year of uncommonly early spring—all for a dollar and a half.

With innate Swedish sense of the fitness of things, the flower tables are nearer to Orpheus and the Concert House façade, while farther away are ranged the summer stalls of fresh fruits and berries: boxes of luscious dark-red cherries, green and white gooseberries, lingon berries, blueberries, and yellow cloudberries from beyond the Arctic Circle and, best of all, raspberries at twenty-five cents a quart, and the more expensive incomparable wild strawberries.

Still farther away from the esthetic side of the square come the profusion of summer vegetables, the cauliflowers, tomatoes, string beans, red cabbages, beets, and twenty varieties of herbs, with umbrella-long clusters of feathery dill, with which the Swedes season crayfish and garnish salmon.

Cultivated mushrooms, and those gathered in the forests, make an especial impression in their abundance. There are large and small varieties, pink, beige, and chamois-colored, and bushel mounds of delectable golden-trumpeted chanterelles, like those I have often gathered in New Hampshire woods.

Still farther away from the pillars of the Concert House is a roofed hall, in which are spread glittering delicacies of sea and lake and inland stream that help to make Swedish smörgåsbord renowned: silver salmon and sardines, green sea pike and lake pike, red fish and sole, perch and mountain trout, large Norwegian herring from the North Sea, and the small Baltic herring (strömming), Ingrid Bergman's favorite food, and eels that are considered a very special delicacy when properly smoked.

In the meat and game department, besides the conventional beef, mutton, and pork, one can buy reindeer steak and venison and wild duck, hazel hen, woodcock, quail, and pheasant. And for those who want to save kitchen bother there is the delicatessen, with Swedish meat balls, foie gras and truffles, a dozen kinds of sausages and cheese, and shrimp that have been boiled at sea in sea water.

It is nice to sit in the sun on the steps of the Concert House and watch the commerce in flowers, with everything attractively displayed, with little flags flying on the counters, with no haggling, no crowding, and the apple-cheeked countryfolk making a pleasure of selling.

In neither traffic nor spirit was there in 1946 any outward change in Hötorget since 1939, but underneath, far below the stone paving on which flower tables stood, there had been a revolution. The rocky substrata had been blasted out and Sweden's largest air-raid shelter constructed beneath the very ground from which the music of Orpheus seemed to be drawing the ghostly group back to life. When the danger ceased in '45, the shelter was turned into a most needful and commodious underground parking lot. Without self-consciousness I could breathe a prayer that no shadow of inimical bombers would ever fall upon this bright market square to make a discord in the melody heard or unheard and break the rhythms of Sweden's blessed peace.

TOWN HALL WITH DEVOTION

Sweden has been peculiarly blessed in its abundance of first-rate twentieth-century architects, both those of the modern functional style and those of the so-called "romantic national" or "new traditional" school. Besides the Concert House, built in 1926, Ivar Tengbom designed the strikingly modern Högalid Church, and one of the world's most beautiful office buildings for the Swedish Match Company, both marked by elegant simplicity. E. J. Lallerstedt was architect for the Technical College, and Aron Johansson conceived the handsome Dansvik Home for the Aged, splendidly situated on the outer harbor. In the Municipal Law Courts Carl Westman made a modern adaptation of various Vasa Period motifs, while Torben Grut in designing the Athletic Stadium for the 1912 Olympics recalled Visby's medieval town wall. Of the leading architects since 1910, in my opinion only one, E. G. Asplund, made a sorry mistake when he designed the Municipal Library in a freakish functionalist style, making it resemble a gas tank or a brown top hat, as you choose. Yet the very able Asplund, who went wrong in the library, was one of the leading spirits in promulgating the idea that modern housing and furnishings were to be in harmony with each other and in accord with the requirements of accelerated modern living. And before he died, in 1943, Asplund redeemed himself by the inspired architecture of the Stockholm Crematory with its spectacular hillside calvary, its extensive classic-modern ambulatory with the slender square columns, its three chaste chapels, large, medium, and small, and its tiers of intimate flowering courts lined with niches for cinerary urns. Asplund conceived a far more beautiful setting for modern dying than for bookish learning, and in this crematory he proved that "modern forms can express immortal values."

The most impressive building erected in all North Europe in this century is Stockholm's Town Hall. It has made sure a place among the Swedish immortals for its architect, Ragnar Östberg, who first dreamed of such a structure in 1893, began it in 1911, and saw it completed in 1923.

As setting plays an important part in all Stockholm's public buildings, the site of the Town Hall on the island called Kungsholmen could hardly be better. It is so placed on a tip of land thrusting out into Lake Mälaren that it can be seen from most of the wind's twelve directions. By day its splendor is doubled in the mirror of the lake, and at night its illumined outlines are pricked out in rippling gold on the darkened surface of the water. Built of hand-made brick of a mellow russet-red, like some rediscovered from Gustavus Vasa's time, the Stockholm Town Hall is vast in its proportions. At the southeast corner its majestic squarish tower rises three hundred and forty-odd feet, slightly diminishing as it ascends to a belvedere topped with the three golden crowns.

Few of the great architects who built churches in the fourteenth century for the glorification of God could have been more imbued with a sense of devotion than were Östberg and the artisans who helped him create this contemporary masterpiece for the honor and glory of modern Sweden. Conceived on a magnificent scale, it was executed magnificently with a kind of patriotic fervor. During the construction Östberg and many of his artisans thought of little else; for periods they slept at the place, so that their whole beings might be subdued to the very quality of their work. The cost was just under $6,000,000, small indeed for a structure of such magnitude, but considerable for a city no larger than Stockholm. (To duplicate the work in America today the estimated cost would be some six to eight times more.) When the price of copper went skyrocketing in World War I and there were not sufficient funds to complete the roof, citizens contributed copper plates at $6.00 apiece. Each plate is numbered and registered in a Book of Honor, with the name of the donor inscribed beside it.

At small salaries, Östberg had the assistance of the nation's top designers and craftsmen, who were inspired to reach beyond themselves in this expression of what he termed "the new traditionalism." Each detail was carefully thought out and executed: a staircase lighting fixture, the leatherwork in the library, the needlework in the tapestry room, the mosaic of the gold banqueting hall, in which more than a million pieces of colored stone were set to make pictures in a glitter of gold something like that of St. Mark's in Venice. Einar Forseth worked the mosaic. Prince Eugen did murals for the long gallery. Elsa Gullberg designed and executed rugs and textiles. Carl Malmsten wrought inlaid furniture of Swedish cabinet woods. Baron Fleming fashioned sumptuous ornaments of silver.

For all my appreciation of interior excellences, I prefer, however, the timeless exterior with its grandeur of masonry. I like the paired pillared arches of the noble colonnades, the regal open halls of hand-chiseled brick, the Italianesque terrace with square patches of green lawn between patterned marble walks, and at a far corner the one grand rounded column bearing aloft Christian Eriksson's statue of Engelbrekt. I enjoy sitting on a marble seat in the waterside garden and looking across the blue water to historic Riddarholm Island with its fine old buildings the color of yellow plums and persimmons nipped by frost. The lake laps gently just below the long marble balustrade, on which alighting sea gulls make their own sculptural adornment, not far from the garden statues by Carl Eldh of Swedish firsts: Strindberg, the dramatist, Fröding, the lyric poet, and Josephson, the painter.

All during the first World War, while men of many other nations were bent on killing and destroying, Swedes calmly proceeded with the erection of this monument to art and beauty. With the devoted cooperation of Swedish masons, carpenters, weavers, dyers, artisans, artists, and landscape gardeners, the building begun in 1911 was completed and furnished in twelve years. The "new traditionalism" in Swedish architecture thus reached its flowering just as the style that came to be known as "Swedish Modern" evolved. The Town Hall was dedicated on Midsummer's Eve of 1923, the four hundredth anniversary of the coronation of Gustavus Vasa.

By that time the Social Democrats had become the dominant political party. Though I have never met a Swedish Socialist who was not proud of Stockholm's Town Hall, perhaps it was well the structure was finished when it was, for the Socialists declare themselves in theory opposed to excessive ornamentation and display involving conspicuous expenditure. Certainly after 1923 the major emphasis in construction has rightly been turned to modern apartments for the comfort of ordinary folk. By midsummer, 1946, the citizens of Stockholm as a whole were probably better housed than those in any other city of the globe.

ALL THIS, AND FINE FOOD TOO

In Stockholm one is assured not only of fine views and good beds and politeness, but of excellent food at reasonable prices. "There is nothing which has yet been contrived by man," Samuel Johnson once declared, "by which so much happiness is produced as a good tavern." And any man who enjoys eating well in pleasant surroundings will find Sweden superbly equipped to content him, for the skillful preparation and attractive serving of food is looked upon by Swedes, as by the Danes and the French, as a prime amenity of civilization. Stockholm is replete with good restaurants, and at least a score of them are so situated that one may also feast his eyes on beauty while he regales the inner man. The choosing of the place to dine becomes a joyous task, the selection depending on the time, the convenience, the weather, and the mood.

Some restaurants lie along sea water, others are set on wooded hills embowered in rhododendrons, one, the Mosebacke, commands an incomparable view from the edge of a high cliff. There are garden restaurants, and restaurants on roofs, verandas, and sidewalks and in eighteenth-century cellars. Some are smartly ultramodern, some rich in the atmosphere of an elegant past, some with little to recommend them but the wonderful food.

The superiority of the cooking in Sweden, as in Denmark, may be considered merely another manifestation of the high level of Scandinavian culture—an example of the value of education. All Swedish women are trained not only to run their homes with a certain perfection, but to be first-rate cooks themselves, even the ladies of royal blood. In the best restaurants the very menus have a kind of distinguished selectivity. Each dish from soup to sweet seems to have been given special thought. Swedes are fortunate in having an abundance and variety of seafood, and they make the most of fish from simple broiling with lemon-butter to elaborate preparations with subtle wine sauces. Good cuts of meat are generally accompanied by some rich brown or herb sauce. The full-flavored vegetables, which mature rapidly in the extended hours of summer sunshine, are often prepared in the French manner, for Swedish chefs study abroad as well as at home. While the delectable raspberries and strawberries are most popular summer desserts, whether served *au naturel* or with heavy cream or frozen cream, the Swedish cakes and pastries are works of art. Even the baked apple becomes something special in Sweden when it is rolled in melted butter, stuffed with chopped almonds, and served with an innocent-sounding vanilla sauce made of pure cream, pure butter, and beaten whites of eggs. Almonds are much used for seasoning, as are Burgundy, sherry, and brandy, as well as Parmesan cheese, and a score of herbs.

In Sweden one cannot help but revel in the excellent food—in such gastronomic delights as lobster *soufflé* served with a cream sauce of small oysters and tiny shrimp, or a black soup made of goose blood, giblets, stock, and Madeira. Blessedly one's enjoyment at table in Stockholm is not constrained as in Paris and so many other places by the accusatory thought that other citizens may hunger. For every Swede eats sufficiently. Though the diet of the poorest families may be mainly fish and potatoes, bread, milk, fruit soup, beer, and coffee, with occasional treats, it is adequate and nourishing.

None of the Stockholm restaurants are ruinous in price, and some are extremely reasonable if meals are taken without alcoholic beverages. Though Bellmansro in the Deer Park, the top restaurant in Stockholm, is expensive, at fashionable Cecil, Rosenbad, the subterranean Golden Peace, and Operakälleren one gets a meal—without wine—to remember for $2.00. At Konstnärshuset (The Artists' House), noted for its original murals and gay atmosphere, the prices are considerably more moderate. On the Grand Hotel's large veranda café, facing another of the world's most memorable metropolitan views, I lunched in 1946 for as little as sixty cents and dined for $1.00.

In numerous parts of the city scores of Norma restaurants, owned and operated by the Stockholm Cooperative Society, supply good, tasty food in pleasant surroundings at extremely moderate prices for both working men and the general public. In 1939 the railway-station restaurant was an eye-opener to me: for fifty cents I had thirty choices of smörgåsbord, dishes with hot meat and vegetables, dessert and coffee.

The traditional Swedish luncheon begins with smörgåsbord; and in taking smörgåsbord, one begins with herring, bread, and butter, generally accompanied by a small glass of ice-cold *brännvin* or schnapps. The strong colorless spirits relaxes tension, loosens the tongue, stirs the appetite, and puts one in amiable mood. A glass of schnapps is the wherewithal of a friendly skål. The ceremony of skåling, symbolic of welcome, wishing your companion health, goes back to Viking times, though no one knows the precise derivation of the word. While today skåling is losing some of its dramatic seriousness and is done with a kind of cavalier casualness, it is still a custom far more honored in the observance than the breach.

Before the war, besides the herring, one had a bewildering choice of dishes from the smörgåsbord table. After the wartime rationing began each patron had to content himself with three dishes of hors d'œuvres brought to his table. At the first luncheon of my 1946 visit the smörgåsbord menu at the Mosebacke Restaurant consisted of anchovy au gratin, smoked salmon, vegetable salad in mayonnaise, smoked reindeer meat, sardines, cheese, and mushrooms in pastry shells, besides the inevitable pickled herring. With any three of these and Swedish hard and soft bread as a first course, one could hardly feel the pinch of deprivation, particularly when the main course was filet of sole in some marvelous sauce and new potatoes and cauliflower, followed by wild strawberries and frozen cream.

It is not only in Stockholm that good taverns with good food are to be found. One is fed well at almost any provincial inn. At the Stadshotell in the small city of Karlstad and at the Gyllene Uttern (Golden Otter) a couple of miles south of the idyllic village of Gränna, I have had meals as remarkable as the best in the capital.

HISTORY IN THE OPEN

Summer evenings in the capital are so salubrious and delectable that one walks to engagements whenever he can, and often he learns something new as he goes. My first evening, on the way to dinner with a Swedish friend at the Cattelin Restaurant in the Old Town, I was struck by a congregation of some sixty people on a steep short side-street, grouped about a bareheaded man, who stood halfway up a stepladder. He was neither a soap-box orator stirring people's passions (such things hardly happen in Sweden) nor a street evangelist (though the Salvation Army does operate). He was a peripatetic historian, speaking under the auspices of the Society for the Preservation of the Old City, giving an alfresco lecture to a street audience. At the moment of our passing, his discourse had to do with the habits of a favorite of a long-dead king as well as some architectural detail of an ancient upper-story window to which he pointed. In the group, which was made up of persons of all ages, I noted more than a score of bareheaded, athletic-looking youths, all a trifle larger than life size, listening with respectful attention, some taking notes. To me it was an interesting commentary on these days of advanced social welfare in Sweden that young men took so much interest in their city's history.

In the small radius of "The City Between the Bridges" there was plenty for the historian to remark, for this island was the original site of Stockholm, founded in the 1220's by Birger Jarl.

Just beyond Storkyrkan, Stockholm's oldest place of worship, which dates to 1260, and where all the coronations since 1740 have taken place, a narrow street leads into Stortorget with its stepped-gable houses. It was in this market square that the infamous "Blood Bath" was staged in 1520. After a long and violent siege by Christian II, King of Denmark, as well as of Sweden and Norway, on the promise of full amnesty, Christina Gyllenstjerna, gallant widow of the Swedish opposition leader, Sten Sture the Younger, had opened the city gates. Two months after the surrender King Christian summoned the foremost representatives of the Swedish nobility, clergy and burghers to a "fête of reconciliation" at the palace. When the guests were assembled more than eighty of the nation's chief noblemen, bishops and burghers were seized, accused of heresy, condemned, formed into a queue, and beheaded as expeditiously as executioner could wield his ax. Today, on the north side of this quiet old square stands the Stock Exchange, erected in 1773, and in the upper floors are the headquarters of the Swedish

Academy, in whose ceremonial hall the annual recipients of the Nobel Prizes in Literature are selected.

From Stortorget radiate narrow, twisting, picturesque old streets, hardly more than alleys, with the shadowy atmosphere of a stage set of the gas-light era. This close-packed section makes a striking contrast to modern Stockholm, with its galaxies of bright and airy apartment houses, where abundant fenestration is a prime factor in architectural design.

In a nook of the Old Town, bordering a pretty four-bridged canal and facing the Riddarholm Island, stands Stockholm's most charming relic of the past, Riddarhuset (House of Nobles). Built in the seventeenth century in the richly ornamented style of the Dutch Renaissance, and crowned with a grandly arched copper roof, it remains in its original grace. On the wall of its assembly hall are hung the painted coats-of-arms of all Sweden's noble families. The armorial bearings of the various great families from the past number over twenty-eight hundred, but today only seven hundred noble names survive and carry on.

A few of the escutcheons, like those of the Lewenhaupts and Wachtmeisters, are also to be found in the Riddarholm Church, the most conspicuous building on Riddarholm Island, where the kings and queens lie buried and tattered banners from famous victories hang.

Compared to Westminster Abbey, the Knight's Church in Stockholm is small indeed, and one needs no more than a half-hour's pause here, particularly if he goes with a Swede who can tell him much in few words. And most of them can. For Swedes have an active knowledge of their past. Their civilization is based on learning. A stranger should know something of old Stockholm and its history in order to realize that in changing the social order the Swedes of our times have been as adventurous in their way as their warlike ancestors.

MAKING THE MOST OF SUMMER

Because of the long dark winter months, Swedes make the utmost of summer. Everyone who can, leaves the city for a hut in the woods by a lake or an island cottage in the Archipelago. Those who remain at work through the weekdays snatch as much sun as they can at lunch time, not only in the open-air cafés and on park benches, but on stairs and sea walls, or leaning against the bronze legs of sculptured kings. At the seaside children go naked all day long, while adults wear the slightest tributes to convention and swim in the nude behind screening rocks. In the city's wading pools (a most popular one is close by the Municipal Library), it is quite *de rigueur* for youngsters under seven to splash about in their birthday clothes.

There is something of the Hellenic spirit in a capital that sets an open-air swimming pool (Vanadisbadet) in the slope of a hill, above a busy thoroughfare, where straight from shopping or business one may ascend for a swim in fresh water. The upper terraces are strewn with mats and deck chairs for sunbathing. Since many offices and most factories close at four o'clock in summer and since the sun shines bright until nine in the evening, citizens can get their full share of sun-ray vitamins without having their vacation at the seaside.

A pleasant way of taking the sun fully dressed is in the open sight-seeing motorboats, which move through the historic waters and canals, making circuitous half-hour and hour tours within the city precincts, or going farther to Drottningholm, or to Gripsholm Castle, three hours away on Lake Mälaren. While Swedes have no American passion for automobiles, they dearly love boats—and many a workingman in the city owns a motorboat. One sees lines of them fronting apartment houses which give on water. Even when the owners cannot afford or get rationed gasoline for long rides, they like to sit in the motionless boats after work hours, enjoying their leisure with their families or entertaining friends with coffee or beer.

For citizens who have neither boat nor seaside cottage, the famous Colony Gardens on the outskirts of Stockholm provide sunny recreation, if the owners like to dig in the earth and raise vegetables and flowers. For an annual rental of a pittance a man gets a tiny plot of ground, on which he erects a tiny house, only big enough to store his garden implements and hold a cot and a table and chairs. Here he may shake off factory or office fatigue by raising asparagus, rhubarb, or strawberries, jonquils, phlox, or gladioli. The family often comes for picnic suppers or spends whole Sundays cultivating the garden or merely luxuriating in the out-of-doors.

For those who want entertainment on a large scale, Djurgården, one of the city's largest islands, is almost all recreation park, although some private villas and some foreign legations and Stockholm's number-one summer restaurant, Bellmansro, cluster in the northwest section not far from the Nordiska Museum.

Wooded Djurgården, once a royal hunting preserve, has been a pleasure park since the seventeenth century. Its greatest attraction is Skansen, an open-air museum that covers many square miles. Conceived by Arthur Hazelius, it was opened in 1891. He brought centuries-old houses from various provinces and fitted them with the proper antiques, so one merely strolls about to see how Swedish life was lived in the past on manorial estates and farms, and also how present-day Lapps live above the Arctic Circle. An authentic eighteenth-century pharmacy with all the fixtures, a glass blower's home, and an ancient tannery are among the countless attractions.

Besides the acres of exhibits, there are children's playgrounds and a zoo, an aviary, a modern art gallery, restaurants with glassed-in verandas, and open-air cafés with dance floors and splendid night views of Stockholm. On certain days folk dances are performed by especially trained young people from Skåne or Dalarna. One of the best seasonal entertainments is the open-air theater, where some of Sweden's finest actors appear. My second night in Stockholm in 1946, I saw a charming production of *A Midsummer Night's Dream,* with a slender, golden-haired Titania as exquisite as one could have imagined, and with settings by Sigvard Bernadotte, Crown Prince Gustav Adolf's second son. When the night air became chilly, spectators rented woolly blankets to wrap about their legs. But the Queen of the Fairies, clad only in a scanty yard of diaphanous azure chiffon, had nothing but the audience's admiration and applause to warm her white midriff and lovely bare thighs.

STIMULATION IN THE ARTS

While in the warm months Swedes take their music and their drama alfresco as well as their dancing and history, for at least nine months of the year Stockholmers may be regaled nightly within doors with a play, an opera, or a symphony concert. Esteem for theatrical and operatic art has been a Swedish tradition since the latter part of the eighteenth century when Gustav III founded the Swedish Royal Opera and the Royal Dramatic Theater. Today both are royal in name only; they are very much for the people, and subsidized so generously by a socialistic Government that a city of 700,000 inhabitants can boast of performances of the highest artistic standards.*

Whereas the Metropolitan in New York is able to present opera for only five months of the year, in Stockholm the season runs for almost ten months, and the repertory comprises practically the entire range of "living" operatic works. Among other performances in Stockholm I have seen *La Bohême* with Jussi Björling, *Carmen* with Gertrud Pålsson-Wettergren, and *Siegfried* with Set Svanholm. Madame Pålsson-Wettergren had already sung *Carmen* at the Metropolitan; Jussi Björling is now its leading lyric tenor, and Set Svanholm a much admired Siegfried. Among other noted Swedish artists the Metropolitan has lured are Kerstin Thorborg, Torsten Ralf, and Joel Berglund, who has recently accepted the position of director of the Swedish opera.

Built in 1898, to replace the small but more beautiful neoclassic structure of King Gustav III's commission, the Royal Opera is prominently situated on Gustavus Adolphus Square across the water of Norrström from the Royal Palace, in the very center of the city's heart. Its richly decorated interior includes a bust of Jenny Lind, the greatest Swedish voice of all times.

Less than a ten minutes' walk away, the Royal Dramatic Theater occupies an entire block at the beginning of Strandvägen, facing the blue bay of Nybroviken and flowery Berzelii Park. The theater was built in 1908, the first year of the present king's reign. Both the marble exterior and the ornate auditorium are a marked contrast to Sweden's modern architecture, born less than two decades later. Soon the capital is to have a playhouse purported to be as modern and as exciting architecturally as the Municipal Theater in Malmö.

Swedes take their dramatic and operatic training with high seriousness. Winning a scholarship to the Royal Dramatic Training

---

* See section "For the General Welfare."

Academy is the most coveted honor among aspiring young actors. Exceptional talent is the requisite. In mid-August the school holds an annual competition for girls sixteen years to twenty-two, and boys seventeen to twenty-two. Out of the hundred-odd applicants admitted to the grueling series of elimination tests only eight are selected for the three years' training given on the top floor of the theater building.

Greta Garbo, Ingrid Bergman, Signe Hasso, and Viveca Lindfors, the cinema stars, all received their instruction at the academy. But Bergman left before she finished her course to play in Swedish movies and then went to quick success in Hollywood. Director Rudolf Wendbladh, who studied in Russia under Stanislavsky, feels that a potentially great actress was damaged by her too hasty flight to films and stardom.

Sweden's Dramatic Training Academy became internationally known when its pupil Greta Garbo (1922 and 1923) made world fame on her first movie in Hollywood. After the former salesgirl's meteoric rise, talent scouts, not only from the States but from France and England, began periodic visits in Sweden.

Every few years some of Sweden's most successful players are beguiled by foreign offers. The State expects this and does not murmur or resent the money spent on their training, for it knows that Hollywood attractions like Bergman and Garbo make excellent cultural propaganda wherever they appear. And there is still a plentitude of expert stage performers left at home to satisfy the Swedes.

Such distinguished directors as Olof Molander and Alf Sjöberg produce everything from Sophocles, Shakespeare, and Strindberg, to Sartre, O'Neill, Saroyan, and Marc Connelly (*Green Pastures* was a tremendous success). Many a Broadway play is put on in Sweden within a few weeks of its appearance in New York, not only in Stockholm, but simultaneously in smaller cities with different casts. The Swedes are avid patrons of the theater and opera, and they import the finest American and European films.

During the last four decades the governmental authorities, whatever political factions they represented, have taken increasing interest in the Swedish theater. And, today, under the Social-Democratic regime almost a million dollars is appropriated annually as State subsidies for dramatic and operatic companies and symphony orchestras.

Stockholm is almost as rich in museums as in children's wading pools, for forward-looking Swedes use them for cultural instruction. Some are State-created, some given by private citizens. There are good ones of many categories: art, military, ethnographical, scientific, Egyptian, postal, Far Eastern, railway, maritime historical, natural historical, musical historical, and a vast Royal Armory containing weapons from the time of Gustav Vasa. But the only one to which I pay return visits is the National Museum of Art set gloriously at the end of the little peninsula of Blasieholmen, that looks across the water to the Royal Palace and Sergel's statue of Gustav III, who began the collections. Constructed some nine decades ago of limestone and marble in Venetian Renaissance style, it is most agreeably arranged and very easy to wander through. While it possesses some of the important works of Rembrandt, Rubens, Hals, and El Greco, and an excellent French collection including Manets, Renoirs, Gaugins, and Cézannes, visitors to Sweden are chiefly interested in six Swedish painters active since 1880. These six are Ernst Josephson, the foremost portrait painter; Carl Larsson, the most beloved for his refreshing views of Swedish home life; Helmer Osslund, the unforgettable depicter of Lapland; Prince Eugen, Bruno Liljefors, and Anders Zorn. Though Bruno Liljefors is one of the world's best animal painters, the prolific Anders Zorn * is really the only Swedish painter who has ever won much acclaim outside his own country, and he has a whole museum to honor him in his home province Dalarna.

HOW GOOD TASTE IS CULTIVATED

Wherever I went, whatever I did in Stockholm, I continued to be impressed by the good taste not only in public buildings, shops, motion-picture houses, schools, and restaurants, but in private homes of both the well-to-do and the wage earners. While Swedes inherently possess an extraordinarily good color sense, a movement was started more than a century ago, in 1845, to improve the taste of

---

* See section on Dalarna.

the citizens by promoting good design. Just at the time the late-arriving industrial revolution was superseding the old craft guilds, the Svenska Slöjdföreningen (Swedish Society of Arts and Crafts) was founded. It straightway established a School of Industrial Design, and, through the remainder of the century, arranged exhibitions and offered numerous contests for design and workmanship.

But it was not until 1914 that the society's current program was launched under the stimulating leadership of Erik Wettergren, the present director of the National Museum. His slogan, "Artists for Industry," gave fresh impetus to the striving for better design and taste. In the early 1920's a still more striking slogan, "More Beautiful Things for Everyday Use," was devised by Gregor Paulsson, the president of the society, and Swedish manufacturers began to employ leading artists as designers. Soon the happy result in style and quality was obvious, not only in articles of glass, ceramics, wood, and metal, but even in machine-made textiles.

It was in 1925 in connection with the Paris Exhibition of Modern Decorative Arts that Erik Wettergren first spoke to an international audience of *"l'art décoratif moderne en Suède."* "Swedish Modern" is a style evolved from esthetic and social efforts to raise the standard of the Swedish home and improve the quality of home furnishings. It stands for natural form and honest treatment of material, as well as a pleasing clarity of line and a certain smartness. As light walls, with pastel or clean, clear colors are standard in the new apartment houses, so blond wood is almost essential in modern Swedish furniture. When Swedish designers sought to bring applied art into harmony with modern man's needs, the simplicity of the functional became obligatory.

Akin to the nation's social policy, the goal of the society was, and is, to "by-pass former conservative exclusiveness," and create pleasing and comfortable surroundings of good taste for everybody. Economic considerations have, perforce, influenced esthetic considerations. To realize the ideal of "more beautiful things for everyday use," it was necessary for manufacturers to produce good furniture and household effects at prices the masses could afford. Even if his means are quite small, a Swede today can furnish his house simply with good taste, for standardized mass-produced articles of good quality designed by first-rate artists are widely available. Whereas

American manufacturers and storekeepers seem willing to give the public whatever vulgar and shoddy products it demands, Swedish merchants attempt to keep both cheap and expensive atrocities from the market. The hideous fancy living-room suites in garnet velour and golden oak that one can buy from Lake Michigan to the Rio Grande cannot now be found in Sweden at any price.

The new style has brought about a reaction against ornate embellishments and clutterings of bric-a-brac. In the modern Swedish living room one finds only a few carefully chosen decorative objects in glass, pewter, or ceramics, two or three good pictures, and as attractive hangings as the owner can afford.

Since 1930, aided by the industrialists, the society has carried on an extensive propaganda to improve public taste by exhibitions in all parts of the land, by illustrated lectures, by study circles in home decoration, and by various publications like the magazine *Form*. The organization has its professional unit, composed of artists, architects, and industrial designers, and its producers' unit, composed of great and small manufacturers of industrial art goods. It has also its section of municipal councils and its branches are open to the general public interested in promoting good taste.

Today a surprising amount of discrimination is exercised by simple householders in the choice of a chair, a picture, a rug, or tableware.* Though the man of small income cannot afford such things as handblocked linen draperies by Sven Markelius, a silver tobacco jar by Baron Erik Fleming, or a pewter-framed mirror by Estrid Erikson, he is able to appreciate and admire them. And the average Swede seems better able than most men to distinguish between real and false value.

Two of my favorite shops, which exemplify phases of Swedish Modern at its best, date significantly from the mid-1920's, when Wettergren first used the term that coursed the globe. One, Atelier Borgila, is owned and operated by Baron Erik Fleming; the other, Svenskt Tenn, by Estrid Erikson. Both proprietors are their own chief designers. But in one respect they differ widely: Fleming works in silver for the luxury trade; Miss Erikson, who works chiefly in pewter, also sells virtually everything one needs to fur-

* See section on Cooperative Housing.

nish a home except refrigerators, vacuum cleaners, and bed sheets.

Fleming's small show room on Sturegatan is a gem in itself. Lighted by a great rounded corner window from ceiling to floor, it is carpeted in gray velvet of an unusual shade and its show cases are lined with silk the pale-green color of tulip stems. The first time I saw the shop, silver bowls filled with white tulips set on modern pedestals made the decoration.

Erik Fleming, who once got a degree in engineering and was planning to be an architect when he discovered in himself a talent for creating art objects in silver, is an artist and craftsman in the Renaissance sense that implies intimate collaboration between master and workmen. He works carefully with his men on the execution of his designs. The artisans in his workshop number less than a score, for he refuses to produce on a large scale.

Though undoubtedly influenced by the modern work of Denmark's late famed Georg Jensen, Fleming's is a highly personalized style. His cachet signs all objects issuing from his shop. Fascinated by the full luster of silver surfaces and chary of ornamentation, he sometimes uses nothing more than an exquisitely designed monogram to make the decoration. His creations are inherently chaste, with that kind of elegance of simplicity found in sharp-cut early eighteenth-century English design. But often, with his infallible taste, he will give his imagination full play, and sometimes he puts a sparkle of humor in his pieces.

Besides his own regular wares for sale, Fleming makes objects on order for special persons or occasions. They may range from a wedding ring or a pair of cuff-links to a magnificent silver crosier mounted with precious stones like that one he made for the cathedral of Strängnäs at the expense of Baroness Falkenburg. Commissioned to make the peoples' wedding gift for Prince Gustav Adolf and Princess Sibylla, he designed a simple but beautiful table service, comprising 811 pieces, suited to "a princely court in a democratic age."

Though Fleming's attitude and work are thoroughly aristocratic, his exquisite products have had their influence on Swedish democratic taste.

What he did to revive the art of the silversmith in Sweden, Estrid Erikson did for pewter. In 1924 she started a modest shop known as

Svenskt Tenn, at first selling only pewterware designed by herself. Her shop on Strandvägen, close to the Dramatic Theater, and overlooking the sparkling water of Nybroviken, now occupies the full four stories of the building. With trellises of green-growing vines for decoration it is quite enticing, and besides distinctive objects and textiles by other noted Swedish designers there are displayed carefully chosen products from the ateliers of Florence and Paris that blend with Swedish Modern.

As a girl Miss Erikson * had been interested in ancient cultures and traveled far to see beautiful things, collecting ideas as she went. Then she studied at the Technical School in Stockholm to get a fundamental knowledge in the technique of creating artistic objects. There is a clean-cut refinement and restrained elegance to Estrid Erikson's creations, like those of Baron Fleming, but she often makes use of peasant motifs in a sophisticated, modern manner. Like him too, though to a less degree, she is in close contact with her craftsmen who carry out her ideas. She has had the more influence in improving Swedish home decoration because she is not at all aggressive, but a modest woman of unusual charm and gentleness, more like a hostess than a director. For two decades now Svenskt Tenn has been a criterion for Swedish modern taste, and Estrid Erikson's delicate color combinations and simple, distinctive designs have spread all over Sweden, and beyond to other lands, for English and American clients come to ask her advice about decoration, as well as to buy.

EXCURSIONS AND CARL MILLES

As pleasing as Stockholm is within its corporate limits, its attraction is so enhanced by memorable surroundings, that one is continually lured to make excursions. I know of no city that holds more treasured spots within a radius of forty-one miles. Small steamers and motorboats are continually departing from one of four

---

* In 1946 she married for the first time, changing only the spelling of her name from Erikson to Ericson, since her husband is Sigfrid Ericson, captain of the *Gripsholm*. While Captain Ericson continues to command his ship, his wife continues to make and sell beautiful things.

focal points within Stockholm to near destinations on the sea or to some idyllic and historic spot on Lake Mälaren.

To the south and west of Stockholm on Lake Mälaren are two of Sweden's finest castles, the graceful Drottningholm, where the King resides in winter, and the massive Gripsholm, now a national museum stored with the personal belongings and portraits of dead monarchs and their queens. Between them, on its own little island, is Birka, a noted trade center in Viking days and the spot where Christianity was first preached in Sweden in 829. Today it is hardly more than a congregation of ancient graves backed by a beautiful birch grove. Farther to the west and three hours by boat from Stockholm's Town Hall is Strängnäs, with a Gothic cathedral dating from 1291 and containing priceless old church silver. It was in Strängnäs that Gustavus Vasa was elected king in 1523, and here the Lutheran Reformation was first preached in Sweden. Today the quaint town seems to have achieved a complete, mellifluent peace, religious and political.

North-northwest of Stockholm on a narrow arm of Mälaren is Sigtuna, now a picturesque village with the ruins of medieval churches, but once one of Sweden's most important towns and first mentioned in the chronicles of the year 900. Today boarding schools flourish in its mellow atmosphere.

Though one cannot reach Uppsala by pleasure boat, it is a quick, pleasant trip by car only forty-eight miles north of Stockholm. Once the most important town of Sweden, it is now only the smallish capital—30,000 inhabitants—of the province of Uppland, but still the nation's foremost university center. The dusty-pink castle built by Gustavus Vasa on a rocky plateau and the grandiose "restored" cathedral dominate the town physically, but the pursuit of learning and the ghosts of great names pervade the atmosphere. In the castle's hall of state, Queen Christina made her dramatic abdication. Behind a golden grille in the cathedral lie the bones of St. Erik, Stockholm's patron saint and king of Sweden around 1150 and, back of the choir, those of the great Gustavus Vasa. In opposite chapels are buried Sweden's two most distinguished sons who were not warrior-kings: Emanuel Swedenborg, the scientist and mystic, and Carl von Linné (Linnaeus), the botanist. The only Swede dying within the last hundred years considered of sufficient eminence to be entombed among the immortals was Archbishop Nathan Söderblom, laid to rest here in 1931. Often called the foremost Protestant churchman of modern times, the good man continued to his dying breath to declare that some day people would come to their senses and have one church, one God, and one peace for all the world.

Besides the mortal cases of the great spirits that brought victory or sweetness and light to Sweden, the chief treasure of Uppsala is a book in the university library. It is one of the world's rarest volumes, the Codex Argenteus, a sixth century New Testament in the Gothic language, written in silver letters on a reddish-purple parchment. While the Swedes about Uppsala were worshiping Odin, Thor, and Freya at primitive pagan temples, the Balkan Bishop Ulfilas was preparing the text for the world's most beautiful Bible. In the land of the Czechs, soldiers of the late Gustavus Adolphus found the silver-bound Holy Book, which is our key to the Gothic tongue, and bore it to Uppsala as precious loot in 1648.

At Old Uppsala two miles north of the town once stood the most magnificent pagan temple in the Northern Countries. The place was then the capital of the kingdom and the seat of royalty, where successive kings dwelt before historical records began. Nothing from the ancient days is left standing except the three huge burial mounds sixty feet high dating from the Iron Age.

The charming, garden-enclosed town house of Linnaeus, the university's most eminent professor of all times, is now a museum. And so is his summer home at Hammarby five miles away to the southeast, where he lived and lectured in the garden to foreign disciples, seated on a straddling chair of his own design. The walls of one of the sitting rooms are papered with Linnaeus' paintings of plants. And over the door of his bedroom, in his own handwriting in Latin, is an inscription which reads, "Live blamelessly, God sees thee." Of the three hundred specimens of plants and trees sent to him by Catherine the Great for his garden, only two from Siberia still flourish, one being a Siberian apple, whose fruit is smaller than the crab.

A student from Värmland who accompanied me to Hammarby reminded me that Linnaeus' birthday was May 23. "I think perhaps that is why he had such a keen sense of spring," he said. "He was born just when the cuckoo first announces the season—when the rye has put out one leaf, but not two."

The atmosphere of this evocative old town, breathing history from its stones, is kept ever fresh and stirring by the extracurricular activities of four thousand students, who have lusty lungs for singing and who frequent the pleasant beer gardens by the river. The white student caps of the undergraduates give an accent of youth to the old streets, as well as to the houses of the "Nations," which are like fraternities except that they are neither elective nor exclusive. Every man automatically belongs to that one representing his home province, and he makes what recreational use he will of the club house endowed by the alumni of his "Nation."

Lidingö, an island almost as extensive as incorporate Stockholm and only a quarter hour away by car across bridges, is chiefly visited because it is the summer museum home of Carl Milles, the greatest Swedish sculptor since the eighteenth-century Sergel. The house stands on a promontory, high above the blue-green expanse of salty Lilla Värtan, facing piers and industries. But as industry in Sweden rarely makes for ugliness, but generally benefits the landscape, so here the smokestacks and multiwindowed walls, with freighters at mooring, do not offend the view by day, and by night enrich it. On the island, the Milles house has the athletic training center of Bosö for neighbor, quite fitting for the man who creates magnificent bodies out of metal and marble. On a jutting, rounded level of the Milles garden, stands a replica of "The Sun Singer," the heroic bronze gleaming in the sunlight like a signal for the ships that come and go.

Built at a bad romantic period early in the century, the house is no specimen of architectural beauty, and ever since the artist moved in, in 1905, he has been changing it. But the courtyards and gardens, the galleries and sunken terraces are so seductive that one hardly notices the architectural faults of the house itself until the master points them out.

Though, since 1931, for nine months of the year Milles works and teaches at Cranbrook, that oasis in American art at Bloomfield Hills near Detroit, he and his wife come to Sweden for the summer when they can. When I called at Lidingö, he himself received me and showed me about. I had met him a few weeks before, at a small luncheon in New York, the day before he sailed for and I flew to Sweden.

He was in fine form, glowing with pleasure at being back in Sweden, despite his casual insistence, "The earth is my country." Though he was seventy in June of 1946, the white-haired, stocky Milles has powerful shoulders and a deep chest. His own strong features suggest rugged sculpture, but they are as mobile and expressive as a good Shakespearean actor's, and his eyes have the glow of a seeking seer. Milles is a fascinating talker, if he finds a sympathetic listener. His close friends say his conversation has a mighty range, but he generally gets in something about life after death, the stars, or water, for which he has a passionate affinity. He thinks perhaps he is so moved by water because he was born on the first day of the water sign Cancer. His friends say he is "angel-haunted" too. And he enjoys creating angels, as much as all sorts of recognizable and imaginary sea creatures, dolphins, tritons, mermaids, and fantastic fishes.

The manual labor of Carl Milles is evident not alone in the specimens of sculpture at Lidingö, but in the garden walls and walks and the exquisite little shrine to the Virgin he made for Olga, his Catholic Austrian wife, on her fiftieth birthday. A consummate tenderness and delicacy went into the conception and the making of the shrine, which is set in the side of a shrub-studded knoll and approached by an original narrow flight of stairs, bordered by lilies-of-the-valley.

The rich mosaic floor of the front drawing room of his house Milles laid entirely with his own hands. It took him years to do the intricate job of making Swedish wild flowers bloom in the colored stones. The rooms beyond the first drawing room descend to different levels, and finally reach his workshop. On the way we passed through a carefully selected museum, with special treasures in Grecian marble, Florentine bronze, and Austrian wood sculpture. One of the loveliest of the pieces was a thirteenth-century madonna in wood he found in Innsbruck. On a work table I admired a model of the Swedish hero Engelbrekt. "Ah, yes," he said, with a shade of resignation in his voice. "I received a prize for it a long time ago, but, alas, it was never executed. This happens often with me."

I wondered about his living models. "But I never work with models," he said with quick emphasis. "I do not need naked men and women to pose for me like a photographer. All comes out of my imagination."

When I asked him at what age he started modeling, he replied, "At the breast of my mother, I think."

When we had seen the museum rooms and the guest wing, where the poet Yeats and Hugh Walpole and a nephew of Gandhi had stayed, we sat on the front Italianesque terrace on the wall of the oblong pool from which rose water lilies and aquatic Milles figures. "Fate, it seems, has directed me all my life," he mused. "In my youth I was often quite miserable. My father did not want me to be a sculptor. He arranged for me to go to Chile on some business. I got to Marseilles, but I simply could not take the boat for South America. Fate would not let me. Eventually I got to Paris. I lived there for sixteen years. I was so poor I had to sleep on the floor of a humid greenhouse, all glass, in a small back yard surrounded by buildings. I was a waiter in a restaurant. I helped build houses and make coffins. I did almost anything to eat. But I also studied history and astronomy. And then I met the great Rodin. He let me live in his studio and work under him. I did not write home for six years— not until I found myself. Then I won a competition for a statue of Sten Sture the Elder to be erected at Uppsala.

"When I finally came back to Stockholm, Swedes seemed strange to me. They were so conventional. At dinners, my God, how mannered they were! I think the Swedish youth of today is much better. I like young people enormously. In Cranbrook students can come at any time to discuss things with me—anything except politics. I hate politics. We talk about art and the stars, mysterious things. 'My friends,' I often say to them, 'don't decide to march all by yourself. Let destiny guide you.'"

Milles rose to save a winged insect struggling in the water, scooped it up carefully with a leaf, and set it at liberty. "I never read newspapers in the States or in Europe. I never dare. They make the world sound so terrible. I read periodicals like *Punch, Le Rire, Simplicissimus*. And, of course, I rarely listen to a radio. Radios are more horrible than the papers. Even as it is, I have sleepless nights thinking of the troubles of the world." He paused, and then smiled. "But in the morning when the sun shines and the birds sing, as now—everything looks good and is filled with hope again!"

He offered me a cigarette. "I shall not speak about the war, but I am ashamed about us white people. I feel as Gorky when he wrote his six letters about *his* people. We still live in the Middle Ages or in a worse period. I try to turn my soul to the 'Agnosto Deo,' and become a religious pagan. Often for consolation I point my telescope at one of the billions of galaxies. It helps me wonder and think. And I have my microscope too, to enter the small world, for which I praise God."

A shadow from a leafy bough had fallen across us, and we moved to a sunny edge of the pool.

"To go on with the Swedes. They are mannered, yes—and they have their faults. But they are lyrists and have a real sense for the arts. They are philosophers in the way they need to be to live in a country with a bad winter climate, with so little sun six months of the year. Far from the great centers of culture, Swedes have had to create their own, and they have done well."

A message interrupted our talk. There was something my host had to attend to at once. He sighed and smiled resignedly. "Fate has made me a man who is, year in and year out, hard-working. People put on my seventy-year-old back more and more and still more and more."

But my taxi had come, and we strolled towards the high gateway of the outer courtyard.

"Before you go," he said, "I must tell you about a fountain in silver pewter I am going to make for the Houston Museum in Texas. It will be very beautiful, I think. It represents the Tree of Paradise when the angels deliver us in the crown of the tree, and we are very astonished as we look around. And this you have never seen before: the water will just *drop* down from the tree—just dropping water, which is so beautiful to listen to. The Arabians used this idea for their small marble fountains, where each drop gives out a different sound. My little eight-foot fountain will in reality be for youthful people—just to sit around and look and listen and contemplate—and maybe talk quietly as we have been doing."

He caught my arm after I had said good-by. "I have lived in many countries in many conditions, and in reality there are no great differences in people. I have been the poorest of the poor, and I have also tasted the so-called 'better' life with the rich, and I know it does not matter whether you are without coins or have riches— for either way it only matters how you think and how you do. The only thing I hate is unkindness and stupidity—snobs and cynicism and intelligence alone *without* heart. But what is more wonderful than the intelligent heart?"

A KEY FROM THE CROWN PRINCE

As I drove back to my hotel, the last words Carl Milles said to me kept running through my mind. I wondered how far "the intelligent heart" was responsible for the harmony in Sweden's contemporary way of life. Warmth certainly did not seem to be the most notable characteristic of the level-headed Swedes. And yet in thinking of some of the most influential leaders I talked with, both in 1939 and 1946, the phrase did have significance.

There was no doubt in my mind but that intelligent heart motivated August Lindberg, the head of the Labor Federation, and Gunnar Andersson,* the head-elect, and Gustav Möller, Minister of Social Welfare. And on reflection it certainly seemed true of Per Albin Hansson,* the Social-Democratic Prime Minister. While Gunnar Myrdal's brilliant gifts did not show to best advantage in his job as Minister of Commerce because he had no passion for business, his interest in the happiness of his brother-man was profound and genuine. As I went down a mental list of prominent Swedes I had met, I recalled my first visit to the palace in mid-March, 1939, when Crown Prince Gustav Adolf received me because of letters from a mutual friend in England. For it was the Crown Prince who gave me a significant key to understanding the social well-being of the Swedish people.

The American minister, Colonel Frederick Sterling, had been somewhat concerned about the protocol of my appointment with His Highness. He offered me his own morning coat and striped trousers, which would have fitted me well enough. But I wanted to go in my own clothes. I had heard the Crown Prince was not too

* Gunnar Andersson and Per Albin Hansson both died in the fall of 1946.

punctilious about ceremony, and when calling on Pauline Brunius, the director of the Royal Dramatic Theater, the day before the scheduled meeting, I told her my dilemma and asked her if a dark business suit with a white pin stripe would not be acceptable garb to His Highness at eleven o'colck in the morning? The great lady said she was attending a dinner party with the Crown Prince that evening and she would tell him I did not possess a morning coat and ask if he would not receive me in a business suit.

Because Mr. Sterling feared that I might be a bit late or a bit too early, or go to the wrong entrance, he kindly sent me in his limousine, after giving his Swedish chauffeur precise instructions where to deposit me. I was driven to the north entrance within the main courtyard of the palace. Uniformed guards ushered me to a door three steps up from the stone paving of the loggia into a small reception room, where another uniformed official took my overcoat and hat. Then another door up three more steps was indicated, and I was led into the office of the equerry, a dapper, smiling man with splendid teeth and a huge distinguished nose. He graciously asked me to be seated, while he went up three other steps to a still more inner room to announce me to His Highness. It happened to be a very busy day, for the Crown Prince was regent while his father the King was on his vacation in Southern France.

Before I clearly saw the Prince himself I remarked with relief his dark-blue flannel business suit with a fine white pin stripe. He was well built and of good height, but nothing like so tall as his father or his brother, Prince Wilhelm. He had a friendly smile and he wore horn-rimmed glasses, which helped give him the look of an alert archeologist or a professor of economics. (I knew that archeology and economics were his special interests along with art and fishing.) On his desk was the letter Lady Astor had written in my behalf, and we laughed about the illegibility of her impulsive handwriting, as he confessed he doubted if the Government decoders would be able to decipher completely one of her dashed-off missives. Straightway he began to ask me about the United States' interest in the Scandinavian countries. I told some of the aspects of Sweden's democracy I had come to observe for myself. Then I asked him directly what had been the motive force that led Sweden to such advanced standards for the general welfare.

The youngish, sixty-year-old Prince, whom the conservatives often call a socialist, reflected for a moment. "Very briefly," he said, "to understand what has happened in Sweden, one must go back to the time when we were a world power. The change in the national thinking began when we lost Finland to Russia in the early part of the nineteenth century. Then when Norway separated from Sweden in 1905 it was such a terrific shock to the country that the Swedes woke up, as it were. We gave up forever any faintly lingering thought of again becoming an imperialistic nation. We began to turn all our attention to internal work, to improving the home stock and home conditions. We put all our energies into making the very most out of our own resources and ourselves.

"Some of the achievements must be accounted for by the natural gifts of Swedes for organization and for mechanical ability. When the World War came with its blockades and restrictions, it taught us to become self-sufficient. We learned to work the land better, to produce more on small acreage. We experimented and strove to produce better grains. Formerly, we got most of our seed from England; but we so improved on the quality that England now buys seed from us. So it went. And after the war was over we began building moderate-rent apartments with new amenities and set about really to create a more abundant life for the general public. It became a kind of national ideal to improve the quality of the Swedes themselves, their health, their taste, and their design for living."

He smiled—and said, "You understand, I cannot speak of the politics of the matter—in these democratic days politics is not within the royal prerogative. But you see how it has gone. When a small country gives up all imperialist ambitions, then it can really accomplish good and substantial things for its own people."

Though we talked for an hour and a half, these first sentences stuck emphatically in my mind. I knew Mr. Sterling perhaps needed his car, but the Crown Prince generously detained me when I made moves to leave and asked me many questions about America and the South. Finally, he gave me a list of important persons I should meet, including, most importantly, the head of the Labor Federation, and he asked his equerry to make appointments and write to some people I should see in other parts of Sweden. At the very last he said I should meet right away his close personal friend, the publisher and art collector, Torsten Laurin, and he took the telephone himself and made an engagement for Monday.

As I drove out of the palace courtyard in the March snow flurry, one sentence of the conversation, said with an almost whimsical smile, re-echoed in my ear: "I don't see how we *could* be more democratic, do you?"

Now, seven years later, as I watched from my hotel window the king's guard march up past the Opera and across the North Bridge to the palace to relieve those on duty, I thought of what Karel Čapek had said to a Stockholm reporter: "It must not be difficult to be king here, for it is certainly not the worst of jobs to govern people who are gentlemen." And reflecting on the Crown Prince's words and attitude in 1939, and Carl Milles's "intelligent heart" phrase of half-an-hour past, and what I had learned of Swedish democracy in the years between, it occurred to me that Sweden's Golden Age was now.

The present is a finer period than that of Gustavus Vasa or the fighting hero Gustavus Adolphus or the glittering art-patron Gustav III. For their times were great for the privileged, and these are good for the entire commonwealth. While the nation could not have spared those special kings with their special gifts, these less glamorous decades have more to say to a troubled world. The rise in living standards for the masses, the gratifications of social security, the modern renaissance in architecture and decorative arts, with the vast-scale construction of cooperative apartments and Government-subsidized garden cities, have all come about during the reign of Gustav V. Yet for all the social experimentation, the Swedes have never failed to cherish excellencies that abide in the old and the tried. With a Labor Government in dominance for many years, distinction is still highly commendable in Sweden.

As I looked out across the city of space and grace, which custom could not stale because of those very attributes, there seemed to be comparatively little conflict in the Swedish mind and spirit. Even the briefest visit to Stockholm, I thought, might inspire the stranger with hope for mankind's future.

2.

Dalarna, Heart of Sweden

A philosophy, like human life itself, cannot be imprisoned in a formula of words. It too must be living, growing, changing. It must combine the logic of the mind with the wisdom of the heart and merge both with the spirit's intuition. It must be strong enough to make science the servant of man, not his master.

—CHARLES A. LINDBERGH

JÄRNBÄRALAND OF THE SAGAS

ALMOST EVERY COUNTRY great and small has some segment or province for which admiring strangers, as well as its own people, have a special affection. In England it is Devon. In America it is Virginia. In Denmark, the island of Fyn. In Sweden it is Dalarna, or as the English call it, Dalecarlia. Either name has a lovely sound that suggests the charm abiding in the region coursed by the river Dalälven. Swedes of all latitudes have their own pet epithet for the province: "The Heart of Sweden."

Geographically Dalarna lies a little south of the heart of the elongated country and somewhat north of the center of population density. It is the most beloved of the provinces because it is the most "typically Swedish" as well as the most colorful. Its sturdy, blue-eyed people have accepted what they need of mechanical devices without disturbing the familiar contenting rhythms. As modern industrialization has come to Dalarna, the mighty blows of water-driven forge hammers no longer disturb the stillness of the forests, and the waters of the many falls have been sidetracked into power-house flumes. But one still finds the same cheerful red farmhouses with hand-carved gables and gaily decorated porches, and cupboards

46

and hall clocks painted with tulips and roses. One can see timbered haylofts dating from 1500, and beautifully carved fifteenth-century reredoses in old blue and white churches. High in the hills at the *säters,* from Midsummer to Michaelmas cowgirls still yodel on long birch-bark horns for their cows. The leather-tailors of Malung, who for centuries fashioned garments out of sheepskins and goatskins, continue to ply their trade, and today make fur coats for the military and sport coats for women. The charcoaler spends his winters deep in the forest remote from the world of man, practicing that ancestral art that requires long apprenticeship, for charcoal is yet in great demand in the refining of high-grade steel.

The fact that Sweden's largest ironworks and paper mills and second-largest iron-ore deposits lie within its boundaries does not change the impression that Dalarna is a pastoral land with picturesque farmhouses behind the birch-bordered roads, where yellow nightshade enlivens the ditches and the stout old fences of slanted split spruce rails. The mountains climbing in the west towards Norway, with their spectacular Alpine scenery and fashionable ski resorts, merely accentuate that smiling quality of the Dale land.

For all its industrial activities in the east and its steady flow of tourists, Dalarna has cherished its traditional peasant culture more than any other province. It is one of the last parts in Sweden where women continue to wear their bright provincial costumes to church and to parties. In present-day handicraft work, in lace-making and the weaving of wool and linen, old motifs and patterns are quite naturally followed. Though Dalarna is inherently conservative, it is from this region that many national popular movements came, massed determinations to take no nonsense either from Swedish kings or would-be oppressors from abroad. In the fifteenth century this romantic province was the birthplace of Sweden's modern independence, inspired by the mine-owner Engelbrekt Engelbrektsson, who summoned the first Swedish Riksdag ("Parliament") in 1435, and who is considered Sweden's foremost medieval statesman. And it was the Dalarna peasants who helped to change the course of Swedish history in 1521 when they massed to support the revolt of Gustavus Vasa against a Danish king.

One of Sweden's largest provinces, yet with only 280,000 inhabitants, Dalarna has about everything except skyscrapers and roller coasters. Even the old proverb which says, "The oak tree, the crayfish, and the nobleman do not flourish north of the river Dalälven," is not absolutely true in fact. Its economy is uncommonly well balanced and has been so for centuries. A rich agricultural district with sleek cattle and full-eared grain, it possesses also abundant timber lands and swiftly flowing rivers to bear the felled logs to the mills. Sweden's oldest mining district, Dalarna is that Järnbäraland, "iron-producing country," of which the Icelandic sagas sang. An extant document shows that the world-famous copper mine, Stora Kopparberget, at Falun was worked before the middle of the thirteenth century. After the discovery of copper "under the moss and pine roots" this previously neglected part of the country suddenly gained marked interest for kings, bishops, and foreign merchants. By the fifteenth century, prosperity from mining, supplemented by agriculture, brought a relatively high standard of material living. A great building activity then ensued, and churches were erected through contributions from rich mine-owners. In the sixteenth and seventeenth centuries came the manors, not of titled families or landed gentry, but of the proprietors of mines and ironworks. Old tales are still told of those powerful industrial squires who sometimes ruled their parishes as if they had been personal dukedoms and who rode to church on horses shod with silver shoes. The "great period" of Dalarna came at the end of the seventeenth century and lasted through the eighteenth, when the goldsmiths of Falun and Hedemora could hardly fill the orders for church ornaments in silver and gold, and even farmers and miners bought silver drinking mugs and goblets for their ale and *brännvin.*

The words "underprivileged" and "proletarian" have no meaning in Dalarna. Many of the free-born Dalecarlians have owned their own land since before the beginning of Swedish history, and have never been attached to castled estates like certain families in Skåne. They are a strong-minded, straightforward people, seasoned with ready wit. They care little for the outside world and are quite content with the world of their own making, though the peasants have never hesitated to go in protest directly to the king if some State business merited their disapproval.

Naturally buoyant in spirit and hospitable, they are yet incorrigibly independent and little impressed by eminence. "The Dalarna peasant," wrote Hans Christian Andersen, "has the feeling of an ancient line, that he is nobly born. Once when one of the grandsons of King Carl Johan was in Dalarna, an old peasant came up to him, pressed his hand, and said, 'Please greet thy old grandfather for me at Stockholm.'" A few years ago when the popular Crown Prince Gustav Adolf was taking a brief autumn vacation at Hotel Siljansborg, he remembered a farmer of the neighborhood who had impressed him from among a group that had come to the royal palace to lay some case before his father, the King. So he sent his equerry and the hotel porter to bear the amiable command to an audience the next day. The emissaries returned somewhat chagrined. The old peasant had said he was sorry, but he could not come the next day, because he had made his plans to drive to Falun for his winter's supply of liquor. However, he added, if His Highness was still about on Thursday or Friday, he might be able to get over to see him on one of those days.

The influx of tourists during the last three decades has not disturbed the even tenor of the Dale folk, who seem impervious to exploitation or to blandishments of any kind. This popular region is both summer and winter resort, and possesses more good hotels and pensions than any other province. During the first three months of the year Swedes from the south go to Dalarna to avoid the slush and enjoy the northern snow. In summer they go for the coolness and to celebrate the once pagan festival of Midsummer (June 23-24), now blessed by the Church as "St. John's Day." For nowhere else in Sweden are to be found such gala Maypoles, such lilting music, such spirited dancing, such brilliant peasant costumes.

To get the full flavor of Dalarna, the province should be twice visited, during the snow and again in summer. I first saw Dalarna in mid-March of 1939, when the landscape was heavily wrapped in white, and again in late July of the postwar year 1946, when summer was in full flower and there was virtually no night. It is impossible to say which is the more delightful time.

In winter one generally goes by train straight to the heart of Dalarna, to Rättvik, on Lake Siljan. The journey from Stockholm takes something less than five hours. In summer thousands bicycle, the men almost invariably stripped to the waist, the women scantily clad, to get the full benefit of the tanning, vitalizing sun. Those who own a car, or who can afford to hire one, drive. In 1946 I was fortunate in having Swedish friends provide me with a commodious Buick, a chauffeur who spoke four languages, and a personable young man named Gunnar Rosvall, who spoke seven languages, to act as guide and companion.

The first important town one comes to in Dalarna is Hedemora. In early days it was the only town, receiving its charter in 1459, though it had been licensed to hold fairs long before that. Hedemora has ever been noted for its cottage industries, its rag carpets and hand-woven linens. The large brick church dates from the latter part of the fifteenth century, and there is a nice old town hall, as well as many fine old mansions. But we visited only the brand-new furniture factory of Alvar Aalto, the Finnish architect, who had brought some of his best workmen here after Soviet Russia blighted affairs in Finland. There is no finer modern furniture turned out in Sweden, for Aalto is unsurpassed in modern design and use of material.

After some neat farms with flowery meadows comes Domnarfvet, the largest ironworks in northern Europe. Besides its electrical blast furnaces, Bessemer steel works, and rolling mills, it holds a pleasant village that is one of the numerous models of Swedish social organization. The housing problem of the workers, caused by mass production, has been given great consideration. The Building Society of the company has attempted to retain the artistic traditions of the Dalarna peasantry, and at the same time to provide modern conveniences and comforts. The country-cottage charm of crisp curtains, hand-woven fabrics, embroidered towels, and bright copper utensils is echoed in the houses of the industrial workers.

Falun, the chief town of Dalarna, with a population of only 15,000, is set attractively between two lakes. In tradition and history as well as material wealth it is richer than most Swedish towns. Its special distinction comes from the fact that it grew up at the edge of the famous Stora Kopparberget ("Great Copper Mountain"), which has been called "the eighth wonder of the world from the Middle Ages." The bright metal from these mines helped to finance the wars that once put Sweden among the Great Powers of Europe. And because so many foreign tourists have wanted to gaze on the mammoth hole in the ground from which copper was extracted for seven centuries, the Mining Company has built the Grand Hotel in the modern part of the town to accommodate visitors. Its public rooms are decorated by well-known Swedish artists. Its dining room, with two levels like a theater with a balcony, is all glass on the side that looks out on a fountained garden. There is also a long veranda embowered in flowers, which is particularly nice for tea or dining alfresco while the orchestra plays folk music.

Today, though the opulent veins of copper are exhausted, the mine still yields a valuable yellowish iron pyrite, the children's "fool's gold," and red ocher, the famous "Falun red," of which so much paint is made. The hematic pigment was discovered in the dim past when a wandering goat returned to its herdsman marked with a rich deep red caused by a forest fire oxidizing the surface copper of the mountain. Through the centuries it spread in its usage to Sweden's barns and farmhouses. Without this Falun red the landscape recognized and loved as "typically Swedish" would be something quite different.

In this province of archeological and art museums (there is one kind or another in every town), Falun's Bergslags Museum holds special interest. Constructed around the old mine-manager's house, it sits brooding at the edge of the mammoth hole from which the copper was dug and affords remarkable illustrations of the history of mining, beginning with Exhibit Number One: the five-sealed document in parchment dated June 16, 1288, entitling the holder to an eighth share in the mining property.

After being worked for six centuries without proper shoring, the honeycombed hill caved in one day, and by the grace of Heaven no one was hurt, for Providence had timed the event to coincide with the celebration of Midsummer Day, 1687, while the sixteen hundred miners were all out dancing.

The world's oldest stock company, still known as Stora Kopparberget, flourishes today without copper, and does a mighty business in timber, paper, and iron.

Within a few miles of Falun to the west and southwest on the swirling waters of Dalälven are grouped important industrial establishments: sawmills and hydroelectric power stations and the Kvarnsveden Paper Mill, the largest of its kind in Sweden.

Three miles east of the town is the manor of Sveden, one of

numerous old manorhouses erected by mine officials. Here the bishop father of the famous religionist Emanuel Swedenborg was born in 1654, and here in the "Wedding Hall" Carl von Linné (Linnaeus), the world-renowned botanist, was married in 1739. Less than three miles to the northeast is the pretty village of Sundborn, with the house of Carl Larsson, who, because of his heart-warming depiction of Swedish family life, is the most beloved of Swedish artists.

Across the beautiful Runn Lake, five miles to the southwest of Falun, stands the Vika church, Sweden's finest monument from the end of the Middle Ages. It contains thirteen rare pieces of medieval wood sculpture, and its walls and vaulted ceilings are covered with richly detailed murals in chalky pastel colors. As Rosvall said, these are *the* murals of Sweden.

Though Falun is a center for excursions leading as far to the east as Sandviken, Sweden's best-known steel mill, and to the city of Gävle on the Baltic Sea, it cannot equal in tourist affection the area around blue Lake Siljan, which is indeed the core of Sweden's heart.

HOTEL ON LAKE SILJAN

Just before dinner we arrived at Hotel Siljansborg spread on a rise above the lake, a couple of miles beyond the village of Rättvik. The metamorphosis of summer had made such transformations that I hardly recognized the place I had loved when it was deep in snow. Now all was luxuriant verdure, cultivated blossom, and terraces with lily pools and inviting nooks. Some guests were returning in bathing togs from the lake, and others in summer attire were on the verandas waiting for dinner. But Britt Arpi, the still young, fair-haired directress, was at the door to welcome us just as she had been on a March afternoon in '39.

Siljansborg owes much of its distinction and popularity to the personality of the two women who have been in charge since it was first opened: Fru Sigrid Arpi-Bertil, now manager of Hotel Stockholm in the capital, and her daughter Britt, who assumed full directorship while still in her twenties. When in high school Britt Arpi set her heart on becoming secretary to Ivar Kreuger, the match king and financier, and later prepared herself for the job by studying languages in France, Germany, and England. Then, the very week she was to have an interview, came his sensational suicide and the subsequent disillusioning scandal. So she turned to hotel management as a profession, and with Swedish thoroughness worked at quality hotels and restaurants in both Stockholm and London in every capacity from chambermaid and kitchenmaid to receptionist. She then succeeded her mother, who had made Siljansborg a favorite resort of discriminating Swedes as well as foreign visitors.

After dinner, to stretch our legs, Rosvall and I took a walk up into the wooded hills where Thérèse and I had walked in the March snow and heard the strange crying of a hungry baby fox. But this July evening we heard only the murmurings of contented birds, and we picked wild strawberries that grew in profusion in the deep leaf mold of centuries.

Returning by a circuitous route past sloping farms, we saw that the golden wheat was sometimes studded with bluebells and blue cornflowers, and along the fences the overpoweringly sweet elk grass was still attracting the honeybees. The barns and houses were all painted the same rich red, which made them look uncommonly cheerful and prosperous, but without snow they had lost something of their picturesque appeal. In the midst of green summer I continued to recall nostalgically journeys in the time of snow when my wife and I first visited Dalarna.

It was in 1939 on March 21, the day spring officially arrives in the almanacs, that Thérèse and I had arrived at the station of Rättvik in a faint afternoon flurry of snowflakes. Everything was white and red like a Santa Claus costume, as we drove through a frosty storybook land to Hotel Siljansborg. Snow blanketed the rolling hills, and the roofs of the red barns and cottages glistened with white. Between the farms birch trees stood naked and graceful with their ankles deep in snow, their milk-white trunks striped daringly with black like a zebra's flank.

In our hotel room, on a table between two large windows, were daffodils, narcissi, and pink tulips for Thérèse. The windows opened on a balcony overlooking the white garden, the ice-sheeted lake beyond, and the distant blue-white hills. As Thérèse said, the world looked so still—and purified.

While we stood gazing for some time at the white enchantment, a figure appeared at the lake's edge and pushed off on a "kick-sled" across the ice. Like some far-off phantom emerging out of the hoary dusk, another figure with a similar sled then took shape and approached the first. The two men met, held secret colloquy away from the shores of man, concluded their business, waved brief fare-wells, and returned in the thick-gathering twilight the way they had come. Though the scene had no special significance for us, the strange transaction on the lonely stretch of ice was sharply etched in our minds in contrast to the warming cheer of the hotel's hospitality.

Winter or summer there is a kind of amiable house-party atmos-phere about Siljansborg. For those who do not take breakfast in their rooms, the meal is set out in the English country-house man-ner on buffets. On winter evenings coffee is taken in one of the several drawing rooms or the library, where one gathers with his own little circle of friends, old or new, around open birch-log fires or away in farthest corners. To remind one that this is Dalarna, the waitresses wear the native costumes with linen neckerchiefs and lace headdresses. The girls wear them authentically according to their own parishes, for they are all from the near countryside.

SLEIGH BELLS AND THE FARMER'S WIFE

Seasonable excursions are continually being arranged for guests. Our second afternoon Thérèse and I went with a sleighing party to a place high up in the hills. A new Swedish friend named Ambra—a glamorous, golden, high-spirited young woman—sent Thérèse a covering for her head, a white woolen cap and a peaked white goatskin cap to go over that, for it would be cold in the open sleigh. Five minutes before the appointed time we looked out of the upper window at the head of the stairs and saw another storybook picture. Grouped like the figures on a clock dial around the snow-covered circular drive were twelve gaily painted double sleighs, piled with yellow and red pillows. The sorrel horses blew their breaths into the frosty air, and the stalwart drivers stood with the collars of their fleece-lined coats turned up over the ears to meet the edge of their pulled-down sheepskin caps.

Our tall rubicund driver helped Thérèse into the sleigh and then motioned her to snuggle down and lean against the pillows at the back. He wrapped her feet and legs in a soft green blanket and pulled two noble fleece-lined covers up about her, tucking her in like a baby. He next went through the same routine with me beside her. And then with Count Trompi, the hotel's ski master, and with Ambra, resplendent in white fox coat and ermine toque. These two were put at the opposite end of our sleigh, facing us and traveling backwards. In the posture one assumes in a gondola we half-reclined, as luxurious, peaceful, and excited as if we were to view for the first time sights on the Grand Canal.

Off we went at what is called a merry clip, the honey-colored manes of the horses flying in the wind and the strings of bells jingling like a Christmas chorus from twelve sets of harness. The motion of a holiday sleigh behind a fast horse on a frosty afternoon is something to induce smiles and little thrills of pleasure all the way. When we took the curves, our sleigh slipped and skidded on the icy roads with just enough uncertainty to give a pleasant fillip of danger. Sometimes we came so close to whitened branches of fir trees that they brushed the horses' flanks and flicked snow against our cheeks. From our low position, hardly a foot from the ground, the stark whiteness of the landscape rising about us was more impressive than that of gilded walls in Venice.

As we reached high country, here and there on the hilltops stood the gray log huts of the *säters,* in which the cowgirls live, while tending cattle and making cheese during the summer pasturing. In a small clearing among firs and gray alders the twelve sleighs drew up before a large one-room cottage owned by the Swedish Tourist Association. It was like hundreds of others erected about the country for the convenience of hiking vacationists. A bright fire burned in a corner fireplace, where the short split birch logs were up-ended in the usual Swedish manner. The aroma of good strong coffee mingled pleasantly with the cleansing aromatic odor of burning birch and pine cones, for Miss Arpi had preceded us to get things ready. At a long table covered with blue and white oilcloth we sat down, forty-odd strong, to eat cake and drink coffee. Having lost their natural reserve and restraint in the invigorating ride, the Swedes chattered like Danes and actually addressed other Swedes to whom they had not been formally introduced. Musicians appeared and made music with old-fashioned country instruments, the harp and buckhorn, the bagpipe and fiddle. In the late afternoon, after the place had been cleaned and the wood box filled for the next occupants, we drove home through the chill atmosphere to the tintinnabulation of the twelve sets of bells and a different song in each sleigh.

The next day, not by sleigh but in a small chartered bus, a group of us went to visit a typical Dalecarlian farm. The place had been in the same family since 1590. One wing of the old house had been left intact as a kind of museum. Its walls were much decorated in Dalarna baroque, and bright painted shelves held antique pieces in pewter and copper. Behind the fireplace were built-in bunks where in olden days stranger-guests were invited to sleep. The widow proprietress, wearing her accustomed peasant costume, was an energetic, homely old woman with rough red skin, bad teeth, and a merry twinkle. She showed us first the part of the house the family actually lived in. The old-fashioned kitchen had been modernized to the extent of electric lights, radio, cream separator, and a stainless-steel sink. It was scrupulously clean, and pots of flowers lined the window ledges. In an open cupboard under the stove two sleepy kittens stretched themselves in household comfort.

With the temperature outside at zero centigrade, the old housewife's bedroom was warm, though there had been no fire in it since the evening before. The little tile stove retained the heat all day, and the fires were made only at night. But the double windows were kept airtight. Though most Swedes are fanatical out-of-doors enthusiasts, for seven months of the year the peasants never let a breath of winter air slip into the houses, if they can help it. And for all the shining cleanliness of this place, the atmosphere smelt stale like slightly rancid milk.

The dining room was definitely cold because it was used only on special occasions. But there we were invited to behold the silver loving cups jammed together on the sideboard thick as a wild spruce forest. The old lady was more proud of them than of her own heirlooms, for they had been won by her various farmer sons in bicycle races.

Thérèse and I were the only ones who wanted to see the cows. Though the cow stable across the courtyard was cleaned daily like the house, the manure odor was somewhat suffocating. For seven months of the year the five fat cows were stanchioned in stalls far narrower than jail cells. Our visit caused great interest among the bored beasts, who nearly twisted their eyeballs out of their sockets trying to get better looks at the strangers. One unstalled yearling rose to lick the old lady's hand out of affection and respect. And as it tried to follow us, it stepped on two pert pigs, pink as rosebuds. The pigs squealed wildly, not from hurt, but from excitement at the broken monotony of long incarceration.

The rest of the crowd, not as interested in bucolic winter arrangements as I, had strolled back to the bus, but I wanted to take the old lady's picture. Just as I had her placed by a fancy carved porch pillar, she threw up her hands and rushed away, insisting that she must put on her proper headdress. Thérèse said she imagined it must be some antique flowery thing. The bus horn blew, and blew again. Still the old lady did not return. At last she appeared with a kind of plaited rope, which she began winding about her hair ritually. The usually well-mannered, patient Swedes in the bus now blew the horn somewhat impatiently, for they were cold. But the old lady wound with Swedish imperturbability, though she, too, heard the motor start. At last, when I thought the bus might really leave us, the old lady triumphantly tied a white rag peasantwise over her head and under her chin so that the wound rope was completely hid. Then she grinned snaggle-toothed and nodded for me to snap her picture.

CHURCH, MINK, AND A LAUREL WREATH

On Sunday mornings the hotel guests usually go to church either at Rättvik or Leksand, largely to see the native costumes. Both churches are happily situated. The Rättvik church does not stand in the midst of the village, but on a low promontory projecting into the lake. The main body of the building has been there since 1300 and the groined vaulting dates from the fifteenth century when the religion was Roman Catholic. In olden times those who lived around the lake came to church in summer in long boats equipped with ten pairs of oars. Those who came by sleigh or carriage had their stables near the church. These small wooden huts, a hundred strong, still stand grouped like a miniature hamlet. It was in this churchyard of Rättvik in December of 1520 that Gustavus Vasa, "the father of modern Sweden," first pleaded with the peasants of Dalarna to support him in a revolt against the Danish king. An eighteen-foot stone shaft set on a barrowlike mound in Old Norse style commemorates the event, and it is surrounded by a dozen lesser stones inscribed with the names of the twelve persons who helped him escape from the Danes.

For our first Sunday service, however, we went to Leksand rather than Rättvik. The church grounds are entered through handsome wrought-iron gates with shingled pillars. The approach to the church is an avenue of four rows of gigantic birch trees planted early in the nineteenth century. This crisp Sunday the leafless branches did not seem at all like "bare, ruined choirs," but sparkled festively with ice particles like brilliants, while the ground beneath was spread with a deep, velvety carpet of snow. The white church with the black bulbous turret had been built in 1709 under the inspiration of a rector who had been attracted by Byzantine architecture in South Russia, where he had served as chaplain in the armies of Charles XII.

We went early to watch the congregation gather. The women wore short white lambskin jackets and black skirts with the apron panels embroidered in narrow vertical stripes of different colors. The married women had old-fashioned white caps with many ribbons; the unmarried women, red or flowered caps. Widows were to be recognized by bright-yellow aprons and white veils, very fetching indeed on the younger ones, and quite a contrast to the funereal, crapy black of widows in Stockholm.

The church was just comfortably full. Since earliest times the Dale folk, noted for clinging to old parish customs, have had a good record for church attendance. In olden days even the severest winter never stopped them; for when it was coldest, they felt a moral obligation to go to help warm the unheated church with their bodies. Today, though the church is furnace-heated, the parishioners come just the same. The singing was mighty, true, and impressive. For generations the men of Dalarna have been renowned for their fine voices and choral singing. Jussi Björling, the Metropolitan Opera tenor, comes from the region and before he learned operatic arias he sang the good old Lutheran hymns. For his text the dark-haired minister had chosen a verse from Proverbs, "And he that is of a cool spirit is a man of understanding." It struck me as being both strikingly Swedish and of particular significance in the charged, war-imminent year of 1939.

After the service we lingered a little in the serenely ordered cemetery, which is particularly admired in summer. For me one inscription on a headstone seemed to say the thing better than the others.

> How sweet to have lived,
> How beautiful that one can die.

Adjoining the churchyard cemetery is the home of Dr. Axel Munthe, physician-in-ordinary to King Gustav, and author of the international best seller *The Story of San Michele*. Built in old manor style of white stucco with black metal trimming and a black roof, the house is charming behind its white brick wall, with an avenue of birches leading to it. The author-physician said he found the Leksand cemetery the most satisfying in all the world and expected to rest eternally in this very heart of Sweden's heart.*

The most admired personage of the district is the Nobel Prize poet Erik Axel Karlfeldt, who died in 1931. His farm lies on the old highway between Leksand and Rättvik near the hamlet of Sjugare. Here his widow and son continue to live in the old home. Miss Arpi had asked permission to bring Thérèse and me, and we stopped there to pay our respects on the way from church. The garden, noted as one of the loveliest in Dalarna, was now masked by winter and further disguised by something quite unnatural. Numerous small cages, set in parallel rows and following the slope toward the frozen lake, housed mink, whose pelts the Karlfeldt son planned to sell in the London market. Swedes were somewhat resentful of the business that sullied the Karlfeldt garden. The acrid odor of live mink, they said, was most unsuitable incense before the shrine of the lyrist who so happily had captured in melodious verse the rich humor, the wisdom, and the grace of Dalarna.

Young Karlfeldt was busy in the little carpentry shop, making more cages to house more mink. He was working fast, for it was

---

* On February 11, 1949, at the age of ninety-one, Dr. Munthe died at the Royal Palace in Stockholm, where he had been the King's guest since 1943.

the mating season and each mink skin would bring fifty-six shillings or more. Mrs. Karlfeldt showed us everything from the fierce little beasts in the cages to the homey drawing room with its antique peasant furniture, its old copper and pewter. We saw the study where the poet wrote by a large window overlooking Lake Siljan— and on his desk lay the laurel wreath, the medal, and the citation from the Nobel Committee. In 1931 the prize had been awarded posthumously, and the $40,000 material part of it helped preserve the poet's home. But the mink industry was deemed a necessity for family expenses. On my return in 1946, however, the cages had been removed to ground less sacrosanct and the air was fragrant with flowers.

WAFFLES ON ANNUNCIATION DAY

Though Sweden went through the Reformation and turned from Catholicism to Lutheran Protestantism with no bloodshed and virtually no pain, the people clung vigorously to household celebrations of certain religious festivals like Incarnation Day. On March 25, celebrating the Annunciation when Mary received assurance from the Angel Gabriel that she was to bear the Lord, all good Swedish housewives serve waffles with strawberry jam.

In honor of the feast day Miss Arpi had a small dinner party for us, to which she asked Ambra and Count Trompi, Dr. Carth, director of one of Stockholm's hospitals, Stig Engelbert, a lively, red-haired young jeweler, the young Countess Wachtmeister, the director of a cellulose plant and his wife, and old Mr. Knut Nyblom, the ballad singer, whose professor father had been mentor to Prince Eugen.

The skåling began with the cocktails before the smörgåsbord, the hostess welcoming us to Siljansborg. With the fish the skåling was done in white wine, and now the hostess made another little speech of welcome. After the main meat course with red wine came the big speech of welcome, with praise of Dalarna, love of the land, and hopes for our pleasure in the province. Then everybody looked into everybody else's eyes, drank, looked again, gave slight bows as glasses were set down.

Swedes react happily to alcohol. Everybody became more and

more amiable and relaxed and talkative. All the men skåled with Thérèse. I skåled with all the women, except the hostess, whose privilege it is to invite the skåls herself.

"When I was a young girl and very shy in London," Miss Arpi said, "at a dinner party no one would drink with me. Being a guest, I dared not drink unless the hostess or some gentleman invited me. As the evening wore on, I grew more thirsty and miserable. At the end of the meal there stood my row of four full glasses. Finally, when I saw we were about to rise from the table, in desperation and pique, I took each glass as it came and drained it to the dregs. Later I learned that in England ladies drank wine as they pleased, without having to wait, as Swedish women do, for a skål from a gentleman."

For the last course came the hot waffles and strawberry jam, the traditional dessert on the Feast of the Annunciation—why, no one present could recall at the moment.

"Today in Sweden is called *Vårfrudagen,* 'Wives' Day,'" said Mr. Nyblom, as if that helped.

"But why?" I pondered aloud. "The Virgin Mary was not married at the time."

The old gentleman's ruby cheeks lost their color, and he stared at me in amazed horror. Then he bethought himself and at last exclaimed *"Ja-so!"* and he could not help but smile.

Dr. Carth explained that Mr. Nyblom had slipped up as a linguist, and that *Vårfrudagen* did not mean "Wives' Day," but "The Day of Our Lady," though, of course, *fru* did also mean "spouse." "In the Lutheran church," he added, "the Feast of the Annunciation is called officially *Marias Bebådelsedag,* or literally 'The Day of Mary's Advance Information,' which sounds a bit prosaic, God wot."

In the blue and white parlor we gathered for coffee and skåled for the last time, the men with brandy, the ladies with crème de menthe. Then the seventy-year-old Mr. Nyblom sang songs to his lute (made in 1799), and despite his cracked and trembling voice, his artistry delighted us.

In the midst of a rendition of a song of Carl Michael Bellman about taking breakfast with Ulla Winblad on a summer's day, he broke off suddenly. "I know why we eat waffles and jam today!" he cried out. "My professor father told me when I was a little boy. In the north of Sweden *Vårfrudagen* became pronounced more and more carelessly until it sounded like *Våfflordagen,* or 'The Day of Waffles.' The original meaning had been lost. Hence waffles and jam." It was the climax of his performance.

A village orchestra played dance music in the big drawing room, and everybody seemed in as gay a mood as at Midsummer. Stig, the red-haired young man, joked and laughed and danced as un-restrainedly as an American college youth, and pounded out swing music on the piano in a most un-Swedish manner, when the orchestra took an intermission.

After ten-o'clock tea and sandwiches a dozen Rättvik girls and men came in their native costumes to put on a repertoire of Dalarna dances. The men wore flowered waistcoats, bright-blue jackets, and yellow knee breeches of doeskin with white stockings, which set off their virile country legs. The pretty girls wore almost all the colors of the rainbow, including the blue of their peaked caps, which about 1935 had inspired Schiaparelli hoods on evening wraps.

> The coat-tails they fluttered, the aprons they flew,
> And braids were a-flapping and skirts flung askew,
> While the music would whimper and drone.*

But the swishing of skirts, the stamping of feet, and the twirlings under a man's upraised arm could not obliterate the redness of the hands of those light-foot girls who were dairy maids and washer-women. The girls enacted little dramatic pantomimes with spirit, though they could not equal either the grace or the abandon of the men dancers, "who are nimble at tossing a girl at the skies, and at catching her when she comes down." Except for the lack of a multi-ribboned Maypole, we might have been celebrating St. John's Day at Midsummer instead of the Promise of the Lord's Coming in snowy March.

SKIERS IN THE WILDERNESS

Snow is a profitable commodity for hotel business in the Lake Siljan district, for skiing is one of the chief attractions from January to April. All of the three best resort hotels, Siljansborg and Pers-borg near Rättvik, and Långbersgården at Tallberg, provide ski

* See Charles Wharton Stork's excellent translations of Fröding's poetry.

instructors for their guests. But skiing is by no means the be-all and end-all of a winter vacation in the Vale of Siljan, as it is at the great hotel with the jawbreaker name, Kur-och-Högsfjällshotellet at Sälen high in mountains near the Norwegian border. Since its completion in 1938 Sälen has been the most fashionable ski resort in Sweden, patronized by British and Danish nobility as well as by Swedish sportsmen.

Three motorcar loads of us drove from Siljansborg to spend the day at Sälen, but only the more expert took along their skis, for the mountain slopes there are steep. Much of the road lay through deep snow country and cut through forests of spruce and pine. When we came upon houses they were of square-cut logs, unpainted and weathered a silver gray. With their barns and stables built around courtyards, they resembled animals huddled together for protection against wolves and bears. The most stirring to the imagination was a long gray timbered farmhouse renowned as one of the places in which Gustavus Vasa took refuge on his flight. After four centuries it stood steadfast, alone and enduring on its sloping hillside, its roofs having borne the snows of more than four hundred winters.

Past this house the famous Vasa Ski Race has its course at the beginning of every March. The race commemorates the decision of the Dalarna peasants to back Gustavus Vasa in his proposed revolt against the Danes, and to send two ski-runners from Mora after him in January, 1521. When the two caught up with the fugitive patriot at Sälen, the fortunes of Swedish history turned. Today the ski-runners, in reverse order, must cover the distance of fifty-six miles over the mountains and through the forests from Sälen to Mora. This sporting event is a kind of national and patriotic festival, and every year crowds come to witness the finish at the Gustavus Vasa statue in Mora, where the champion is wreathed with laurel.

The last lap of the motor journey to Sälen is up a winding narrow road between snowbanks high as a wall and hard as a rock. Beyond the village the resort hotel sits on a bare plateau with mountains rising spectacularly all about it. In style it is functional in the extreme. Inside, it is garishly decorated in a bold and heavy-handed modern manner. "The manager is Norwegian," the

Swedes say, as if explaining the clashing colors. The whole thing seems an anomaly—this extravagantly modernistic structure in the wintry wastes, with smart guests lunching in their smart ski togs and dressing for dinner.

But out of the vast plate-glass windows of the dining room we look upon a stirring sight. A great slab of white mountain rears up precipitously. Stunted trees resembling dwarfish men punctuate the camellia whiteness. Dark human figures move slowly up the incline or flash down like zigzag crayon streaks on the white paper of a tilted drawing board. At first the only way one can distinguish the dwarf trees from skiers is by movements.

Count Trompi and five others from our party had headed straight for the mountain on arrival. As we grew accustomed to the scene we could recognize Trompi descending in skillful curving slaloms and then shooting straight into the valley out of our sight. "You see," said Ambra as he descended, "skiers, like ballet dancers, need trained legs and also the hearts of lions." "But if you do not ski," she added, "there is nothing to do here but look at the snow and eat yourself fat."

The luncheon in this remote northern wilderness was memorably delicious and a tribute to the management. For smörgåsbord: Russian caviar, lobster mayonnaise, lamb kidneys from the chafing dish, several cheeses, and a green salad; for the main course: beef tenderloin and fruit salad; followed by coffee and cakes and cherry brandy served on the sun veranda.

ANDERS ZORN LIVES IN MORA

During my stay in Dalarna in 1946 I continued to recall nostalgically excursions in the snow in 1939. But historic Mora, at the lake, is the one place that improves with full-bodied summer. Perhaps it is the pervading influence of the zestful artist Anders Zorn, who painted the buxom peasant girls with a Rubens-like exuberance. Though Mora has existed since the Middle Ages, when it was a trading post between Norway and Finland, the town is as much Anders Zorn as Stratford-on-Avon is William Shakespeare. It is the Zorn house, the Zorn garden and Zorn grave, and the Zorn pictures that tourists come to see, rather than the fifteenth-century church with its tower by Nicodemus Tessin, a gift from Charles XI to the local peasants in 1673. Though Gustavus Vasa spoke the words here at New Year's, 1521, that subsequently resolved the farmers to send ski-runners to bring him back to lead the fight for independence, it was Anders Zorn who made the hero's noble statue and set it on the very spot where he harangued the crowd.

In the excellent Zorn museum, opened in May, 1939, hang many of the most famous Zorn paintings. Just outside of the village at Skeriol stands the Zorn-created out-of-doors museum of old Dalarna dwellings, dairies, lofts, storehouses, wells, together with relics from the Stone and Iron Ages. Close by is the Folk High School and Agricultural School established by Zorn and supported in perpetuity by his estate. The vitality of the artist, who died in 1920, continues to pulse through Mora today. And a highly intelligent woman doctor of philosophy, Gerda Boëthius, tends the fires of the Zorn sanctuary like a vestal virgin. She is his art executor, as well as directress of the art museum. She lives across the river in a charming old house to which Zorn's widow gave her a deed one morning when she was invited for breakfast. In the paneled dining room of 1793 Dr. Boëthius entertained Rosvall and me at luncheon and answered my questions about the artist.

Anders Zorn was born in Mora in 1860, son of an unwed farmer's daughter by a German brewery worker. He was brought up on his grandfather's farm at Utmeland, a mile and a half to the north, that same Utmeland that is famous for one of the narrow escapes of Gustavus Vasa. There Margit, wife of Tomt Matts, hid Vasa in the cottage cellar and fooled the Danish pursuers by placing a vat of Christmas home-brew over the trap door.

Besides a mighty gusto for living, Zorn was endowed with a variety of talents, which won him world eminence with brush, pen, chisel, and etching needle. After many years of foreign travel he returned to his home village with his wealthy, cultured Jewish wife, Emma Lamm, of Stockholm. The lady shared Zorn's enthusiasm for preserving the cultural traditions of Dalarna and gave unstintingly of her money and her time. She helped further the handicraft work, and in arranging the annual musical competitions at Gesunda, which were a part of Zorn's vigorous campaign to collect and preserve the local folk music.

Emma Zorn had rare wifely understanding of her artist husband's seeming needs. She let him retain the illusion of freedom and never pried into his relations with his models. Of only one she may have been jealous, the one he had loved in his bachelor days, a slim one, whom he never desired to paint in the nude. This woman was still alive in 1946, and despite her white hair, as fresh looking as a field flower. When I was taken to call at her ancestral farm, we found her pressing a granddaughter's frilled lawn dress with an electric iron. Dressed in a color that matched her forget-me-not blue eyes, with delicate features and a fine-textured, pink and white complexion, she was as pretty as she was full of natural grace. If Zorn could see her now, I thought, twenty-six years after his death, he would surely want to paint her in her sun-splashed yellow kitchen, where flower boxes lined the window ledges and an odd kind of country charm pervaded the atmosphere.

That Zorn was as successful in portraying old ladies as desirable young girls, one can see from studies he made of his mother both in oil and bronze. Apparently this mother, who had the respect of her neighborhood, was a remarkable woman, despite her lack of education and her youthful indiscretion that resulted in the creation of Zorn himself. She was worshiped by her famous son until her death at the age of eighty-two. As if further to point the attachment, Providence arranged that the mother and son should die and be buried in the same year, 1920.

No Swede has warmed both hands before the fires of life more expansively than Anders Zorn. He reveled in light: sunlight, gas light, firelight. His naked peasant girls, bathing at sunrise or sunset or in the full flame of noon in some rippling river or emerging from a bath in a copper tub before a crackling fire, reflect his appreciation of luminous flesh. His amoral models are golden and rosy with health, with well-fed rumps and curvaceous breasts and midriffs. Doubtless it was because, as Dr. Boëthius said with a twinkle, "Zorn believed ample stomachs reflected the light in the best way."

Though Zorn's nudes are his best-known subjects, he painted far more clothed figures than naked. Next to flesh tints, red and green were his favorite colors; he got an especially evocative subtlety into them, as Rembrandt did with browns and yellows.

With many critics Zorn ranks even higher as an etcher than as a painter in oils. But he was highly successful, too, with aquarelle and pencil drawing; and he carved figures in wood and stone and made statues of bronze. Almost everything he did had a sensuous vibration, and wisely he eschewed spiritual interpretations and religious themes. Zorn was of the earth, though not earthy in any grimy sense. He depicted a land of milk and honey, of simple abundance, where folk of abounding health and good spirits danced after work. His heartiness is expressed with taste, for the joy Zorn took in being a human being was never vulgar. Completely opposite to the tortured probings of Sweden's great dramatist August Strindberg, Zorn's productions radiate an incorrigible optimism.

Zorn reverenced the old, and for his studio he set up in his garden a beautiful timbered "fire-house" from about the year 1100. The Zorn dwelling house, constructed in accordance with the ancient tradition of Swedish carpentry and wood architecture, has tarred timbered walls and a steeply sloping roof with decorations of dragon's beaks. From the outside the Zorn house is odd-looking rather than attractive. Inside it is cluttered with a few beautiful objects and with scores of things of doubtful taste, like those which artists everywhere seem to have collected in the decades around 1900.

Since the recent death of Emma Zorn the artist's home, with all the intimate appurtenances of daily living, is now open to the public. The guest towels and the soap and the chamber pots in the bridal-like white guest room seem awaiting imminent arrivals. The lofty billiard room, with its thronelike spectator seats and bookshelves that can be reached only by towering ladders, looks as if Zorn might return for a game or a volume at any moment. In the dining room the table is set as if for expected guests or unexpected ones who might not even have bothered to call No. 4 on the old-fashioned telephone.

The Zorns lived no life of artistic seclusion, but took an active part in social as well as municipal and provincial affairs. Their house rang with the merriment of guests, celebrated personages from Sweden or abroad, and local old-time friends. The much-traveled Anders Zorn found his native Dalarna, and particularly Mora, as tempting a playground as any in the world. And like Zorn, vacationing Swedes find Dalarna delectable, each having his most favored spot.

After all-day summer excursions I was ever as pleased to return in the evenings to Siljansborg as I had been when March snow lay thick on the earth and the lake was a sheet of ice. Standing at the window my last day, looking out at the water sparkling with the gold of sunset, I watched two gay pleasure steamers meet and exchange greetings, as one returned to Mora, the other to Rättvik. I recalled my first view of the lake, when the figures on "kick-sleds" had emerged, met, conferred on the lonely white waste, and then returned in the twilight the way each one had come. With human activity or without, in one season or another, the lake was a picture that never failed to delight. I thought of what Hans Christian Andersen had written as a tourist: "Painter and poet, shake hands and go up to Dalarna. That country is rich in beauty and poetry, and richest at Lake Siljan."

Some foreign visitors go to Dalarna for sport rather than for beauty. Some go for utter *dolce far niente,* rather than merrymaking. One may treasure in memory a special boating party on the lake, or a view of an incomparable sunset from the belvedere of Långbersgården, or the twirling dancers about a Midsummer Maypole, or a torch-lit sleigh ride through the white and silent forest. Whatever one's experiences, if there is response or affection in him, he is bound to leave a bit of his own heart in this heart of Sweden.

3.

The Spell of Värmland

It is a sweet land, this Sweden; but haunted a bit in places.

—KAREL ČAPEK

GUN FACTORY IN THE MEADOWS

"THE SWEDES more than the other Nordic nations," Sigrid Undset once said to me, "know the desire to create an imaginary world above the real one. See how the lyrist Carl Michael Bellman lifted the underworld of his Stockholm into a realm of golden clouds of beauty and music and melancholy." And as the songs of the beloved wastrel Bellman turned the traffic of sailors' dives into a roseate region of enchantment, so, in her stories, Selma Lagerlöf cast such glamour over the province of Värmland that today travelers often remark the region with the author's eyes as much as their own.

Since the publication of Lagerlöf's *Gösta Berlings Saga* in 1891, the novel has been the key to the spell of Värmland. To visit the province without reading the book is to miss half the enjoyment. As Christopher Morley once whimsically carried Shakespeare's *The Tempest* about with him as a guidebook to Bermuda, many Swedes and many foreigners take a copy of *Gösta Berling* to Värmland, and two maps of the Fryken Valley region, one with the true geographical names and one with the nomenclature of Selma Lagerlöf.

Värmland's western boundary marches with Norway's eastern mountains, and her southern parishes lie along Lake Vänern, Sweden's largest lake. The province has been peculiarly well supplied with the three natural resources which contribute most to Sweden's economy: the soil, the forests, and iron. The exploitation

69

of these factors has made for a heritage of culture and gracious living.

Fact and fancy, shrewd practicality and idealism, a love of land and of masquerade, high spirits and dark tinges of melancholy make odd paradoxes in the life of the workaday region. This province of old ironworks and new cellulose mills and one of the world's great arsenals gave birth to Sweden's two greatest poets, Esaias Tegnér and Gustaf Fröding, and to its most noted historian, Erik Gustaf Geijer, as well as to its most popular novelist, Selma Lagerlöf. Värmland was also the birthplace of the engineer John Ericsson, inventor of the revolving gun turret and designer of that cheese-box-on-a-raft *Monitor* that helped to turn the tide against the Confederacy.

It was largely because of Selma Lagerlöf that we visited Värmland twice in 1939—in the spring of late May, when she was still at her winter home in Falun, and in the summer of early July, because she had returned. We were the last Americans to see her, for she died in March of 1940.

On May 22nd we entered the province of lyricism and big business from the east by way of Bofors, the internationally famous munitions works whose output of guns during the years 1940-45 so mightily strengthened Sweden's defense that Hitler felt his losses might be too severe to risk. Like most Swedish factories, Bofors has a charming setting. The hills about were dotted with the graceful fascicled larch trees and the meadows were bright with yellow flowers called "golden wives." The pleasant houses of the workmen who manufactured the death-dealing instruments were arranged informally along new-made winding streets cut through little forests of silver birch.

On the hills sat the director's splendid manor and the homes of the high officials. Evert Wijkander, the director, was one of those tall cultivated Swedes we had come to expect to find among the industrialists, but he also was handsomer than any of the others. We lunched with him on woodcock in the private dining room of a new 1,500,000-kronor hotel built to entertain buyers of guns. William Batt, the dynamic head of the U. S. branch of S. K. F., the Swedish Ball and Roller Bearing Industry, made the sixth luncheon guest that day with Count Trompi and Ambra, who were driving us from Örebro to Karlstad.

"You may be sure," the amiable Mr. Batt said to me with a grin, as we drove about after luncheon inspecting the workers' houses and the various amenities, "these Swedes haven't done a thing for labor they weren't forced to."

"Well, in any case," I said, "it's nice to see the curse taken off industry with these neat gardens, winding streets, and recreation parks. I wish you American industrialists would take a whole fistful of leaves from the Swedish book.

"And look," I added, "at the faces of the workers. They all have happy and contented expressions."

"The boys ought to, the way they work," Batt said amiably.

When Director Wijkander later took me alone through the factory, I saw what Batt meant. The workmen moved with a slowness and deliberation that astounded even me, who came from the South where people do not hurry. Everyone I remarked seemed like a W.P.A. worker. But these men differed in a main essential: they knew well what they were doing and they did it expertly. The presence of the passing director or of a foreman stimulated not the slightest impetus to their movements. I was all for telling Mr. Wijkander to have the foreman jack them up, for some of them seemed to be merely standing about daydreaming, perhaps saving their energy for helping with the construction of their own houses or for working in their vegetable plots or for playing an athletic match on the sports field. Well, the war was not on yet, and Sweden was in no danger of invasion. When Sweden really needed defending, these men were to work with patriotic intensity and devotion.

Since visitors were not admitted into the plant, I was informally sworn to secrecy in regard to anything connected with the machinery of gun manufacture. But since I was utterly lacking in scientific talent, it was all like descriptions of another planet written in undecipherable language.

The metallic actuality of what I beheld was to me akin to a dream phantasmagoria through which I wandered. Among other fabulous devices I saw the new electro-steel plant equipped with a 15-ton furnace, and the steel foundry, the largest in Scandinavia. We wandered under erected 75-mm. antiaircraft guns and beneath 25-mm. naval guns in double turret. I saw field howitzers and mountain howitzers, armored turrets and torpedo air vessels, illuminating shells and tracer shells, mine bombs and incendiary bombs. I gazed upon nitroglycerine and nitrocellulose powder and explosives like penthyl, tetryl, bonite, TNT, and dynamite. During the walk through the spotless galleries and well-scrubbed corridors of potential hell, the air was now and again rent with battle roar. Three miles from the works are the Bofors proving grounds, twenty miles long, where continual testing of new types of shells, fuses, and gunpowder break the pastoral peace.

And as we walked, Mr. Wijkander, urbane, informal, looking every inch a man of distinction in his well-tailored tweeds, explained this or answered that question. Bofors was far from being a come-lately concern. The first furnaces and forges, he told me, were set up here in 1646, not so long after the Pilgrims arrived at the Rock they called Plymouth. The choice of location was made because of near-by waterfalls and surrounding forests with plenty of fuel and, of course, the iron ore, which was not far away. The big days began in 1894, when Alfred Nobel acquired control of the works near the end of his career.

We spoke of the paradox of the great Nobel, inventor of explosives and a peace-loving idealist, a man with a passion for Shelley and the Swedish lyric poets, an astute financier, who had contempt for Mammon and who became one of the richest men in Europe.

In short order Nobel had made Bofors one of the world's munition centers. When he invented dynamite, he conceived of it as a helpful agency in industrial blasting. And when he created smoke-less gunpowder and other armaments, he hoped the very destructiveness of his inventions would so appall nations that wars would become obsolete. In 1892 he told a member of the Bern Peace Conference, "My factories may end war sooner than your congresses. The day when two armies can destroy each other in a second, all civilized nations will recoil from war and disband their armies."

Possessing a compassionate love for humanity, for his own personal life he never cared greatly. "Alfred Nobel—a wretched half-life," he once penned his autobiography in a single sentence, "should have been choked by a humane physician when he made his entry into life, howling."

A dreamer, devoted to foreign travel, he never married, but he so adored his mother that he would rush back from far corners of the globe to celebrate her birthday with her. When he was seventeen, he made his first trip to the United States partly to visit the Värmlander inventor, Captain John Ericsson, and observe his various mechanical inventions. Here in 1858, three years before the Civil War commenced, he saw the plans for the *Monitor,* and it was while in the United States that he conceived his youthful idea of disarmament among nations.

Nobel died just before the twentieth century began, leaving his vast fortune in trust to reward annually outstanding benefactors of mankind, among them persons who have done most for the furtherance of world peace. Happily he was spared awareness of the ghastly carnage and corroding hates of the two World Wars. He missed horrible imaginings of a possible third World War with atomic weapons that might wipe out not only armies in a minute, but entire nations.

In 1939 at Bofors, Nobel's ideal of complete disarmament and his belief in civilized men ultimately coming to their senses never seemed more ironic. But in the sunshine of a May afternoon, driving through the heart-lifting Värmland countryside, irony was no more fitting in thoughts than antitank guns were on the plowed fields where seed sprouted like a green dew.

HEADQUARTERS FOR BUSINESS AND ROMANCE

Karlstad, the capital of Värmland, lies conveniently on the State Railways line between Stockholm and Oslo, sixty miles from the Norwegian border. Few are the visitors to Scandinavia who do not stop for a few days at Karlstad, making headquarters at the Stadshotell and taking excursions by motorcar, bicycle, bus, or lake boat into the Selma Lagerlöf country.

The provincial capital, with a population of 28,000, is thrice-blessed in its waterside setting. It lies at the head of Lake Vänern, Sweden's largest lake, at the mouth of the swift-running Klarälven River. Karlstad is the oldest town in the province, receiving its charter in 1584; known as Tingvalla during the Middle Ages, it has long been a significant trading center. In the nineteenth century a fire wiped out much of the old town; and in the new municipal planning the streets were made wide, the squares spacious, the parks plenteous. Though an active commercial center, substantial beauty in architecture and green breathing space so prevail that Karlstad seems like a leisure town. The Stadshotell, the largest provincial hostelry in Sweden, is beautifully situated with an extensive view of the great river, where the flotillas of logs pass under a many-arched eighteenth-century bridge to the cellulose mills six miles below. Historically, Karlstad is not important except for a single momentous occurrence. Here in 1905 negotiations between Swedish and Norwegian representatives ended in the peaceful dissolution of the Union that had joined Sweden and Norway under the same king. The Norwegians were preparing to secede and had begun to fortify their borders. War seemed inevitable between the sister countries, in which there had been no foreign war for almost a century. But Swedish Labor threatened a paralyzing general strike if Sweden took up arms against her recalcitrant sister. So the reasonable Swedes reluctantly and sadly let Norway separate and become a nation apart.

In the sixteenth century Karlstad had already assumed some importance as the outlet for the numerous iron foundries that sprang up in the vale called Fryksdalen with its forty-three miles of narrow lakes. At the beginning of the eighteenth century eighty per cent of England's iron requirements were met by exports from Sweden, and much of the hammered pig iron came out of Värmland by way of Karlstad across Lake Vänern and thence to Göteborg and the North Sea to English ports.

Our room at the Stadshotell was in the long wing that gave on the river. It was a charming room, with French furniture, gray hangings, and pale-blue walls—everything in excellent taste. The little balcony overlooked the water where felled logs from the upland forests came drifting by. In the flame-colored sunset they resembled great round bars of greenish gold.

Trees are really the green gold of the country, for forest products are today the prime factor in the economic life of Sweden. The potential value of wood was discovered after the middle of the nineteenth century, just as the day of the small iron foundries was ending in Värmland. And many of the country manors and the town mansions, which had come from iron fortunes, are now occupied by men whose high estate is based on wood.

On arrival we had been received not by one but two pretty young hostesses, a special innovation of Henry Odén, the hotel's gentleman manager. They had trained for their jobs with Scandinavian thoroughness, just as Odén himself had, for the hotel had been under the same family's management for almost half a century. The Norwegian girl had served her apprenticeship in Oslo's Grand Hotel, where her uncle was manager. The Swedish girl had worked as chambermaid at the Grand Hotel in Stockholm, had lived in England to perfect her English, and had been employed in various capacities at sports hotels at home and abroad. Both hostesses were cultivated and knew well the region's history, which was an essential in a province where the romantic and literary background is the tourist's magnet. Everything was done with tact and a kind of natural deprecating grace, which made hotel guests feel as though they were being entertained by the young daughters of a country estate.

That first evening, at one of those perfect Swedish dinners with a slight French accent, Odén gave us a hint of the temperamental make-up of the Värmlanders. He told us that small bands of wandering Tartars had once come into the land from the northeast. Then Finns settled in the northern and central portions of the province, but in time they were run up into the hills by the Swedes, and became wildish and got the reputation of wizards. In the seventeenth century Belgians were imported to teach the settled Swedes more about iron production. So in some Värmlanders there may be found a strain of Walloon or Finn or even a *soupçon* of gypsy. Not as utterly homogeneous as the other Swedes, Värmlanders are on the whole more friendly, more romantic, and a little madder.

Though Swedes in general are noted for their remarkable patience, the Värmlanders are not. If they do not understand a thing right away, they dismiss it forever. If they do not get what they desire immediately, they throw away all hope of it. Värmlanders are supposed to have prophetic dreams, as once when the poet Fröding told his mother of a dreadful dream of famine, and she said, "Get all the cash you can and buy grain." They bought, the famine came, and they were rich.

It was in this province, where the real and unreal are not always sharply defined, that strange legends grew and the characters peculiar to *Gösta Berlings Saga*. It is quite likely that if Selma Lagerlöf had been born and reared in some other Swedish province, she might never have attained special fame. But here she found bewitching folk tales crying out for preservation and characters of unforgettable flavor.

THE KEY TO THE SPELL

The next morning, with Odén and both hostesses, we went for an all-day motor tour of the Gösta Berling country. To give us the full benefit of the May sun, Odén put back the top of the car. Spring was merging into summer. The hawthorn was still in bloom. The odor of lilies-of-the-valley scented the hillsides. Some fields were white with the fragrant weeds called "almond flowers." Plowmen were turning by black earth, opulent and moist. The horses pulled the plows as if for joy and white butterflies swarmed ecstatically. On the roadsides farmers and children responded cheerily to the waves and shouted greetings of the hostesses, and we saw that Värmlanders were more friendly with strangers than other Swedes.

I carried two maps of that region between the Fryken Lake and the Klar River, the Gösta Berling country. One was the official Swedish, the other marked with those fictional names of the *Saga*. Between them, with the help of the hostesses, I amalgamated the contemporary places with the storybook events, like the chase of Anna and Gösta by the famished wolves, the kidnapping of Countess Dohna, the bitter auction at Borg.

From the south one starts at the lovely white church of Östra Ämtervik, which is the Svartsjö of the *Saga* and the real burying place of the Lagerlöfs. Herresta Hall is the Borg of fiction, and Sandsberg is Björne, the manor of the heroine Marianne Sinclair. The Bro of the story is the delightful resort town of Sunne, where today the little lake steamers *Gösta Berling* and *Selma Lagerlöf* tie up near the hotel. "Here is the parish of Bro," writes Lagerlöf, "in this land of wealth and joy, where the estates lay side by side and the great iron foundries adjoined one another. . . . Oh, life was one long dance of pleasure along the shores of Löfven Lake!"

Sunne is the very center of Gösta Berling land and lies only three miles from Rottneros Manor, the Ekeby of the story. This most important house in the novel was the one in which the Major's amazing wife lived and kept her twelve cavaliers in luxurious idleness in the guest wing. "She is the richest woman in Värmland, and as proud as a queen. She loves song and the music of violins. Cards and wine she likes, and a table surrounded with guests. She likes plenty in her pantry, dancing and gaiety in her halls, and to have the cavaliers' wing full of her pensioners."

Thus the author speaks of the Major's wife, who pleasured herself so bounteously to forget the loss of the only man she ever loved. And that devasting, poetic rake, Gösta Berling, who became one of her cavaliers, explained the carefree way of life thus: "We empty our mountains of their iron and fill our cellars with wine. The fields bear gold with which we gild life's misery, and we fell our forests to build pavilions and skittle-alleys."

In Ekeby, though we knew the separate cavaliers' wing had burned long ago, we had naturally expected a handsome house and a romantic garden. But instead of finding the place under a spell, it was remarkably familiar. Rottneros Manor was pure Virginia. The stately brick house painted white, with four massive Ionian columns towering to the top of the second story, was a variation of the architecture repeated hundreds of times in Southern ante-bellum houses. Even the vast sweep of lawn in front with the great shade trees and the lawn which sloped to the steel-blue lake at the back looked just like Virginia. The back façade with the balustraded veranda was completely Southern, and the clustered apple trees in bloom again recalled Virginia in April. "This, in Sweden!" Thérèse exclaimed. "It is pure Old South. Bring any Negro mammy here blindfolded, remove the handkerchief, and she would know this was home."

But though Rottneros Manor is one of the most splendid of the Värmland houses, it is not really so fine as scores of houses still to be seen in the South. And some of the so-called manors of the region are indeed simple—the one in which the old Countess Gerten danced with the Devil on New Year's Eve was merely a plain two-story house built in 1650 of wide wooden planks set vertically. Some of the gentry who still inhabit the manors are more or less impecunious, for the iron ore that made their ancestors rich has been exhausted. But they have their parties and dances, their moonlit sleigh rides and rounds of visits, and the men ride horseback and go on moose hunts in the hills to the north beyond Södra Finnskoga, the mysterious and lonely fen country, where the ministerial original of the Byronic Gösta Berling lived and worked.

Mårbacka, Selma Lagerlöf's home, which is the Lövdala of the *Saga,* lies about ten miles southeast of Sunne. It is, of course, the best-known private residence in Sweden. The author has written several books about the place in her childhood. But today the stucco house is much grander than it was when she was born there on November 20, 1858, in a two-story frame house painted the country red.

Mårbacka had been in possession of the Lagerlöf family for almost three centuries. But shortly after the death of the author's retired army officer father, the place had to be sold. Lieutenant Lagerlöf was a gay-hearted, expansive fellow, who squandered his wife's wealth and his own inheritance and failed in all his impractical schemes for improving production. As the bachelor Alfred Nobel adored his mother, so the spinster Selma Lagerlöf worshiped her dashing, lovable father, and kept his memory ever green by celebrating his birthday on August 17th decades after his decease. While she taught school, it was her chief ambition to wipe out her father's failure by retrieving the estate. And, besides, she personally suffered acutely the loss of the home place.

Many have seen the home of their childhood return their gaze like a wounded animal [she wrote]. Many have felt themselves guilty when they have seen the old trees dying away in the grasp of the lichens and the garden walks covered with grass. They could have fallen upon their knees before the fields, which formerly were covered with rich harvests, and begged them not to blame them for their shameful condition.

No place on earth is so wretched to enter upon as a ruined home.

Oh, I beg you—you who guard the fields and meadows and parks and the happy flower-gardens—guard them well! With love and work! It is not well that Nature should sorrow over mankind.

So the material incentive that spurred the young schoolteacher to labor on her stories was not so much to escape classroom drudgery as to buy and restore Mårbacka. The lady did not earn enough from her writings, however, to achieve all her heart's desire directly; but on winning the Nobel Award for Literature in 1909, with the $40,000 that went with the laurels, she was able to secure the estate and re-do the house as her father had dreamed. And here she spent the distinguished last three decades of her life in comfort and satisfaction.

With its creamy stucco walls and gabled black metal roof, Mårbacka is built more in the traditional Swedish manor style than Rottneros. Across the front veranda rise five sets of double Doric columns. Though the house was large enough to shelter most of the Lagerlöf relations, after the death of her aged mother Selma Lagerlöf resided alone with a secretary and servants, received visitors rarely, and shied away from interviews as assiduously as Greta Garbo.

Tens of thousands of persons from many lands, however, made pilgrimages to Mårbacka, and some even peeked in the windows and tramped over the garden. Finally a restraining chain had to be stretched across the driveway entrance about a hundred feet from the house. The chain could easily be dropped or crawled under or vaulted, but its cool, ordered links served as well as the flaming sword at Eden's gate. No Swede at least would ever go where he was asked not to, and aggressive foreigners seemed caught in the spell of Swedish lawfulness and respect when they approached Mårbacka. So for the last years of the author's life a single stretched chain protected the house's privacy, even when the chatelaine herself was absent at her winter home in Falun, where she was in this May of 1939.

Henry Odén, a friend of long standing, did not hesitate to drop the chain for us, and he received a warm welcome from the old gardener, who led us to the back garden. There we beheld a sight worth many miles of travel. Selma Lagerlöf's great cherry tree was at the climax of blooming.

I had not known that a cherry tree could grow to such proportions, or that a single tree could so dominate a place with luminous beauty and make everything for miles about seem of less consequence. As spectacular as a white peacock in full fan on green turf, it yet looked as hospitable as a sheltering shade tree in a family backyard. Its myriad white blossoms, ethereal, vibrant like starlight, were prodigal with promise of rich earthy fruit. For a long time we gazed admiringly from one angle and then another, until the old stooped gardener grew inches taller with wondering pride, as if his personal ministrations had called forth this magic snowdrift that enthralled us.

The radiance of the cherry was almost compensation for our disappointment in missing Selma Lagerlöf. And Odén now invited us to stop by Karlstad after our trip to Norway, promising that the lady would receive us, if she was not confined to bed. The gardener said she was sure to be fine after Midsummer, she always was.

As we drove away, Odén told us that the old man had never ceased to be perplexed about his mistress's source of income and her fame, which brought carloads of people to stare across the chain. Once in earlier days when he was working under her study windows and the maid was gathering flowers, the author heard him ask the girl, "Why is it really that our Selma is so famous?"

"It's her books," the maid said.

"Yes," he replied dubiously, "so they say. But she tells a lot of lies in them, now don't she? I've tried telling lies, too, but no good ever came to me from 'em."

THE WHITE MANORS AND PULPWOOD

We found it noteworthy that Sweden's three foremost writers in their fields—the romantic novel, history, and lyric poetry—were all born within a comfortable sleigh ride of each other and came from upper-class families and modest manors. Esaias Tegnér, the chief epic poet, was born farther away, at Rämen, north of Filipstad, and came from a manse.

Ransäter, the ancestral home of Erik Gustaf Geijer, Sweden's top historian, is about ten miles from Mårbacka. Whereas Mårbacka in the 1911 restoration became something quite different from the original "two-horse, ten-cow farm," Ransäter remains more or less as it was at Geijer's birth in 1783. The place is distinctive in that it is the only one-story manor in Värmland, and its long low white façade is uncommonly charming. Two white wings at the back mark the symmetrical boundaries of a patiolike garden, and stretching beyond are two servant wings, pleasingly proportioned and painted the country red. The grounds are scrupulously kept, and the interior has been restored to give an impression of life in a cultivated Värmland home in the early nineteenth century, when Geijer became renowned not only as a historian and a professor at Uppsala University, but for poetry distinguished enough to put him among the first ten of Sweden's poets. But Gustaf Fröding, who sang of Swedish peasant life against the Värmland background, outranks them all as a lyrist, and his house seems peculiarly fitting for a poet who brought a new and delightful melodiousness into the Swedish language. We saw it to advantage in the soft light of late afternoon.

The dwelling of Fröding (1860-1911) stands just as he knew it, a white two-story house with eight square half-columns reaching from ground to roof and built into the façade, which is constructed of extra-wide planks upended and treated after the board-and-batten manner. Like Geijer's home, the house gives out a most pleasing aura of symmetry. It is reached by a wide flagstone walk, broken by a beautiful square well of white marble with flying gulls in bas-relief. The walk is bordered by spaced poles, twelve feet tall, where roses climb. A pair of slender lions sculptured in white stone are seated on either side of the wide entrance to the flagstone terrace before the small veranda. Fruit trees in white blossom made the perfect landscape decoration in May.

"What an extraordinarily chaste and clarifying house," we said. Yet Fröding, so gay of heart, with such superb ear for rhythm and living in such harmonious surroundings, strangely was overcome with that vein of Swedish melancholy that runs like a bitter counterpart through his sweetest songs, and his later days were spent in a mental mist, though he partially recovered before his death.

As I admired the dignified but graceful proportions of the poet's home, I thought of the insistent symmetry of all the Värmland houses. It appeared as if the builders felt they must have balance above all else in this province where the landscape skips like a madcap, with linked lakes and meandering rivers, with black bogs and white cascades, with flowery plains and spooky woods. The demand behind the ordered architecture seemed as emphatic as that longing for the primitive that makes ever-recurrent pulls at the hearts of urbane Swedes and commands them to commune with forests or lie naked on rocks at the sea's edge.

✦

The flush time of the small private ironworks which left their stamp on the culture of Värmland was over, as definitely as that of the cotton plantations of the Old South. The iron mines that are not exhausted are in the hands of large companies. Today the forests of Värmland are its chief wealth, just as wood products are the leading factor in Sweden's economic life and account for almost half of the country's export.

Nearly sixty per cent of Sweden's area is covered with forests, mostly of pine and spruce, the raw material of cellulose, of paper and artificial silk. The number of standing trees is approximately five times the population of the globe—five Swedish trees to each of the world's inhabitants. But since there are no more primeval areas to be tapped, the supply is regulated by compulsory replanting and national reforestation. Though the annual cutting is heavy, it is not excessive, because it is strictly administered by law, and in typical Swedish fashion an extraordinary equilibrium is kept between growth and felling.

Sweden is peculiarly fortunate in natural aids for the transporting of timber. The winter snows greatly facilitate the dragging of logs through the woods to the banks of frozen rivers, where they await the melting of the ice to be launched on their watery voyage. The spring thaw brings the mountain flood and hastens the transportation. Artificial timber-floating channels have a combined length of some 21,000 miles. The sum total of transport expense by the floating system is only one-seventh of what it would be by rail.

All the large companies employ scientifically trained forest staffs, who spend the greater part of their lives in the woods. The logging gangs far up-river—"those tall, silent, stalwart Swedes" who are the pith and sinew of the race, a great reservoir of national strength—start the logs on their downward trip, each with its own special mark like the brand on a Western steer. At arrangements called "timber booms" near the mouths of rivers the floating logs are sorted out to the different owners according to the markings.

The Värmland visitor more interested in the actual workings of cellulose mills, paper mills, or sawmills than in the ceaseless summer pageantry of floating timber rafts may indulge himself to his heart's content. For he will be welcomed at various sectors of the province's wood business centered in three great companies: Uddeholm, Billerud, and Mölnbacka-Trysil. He will find everything up-to-date, in technical equipment and industrial management, in attractive housing and amenities for workers of all categories. Swedes have been foremost pioneers in wood industries. It was a Swede, C. D. Ekman, who built the world's first sulphite mill in 1874, when Selma Lagerlöf was just sixteen and reveling in tales of the golden era of the ironmasters. Six years later Alvar Müntzing invented methods for producing sulphate pulp, from which kraft paper is made. And today Sweden is the world's largest exporter of both sulphite and sulphate pulp, the sale of which has mighty significance in keeping up Sweden's high standard of living.

JOHN ERICSSON AND A FOLK SCHOOL

Like their natural taste for lyric poetry, Swedes are born with uncommon mechanical ability and inventiveness. But Sweden has let many of her great scientists slip away to other lands. One of the most noted emigrants was that Värmlander John Ericsson, renowned in the history of the United States as the designer of the *Monitor*. His remains repose in his native heath at Filipstad, a pleasant motor ride from Karlstad.

Filipstad sits cozily beside a blue lake in the shadow of green mountains. The town was founded in 1611, the year that saw the publication in England of the King James authorized version of the Bible. It is a pretty little place with a Tessin church, a series of bridges, quantities of swimming ducks and bright-yellow pansy plots. In the suburbs are the memorably picturesque ruins of an old smelting furnace. But the hillside cemetery, crowned by a great ugly tomb of John Ericsson, is regarded as the summit of local attraction. Watched over by a gigantic glaring American eagle in stone, the casket in the mausoleum is draped with the Stars and Stripes, for John Ericsson became a citizen of the United States and spent fifty of his eighty-six years in New York.

The inventor was born (in 1803) twelve miles from Filipstad at Långbanshyttan, where his grandfather was chief engineer at one of the near-by iron mines. His father did not amount to much as a money-earner, so his mother became a boarding-house keeper at a place where her young son John and his older brother Nils could find employment. This Nils, too, was to become distinguished as an engineer and to gain the epithet of "Father of Swedish Railways."

As a schoolboy, John revealed his mechanical genius, and at the tender age of twelve he was employed as a regular draftsman with the Göta Canal Company. At fourteen he was boss of four hundred canal workmen. When he was twenty-three he left for England, after the King, Charles XIV John, had ridiculed his offer to build an iron-clad vessel to protect the Swedish coasts. In England he built a locomotive, the *Novelty,* which he entered in the famous competition in which Stephenson's *Rocket* won the prize. At thirty he patented a screw propeller, and he invented the steam fire engine, and much later the revolving gun turret. Jealousy from English scientists helped to send him to New York in 1839, when he was thirty-six. During the Civil War his design for an armored ship was accepted by the United States Navy Department. This turned out to be the famous iron-clad *Monitor,* which defeated the Confederates' *Merrimac* in March, 1862, and proved a significant factor in the ultimate Union victory. After his death at the overripe age of eighty-six, Ericsson's body was brought back with great ceremony on a United States battleship to rest in his native Värmland.

Like many notable nineteenth-century successes, John Ericsson was largely self-educated. But along with the democratization of Swedish society in the 1860's and the franchise reform arose interest in further education for the agricultural class, so that the people might become equipped to exercise their new influence in State and local affairs. Following more or less the Danish pattern of folk school, which had been in existence since 1844 under the inspiration of the great Bishop Grundtvig, the first people's college was established in southern Sweden in 1868. By 1939 there were fifty-six of these folk high schools receiving State aid.

After Filipstad we went to visit the Folk High School at Molkom. The well laid-out grounds were at their best, with the fruit trees in pink and white blossom. Like the Danes, the Swedes know how to utilize fruit trees for beauty in landscaping. Small tables with chairs were scattered here and there on the dappled lawn, where we had coffee with the headmaster Bransén and his wife. The delicious hot cookies had been made by students in the home-economics department.

Folk high schools have the purpose of giving further education to farm youths who generally stop their schooling at fourteen to sixteen. They provide a kind of continuation course after an interruption of years of work. The students are usually from sixteen to twenty-five years old, and they come thirsty and eager for more knowledge. They read, study, and attend lectures, but they take no examinations.

The subjects which are compulsory for the first-year course, the headmaster told us, are Swedish language and literature, history, sociology, geography, natural science, hygiene, gymnastics, and singing. The winter course for both male and female students lasts twenty-one to twenty-four weeks. In summer, courses in housewifery are stressed. The methods of teaching are left to the headmaster and his staff. There is close contact between mentor and students, and only those with an aptitude for teaching and love of their fellow-men are chosen for instructors. Expenses are remarkably low. The girls pay about ten dollars a month for tuition, board, and lodging. Needy students are given the course entirely free.

As we sat under a blossoming apple tree, drinking coffee, and eating cakes served by two of the girls, we listened to the headmaster and his wife talk about the work. Many of the girls had never left home before. A few came from other provinces. They seemed vibrant with eagerness and appreciative of everything. It was all very simple, the headmaster's wife said—simple food from the school vegetable garden, lots of milk, a cheery atmosphere. Yet how fine-looking and how tastefully dressed were these girls from humble farm homes.

The lectures covered both Swedish subjects and world subjects, Mr. Bransén said, with emphasis put on making the students unprejudiced, generous human beings, with a richer capacity for living.

"Many a shy girl from a remote country farm," Fru Bransén said, "or a boy from the deep forest gets a new kind of initiation into world knowledge as something beyond rural or provincial knowledge. Here natural obstinacy, or suspicion, or shyness, melts away."

After a visit to lecture rooms, dormitories, kitchens, where all was order and cleanliness, Mr. Bransén invited me into his office. "Now it seems I must instruct myself in something I don't like. This weird-looking object came from some Governmental agency this morning. I am told to learn how to adjust it so that I can instruct others if need be." He displayed on his desk a black and gray contraption, with an insectlike proboscis ringed with aluminum. It was a gas mask. So the peace even of rural Sweden might conceivably be thrown in jeopardy by foreign machinations! But together we laughed off the likelihood of any such preposterous evil—much as Alfred Nobel might have done.

SELMA LAGERLÖF AT HOME

When we returned to Mårbacka the fifth of July, the refulgent beauty of the cherry tree in flower was weeks past, but midsummer, Selma Lagerlöf's favorite season, had settled on Värmland. The roads were bordered with chervil and blue and yellow midsummer flowers. Sleek black cows with gold-colored horns feasted on green meadows studded with daisies and ragged robins. Vacationists, wearing white caps, cycled bare to the waist with the sun baking their torsos like biscuits. Sparkling timber rafts covered the surface of the rivers like long corded rugs. Birds sang in the hedgerows and the gardens were blazing with multicolored bloom.

Selma Lagerlöf sat on her sun-splashed veranda dictating to her Austrian secretary, a pretty, slender, dark-haired girl who looked like a young Wally, Duchess of Windsor, in Tyrolean peasant dress. Though the day was quite warm, Dr. Lagerlöf wore a long white knitted sweater that reached almost to her knees. Across the back of her chair was folded a fringed blanket of white cashmere. Wrapped about her throat many times was a blue chiffon scarf. Her feet, encased in high-top country walking shoes, rested on a low footstool beside a lazy white Eskimo dog named Karr. The girl's fingers paused above the typewriter keyboard and Selma Lagerlöf rose slowly to greet us.

As she gave us a kindly but searching glance from her unspectacled shrewd gray eyes, I thought at once how absolutely Swedish she was; that face could have been produced nowhere but in Sweden. It was a naturally plain face made beautiful by character.

The moment she spoke and held out her small hand we felt completely under her spell. We were unprepared for such genuine sweetness. We had expected the only woman ever elected to the Swedish Academy to be somewhat austere; but I cannot think she ever was. Her inherent Swedish shyness and reserve she covered up in graciousness. Partly because of her frailty and her years, but more, I think, because of her own gentleness, she inspired tenderness and protectiveness. As she showed us about the ground floor, an aura of humility emanated from her, as if she had never become accustomed to the blessings Providence had showered upon her: the fame, the security, the admiration of foreigners.

The walls of the cheerful drawing room were hung with family portraits—generations of clergymen, who were also dirt farmers and who married daughters of other farmer-clergymen.

"We were not from a noble family, you know," she said. "Good, but not ennobled."

"All these ministers in the family," I said, making a little joke, "perhaps that is why you are so good."

She smiled. "I doubt if I am good, but I know I have gratitude. And I think gratitude is an excellent quality. We can derive benefit only from what we have the capacity to be grateful for."

As I glanced almost wonderingly at some of the foreign editions of her books in the study, testimonials of her widespread success, she seemed to read my thought. "It all came from here," she said simply, pressing her heart, "all from here. You know I was just a schoolteacher, such a poor little schoolteacher, too."

The schoolteacher had indeed gone far. There was no man alive in Sweden who approached her in world literary fame. The great August Strindberg, who was only nine years older than she, had died in 1912. Now in her eighty-first year, like Rudyard Kipling she had enjoyed a quarter-century of fame as a living classic. Uppsala University had conferred a Doctorate of Literature on her in 1907. In 1909 she became the first woman ever to be awarded the Nobel Prize for Literature, and in 1914 she was the first woman ever elected to the Swedish Academy. Her success began in 1891, when she was thirty-three. With a group of Värmland tales strung together she won the prize in a national magazine contest. These were added to and published in book form as *The Saga of Gösta*

Berling, which still remains her most popular novel. At first the book made little stir in Sweden, for since the publication of Strindberg's *The Red Room* in 1879, realism had become the vogue in Swedish literature as it was on the Continent. *Gösta Berling,* with its wild romanticism, its beauty and idealism, was launched courageously at a time when naturalistic sordidness and cynicism seemed to be demanded by critics and public. But after the great Danish critic Georg Brandes discerned the book's rare virtues and commended it highly, the Swedish public took renewed interest in it. King Oscar and his artist son Prince Eugen admired the book and arranged a royal scholarship for foreign travel for the author. When she returned, she never went back to the schoolroom, but poured all her energies into her own fictional creation.

The seeds of a literary career were well sown when Selma was a tiny tot listening to her grandmother telling tales from the corner sofa. Almost until the very morning she died, it was her pleasure to tell the Lagerlöf children marvelous stories. And then Aunt Ottiliana Lagerlöf refreshed the children's memory with other versions of the grandmother's tales and told countless new ones, which Selma was to present in print later transfused with her own fanciful imagination. It was from her grandmother, however, more than the ancient sagas, that she got her special persuasive manner of taletelling. The grandmother was supposed to believe her own stories and the author says that when the old lady told something very wonderful, she would look deep into the eyes of the little children and say, with the utmost conviction: "All this is as true as that you see me and I see you."

A precocious, grave child, who could not play about because of a hip disease, Selma read prodigiously. After perusing Mayne Reid's Indian story called *Osceola,* a powerful desire to write a novel was born in her. Of course she already knew all of Hans Christian Andersen's fairy tales; and at nine, while taking medical treatments in Stockholm, she came upon Scott's novels in a relative's library. But because she spent years dabbling at poetry, she did not publish any prose fiction until she was thirty-three. As she followed *Gösta Berling* with numerous books, her fame spread until she far outsold every author in Sweden, and her work was translated into thirty-four languages and dialects, including Arabic, Yiddish, Lettish, and Bengali.

In the 1930's she was still producing, but her best work had really been done before World War I. The tragedy of mass killings among civilized people weighed so heavily on her heart that she lost something of her creative power. She could never understand "how in the world of grown-up folk there could be room for a real hatred."

The three books of hers which appear most likely destined to live were published in 1891, 1901-02, and 1906. They are respectively: *Gösta Berlings Saga, Jerusalem* (two volumes), and *The Wonderful Adventures of Nils,* a classic for children in any land.

The story of Nils Holgerson and his wild goose resulted from a pressing invitation to write a Swedish geography for schoolchildren. Instead of doing it the conventional way, she conceived the idea of turning a naughty boy into an elf and sending him on the back of a gander named Martin to the various provinces of Sweden. In the guise of an adventure story she not only set forth lessons in geography, but sketched the character of Swedes in various latitudes and landscapes, and got in many homely moral lessons for boys and girls without seeming to preach. This book has delighted children and grown-ups in far-flung regions and sold best among her best sellers.

In the library, where I remarked first editions of Strindberg dramas and Gustav Fröding's poems, I thought it interesting that these three foremost Swedish authors should have been born within eleven years of each other—Lagerlöf late in 1858, Strindberg early in 1849, and Fröding in 1860. With Fröding, who sang inimitably of peasant life against a Värmland background, Lagerlöf had much in common. But she and the city-reared Strindberg could not have been more antithetical in their art and life.

Selma Lagerlöf's roots went deep into Värmland's loam, and she knew simple values, as the cynical Strindberg, with all his re-inforced armor of intellect, never did. Born the son of a one-time barmaid, rootless Strindberg was nurtured in noisy, crowded city quarters and spent his life in furious revolt against his environment. But later, when he might have escaped to remote rural peace, he seemed magnetized to city turmoil. He continually stirred up hatred between the classes (while Branting, the great Social Democrat, was bringing about orderly reforms), he was thrice divorced, and he alienated virtually all his friends.

Early in her career Lagerlöf learned self-discipline, purged herself of egotism, and lived in harmonious concord with herself. Strindberg was as thoroughly obsessed with his own ego as any man who ever achieved fame, and what he wrote was more than often motivated by his own personal disharmonies and psychological complexes. Where Strindberg probed the abnormal in a naturalistic milieu, Lagerlöf sketched the workings of the normal mind in highly romanticized situations. She presented the fantastic with the familiarity of convincing fact. He often revealed reality like some distorted phantasmagoria. Where she was attuned to the past, he was as intensely contemporary as his own erratic heartbeat.

Strindberg is, of course, infinitely the greater artist. For Lagerlöf never became expert at plot construction, and none of her characters is fully realized. Yet she is a born storyteller; and as one reads, he gets the impression that the narrator is speaking, telling the tale, rather than writing it, following the oral tradition of the scop entertaining Vikings and their ladies about a winter's fire. When she leads us into a magic world of fancy, she herself never loses her way or forgets the key to the maze she has created for the reader's delectation. She seems to smile quietly to herself, quite aware of what she is doing, even when she allows her style to become overwrought with a downpour of exclamation points. The faults of her style are easily discerned. The virtues elude analysis, for her naïveté is deceptive. In her disarming simplicity she is as audacious as the profound and shocking Strindberg.

While Lagerlöf cannot be compared with Strindberg in genius, yet this seemingly artless stylist well exemplifies Willa Cather's criterion for fiction: "Every fine story must leave in the mind a cadence, a quality of voice, that is exclusively the writer's own, individual, unique." And her almost childlike humility opens gates to spiritual understanding, which the brilliant Strindberg with all his insight and intellectualism never glimpses.

Though Lagerlöf was indubitably a sentimentalist, with a strong moral conviction in the ultimate conquering power of goodness and love, she possessed a healthy sense of humor and a shrewd understanding of man's vanities and foibles. Her poise and her firmness of character helped to secure her fame and to endear her to the orderly Swedes, who set great store by simple truths, traditions, and love of home and country.

I was interested to find that a gentle harmony pervaded the author's personality and her home, as it does the ends of all her books, and that she maintained her keen sense of practicality. As we were about to leave, Henry Odén told her that he had built a new dining room onto his hotel. She smiled, and said somewhat crisply, "I hope it is more convenient to the kitchen than the other one."

I stopped before a great stuffed wild goose that stood over the hall mantel. "This, of course, is the original gander that carried Nils Holgerson about Sweden," I said.

"The very same." Then she added, "A schoolboy who liked the tales shot it, and had it stuffed and sent to me."

Out on the veranda again she let me take half a dozen pictures of her with my Leica, the last pictures of Selma Lagerlöf ever taken. "They say I am not as well as I should be," she said, "so they are giving me injections of vitamins. But I really think sunshine is a better medicine."

I thought of a line she had written on the first page of *Jerusalem*: "What more does one want than sunshine and fair weather to make him happy as a child of heaven?"

When she came to the edge of the veranda to say good-by we spoke of the beauty of her pastures decked with field flowers. Thérèse said, "I think the flowers must be the reason for the extra sweetness of Värmland butter."

Selma Lagerlöf's eyes twinkled and she said, "It is a pretty thought, and for a long time I myself so believed. But if you notice closely, you will see that the cows nibble all around the flowers and leave them untouched. Not for esthetic reasons, but because they just don't like the flavor of flowers."

As we laughed, a farmer's boy arrived with the morning newspaper and handed it up to the secretary. It seemed as if a shadow passed over the frail figure of Selma Lagerlöf, who was standing in a shaft of sunlight, smiling gently.

I had glanced at a paper at breakfast and had noted dark intimations of war on the first page. "I do hope," I said, "that whatever may happen in the world, the peace of Sweden and Mårbacka will not be broken."

Selma Lagerlöf looked off for a moment and her eyes became dim and absent. "No," she said sadly, "I'm afraid these are not very comfortable times we live in." Then she added more brightly, "But they are interesting and even momentous times. In the years to come much will be written about these uncertain times in which we now live."

Selma Lagerlöf lived just long enough to know the first months of the war, and to donate her Nobel Award gold medal to be melted down to contribute aid to innocent sufferers of devastation. Happily, a few weeks before the invasion of Norway and Denmark, she died on the sixteenth of March, 1940.

Mårbacka straightway became Sweden's foremost literary shrine. In the summer of 1947, seven years after Miss Lagerlöf's death, more than twenty-seven thousand visitors, including travelers from many parts of the world, came to look at the birthplace and dwelling of the internationally famous author, so beloved by her countrymen. So one may believe that the glamour of fantasy which Selma Lagerlöf cast over the Värmland landscape will not be soon dispelled.

4.

Lapland, "Where Our World Ends"

When I reached this mountain, I seemed entering on a new world; and when I had ascended it, I scarcely knew whether I was in Asia or Africa, the soil, situation, and every one of the plants, being equally strange to me.

—LINNEAUS—Journey in Lapland

ACCORDING TO the Swedes themselves, the climax to Sweden's tourism lies almost a thousand miles north of Stockholm, far above the Arctic Circle. The British discovered its peaceful excitements a decade before the war, but few Americans venture into Lapland, though today it is as easy for the comfort-loving traveler as it is for the rugged whose symbol is the rucksack.

We know that three adventurous Frenchmen, including the dramatist, Jean François Regnard, visited the remote region as long ago as August 18, 1681; for in the little church of Jukkasjärvi, the oldest village in Lapland, the indefatigable travelers inscribed in Latin, "Here we stand, where our world ends."

We have no record of their means of transportation, but at the beginning of the twentieth century traveling conditions in Lapland had advanced to the stage where the famous Dr. Axel Munthe could write in remembrance:

It was quite an easy and comfortable journey this time of the year. Eight hours' ride through the forest to Rukne, three hours downstream in Liss Jocum's boat, six hours on foot across the mountain to the church village, two hours across the lake to Losso Järvi, from there eight hours' easy drive to the new railway station. No passenger trains as yet, but the engineer would be sure to let me stand on the locomotive for two hundred miles till I could catch the goods train.

Today one can travel on a commodious passenger train equipped with private bedrooms. The express leaves Stockholm daily, and within twenty-four hours one arrives at Abisko with its tourist hotel 937 miles to the north. The first of March the skiing season opens, and in June come the summer vacationists: the hikers, the hunters, the watchers of the midnight sun.

On a map of Sweden one sees that the northernmost and largest province called Lapland holds almost a third of the kingdom's entire area. It has approximately the area of Pennsylvania. Cut off from both the Atlantic and Arctic Oceans by a slim curving arm of Norway, it is separated on the east from the Gulf of Bothnia by Norrbotten and Västerbotten. These three districts together are known to Swedes as Norrland, and constitute almost sixty per cent of the country's area, with no more than eighteen per cent of the population. Lapland is the most sparsely settled province, with about one inhabitant to the square mile. Lapps live in all three provinces, but their entire number in Sweden is only some 6,240, including both the settled Lapps and the nomads with their reindeer herds. (Norwegian Lapps number about 20,000 and the Finnish Lapps hardly 2,000.) The Lapps, who have been in the region since about 500 B.C., are outnumbered six times by people of Finnish descent. The municipality of Kiruna, the great iron center, which achieved a population of 11,000 as early as 1909, holds more pure Swedes than there are Lapps in all Sweden.

The Swedes who live in Lapland look just like the blue-eyed, fairhaired Swedes in the south, though they seem to have broader shoulders and to be more taciturn. Those who have homes in the lake-dotted hinterland away from the settlements work their little farms, raise oats, barley, and potatoes, keep a horse and four cows, hire out as foresters in winter, and add to their slender income by running motorboats for occasional tourists in summer. They are unfailingly courteous, and as hospitable as their simple amenities permit.

Much of Lapland is waste, with nothing to recommend it but invigorating air and wild virgin beauty under the winter moon or the sun of midsummer nights. But vast quantities of trees are felled and floated down swift-running rivers to pulp and paper mills. The northern provinces contribute much more to the national economy than timber and romantic scenery. At Boliden is Sweden's great gold mine, and clustered in Lapland are Kiruna and Gällivare and Malmberget, with the world's richest iron-bearing mountains. The horsepower of tumultuous waterfalls of Lapland, the "white coal," has been harnessed at Porjus to electrify not only industry and the railways, but to bring light and labor-saving devices and radios into humble rural homes.

For many years Lapland has been paying off in national health-giving properties. Youngsters and oldsters hike, with maps and compasses, to keep themselves fit throughout the year. The Swedish Tourist Association has provided free shelters over hundreds of square miles of challenging terrain. Where hikers want to make big jumps, there are bus and motorboat services. Riksgränsen, the farthest-north railway stop in Sweden, has become a skiing center, for snow remains longer here than in any ski resort in the world. In some seasons it remains even until midsummer, when folks ski at midnight by the light of the sun.

For those whose time is limited, there are several scheduled airplane flights a day from Stockholm to the far north. Instead of going by train, my Swedish friend Allan Kastrup and I telescoped distance by taking the plane to Luleå, 730 miles northeast of Stockholm on the Gulf of Bothnia. From Luleå one may proceed by train on a bias that cuts sharply north-northwest through the Polar Circle to Kiruna, and thence to Abisko and on to the Norwegian port of Narvik.

In the late afternoon we took off from Bromma Airport, and as there is no night in the northern summer it is an ideal time for clarity of vision. The plane flies along the variegated and many-islanded coast washed by blue Gulf waters and then traverses thousands of wooded acres, broken by silvery lakes and fertile pastures and by modern pulp mills, all lying like pieces of a jigsaw puzzle neatly fitted together.

We made only one stop at a halfway point between Sundsvall, the one town of the province of Medalpad, and Härnösand, the ancient seaport of southern Ångermanland. The two provincial capitals lie not forty miles apart. Rich both in forest and fertile soil, the region is noted, too, for its fascinating scenery up the long Ångermanland River, where excursion boats ply and acres of logs come floating down to the coastal pulp mills from as far away as the Norwegian border. From these regions come those tall, silent lumberjacks of Sweden known for their virility and good looks.

Northward the air route lies over more treetops and lake water and four more rivers, with little seaports marking their termination. Twenty miles inland from Skellefteå, in a bleak forbidding area, lie the mines of Boliden, with gold, silver, and copper, and ores containing arsenic. Discovered after 1920, Boliden yielded more gold in two decades than has been mined altogether in Alaska. Today it is the foremost gold-producing mine in Europe.

At half-past nine when we landed at Luleå, it seemed no more than late afternoon. The landing field was surrounded by myriad stalks of magenta midsummer flowers, which resemble wild phlox and larkspur. Whether you approach the town by the ferry or the long river bridge, the way has northern charm. Founded by Gustavus Adolphus early in the seventeenth century, Luleå is a pleasant, solid town, with a population of 14,000. The seat of a bishopric and the summer depot for iron ore from Kiruna and Gällivare, it is a lively seaport from May until November, when ice cakes the Gulf.

Kastrup had prepared me for everything except for the atmosphere of the Riviera, when we dined at half-past ten on a roofless veranda off from Stadshotellet's winter dining room. Our table was set close to the fluted iron balustrade, whose pillars supported blue and white porcelain jars spilling over with pink geraniums. Edging the balustrade and making a decorative screen were the gently quivering tops of silver birches. In a shell-like pavilion at the end of the terrace four musicians played Viennese waltzes and haunting pieces by Sibelius, whose country lay just across the Gulf.

We dined on fresh salmon, filet mignon, and raspberries with frozen cream. While we ate dessert, the darkest time of night came at half-past eleven. But yet no electric light was necessary, and each raspberry was as clear in detail as the daisies in the table vase, though there was no illumination beyond that from the starless firmament. Guests lingered over dinner as if to taste the full flavor of this ultimate season when the strange light touched ordinary, everyday things with glamour.

For coffee we moved to a larger and higher terrace built onto another part of the hotel. Here, entirely above the treetops, were more iron balustrades studded with jars of geraniums. Guests sat in gliders so placed that the occupants could face the northwestern sky, and each glider was provided with blue woolly blankets in case the night air became too chilly.

Out beyond moored boats the still water was the metallic silver color of a salmon touched by the luminous rose of sky. I could read the name of a Danish ship loaded with telegraph poles. It was called *Mary*. In front of the red warehouses two youths were aquaplaning behind two small motorboats, as if it were noon in Hawaii instead of midnight above the 65° parallel.

Like sun-worshipers gathering in the white summer night for some mystic Nordic rite, townfolk come to the hotel's spacious terraces to drink coffee or beer and to watch the almost imperceptible transfiguration of one day into another. And though the parties are gay-spirited, people speak softly. At twelve the music stops and no more food is served on the dining-room terrace, only drinks and coffee in the terrace café. When all service stops at two in the morning, some guests linger on, for it is hard to go to bed on such incomparable nights. At last we tore ourselves away from the midnight spell, and went to our rooms and drew the heavy black curtains to shut out the imminent sunrise.

When I came downstairs sometime after eight, I found that the hotel dining room did not open for breakfast in summer until half-past nine. So I took a stroll in search of coffee past the pretty square and the museum. Within three blocks I found a little corner restaurant called Lundquist's, spanking new and modern, all glass and blond wood. It was filled with workmen wearing caps and white-collar men reading the morning paper. Kastrup trailed me and we breakfasted on coffee and wiener bread and *toscas* with almonds and a jug of rich milk.

The shops do not open until half-past nine. But at that hour a car came for us, and we spent two hours visiting the brand-new Government-owned steel mill and the model cottages of the workers set in the aromatic pine woods. By 1950 this mill would be producing three hundred thousand tons of finished steel a year. At luncheon at the administration building we found potted plants in every available window ledge and vases of flowers on each office desk and table. We lunched on a seven-dish smörgåsbord, followed by broiled salmon caught that morning and creamed spinach from the mill garden.

At 1:09 our train left for Kiruna. We changed to the express at Boden, Sweden's greatest military stronghold, which lies only forty-five minutes northwest of Luleå. The mountain fortifications of Boden are a closely guarded secret. The reason for such a fortress in the far north is, of course, Russia. The lilac bushes that line the street parallel with the tracks were still in bloom in mid-July, and in their half-shade soldiers and their girls sat holding hands.

At three o'clock the train passed Sandträsk, where the world's most northerly sanatorium stands on a hill above a lake. The white cows that furnish milk for the patients were digesting their morning's grazing in the shade of white-barked birches.

At 3:50 we saw a signboard announcing the Arctic Circle in three languages. Then a little red station called Polcirkeln proclaimed that it was 1,234 kilometers from Stockholm.

In the restaurant car where we had tea, electric ceiling fans were running, and, from the wide observation windows, we saw four men swimming naked in a stream.

At Gällivare, with its near-by iron mountains, a group of British salmon fishers left the train, and some hunters going to shoot wild duck and grouse. Three mountain-climbers, who were taking a roundabout way to reach Kebnekaise, Sweden's highest mountain, got off, and four college girls, whose destination was a Lapp encampment in the wilds.

Three male Lapps boarded the train, and I was glad to see that neither modernity nor the recent war had caused them to give up their traditional costume of blue woolen blouses with skirts half the length of their thighs and enormous scarlet pompons on their blue caps. A group of Lapps with a pack of thick-haired Lapp dogs, black, white, and honey-colored, had come to see them off.

Gällivare is a starting point for rugged excursions to lakes and mountain tops and Lapp villages and for the famous Stora Sjöfallet, one of the most imposing waterfalls in Europe. From the town, motor-bus routes radiate in six directions. Gällivare is also the railway junction for Porjus, thirty miles southwest, whose great power station electrifies not only the railway line, but lights most of Lapland, a district large as Denmark.

Between Gällivare and Kiruna the landscape is so barren and desolate that the garden town of Kiruna, lying between the two great iron mountains Luossavara and Kirunavara, seems almost to be a mirage. The flower-boxed station, with the attractive hotel close by, gives a first impression of arriving at some picturebook resort town in the Swiss Alps.

A tall youngish man with prematurely gray hair, and carrying gray gloves, met us at the station. We drove to the Iron Company's guest house, set among trees and hung with gay orange awnings and window boxes of white petunias. I was still more impressed by the emphasis Swedes put on flowers when, in the dining room for the administrative officers and engineers, I saw that each table bore a small white pottery vase filled with forget-me-nots. My astonishment was even greater after dinner when I beheld matured cauliflower, headed lettuce, spinach, beets, and Brussels sprouts growing in open beds in these frigid latitudes, where snow remains through May. The garden walls were lined with columbine and fuchsias, and bordering the walks were golden calendulas, which the Swedes call "ring flowers."

The young engineer, who still carried his gray gloves as he walked among the vegetable beds, explained how the soil was heated by electric coils run under the ground and serviced from Porjus Power Station a hundred miles away. With the sun shining almost the entire night, the maturing time of vegetables was vastly accelerated. As a climax to our amazement, the gardener opened the door of a small glass conservatory. There, in a cubic footage no more than that of the luxurious bathroom at the guest house hotel, grapes grew to the top of the sharp-angled roof as prodigally as in the vineyards of Burgundy. From this little room almost seven hundred pounds of grapes had been gathered the previous year. It was July 18th and some of the grapes were already ripe. With his pocket knife the engineer snipped two weighty bunches for us.

To make living attractive for the staff of executives and engineers, Martin Waldenström, president of the Iron Ore Company, had recently had the interior of the club house redone. Some of the rooms were models of Swedish modern, with hand-woven fabrics and rugs by Elsa Gullberg and furniture by Malmsten. The drawing-room walls were hung with pictures by noted painters, including

Helmer Osslund and Prince Eugen. The library was cozily done with rich chalky red walls and gray wood and comfortable chairs by Finland's Alvar Aalto. The bookshelves were stocked with first-class literature in four different languages. I glanced at two books which had been left lying on a table with book markers. One was Thomas Mann's *Buddenbrooks* in German; the other was *Flora of the Aleutian Islands* in Swedish by Eric Hutten.

At a quarter past eleven we were roused from a siesta to make a journey to the top of the Luossavara to try to catch the midnight sun. The manager drove us through the twilit night along the town's tree-lined streets, where folk still pedaled bicycles, and youths and maidens paused before doorways and at corners saying good night.

"These white summer nights are not so good for romance," I remarked. "There's no seclusion."

"But a winter night lasts six months," the manager reminded me, laughing. "Of course, it's not really all black then; moonlight on snow is brilliant for skiing, and on moonless nights star reflections on the snow make a lovely light."

We left the automobile and walked to a funicular shed, where waited the four-compartment car that bore workmen up the heights. The manager struck a cable with an iron bar as a signal to the operator at the top, and we began the slow ascent.

Like a volcano rising from a plain, the Luossavara stood to itself. On its summit it was like being at the top of the world. Below us to the south lay the town and the lake backed by the vast terraces of Kirunavara, where mining is done sculpturally in truncated tiers. That other iron mountain might have been some stupendous pagan temple created by the Toltecs of ancient Mexico. Now strung with twinkling electric lights and adorned with one gigantic globe at the very top like a stationary planet, it looked more like something in a fabulous land of faëry than a productive iron mine.

Far to the west rose the snowy peaks of Kebnekaise, Sweden's highest mountain. Ten miles to the east beyond the Torne River lay Jukkasjärvi. Through powerful field glasses the distant ancient hamlet seemed only a short walk over the meadows.

The whole northern sky was aflame as if the Arctic Ocean were on fire. Like vaporous breastworks, pearl-pink clouds stretched along the frontier of the horizon, blocking any possible view of the sun itself. Though we were six days too late to see the full sun at midnight, we stared fixedly through the space-devouring lenses, and then with unaided eye, as if intense desire had the power of conjuration. At twelve minutes past twelve the misty clouds parted like drawn stage curtains, and we saw poised in a sea of red-gold ether the convex back of a crimson porpoise. It was only the tiptop of the sun, for its bulk was hidden by the rim of the world, as an iceberg's mass is submerged beneath the ocean's surface. Not until next June could the full golden round be seen at midnight.

We were not too disappointed, however, for the novelty of seeing the sun at precisely midnight was as nothing compared to beholding the wonder of the sleeping world from the mountain top. The flame-tinted sky laid a mystic patina over the landscape. Without benefit of moon or stars, the arctic heavens achieved a glory beyond that of lush tropical nights.

At eleven o'clock that same morning we visited the mines of Kirunavara. The ore is so plentiful that almost all the mining is done from the surface and visitors may watch the miners working the open pits, but when the signal for blasting comes, they must follow the rules of taking cover. Blasting is done three to five times a day. At noon, when most of the men are having their lunches in the safety of stoutly timbered dining rooms, the principal blasting occurs.

One goes up the Kirunavara in another cable car, and peers over stout railings at the man-carved canyon where millions of cubic yards of iron ore have been dug and sent to the markets of the world. Far down in the valleys steam shovels scoop up the rich black ore and little ore cars move on the continually revised tracks. Miners climb and descend ladders like figures in a dream, and men work in pairs, one holding the other for safety reasons, while he does some dangerous task. There is no pressure, no hurry, no tension of increased production. Every move is made with Swedish precision and moderation.

In this region where it is night all winter, powerful electric lights flood the open mines both day and night, and men can work at midnight as conveniently as at noon.

The directors of the company have no fear that the Lapland

supply of iron will be exhausted within a century, for an estimated two billion tons of ore still remains. The quality is so high that the iron content is sixty to seventy-one per cent, as compared with other European ores of only thirty-five to forty per cent. Though Kiruna, the richest of all iron deposits, began its operations virtually "only yesterday," or early in this century, Sweden has been supplying iron from other mines for almost a thousand years.

To make up for the geographical disadvantages of arctic Kiruna, the miners are among the highest-paid workmen in Europe, and there are other compensations, besides those of not having to work underground. First-rate primary schools and technical high schools are provided for the children, and university scholarships are offered. The miners' houses are attractive and equipped with modern gadgets to make housekeeping convenient. The company has provided apartment houses for aged employees and their wives or widows. Most of the workers ski in winter, and go shooting or camping in the summer vacations. There are dance halls and an auditorium for lectures and amateur theatricals. Although there are extensive shower rooms at the mines, the public bathhouse in the town's center is much patronized by all the citizenry. Groups of friends go on certain days, as if to club meetings. For instance, the mine executives try to make it on Tuesdays. One floor of the bath building is the public library, with a good list of titles in English, and many in German and French and Finnish. Before or after an invigorating steam bath miners usually drop into the library to stimulate the mind.

The unique church standing on a hillside was designed by Gunnar Wickman to suggest a Lappish tent. All the light is concentrated at the top, where elongated glass windows are set in the tall gables. Gilded statues of Norse heroes break the brown shingles of the exterior. Some of Sweden's most talented artists like Christian Eriksson, the sculptor, and Ossian Elgström, the painter, have decorated the interior. Prince Eugen painted the great altarpiece, a grove of leafy trees. In the vestry room the visitors' book bears testimony to the number of famous travelers since the consecration of the church in 1912.

Not far from the edifice, within a circle of birch trees, is the simple Viking grave of Hjalmar Lundbohm (1855-1926), the founder of Kiruna. This geologist and doctor of philosophy inspired the development of the mines and laid out the towns in an arctic wilderness with that innate Swedish sense of order and good taste that links beauty and human welfare with industrialization and profit.

On another rise of ground stands the crematorium, where hollyhocks bloom and brick walls are broken with spaces for funeral urns. The crematorium is a special blessing to this area where the ground is frozen too hard for grave-digging for half the year, and where in former days the coffined dead were stacked in the cemetery chapel until the summer thaw.

To get to the village of Jukkasjärvi, we drove through reindeer land that looked like Arctic Finland, with stands of spruce, pine, and birch, and the ground carpeted with lacy reindeer moss, on which the beasts feed in winter. It is clean, removed-from-the-world country, good for deep breathing. Occasionally we passed bicyclists, the men bare to the waist, the sun toasting backs or fronts according to their direction of travel. It seems to be an unwritten code that men must strip to the waist while cycling in summer to store up the sun's benefits against the dark winter.

Although Jukkasjärvi has no special antique aspect, it dates from the beginning of the seventeenth century. Because the houses are of wood, they have been rebuilt from time to time, and the tone of the village is created as much by a noted modern school for Lapp children, a spick-and-span cooperative shop, and a spotless home for aged Lapps, as by the dwellings of weathered wood.

Jukkasjärvi has been visited by foreign travelers since 1681, and during the last three decades hunting parties, including members of the royal family, have come here for Maria Papila's famous reindeer-bone dinners, in which the *pièce de résistance* was a specially prepared dish of marrow of reindeer bone.

We were fortunate to chance upon old Maria Papila herself, as she went under a gap in a fence into a field sprinkled with buttercups. The engineer presented us and we talked over the fence. Maria Papila was a Wagnerian type of woman of mixed Finnish and Swedish blood, with gray eyes like a seeress and huge strong hands now soiled from raking hay. There was something queenly about this peasant woman and a manner reminiscent of Eleanora

Duse off stage. She was old now, and during the war she had given up her little restaurant business by the river. But she invited us to tea and offered to show us mementos of a visit she had made to Berlin years ago as the guest of the Kaiser.

Because we knew she was tired, we declined the invitation, just as a splendid specimen of manhood joined us, with a hayfork over his shoulder. This was her middle-aged son, who had become a Lutheran minister and now preached at the church in Kiruna. He was spending his vacation assisting his mother with the haying and directing two hired men reaping in the field below the Jukkasjärvi church. The Reverend Papila accompanied us to the diminutive edifice at the end of the road where he had been christened. This oldest church above the Arctic Circle was established by Charles IX in 1611, the year in which Shakespeare's *The Tempest* was first performed at court. The present building was erected in 1726.

The names of scores of distinguished travelers whose visits dated from 1681—ranging from Polish princes and Italian marquises to Carl von Linné, the great Swedish botanist—are left on parchment, on wood, and in visitors' books. As far as the record goes, the first American to visit Jukkasjärvi was one who signed himself simply "W. Langhorn, United States of America, July 23, 1787."

In a grove of silver birches stood the little wooden church, surrounded like an English churchyard with graves and tombstones. It was a peaceful place, made sweeter by the flutelike whistle of the dotterel and the Finnish song of two reapers cutting the scented hay in the Papila field that sloped to the river. On the granite slabs and wooden crosses the same names recurred, as if the village had carried on through the years with no more than thirty or forty family names, some Swedish, some Finnish, some Lappish. Though prayer books lying in the pews were in Finnish, most of the people of Jukkasjärvi are trilingual, speaking Swedish and Lappish, too.

In July the majority of Lapps are in mountain pastures with their reindeer herds, but in autumn they return to their winter quarters, and then for a fortnight the church is bustling with funerals, marriages, and christenings. The Feast of the Annunciation on March 25 marks an active time in the icy spring. Lapps come from great distances in their reindeer sledges, bringing the winter's dead, frozen stiff and lashed to tree branches. The bodies are coffined, the burial service read, and a handful of earth sprinkled on each casket, and then the caskets are stored in a pit until June thaws the ground for digging. When the actual burials take place, families and friends of the deceased are far away in the mountains with their reindeer.

Though good country roads lead from Kiruna in three directions, there is no road whatever to Abisko Turiststation, Sweden's foremost resort above the Polar Circle. One walks or rides the train. By railway the journey takes an hour and a half.

Kastrup and I got window seats in the observation-smoking car. After the roadbed began to skirt the long lake known as Torneträsk, a series of magnificent views unfolded. Torneträsk is, to me, by far the most beautiful and exciting of all the Swedish lakes. But it is only for a brief lease in summer that the deep-anchored ice relents under a melting twenty-four-hour sun, and the frosted surface becomes a vibrant cobalt blue. Tier after tier of blunted fawn-pink hills rise behind it, the farther and higher ones marked with snow like spotted deer.

Just before reaching Abisko, Kastrup drew my attention away from the lake view. Dominating the landscape to the left was the stupendous semicircular mountain pass called Lapporten, "The Gateway of the Lapps." The edges of the vast concavity are smooth, and the weather-polished sides of the bare mountains are the color of old silver. It is like a setting for some Norse saga, or it might be the very entrance to Valhalla itself.

At Abisko Tourist Station * the rambling hotel stands in the midst of a wilderness near a canyon cut by a frothing stream, facing the Torneträsk and backed by violet-tinted mountains patched with snow. Built of wood and stained an oakleaf yellow, the hostelry grew up on the spot where temporary shelters were constructed for the men working on the Luleå-Narvik railroad in 1902-1905. It accommodates comfortably 140 guests, and from March to October it is open with full staff. During the winter it operates with a reduced staff. In all seasons reservations should be made far ahead, for there is rarely a vacant room.

The uninitiated, who might well expect a barren icy waste this far north, are amazed at yellow pansies and columbine growing in the railway-station beds, and at the begonias and tulips in the hotel

---

* Burnt down in the Spring of 1949.

gardens. Though I myself had become acquainted with the marvels of arctic blossoming in Kiruna, I was unprepared for the profusion of wild flowers that grew along the lake shore and in sheltered vales and pockets of the foothills. Kastrup, who, like most Swedes, is quite knowledgeable in botany, pointed out a variety of rare specimens, whose names have no English equivalent. But I recognized the white mountain avens with their feathery styles, the sweet-scented yellow violets, the blue gentians, and purplish wild orchids. The most striking of unfamiliar plants were the dwarf Lapland rhododendrons, with stalks no more than three inches tall, but glowing with purple bloom.

Guests indulge in various activities that vacationists enjoy. Some merely laze, taking the sun on the various terraces or "the midnight-sun veranda." Every day parties climb nearby Mount Nuolja, from which one can follow the full route of the midnight sun just above the horizon from June 11 to July 4 or behold a magnificent panorama in any season. Each morning we would see hikers start on a two-hundred-mile trek south on the Kungsleden, "The King's Trail," through wildish country, where the Swedish Touring Club has blazed a trail, built bridges and provided boats, and erected huts equipped with bunks and stoves. A popular easy walk of some five miles towards Norway leads to a tempestuous tumbling waterfall, known as Silverfallet, and just beyond is the village of Björkliden, where the Swedish State Railways have created a vacation home for employees and their families.

Many guests spend their best hours fishing for incomparable Lapland trout. Some take motorboats to seek out Lapp encampments on the northern shores of Torneträsk. The hotel owns its own boat *Abisko,* which makes daily excursions about the lovely lake, pausing before the climax of a waterfall, stopping for picnic lunches at some special spot of interest, or taking hunters on the first lap of their journey.

Kastrup and I did a little of this, a little of that, as the mood directed, nothing strenuous, but taking it all as a kind of rest cure, in which one kept happily on the move. We stretched our legs over irregular miles, and fed our eyes on scenery that would change in color from gold and plum to cream and reindeer-gray, according to the quality of light. We would take after-dinner tramps among rocks and wild flowers, and then sit up late on the terrace savoring the stillness and the ineffable mystery of white Lapland nights. The noontime cobalt of the water would become diluted with mercury color, the snow patches on distant ridges would change from gleaming white to yellowed ivory, and the purple of near hills would become as tarnished silver. The night scene invariably held hypnotic vibrations and stirred up unfamiliar responses. As Kastrup said, "It is comparable in its magic to the powerful and elaborate witchcraft of the Icelandic ballads."

But with all the unearthly magic of this Ultima Thule, the pure air at Abisko is so bracing that the blood and sinews react with an unwonted vigor; one eats with increased appetite and sleeps with a blessed soundness. After three days I could not recall when, if ever, I had felt so well. The Arctic sun seems to have power to dispel worries and to dissolve real or imagined physical ills. Here a man can shake off excrescences of the sophisticate and complex civilizations to the south and greet the experiences of the North as something marvelously clarifying.

5.

Visby and the Enchanting Island

There is not a flower that opens, not a seed that falls into the ground, and not an ear of wheat that nods on the end of its stalk in the wind that does not preach and proclaim the greatness and the mercy of God to the whole world.

—THOMAS MERTON

"NONE OF OUR Swedish towns is comparable to Visby," said Prince Wilhelm. "It is something unique and very special, embedded in an atmosphere that cannot be equaled on the mainland." Because he is a world voyager of note and the author of works on travel, the words of the King's son held special significance for one contemplating a trip to Visby on the Island of Gotland. And Sigrid Undset, the Norwegian novelist, raised her hands in a gesture of delight at the mere mention of Gotland, by all odds her favorite stretch of land belonging to Sweden. "There was a picture of the town wall," said Madame Undset, "with its frowning range of watch towers, in the geography books of my schooldays. Almost as far back as I can remember, I had thought I must go to Visby some day. Yet it was finer, indeed much finer, than I had imagined in advance."

Gotland lies strategically in the Baltic Sea, some fifty-five miles east of southeast Sweden and about a hundred miles west of Latvia and the Gulf of Riga. The kingdom's largest island extends eighty miles in a north-south direction, and at the widest part, the middle, it is some thirty miles in breadth. Its area is sixty-odd times greater than that of Bermuda, the popular little resort in mid-Atlantic.

The whole island has the lure of a memorial, not only because of its scores of medieval churches, but because its palpable history ranges far back through the riches of the Middle Ages, to the

108

austere Iron Age, and beyond through the Bronze Age to the Stone Ages. Experts say the land was occupied by men at least six thousand years ago. One of the ancient sagas names Tjelvar as the first human inhabitant of Gotland, though it had long been known to seafarers as an island of magic propensities, which rose from the sea at nightfall and sank beneath the waters at dawn. But this Tjelvar brought fire to the island and broke forever the spell of disappearance. From Tjelvar's son Gute and his brothers, the people of Gotland claim descent.

The limestone soil, as rich in fossils as in rare wild flowers, has also proved rich in ancient bones and weapons and utensils. Plowed earth has yielded thousands of foreign coins, the earliest dating from the century after Christ. Arabian and Anglo-Saxon coins and gold pieces from Turkey, from the Netherlands, from Portugal, have all been unearthed in the countryside. A sea shell from the distant Indian Ocean and a cup from China have been retrieved along with relics from Iron Age graves.

Since pagan times the islanders ventured far in foreign trade. In the ninth century, we know, they were buying and selling in the fabulous markets of Constantinople, and according to Arab chroniclers, these tall, yellow-haired Vikings from Gotland cut quite a figure with their proud bearing and their heavy gold neckchains. The island itself, however, produced little for sale besides tar and timber, fish and farm commodities; but Visby's men became brokers and its warehouses were filled with goods from near and far-flung lands—furs and wax from Russia, spices and silken stuffs from the Orient.

Though the archeologists and botanists have endless field days on Gotland, as Prince Wilhelm said, the magnet that draws tourists to the region is the town of Visby itself. Visby is, I think, the only place in Sweden for which "enchanting" is the word. That adjective comes unaffectedly to strangers of varying estates and latitudes even after a single day in this least typical of all Swedish towns. "City of Ruins and Roses" is the slogan by which the travel posters blazon Visby's attractions. Trite as the legend has become, none could be more suitable, for the place is a treasury of medieval art and is literally drenched in roses. "Roses bloom here three times a year," one is told; "in June, July, and August." During these months of rose bloom the town's chief activity is to entertain the throngs of visitors, who fly from Stockholm in an hour or come by night boat from Nynäshamn in six and a half hours. The boat train leaves Stockholm for Nynäshamn's docks every summer evening at 9:40. The boat, provided with comfortable staterooms, sails at half-past eleven, and arrives at Visby the next morning at six.

The bastion of Gotland's chalky cliffs rising out of the blue summer sea is an impressive sight. As the antique town emerges into focus, Visby is seen to lie spread on a seaside slope, its face towards Sweden. Flung about it like a tarnished silver girdle is the medieval city wall. From seashore, up along the crest of the hill, and back to seashore, it ranges, almost two miles of mighty masonry, punctuated at intervals by thirty-seven watchtowers. In all North Europe there is nothing like Visby's city wall.

For centuries, commissioned watchers climbed the towers' stairs to spy out danger. Now seaplanes from Stockholm and training land planes of the Royal Swedish Air Force glide over the vacant towers more frequently than the wild swans ever did, making casual mockery of man's efforts at impregnability, and offering airborne travelers glimpses of extraordinary beauty.

But I still prefer the approach by sea, with the walk up from the landing place to Burmeister House, a handsome old three-story half-timber mansion, where in the back garden, with roses scenting the morning air, an appetizing Swedish breakfast is served. Part of this great ivy-clad house with its overhanging upper story dates to the sixteenth century, but it was reconstructed in the seventeenth century by a German merchant named Hans Burmeister, and it has since remained unchanged.

Within a few minutes' stroll in any direction one looks into the face of bygone centuries. In Strandgatan near the square called Donnersplats stands the Gotland Museum in which island relics date back six thousand years. Close by the museum are two splendid thirteenth-century dwellings. A couple of blocks beyond the town hall are the magnificent ruins of St. Catherine's church, erected in 1233. Visby, one notes almost at once, is a triumph of irregularity, its narrow cobbled streets twisting like ramblers among the half-timbered mansions, diminutive cottages of enduring stone, and the gray ruins of great churches. The varied architecture—Romanesque,

Gothic, Hanseatic gabled, Danish cottage—is all laced together with ivy and adorned with roses in season.

The windows of our room at the Stadshotellet looked across the town to a fine sea view. And down in the garden, along pebbled walks, spaced rose trees grew to extraordinary heights. They were as thick with blooms as cathedral chandeliers with incandescent globes. Climbing roses were espaliered on stone walls, twined among the columns of balustrades, allowed to droop over gateways. In the hotel garden yellow roses, pale to deep gold, had chief emphasis.

Most of the rose gardens of public buildings and private dwellings are marked by a predominant color. In some, red roses are seen exclusively; in some, pink; in others, white or yellow. In Visby it is not the custom to cut buds, but only the full-blown roses. To get the ultimate value of the flowering, most of the roses are left until their day is completely done, and every morning gardeners and housewives gather up in baskets the shattered petals from lawns and flower beds.

For all this drenching of a town in roses, there is no sticky feeling of a too-muchness. Too strong an influence from an energetic past mingles with the atmosphere of a stirring present. A refreshing sea breeze blows up the winding streets and is deflected from solid walls that have endured as many hundreds of harsh winters as gentle summers.

The Visby citizens have gone neither soft nor sentimental from existing in a medieval museum set in a flower garden. They are, it is true, less formal and phlegmatic than the Swedes of the mainland provinces. In fact, they seem as friendly and responsive as Danes. "Ah, yes," said a new-made Visby friend, laughing, "but this is summer. In winter, we, too, must be introduced like other Swedes." The alert townsfolk have been shrewd in promoting their antiquities and bathing resorts as tourist attractions. They have done it with discrimination and made conditions for visitors as pleasantly convenient as possible.

Like the majority of Swedes, citizens of Visby have inherent good taste, but a municipal committee on building, Byggnadsnämnden, makes sure that all new construction or reconstruction harmonizes with the town architecture and that imponderable called atmosphere. By law there must be a proper spacing, with provisions for gardens. The height of roofs must be in artistic accord or contrast with other buildings in the neighborhood. The color of paint is chosen for the effect on the street's tone rather than for the gratification of individual fancy. New houses of wood are prohibited, but a few shops of glass and stone in discreet modern style have been permitted. The ensemble of contemporary Visby is a telling example of the value of municipal planning and regulation, where every artistic relic of the past has been preserved and everything recent has been devised for harmony or pleasing contrast.

Up the streets that climb or along those that curl, one can hardly come upon a house that does not seem just right. Roofs project and sag picturesquely. Some roofs are so low that a tall man can reach up and pat the tiles with his palm. (I walked with the six-foot-four son of Austen Chamberlain and saw him do the trick again and again.) Window frames are set askew and old leaded panes reflect the street scene or magnify geraniums in painted pots. Roses droop like portières over both gateways and doorways and have to be pushed aside for one to enter. Gates stand ajar for the visitor's casual delight. In tiny gardens cherry trees grow at the corners and pears are espaliered on old brick walls. On a green turf may be a table for the family to take coffee beside a yellow rose tree six feet high. In the flower beds columbine, foxglove, and pale-blue delphinium are summer favorites. From behind sheer white curtains faces peek at passers-by, fresh modern faces, with here and there an old face that might have graced a canvas of Holbein or Hals.

Few visitors try to remember all the names of the various ruined churches, though an original name may cling to half a façade, a roofless tower, octagonal pillars, or outlines of nave and porches. It is easy to remember St. Mary's at the foot of the hill, for it is the sole church within the city wall that stands intact, and today it serves as the cathedral of Gotland. And one remembers St. Nicholas, because of its famous rose window in the western wall, and because here, where once Dominican friars chanted their litanies, on summer evenings is produced the Visby Miracle Play. Perhaps one may also remember the "sister churches" of St. Lars and Drotten because they lie so close together; and particularly St. Lars, built in the twelfth century in the form of a Grecian cross.

St. Olof's, once a vast and elegant structure, is now little more than slabs of broken walls, half-smothered in ivy, but it is notable because it makes a spectacular rock garden in the south end of the Botanical Garden, where, along with rare plants and exotic trees, simple flowers like love-in-a-mist, gold mallow, and canterbury bells bloom in rich profusion.

One may not recall the name of a certain ruined monastery, but he remembers the massed lilacs in the garden and the ancient mulberry trees, with their vast and venerable branches supported by gnarled props. And no visitor is likely to forget that it was commerce that brought Visby to its eminence at a time in history when religious glorification on earth was a consuming passion of men's lives.

The town of Visby—still the island's only town, and possessing today over one-fifth of Gotland's 60,000 inhabitants—was already firmly established by the twelfth century. It had grown up about a place of pagan sacrifice called Vi. Its importance increased at such a rate that from the middle of the twelfth century to the last half of the fourteenth, it was the dominant city of the Baltic countries. The Gotland Association of Merchants became a power in what was then world trade. By the end of the thirteenth century thirty-odd Baltic, Dutch, and German cities were allied in this association that ruled the business of half a continent. Visby was one of the most cosmopolitan places on the globe. Merchant princes and adventurers from exotic lands, as well as sailors of countless nationalities, frequented Visby, and left foreign legends and alien blood streams, along with quantities of silver and gold. Citizens grew so rich that there were said to be no poor people whatever, except by comparison. Some landowners boasted that they provided silver troughs for their swines' slop. Hundreds invested their tremendous profits in celestial futures, seeking to buy eternal bliss by the erection of great churches. Probably it was because the rich had special need of more and bigger masses to relieve them from the torments of Purgatory that they poured a floodtide of gold into ecclesiastical coffers. It was fortunate for Visby that its era of greatest affluence coincided with that great period of church construction—the thirteenth century, when all Christendom was rearing temples with "an air of completeness and finality," when Gothic pointed windows and spires "almost pure of practical purpose" typified the aspirations of man at his highest. In Visby the offerings were turned into magnificent architectural piles, into choir screens, murals, rich vestments, bejeweled chalices, and all the glittering pomp that troops with magnifying ritual. The ninety churches of the countryside and the eleven within the city walls had all been built by the middle of the fourteenth century, or long before Martin Luther was born and before jealous German cities got the Association headquarters changed from Visby to Lübeck.

Visby continued to be an important member of the commercial combine, renamed the Hanseatic League; and her ships, flying the Lamb-of-God pennants, were still to be seen in every port. But the town began to feel other slings of fickle Fortune. The black plague sneaked in with sailors from infected lands. Summer droughts created dreadful famines among cattle and men. Disastrous fires wrought havoc. Yet for all these calamities, the inhabitants within the stout city walls remained rich like the churches, and believed themselves protected at least from enemy invasion. But in the fateful year of 1361 Gotland's Golden Age was suddenly over with dramatic finality.

In late July the Danish King, Valdemar Atterdag, bent on avaricious pillage, landed with a mighty force a little south of the town. Rather than risk complete sacking and massacre, and in order to make the best deal possible under the menacing circumstances, the wealthy burghers let the invaders enter their portals before Valdemar became too wroth. The legend that King Valdemar forced the citizens to fill two hogsheads with gold and silver in the market place is doubtless as apochryphal as the romantic tale about the beautiful daughter of a farmer called Young-Hanse. This girl is supposed to have fallen in love with the bearded warrior-king when he had earlier visited Gotland in disguise, and to win his favor, she had revealed the weakest spots in the city's defensive wall. For such treachery the enraged citizens afterwards walled up the farmer's daughter in one of the towers to perish by slow starvation. Today this Maiden's Tower is pointed out to visitors.

The historical truth of the attack and the capitulation will never be revealed, but we know that eighteen hundred peasants lost their lives, fiercely defending the city *outside* the walls. The fight occurred on a hot July 27, and to prevent pestilence from sun-heated cadavers, the whole quarry was buried hastily in wet lime in one vast pit close by the Benedictine monastery where they fell. When the mass grave was uncovered a few years ago, breastplates and hoods of chain mail were still clinging to the skeletons of soldiers, while broken bones of boys and old men and a few women, who fought to save the city, show they were unprotected from the piercing arrows and the slashing battle-axes of the Danes. Today visitors who know Latin often stop to read the inscription on the monumental ring-cross that marks the scene of wholesale slaughter. "In the year of Our Lord, 1361, on the third day following that of St. James, the Gotlanders buried herein fell at the hands of the Danes outside the gates of Visby. Pray for them."

In the museum showcases one may look into the fleshless faces of some of the armored slain who fell on that July 27, 1361. The date marked a catastrophic turn in Fortune's wheel for Visby. The proud city never resumed her eminence and glory. In her decline she suffered piratical raids from Germany as well as fights between Sweden and Denmark. Finally, in 1645, Gotland became once more a definite part of the Swedish kingdom. But not until the tourist migration began some three decades ago did Visby begin again to flourish like her roses.

As an antidote to any surfeit of medieval ruins or perfume of roses, two miles to the north lie the sand beaches of Snäckgärdsbaden, one of the favorite bathing spots in Sweden. Here one may enjoy salt sea dips, sun baths in the nude, and quiet walks in the pine woods behind the resort hotel. On the wide beach, sheltered by chalk cliffs and spotted decoratively with smallish boulders and stunted juniper trees, the foreigner notes what splendid physical specimens these Swedes are. There are bullpens for men and henpens for women, where both sexes may sun their bodies thoroughly and tan their skins as they choose, stretching out nude on wooden platforms or in the walled-off compounds of turf or sand. A shy people with their clothes on, Swedes seem completely at ease in scanty bathing attire or naked, recalling the pagan primitiveness of their sun-worshiping ancestors. Those who do not care to hire dressing rooms strip behind boulders or the low-lying juniper trees. Since Swedes are not prying by nature, the undressed do not hesitate to take sunbaths behind the illusive screen of a scraggly juniper bough.

The beach hotel on the ridge—a long rambling structure with gardens sloping towards the sea—is always fully booked. But guests registered at the Stadshotellet in town have the privilege of taking what meals they choose at Snäckgärdsbaden, since both are owned by the Gotland Tourist Association. In the evening on the terrace veranda, one dines and dances, while the setting sun sinks with spectacular effect into the tideless Baltic. At ten o'clock, when the supper crowd arrives, the guests move into the ballroom, but the floor show seems nothing much after the marvelous performance of the sun.

Away from Visby and Snäckgärdsbaden stretches the Gotland interior, where four-fifths of the inhabitants order their lives. Farming is the chief occupation except on the eastern shore with its fishing villages and occasional cement plants. Two all-day excursions by bus or motorcar, one to the north and one to the south, and two four-hour afternoon tours to different destinations in the east are arranged for the convenience of visitors. Any two of these journeys might give anyone except the specialist everything he needs to know of Gotland. But many visitors take all four trips, while some prefer to make privately arranged pilgrimages in the late evening to see a particular church by moonlight or to visit a Holy Well when the nightingales are singing.

Whether the routes run along monotonous limestone moors or through the smiling districts with dairy farms and apple orchards, each tour offers an abundance of medieval churches. From a tower at Jacobsberg, one of the island's high points, 240 feet above the plateau, some thirty churches can be seen on clear days without field glasses.

The rural churches are in better condition than those within the town walls, for they escaped the disastrous fires. Some of the structures, like that of Källunge church, which dates in part back to the tenth century, have been left completely unrestored. In some churches a Byzantine influence is traced in a Romanesque or Gothic building; in others only the expert can tell precisely where the Romanesque and Gothic merged. One lovely old church is surrounded by flat wheat fields, another stands at the edge of a marsh, another is half hidden in a leafy grove. The beautiful ruined Roma Abbey is neighbor to a sugar factory.

Each church building has its own special treasures in stone or wood or glass or fresco painting. But few single objects excite such admiration as the multicolored fourteenth-century crucifix that hangs between the choir and the nave in the great arch of the Öja parish church. Here the unrecorded artist has been able to communicate the religious zeal with which he was inspired while he worked. The transcendental nobility of the Christ, his grief and compassion, are luminous in the face and attitude. This glowing quality is intensified through colors ranging from flesh to green, and red to bronze and pale gold. The cross is encircled by a great solar ring, a wreath of Gothic roses and diamond lozenges. In the upper angles of the cross a crowd of sorrowing angels lean down toward the Son of God. In the longer, lower spaces within the ring the naked Adam and Eve, taller than Swedes, are revealed, first in their disobedience, and then in their expulsion from Eden by a full-clothed angel with flaming sword.

For six hundred years or more simple Gotland farmers have sown and reaped, raised cattle or cut timber within sight of medieval churches. The landowners have ever had a good reputation for husbandry, and except for periods of unusual drought they have been prosperous since the twelfth century. Though today they make use of modern equipment and methods, they cling to many ancient customs and games. While most of the farmers brew their own beer, a few still drink mead (*mjöd*), that alcoholic beverage first celebrated in English literature in the Anglo-Saxon epic *Beowulf*. Today the simple ingredients remain as in the time of dragon-slaying heroes: honey, hops, and water. After half a year of fermentation the mixture is ready for serving.

At a farmer's house where we stopped one day, the amiable wife served us cooling beakers of mead at a table set under a mulberry tree, with thrushes singing in a near-by copse of wild sloes. Though the large barn was new, the land had been in the same family since before the days of records. Sugar beets flourished in some of the fields; wheat grew in others; and an apple orchard contained five hundred trees. But dairying and pig-raising were the most profitable source of income. The pigs were the long lean pink kind like the Danish, bred for bacon rather than pork chops.

"Under Queen Christina in the seventeenth century," the farmer said, "my ancestors paid taxes in oak trees and butter. But now the oaks are gone and we get a better cash price for butter in the Stockholm market than in London."

As the famous botanist Linnaeus found Gotlanders "kind and good-natured," we found the farmer and his wife jolly and accommodating as well. They drove with us to show us some boat graves from the Bronze Age. Large stones had been set in elliptical forms to simulate the outlines of vessels. Within the boundaries of the "death ship" the dead had been cremated and the burned bones and ash deposits collected into urns. The prows of the little fleet all pointed away from the pine forest and towards the sea. In various parts of the island fourscore of these boat graves have been discovered.

Linnaeus had come as an herbalist and discovered a variety of plants that did not grow on the mainland. On the south-shore sands he and his group of eighteenth-century student botanists first saw the gold blossoms of the *Adonis vernalis*. In the twentieth century Swedish children come to Gotland in groups to enrich their school herbariums with rare plants from the island's flora. And young Gotlanders take more interest in their own specimen collections than in church attendance.

At one church where we stopped on a Sunday morning to see a stained-glass window, an intelligent-looking young minister with a mellifluous voice was delivering a sermon before five elderly ladies who made up the entire congregation. But when we passed the village sports field, where old Viking games, like *varpa* and *pärk,* were being played, the place was thronged with smiling people. "Ah," said our host from Visby, "but, you see, Swedes like to use Sunday as a recreation day."

At a village inn on the east coast where we had luncheon, we were reminded of prohibition days in the States when drinks were sneaked. This inn had no license for selling spirits, so we crowded into a small bedroom off the dining room and surreptitiously drank White Lady cocktails poured from thermos bottles. A Visby physician in our party set out a bottle of home-made schnapps for those who preferred uniced aquavit to cocktails. The Swedes enjoyed the clandestine situation as much as Southerners used to do in the time of corn liquor drawn from charred kegs.

The memories of cross-country journeys in Gotland, however, are rarely of personal happenings. They belong almost entirely to visual impressions: of splendid churches by nameless architects reached by dusty chalk roads, of rude but idyllic little harbors, of grottos with fantastic columns, of open-air museums like that one of Bunge composed of a cluster of fifteenth and sixteenth century farmhouses, of Viking pile-dwellings in a lake, of black and gray Fårö sheep grazing, of an eleventh-century frieze or a modern military barracks, of salmon-colored hare's-foot growing out of rock on some remote beach where one does not need swimming trunks.

In the midst of the romantic delights of Gotland one may forget that all the appurtenances and benefits of modern Swedish social welfare are in full force among the islanders, that old-age pensions go to everyone at sixty-seven, that hospitals and schools are modern in method and equipment, and that consumer cooperatives function happily beside private shops.

It is strange that from the centuries of both active and quiescent history only one name of a Gotland-born man stands out significantly. Petrus de Dacia was neither warrior, architect, nor merchant prince. He was a priest of the thirteenth century and he is often called Sweden's first author. While studying in Cologne, he went to the village of Stommeln to pay homage to a girl called Kristina who had acquired an early fame for holiness. The two fell in love, and shortly Petrus departed; but they continued to correspond until her death. And when he was prior of the Dominican monastery of St. Nicholas at Visby, he wrote her legendary life story. The scholar-priest's own purity and loving-kindness show through and illuminate the biography of the pious virgin.

Now on certain scheduled summer evenings in the ruins of St. Nicholas, where this "immaculate mystic toiled and wrote and prayed," a musical drama based on the story of the priest and Kristina is presented. Singers from the Royal Swedish Opera in Stockholm are brought down for the leading roles. The minor parts and the chorus are filled by Gotlanders.

In the first years of the play's presentation the director did not have to go to Stockholm's Opera for his heroine, for the wife of Waldemar Beer in Visby possessed a lovely singing voice and considerable dramatic talent. The idea of the Miracle Play first originated in the Beer drawing room, and, much like the Passion Play of Oberammergau, it remains in considerable measure a community affair.

The drama is enacted against an incomparable permanent backdrop of a towering Gothic wall with a great rose window. Once, so it is told, this window was set with carbuncles that reflected the sunset so dazzlingly that it seemed to mariners as if a constellation had descended to earth. But Valdemar the Dane stole the carbuncles, only to lose them in a tempest. Now at the beginning of the performance the brilliance of the declining sun fills the empty cases with a glowing topaz light; and gradually the incredible blue of the Swedish night sky resets the window with turquoises, while the absent roof is a ceiling of sapphire that loses luster only as ten o'clock approaches.

The technical art of theatrical lighting makes harmonious adjustments with the light from the sky. And though the spectators sit for two hours on hard wooden benches, they are so moved by the drama's haunting quality and the mysterious beauty of the setting that many continue to sit under the lingering spell long after the final tableaux. Only those who are taking the night boat back to the Swedish mainland are impelled to leave promptly.

The night boat sails at eleven, and one just has comfortable time to cover the half mile from St. Nicholas to the dock. Our luggage had been sent aboard by the hotel manager, so we walked directly from the church to the boat. In the faint light it was like moving from one medieval dream into another, as we traversed the ancient twisting streets of gabled houses, with pale flambeaux of roses rising above the garden walls.

In Visby, Swedish farewells recall Hawaiian alohas. At the landing stage to say good-by were friends bearing bouquets of roses, and in our stateroom were more roses with cards from other friends. As the ship moved out into the Baltic, friends stood on the dock and waved white handkerchiefs, and waved and waved. And we waved red roses from the deck rail, until the handkerchiefs were only expiring sparks in the Swedish summer night.

Then the island was washed in darkness and distance until it vanished as completely as in the days before Tjelvar broke the spell of disappearance with his ring of fire. In memory, however, contemporary Gotland would ever remain an isle of enchantment. It had proved something very special, as Prince Wilhelm said, and even more. For Gotland seemed a microcosm, a brief pocket edition of the history of mankind dating back six thousand years, a compact syllabus of destiny's odd vagaries. Man's growth and staggered progress, his acquisitiveness, his spiritual yearning, his fighting heart, his rural contentment were all there explicit, along with his defeats and disillusions and incorrigible love of beauty. In this anxious Atomic Age, Gotland seemed to say, if civilization should blow itself half to the moon with its new lethal contrivances, man himself will yet endure, and, inevitably, flowers will spring up among the ruins.

II

HISTORY: FROM THE BEGINNING TO GUSTAV V

6.

Through Gustavus Vasa

Time present and time past
Are both perhaps present in time future,
And time future contained in time past.

—T. S. ELIOT

WITH THE RECESSION of the northern glaciers more than eleven thousand years ago, people began coming into what is now Sweden. The nucleus of a Swedish population was already well established two thousand years before Christ. Since Sweden has never suffered invasion from any non-Scandinavian folk, its State has developed naturally and uninterruptedly of itself.

The first inhabitants lived in caves, dressed in animal skins, and existed by fishing and hunting. In the Bronze Age (1800 to 500 B.C.), with better tools and some contact with more advanced folk to the south, men began to build rude dwellings and boats, to till the soil and raise cattle.

In the century before Christ, after Julius Caesar had conquered Gaul and Britain, influence of the high Roman civilization began to penetrate into the southern part of Sweden known today as Skåne, which the Latins called Scania, and from which the northern people get the name of Scandinavians. The first mention of Sweden in literature was made by the Roman historian Tacitus in 98 A.D. He speaks of the tribe of the Svear, who centered about Lake Mälaren and the place that is now Stockholm, as *Suiones,* "mighty in ships and arms." To the south of the Svear dwelt the Goths in the present-day provinces of Östergötland and Västergötland, and the Island of Gotland. The two great tribes were often at war with each other, and the Anglo-Saxon epic of *Beowulf* sings of their legendary kings.

125

When, early in the seventh century, the Svear tribe vanquished the Goths, the kingdom of Sweden was formed "through a union of the Svear and the land of Götar."

Gradually the country became organized under one chosen king, who left the farmer communities to run their own affairs except in time of war, when his leadership became absolute and supreme. By the end of the eighth century the unification of Sweden had been realized.

Then, together with their Norwegian and Danish kinsmen, the Swedes burgeoned into world history as Vikings: men who lived in bays or fjords. The Age of the Vikings lasted about two and a half centuries, from 800 to 1050.

The first record of a Viking raid dates to 793, when an island monastery off the north coast of England was raided and plundered with devastating celerity. In the decades following, similar swift plundering raids kept the inhabitants of the English coast in a perpetual state of anxiety and dismay. Soon other lands were to know these flashing forays, and the long narrow Viking ships, with twenty pairs of oars and a single square sail, became terrifying sights to settlements on seas and rivers. The ships were usually manned by half a hundred husky warriors, who killed, looted, demanded tribute. But in time the rovers learned to trade as well as plunder.

Whereas the Norwegian Vikings generally sailed west and north, reaching to Iceland, Greenland, and the North American mainland, the Swedish Vikings pointed their ships to the east. They regarded the towns on the Baltic shores as theirs for loot or commerce. They sailed up the rivers of what is now Russia and established trade routes with protective fortifications.

When they reached the watershed between the Russian rivers they had navigated and those that ran to the south, they had slaves transport their boats the short distance overland and then they rowed on down to the Black Sea and on to Byzantium, and thence to Peiraeus, the famous port in Greece. When the Swedish Vikings found they could not subdue Constantinople, they entered into trade negotiations. The ruler of the Eastern Roman Empire was so taken with the bearing and physique of these adventurous younger sons of Sweden that he asked some of them to form his bodyguard.

Swedes set up the first central government in Russia, and future czars were descended from that Swedish leader known as Rurik. The very name of Russia comes from *"rus"* or *"ross,"* the word for the ruddy-faced, blond-haired adventurers from Sweden. Rurik established his capital of North Russia at Novgorod, while Kiev became the Viking-ruled capital of the South.

The Varangian (Northmen) government in Russia maintained close contact with the Swedish government until about 1050, when the Slavic elements became more emphatic and powerful and absorbed the Swedish. Yet the dynasty established by Rurik, who died at the end of the ninth century, kept the throne until 1578, though few drops of Swedish blood were left in the royal veins by that time.

As the early Swedes chose their chiefs by vote, so did the Viking Swedes elect their kings. A ruler was selected for his qualities of strength and courage and wisdom; but although kings were elected, the choice traditionally went to some member of the royal family.

Except in times of war the king's authority was decidedly limited and he held his high office by the grace of his subjects. He had virtually no control over the domestic problems of the different provinces, whose men democratically made laws, decreed taxes, and administered justice according to local traditions. By a doctrine akin to that known in the United States as "state rights," no section of the country could lay down laws for, or interfere with, the activities of another section.

In the ninth century Christian missionaries from several nations had begun to penetrate among the Swedes. They had been sent largely in the hope that an acceptance of Christian doctrine might soften the Viking heart and stop the depredations. After King Olof accepted the new religion about the year 1000, relations with England, Germany, and France did become more seemly. But though the records are shadowy, Christianity did not quell disturbances between the Scandinavian brother peoples, for the Swedes, the Danes, and the Norwegians combated each other sporadically through the next centuries. Little of the seemingly chaotic period is known with certainty, and in the years between 1000 and 1250 the only events of importance center about the reign of King Erik, a zealous and pious warrior. On a Christian conquesting mission he invaded Finland in 1157, forced the new religion on the vanquished, and annexed the land as a part of Sweden, in which state it remained for the next six and a half centuries. After the king was assassinated in church at Uppsala on Ascension Day in 1160, he was canonized, and became known as Erik the Holy.

Catholicism brought glimpses of foreign manners and customs. And under the influence of the feudal system, which was in full flower in other nations, a new class emerged, the nobility, which had hitherto been merely extensive landowners. Many of the great families in Sweden today trace their lineage to this dim period, and there is no record of their having been ennobled. But most of the Swedish inhabitants were freemen, who had always been free, living in their villages and farming the near-by lands.

The only man of prime importance to emerge from this period was a remarkable fellow called Birger Jarl, who got his son elected king when the dynasty of Erik died out in 1250. But Birger Jarl ruled in his son's name and created good domestic laws with "peace" as the keynote: "family peace" and "church peace" and "peace in government assembly." The most extraordinary of his laws for those ancient times decreed that the daughter should inherit an equal share with the brother.

Birger Jarl is revered as the founder of the city of Stockholm, which was later to supersede Uppsala, which had been the capital long before Viking days. He invited foreigners to settle among the Swedes and he stimulated mining and foreign trade. After his death in 1288 Birger Jarl's descendants succeeded to the throne, though often they squabbled over it, and some were deposed and replaced by relatives. The Folkung dynasty of Birger Jarl lasted until 1364, when a German pretender succeeded in overthrowing it, and brought in with him a great following of greedy German knights.

In the last half-century of the Folkung dynasty, Sweden produced a woman destined to more international fame than Birger Jarl himself or any precedent Swedish male. Born in 1303 and canonized in 1391, she is known as St. Birgitta, or St. Bridget, and the founder of the order that bears her name.

A daughter of one of Sweden's more important noble families, the Lady Birgitta was married at thirteen to a much older man, and she bore her husband eight children before she was widowed. From her childhood she had been devoutly religious, and when at court, where her high rank made her mistress of the robes, her frequent retirement for prayer and fasting caused much comment among the courtiers.

Shortly after her husband's passing Birgitta experienced religious ecstasy, together with the revelation that she should establish a convent and found an ecclesiastical order. She enlisted King Magnus's promise of a royal estate at Vadstena on Lake Vättern as the site for her foundation. Then, in those rude days of uncommodious slow travel, the widow set forth to Rome to seek the Pope's permission and benediction. It took her more than twenty years to get his reluctant consent, partly because the Pope was away at Avignon most of the time with troubles of his own. But the indomitable woman never let up on him until her foundation was assured.

While she was in Rome, the behavior of the Swedish king did not please her at all, and she wrote her disapproval in strong ink. She even suggested a plan for insurrection and deposition. For all her pious zeal, St. Bridget was quite conversant with the events of the day, and she did not hesitate to make herself "the mouthpiece of God's opinion" in political matters.

During her Roman sojourn she set down her *Revelations,* which made her Sweden's first woman of letters, and, next to Emanuel Swedenborg, the most noted writer on religious themes. Her *Revelations* in Latin translations were read throughout Christendom.

The pious woman died in 1372, five years before the actual foundation of her order. But the Order of St. Bridget, which in her mind was to be of such scope as to reform the world, did spread over all Europe until its branches numbered eighty; and in 1949 it still exists in both hemispheres. Her body was brought in an oak coffin by devout followers all the way from Rome to Vadstena. There the abbey was completed just as she had envisioned, with the church separating the building for the nuns and that for the monks. Work had been started on the abbey in 1368, five years before her death, but it was not consecrated until 1430. Then immediately it became a shrine for pilgrimages and a center of learning and ecclesiastical art. Important foreign churchmen came from afar to visit and to study and to plan other establishments. The gallant Henry V of England endowed an Order of St. Bridget in Middlesex as early as 1415.

The German pretender, Albrekt of Mecklenburg, who had seized the throne in 1364, was largely managed by a powerful and avaricious Swedish chancellor named Bo Jonsson Grip, who made the nobility stronger than ever. On the chancellor's death and his burial in St. Bridget's Vadstena abbey in 1386, Albrekt presumed to reduce drastically the tax-free lands of the nobles. His intention cost him the throne.

The Swedish nobles, patriotically aroused at the thought of losing any of their personal possessions, appealed for help to Queen Margaret of Denmark. To secure her military assistance, they elected her their sovereign in 1388. After a decisive battle in February of 1389, the king and his German cohorts were driven from the land. Then Margaret consolidated the three Scandinavian countries under her headship. The Danish crown she had inherited from her father, the mighty Valdemar Atterdag; the Norwegian crown she had from her late husband, Haakon Magnusson, who belonged to the Folkung dynasty. Now with the election to the Swedish throne of her husband's ancestors, Margaret became thrice a queen and ruled over a domain larger in extent than any in Europe.

The abbey at Vadstena continued to be of utmost importance in Sweden's religious and cultural life until 1527, when Gustavus Vasa adopted the Reformation, confiscated the order, and began dismantling parts of the building to procure stones to build himself a fortified castle near-by. Today the north building that housed the nuns still stands, but it has been converted into an asylum for lunatic women.

The years between 1389 and 1521 are known as the Period of Union, but, unhappily, the corollary that it was a contented and harmonious era does not follow.

However, for a stretch of years, former jealousies and enmities were buried in the Pan-Scandinavian idea. In 1397 the nobles met at Kalmar in southeastern Sweden and formally drew up and signed the pact that was to be known as the Kalmar Union. By the terms of the agreement, although the three countries stood combined under one ruler, each nation was to make its own internal laws and govern itself.

Margaret, who, like St. Bridget, possessed the masculine quality of indomitability, was undoubtedly the strongest Scandinavian of her time. No male public official ever worked harder at his job. She used her constructive ability, her diplomacy, and her force of will to make the Union a success and to maintain the royal prerogative.

But the Swedish nobles soon began to complain that the queen's heart-interest was too obviously her native Denmark, and that she seemed purposed to make Sweden a mere dependency. Margaret straightway clipped the discontented nobles' wings by reducing their estates and by setting Danes and even Germans in high Government positions. In 1412, Queen Margaret died, her work of true consolidation far from completed.

Noted for her shrewd statecraft and her sound judgment, Queen Margaret made one most grievous error in selecting for her successor a personable young relative of hers, Erik of Pomerania. Erik did not turn out to have the character Margaret thought she had discerned through his superficial charm. He altogether lacked her abilities, as well as the aura of her dominant personality. In 1405, when he was of marriageable age, she had arranged a marriage with Philippa, daughter of England's Henry IV and younger sister of the dashing Henry V. A beautiful and brilliant girl, Philippa so far outshone her husband in intellectual qualities that he came to hate her. As queen of Denmark, Norway, and Sweden, the young Englishwoman was often forced to take decisive action in State affairs during her husband's many absences. Her good judgments made his weaknesses the more glaring, and sometimes in his jealous rages he would beat her black and blue. Finally Philippa gave up. She retired to the cloisters of Vadstena, where she spent her remaining years and was buried.

Erik was simply not capable of heading the multitudinous affairs of three countries. The only thing he attended to well was the collection of Swedish taxes. Sweden, ruled by bailiffs from Denmark, was on the verge of anarchy.

As the discontent spread to every social class, a leader arose from the mining district of Dalarna. Engelbrekt Engelbrektsson evolved into Sweden's foremost statesman of the Middle Ages.

With heralds sent before, the revolutionary movement swept the countryside and grew into a real war of liberation. Fortifications were destroyed. The hated Danish bailiffs were booted into flight.

The thundering civilian army marched from Dalarna to the capital. But the Council members, who profited by the privileges bestowed upon them by the Union, at first turned deaf ears to the national protest. So Engelbrekt called his own meeting at Arboga in January, 1435. Here the Riksdag ("Day of the Realm") was formed, and all four classes were represented: nobles, clergy, burghers, and peasants. Thus Engelbrekt, who is reckoned as the first great democratic leader of the Swedes, brought about the first representative parliament in Europe, except for the island countries of Iceland and England.

Engelbrekt was elected regent. But before he had had time to draw up plans for national reconstruction, he was murdered by one of the nobles he had enraged.

After his untimely death, for some eight decades, Swedes knew little but strife, both with Danish royalty and among themselves; for the people were sorely divided in their adherence to nationality or the Union.

In 1471 the Danish king was defeated in battle by the formidable young Protector Sten Sture, the only other great name besides that of Engelbrekt during the disjointed Period of Union. Sten Sture became the democratic idol of the people, and he was followed in leadership by other Stures, until one called Sten Sture the Younger was mortally wounded in a battle with the Danes in 1520.

The nationalists in Sweden now had to capitulate to the Danes, and in September, 1520, some eighty-five years after Engelbrekt called the first Riksdag, the gates of Stockholm were opened to the Danish king. The Union seemed preserved. But it was to endure only three more years, and then be dissolved forever.

The Danes now made a fatal error in meting out too severe a punishment to the nationalist leaders. King Christian II had granted amnesty for everything that had taken place during the last Sture-led war. But he broke his word. On a gloomy November noon, after a mock heresy trial, the blood of vengeance began to flow in Stockholm's market place. The gazing citizens beheld the heads of noblemen, bishops, and commoners laid upon the block and struck off. The massacre continued for days, while throughout the provinces other wholesale executions proceeded. In January of 1521 Christian, foolishly believing that his prescribed blood bath had cleansed the land of rebellious infection, returned to Denmark with a smile of satisfaction.

The king little dreamed that at the time of his departure a tall young man of twenty-four was speaking words to the peasants of Dalarna that would lead to the final expulsion of the Danes and the complete break-up of the Union. The young man's name was Gustav Eriksson. Born into the noble Vasa family, he is known to history as Gustavus Vasa, and regarded as greater than any Swede who preceded him. In his teens Gustav had been imbued with ideals of a free people and a Swedish-born king. He had followed Sten Sture the Younger to his court, and in the last war he had been the proud standard-bearer. Captured and imprisoned in Denmark as a hostage, he made his escape disguised as a herdsman. The fugitive had just reached his Swedish home and was in hiding, when his own father's head was struck off in the November executions.

Dressed as a forester, Gustav now set out for Dalarna, that province of independent-thinking peasants and miners, whose patriotism had been inflamed to action by Engelbrekt and Sten Sture.

In the Christmas season he addressed the peasants both at Rättvik and Mora, towns on Lake Siljan. His earnest eloquence aroused no immediate response. The Swedes were so tired of continual disturbance they were ready to endure Danish overlordship for a while longer. In black discouragement, Gustav departed on skis to escape the pursuing Danish officers. Just as he was about to cross the Norwegian border, ski-runners from Mora caught up with him. The men of Dalarna had changed their minds. They would make another fight against Danish oppression, and they asked the young Gustav to be their leader.

After two years of insurrection the last Dane had been driven from Sweden. When the Riksdag met on June 6, 1523, Gustav was elected king.

A century of recurrent strife had left the kingdom bankrupt and prostrate. Herculean tasks confronted the inexperienced sovereign, who was only twenty-seven, when asked to create a new Sweden. By the grace of Heaven Gustavus Vasa possessed the essential qualities. He was of iron constitution and strong will. He could conceive and execute equally well. Practical and materialistic, he was yet foresighted and ever ready to try the untried. It was not in his nature to cling doggedly to the past. Whenever he saw a better way, he did not hesitate to smash tradition. And knowing that his judgments were generally better than those of his Council, he, the revolutionary, made his power dictatorial and supreme.

Gustavus Vasa was an autocrat at a time when the re-emerging nation needed vigor and force in the essential house-cleaning. He labored assiduously himself, and he demanded energetic work from others. He did not inspire affection or love, but a kind of dogged devotion to duty, partly through fear of his stern rebuke.

To refashion the nation on firm foundations, the king's desperate need was money. As he considered every logical expedient for raising cash, he turned speculative and yearning eyes to the Reformation, which Martin Luther had recently inaugurated in Germany. He knew that his contemporary on the English throne, Henry VIII, by adopting the new Protestantism, was bringing tremendous wealth to the Crown through confiscation of the Church estates.

By chance, there was a great preacher in Stockholm named Olaus Petri, who had recently studied at Luther's university at Wittenberg. Petri was promulgating the new idea of freedom from domination by priest and Pope, and the right of each man to seek his salvation directly from God himself. An inherently independent people, some Swedes had already eagerly seized upon Petri's exposition of the new doctrine. Gustavus Vasa gave Petri every encouragement. Together they brought about a bloodless acceptance of Lutheranism. The king became the head of the new Swedish Church and straightway began transferring Church properties, including bishops' manors and the wealth of the convents, to the State.

Having defied the Pope, the king next broke the power of the Lübeck merchants over Swedish commerce. He opened up new international markets for Sweden. He created a navy and an army. And he built castles and public edifices of dignified and solid grandeur.

Sometimes the hard-working king was so discouraged at the fecklessness of human beings that he threatened to abdicate, and to enjoy a pleasant life of merriment far from burdens of State. But the last decades of his life bore the rewarding fruits of his labors in prosperity and peace. After a vigorous, constructive reign of thirty-seven years, Gustavus Vasa died on September 29, 1560.

Though he was hardly a man to be loved for any quality, at his death he was universally esteemed for his mighty service to his country. Indubitably, he is one of the greatest of Sweden's kings, perhaps second only to his own grandson, Gustavus Adolphus, a hero beloved as well as admired.

7.

The Fighting Heroes

Nurture your mind with great thoughts.
To believe in the heroic makes heroes.

—DISRAELI

CONSTRUCTED IN AN ALMOST legendary heroic mold, with large capacities for everything, Gustavus I was thrice married, and by one of his wives he had ten children. So he left a plenitude of direct heirs to carry on the Vasa dynasty. Three of his sons and two grandsons in turn wore his crown, the second grandson, Gustavus Adolphus, being the only one of the five who assumed his grandfather's Christian name. He was the only one of the heirs who measured up to the first Vasa in ability. In grace and heart-warming personality, as well as military strategy, he far surpassed his redoubtable grandsire.

After Gustavus Vasa, sovereignty came by inheritance rather than election. The eldest Vasa son, who became king as Erik XIV, is remembered mainly for his love and display of Renaissance elegance and learning, for his gallant and persistent courtship of England's virgin queen, Elizabeth, and finally for his romantic marriage with Karin Månsdotter, a beautiful nut-seller he discovered in the public market, though some insist she appeared first at court as a serving wench. Such unroyal behavior was sufficient grounds for his ambitious brothers and the nobility to declare the king insane and unfit to rule. So Erik was deposed, and he ended his days in prison, playing his lute for his faithful Karin, until he was poisoned, presumably by the brother Johan III who had succeeded him.

At the age of seventeen Gustavus Adolphus followed his father Charles IX to the throne in 1611, that same auspicious year that saw

136

the release of the King James' version of the Bible. He brought Sweden to her most glorious place in history, inaugurating the stretch of years known as the Age of Greatness, which ended in 1718 with the death of another young warrior-king, Charles XII, who left Sweden shorn of her empire and corroded with despair.

As the Swedish Vikings had regarded the Baltic Sea as their own pond, so did the Vasas. But for almost a century little war had followed little war for possession of its control, Sweden now fighting Russia, now Poland, now Denmark, and sometimes German principalities, and often two or three enemies at once. At the untimely death of his father, the vigorous, tyrannical, cynical, and able Charles IX, Gustavus Adolphus inherited, along with his crown, three foreign wars in progress. Due to his father's materialism, however, the country's condition economically, if not spiritually, was in good repair.

In his first six years the youth's major energies were consumed in concluding peace with Denmark and with Russia: the former, with a loss; the latter, with considerable diplomatic gain and territorial acquisitions as far south as the seaport of Riga. Sweden's principal objective was achieved: the control of Russia's Baltic trade routes. To effect the agreements with his eastern neighbor, Gustavus Adolphus had stilled the Muscovite apprehension that he or his brother Carl Phillip had any fantastic notions of eventually sitting on the throne of the czars.

In 1618, the year after the Russian-Swedish treaty, the general European peace was shattered by the commencement of a religious struggle that grew into the Thirty Years' War. After watching its progress for a dozen years, Gustavus Adolphus himself took the field in defense of Protestantism and shortly became the most renowned soldier of his time.

In the meantime the king worked hard at domestic policies. From the hour of his ascension to the throne, utterly unlike his grandfather, he revealed a remarkably conciliatory temper; and unlike his father, who had a cynical contempt for human beings, Gustavus Adolphus revealed a love of his fellow-men, whatever their estate. His very first act, in 1611, was the promulgation of a Royal Charter by which the Council and the Estates were to have a voice in all questions of legislation. He declared the king and the people were to work mutually for the advancement of the commonwealth. Courts of justice were reformed, and new ones created. The University of Uppsala was put on a strong financial foundation by rich endowments from the State. To the nobility, which had been squelched and suppressed by his grandfather, was accorded its one-time prestige. The king gave encouragement to the merchants, and particularly those who indulged in foreign trade. He invited Scots and Englishmen and Flemings to settle in Sweden with their skills and their capital. The new blood and the new ideas that came into the land proved most stimulating.

Only in one respect did Gustavus Adolphus show himself relentless: he would not tolerate active Catholicism. He said he could not risk internal strife through religious dissensions. Those who openly reverted to the Catholic faith had to seek another country, and anyone found guilty of proselytizing was to be regarded as seditious.

After a decade of putting his house in order, Gustavus Adolphus took up his father's unfinished fight with Poland, and led his forces against his cousin, the Catholic king. As he won successive victories from Riga to Prussia, the great von Wallenstein, Austrian commander of the Holy Roman Empire's forces, became so concerned about the fighting Protestant king that he consulted astrologers, who told him darkly that the Swedes could not be vanquished if they ever fought the Hapsburgs.

But while the Swedish army was engaged in Poland, the counter-Reformation forces in Central Europe were playing havoc with the Protestants. It looked as if the Hapsburgs might soon master all Europe.

When 1630 came, Gustavus Adolphus determined to be the deliverer of the Protestants in Germany from the Catholic oppression. In May he made his farewells to the Swedish people, little dreaming that they were to be last farewells. His blessing on the burghers spoken to their representatives in the Riksdag has been much quoted. "To you," he said simply, "I would wish that your small cottages may become large stone houses; your small boats, large ships and vessels; and that the oil in your pitchers may never run short and fail."

On June 17, glowing with his mission and with the reflected love of devoted subjects, the thirty-six-year-old king set sail with sixteen thousand soldiers "to save Protestantism in Europe." In September he won his first decisive battle at Breitenfeld. This victory broke the counter-Reformation forces, and made him the recognized leader of the Protestant coalition. Gustavus Adolphus now operated with such expedition and brilliant tactical skill that he astounded the whole of Europe. The Imperial forces fell back before him as he marched triumphantly into Würzburg, Mainz, Nuremberg, and Augsburg. Munich, the capital of Catholic Bavaria, capitulated to him in May, 1632, just two years after he bade his Parliament good-by. He had reached the pinnacle of his fame. The "Gold King from the North" had become a kind of legend. Fantastic rumors floated about that he would be made emperor of Germany, as it had once been whispered that he might sit on the throne of czars. The shrewd Cardinal Richelieu, of Catholic France, who had pledged Gustavus Adolphus a large five-year subsidy to assist in the defeat of the menacing Hapsburgs, now became concerned about the ultimate aims of the victorious Swede.

But destiny suddenly broke the chain of seeming miracles. At Lützen, where Wallenstein was settling into winter quarters, Gustavus Adolphus made a surprise attack on November 6, 1632. It was an ominous day of fog that came and went. The king threw himself in the thick of the fight, leading his cavalry and exhorting his men like one possessed. In the encircling fog he got himself completely surrounded by the enemy. A bullet tore into his left arm. As he attempted to retire, another drilled his body, and he fell from his horse. A third bullet crashed into his face and he moved no more.

When Gustavus Adolphus' horse with his empty saddle tore through the Swedish lines like a winged messenger bringing disastrous tidings, the soldiers were momentarily frozen with dismay. Then the sharp spur of grief drove them to redoubled fury of fighting, and they routed the enemy from the field.

There is little doubt that Gustavus Adolphus is the greatest figure in the Swedish chronicles. As man and king, as administrator and warrior, he revealed remarkable abilities. He unified and strengthened his own people; he achieved the Swedish ambition of an empire; he became known as the savior of Protestantism in its most crucial time.

Among his soldiers, both Swedes and mercenaries, he inspired devotion. The tribute paid him by a Scottish officer in his army has been remembered through the centuries: "The king of captains and the captain of kings."

After the death of the leader, who had come to be regarded as invincible, his spirit still animated the Swedish forces on the battlefield. Generals trained by him continued to win victories, as the Thirty Years' War dragged on. When peace was finally concluded by the Treaty of Westphalia in 1648, Swedish troops were occupying parts of Prague, under the command of Gustavus Adolphus' nephew, the Palatine Count, Karl Gustav, who was strangely destined to assume the Swedish throne six years later.

By the Westphalian treaty, which guaranteed liberty of conscience in Europe, Sweden's powerful position in Europe was confirmed. She was now possessed of German provinces and cities, and she commanded the outlets of three German rivers. Again, as in the Age of the Vikings, Sweden was undisputed mistress of the Baltic.

In Sweden the king's death had brought some confusion, as well as consternation and a national mourning. His six-year-old daughter Christina had succeeded him to the throne, while her father's chief adviser, Count Axel Oxenstjerna, headed the regency, and with remarkable skill guided the affairs of State.

It was during the regency that the Swedes made their only attempt at colonization in the New World. On the lower Delaware River, New Sweden was founded in 1638, only eighteen years after the Pilgrims had arrived at Plymouth Rock. But in 1655 the colony was absorbed by the Dutch. Sweden shortly became too engrossed with her possessions in Germany and the Baltic States to make further attempts at colonization so far from home boundaries.

When Christina reached her majority in 1644, she assumed the reins of government. Ten years later, at the age of twenty-eight, she dramatically laid by her crown and abdicated in favor of her cousin, Karl Gustav, of whom she was tenderly fond and whom she had once thought of marrying. Then she renounced the Protestant faith her father had given his life to preserve, and went to Rome to live close to the heart of Catholicism.

Historians are in little agreement in estimating this strange daughter of Sweden's foremost hero. It is well confirmed she did not shirk her queenly duties, but took much interest in the Council meetings, and occasionally offered sound suggestions. Brought up like a boy, she developed into a blue-stocking. Her greatest passion was in cultivating learning and the arts, and she spent large sums of State money in making her court a center for culture. Among the international figures who sojourned in Sweden at her bidding was the famous French philosopher Descartes. Though the great Puritan poet John Milton did not go to Stockholm, he wrote a poem in praise of Sweden's virgin queen.

No one can be sure of the real reason for Christina's abdication, against which even foreign diplomats tried to dissuade her. But certainly one factor was her inability to bring herself to marry and give Sweden an heir. While Christina was extremely pleasure-loving and danced with an almost unseemly abandon at State balls, she found the idea of marriage thoroughly repugnant. She had convinced herself that she would never make a good ruler, for she lacked continuous purpose and execution and, recklessly extravagant, she had no sense whatever of finance. Christina converted herself to Catholicism through her own studies and out of her need to escape from herself and the restless disposition inherited from her Hohenzollern mother. In the barren, boring sermons of the Lutheran clergy, she could not find the spiritual nourishment her disharmonious nature craved.

When Christina's coach passed unceremoniously out of the boundaries of Sweden, the great public did not mourn the departure of their queen. For, in her ten years, she had done nothing to alleviate the distress of the poor, who had been forced to pay more taxes each time she had created more non-tax-paying nobles.

On the road to Rome she paused at Innsbruck to make her formal renunciation of the Lutheran faith and be received into the Catholic Church. For thirty-five more years the one-time queen lived in Rome among esthetic surroundings and distinguished friends, much admired and presumably at peace with herself. She never ceased to regard herself as a sovereign. When she died in 1689, she was honored by burial in St. Peter's.

When her favorite cousin took Christina's discarded crown as Charles X, he found the treasury bankrupt, the people hungry and muttering. But he proved equal to the job of reconstruction. Christina's judgment in choosing a successor was far superior to that of the great Queen Margaret's in the days of the Kalmar Union. Charles turned out to be the vigorous man of ability she wished she might have been. In a war made against him by Denmark he proved himself the nephew of Gustavus Adolphus by his brilliant military tactics, and he won for Sweden the rich southern provinces of the peninsula that had been possessed by the Danes since time immemorial.

The Danes brought the loss on themselves. While the Swedish army was sorely beset by Russian hordes in Poland, Denmark declared war on her cousin country; for King Frederick III hoped to reclaim certain lands lost to Sweden by his father, the great Christian IV. The Swedish King Charles X quickly withdrew his army from Poland to deal with the Danes. Within four weeks the marching Swedish forces had reached Holstein and taken Jutland. A severe cold wave suddenly hit Denmark and with unprecedented celerity the waters of the Belts froze. Against the advice of all his generals save one, Charles decided to risk crossing the new-formed ice and attacking the Danes from the rear. His daring strategy succeeded. The Danes, surprised and crushed, sued for peace. In the peace-making, in which the England of Oliver Cromwell acted as mediator, Denmark lost not only Skåne, but the smaller provinces of Halland and Blekinge, and a western region called Bohuslän.

The annexations Charles X made to Sweden's territory were the only ones to endure to the present day. His able, enriching reign lasted less than six years. Suddenly in February, 1660, the warrior-king sickened and died, at precisely the same age at which Gustavus Adolphus met his death: thirty-eight.

Again, a child—a four-year-old—succeeded to the crown, but this time it was a man-child who became Charles XI. This Charles was neither so attractive nor so clever as his father. But during his long reign the peace was maintained indifferently well, and he increased greatly the State's annual revenues, without oppressing the poor. In fact, the well-being of the peasants improved considerably during his regime. Without radically alienating the nobility, Charles's first significant act was to confiscate a fourth of all their estates for the Crown's depleted treasury. He introduced sweeping social and economical reforms needful for Sweden's stability. For defense, he founded the famous naval station stronghold at Karlskrona and he built a new fleet. In his latter years the watchword of his foreign policy was "peace," constantly reiterated. When he died, Sweden was in excellent economical condition and in possession of her empire. The contributions of Charles XI were sound, rather than spectacular, and his sense of justice has become proverbial in Sweden.

The Swedes were soon to get their fill of heroic ambition and dashing personality in his son and successor, Charles XII, the most controverted monarch that ever ruled in Sweden. Adored by some, and regarded with distaste by others, Charles XII is indubitably an extraordinary if enigmatic figure.

When he succeeded to his father's throne at the age of fifteen, an aura of glamour hung about the vibrant, slender youth. Though he was nothing like so charming, he appealed to the public imagination, much as did the young Edward Prince of Wales in this century. The nation's heart was full of great expectations for a long and prosperous reign, but it was to be blasted with disappointment in the end, for Charles XII, despite his heroism and ability on the battlefield, proved a national disaster for Sweden.

Charles had hardly got the crown about his youthful head, when Denmark, Poland, and Russia formed an offensive alliance against him. Their rulers little dreamed the fighting stuff of which the boy was made. At the age of eighteen he put himself at the head of his troops and routed his aggressive enemies one by one within a single year. First he quickly subdued the Danes. Then he turned his forces against Russia, whose young czar was Peter I, later called the Great. In November, 1700, at Narva, with all the odds against him and vastly outnumbered, Charles defeated the Russians in a snowstorm. The victory was of such brilliance that all Europe was amazed, and the wonder grew because the king-general was only a lad of eighteen. From Narva, Charles turned to punish his third enemy, the king of Poland. With celerity he defeated the Polish forces, occupied Warsaw, and then proceeded to depose the inimical monarch and get the Poles to elect a new king who would be friendly to Sweden.

Hearing of his continual triumphs and incredible swiftness—he took the fortified city of Lemberg in less than half an hour—the great Duke of Marlborough journeyed to Poland in 1706 to confer with the fantastic young fighter, who seemed to know tricks of war beyond the knowledge of the English commander. Marlborough attempted to persuade Charles to leave Russia alone and fight with the Sea Powers against France and Louis XIV. But Charles well knew that Sweden's menace lay to the east. Czar Peter, smarting for revenge, had again attacked Sweden's possessions in the Baltic States in 1703. He was now planning to move his capital from remote Moscow to a spot which was to grow into the city called St. Petersburg. So Charles carefully devised a campaign that would render Russia incapable of harm to Sweden. He aimed to capture Moscow and dictate terms from the ancient capital of the czars.

But the decision to penetrate to Russia's heart proved as disastrous for him as it was later to prove ruinous for Napoleon and the Nazi Hitler. Because Charles had now come to believe himself invincible, he had seemingly discounted the interminable marching of his foot soldiers and the difficulties of supplying food and ammunition hundreds of miles from base. After a first victory over the Russians at Holovzin in Lithuania his luck turned sour. From 1708 until his death ten years later Charles knew little but false hope and defeat.

Russians nipped at the Swedish heels; supply wagons and artillery were lost. Reinforcements could not get through to the king. He was forced to make the Ukraine, with its bread basket, his new objective. But freezing weather took terrible toll of his hungry, weary-footed men, who dropped with pneumonia or sheer fatigue. Played-out animals died in the snow, beside incapacitated men freezing to death. The horrors of the field hospitals were ghastly, as frozen hands and limbs were amputated and the haggard men sent on their way. Bands of Russian horsemen plagued and harried the hobbling Swedes in surprise attacks from the rear, and made havoc of their sleep. The only cheer in the torturing march was that the army was headed south, and that spring would follow winter. At last they were outside Poltava, and it was June. But the crucifying privations they had endured on the frozen trek had transformed the Swedes into mere mangled shadows of their stalwart selves.

Yet before his suffering soldiers had well caught their breath, the impatient Charles ordered a preliminary battle in order to draw the

Russian army to a decisive action. In the skirmish the king was shot in the foot. By the time the full Russian army did arrive, his wound had become gangrenous. Unable to walk or assume full command at this climactic moment of his career, he had his feverish body borne on a litter to the field, just as the hard-pressed Swedes were about to withdraw. The king's presence rallied them and they resumed the fight. But at last they could hold out no longer against the Russian onslaughts. Slashed and bleeding, they turned in panic and stampeded, leaving the king helpless in his grounded litter, surrounded by his dead bearers, with his white bandaged foot sticking up like a strange standard amid the smoke of battle. Horrified, not at his own danger, but at the sight of Swedish backs, the king cried out in dismay and reproach, "Swedes! Swedes!"

Somehow Charles was rescued, and a formal retreat was ordered. At the Dnieper River the ill king was persuaded to cross first. His last command to his army was to follow him into Turkey. But the heroes of nine years of warfare were too numb with exhaustion and despair to face further fighting. Charles had lost his magic spell for them. His all-obeying voice no longer had the power to stir. Sixteen thousand Swedes surrendered to the czar's forces. And soon the flower of Sweden's manhood began the dreadful march to the horrors of prison life in Siberia. Peter had nothing now to fear in making St. Petersburg his capital.

The year 1709 is the blackest in Swedish annals. The twenty-seven-year-old Charles saw the Swedish empire begin to crash like a house of cards. As prisoner-guest of Turkey's sultan, he schemed to save bits of it. He got the Turks to attack the czar, but they feared to penetrate far into the Russian interior. From his Turkish internment Charles attempted to rule Sweden by absolute decree. But certain nobles in Stockholm were making peace without the king's knowledge, and were even preparing his deposition.

In the midst of the domestic plots King Charles turned up dramatically in Sweden in 1715. He had been absent from his country for fifteen years. Still imperious, headstrong, and impatient at thirty-three, he was received with little exultation. As a gesture to compensate for his losses and to regain the popular favor, he determined to take Norway from his old enemy Denmark.

In the dusk of a November evening in 1718, while inspecting the Swedish trenches before the Norwegian fortifications at Fredrik-sten, the king was pierced by a bullet. No one knows for certain from which side the shot was fired; but, at the age of thirty-six, Charles died in the trenches.

Thus ended what is called Sweden's Period of Greatness and the career of her third famous warrior-king. Two years less in time had been allotted to him than to his grandfather Charles X or his great-great-uncle Gustavus Adolphus, both of whom lived to be thirty-eight. For all his place in history as one of the most brilliant youths ever to command an army, Charles XII had managed to lose almost everything the other two heroes had won for Sweden.

It is indeed hard to form an estimate of this exciting young man, who left behind neither wise nor foolish sayings by which to judge him. That he was inherently courageous and superlatively daring, there is no doubt. He saw himself as the savior of his country, and he made wars only on those enemies who started shooting first. He spoke not of demands for new territory, but only of destruction of Sweden's enemies, which became the all-absorbing purpose of his life, and for which end he was willing to forego personal comfort himself and to drive his soldiers beyond human endurance. We have no record of his compassion, but we have a succinct comment on his attitude of absolute authority: "They shall fight when I command them."

For all his meteoric fire, Charles XII is not a sympathetic character. The most famous full-length portrait of him, painted in 1700, is anything but attractive. It portrays him in soldier dress, somewhat stringy in figure, with an excessively narrow, pale face, a narrow chin, a long nose, little squint eyes, and a tight-lipped, contemptuous mouth. His fists are contracted: the left one grasps the hilt of his sword; the right presses his belt, with an elbow aggressively akimbo. The whole figure suggests a repellent cockiness, together with childish arrogance and willfulness, and a restless energy. Even though the portrait was done before he was twenty, it must reveal something of the man.

Whatever the truth about the inner Charles XII, at his passing Sweden's dream of empire was rudely and conclusively shattered. One cannot help but think that the nation would have fared better if the throne had not descended to a youth possessed of such headstrong and daredevilish qualities.

8.

The Age of Peace

Peace hath her victories
No less renown'd than war.

—MILTON

THE HALF-CENTURY, 1719-72, following the death of Charles XII, is sometimes designated as the Age of Liberty and sometimes as the Age of Peace. The nobles and military officers, sick of vain conflicts, took matters in their own hands, abolished the absolute monarchy, and established peace.

Peace, however, did not come to the exhausted nation until April, 1721, when the mighty losses were written off. Because Czar Peter was in a position to make demands, Sweden was forced to cede to Russia Estonia and her other East Baltic possessions—"Sweden's chief bread basket"—and even a strategic part of Finland. After the Treaty of Nystad in 1721, Sweden was henceforth forced to content herself within her earlier boundaries.

Charles, who had left no heir—he was never married—was succeeded by his sister Ulrica Eleonora, Sweden's only other female ruler besides Christina and the Danish Margaret. In a different way, Ulrica Eleonora proved as difficult as her dynamic brother. After two years of wrangling, when she declared herself willing to renounce her royal prerogative in favor of her husband, Prince Frederic of Hesse, the nobles were glad to elect him king of Sweden.

However, they were not pleased with him as a monarch, and the good manifestations of his reign were due largely to the abilities of Arvid Horn, the chief councilor, who turned his attention to creating domestic health and prosperity. Soldiers were rehabilitated on the farms, and their nicked swords beaten into plowshares. New

147

buildings arose. Industry increased more than a hundred fold, and received Government protection. English workmen were imported to instruct the Swedes in the handling of spinning wheels and machines. Paper mills, iron foundries, and dye works did a big business. Foreign trade was extended to the East Indies. Swedish consulates were established in Turkish ports. A new rich middle class of merchants evolved.

The Age of Peace was also marked by the emergence, or rather the flowering, of scientists. Cristopher Polhem, called "the father of Swedish mechanics," was still alive inventing machines, planning projects, stimulating others. His most famous pupil, Emanuel Swedenborg, whose youthful talents had been appreciated by Charles XII, continued until 1772 to astound with his discoveries, inventions, and theories. Because he ended his days as the greatest mystic theologian of his time, the earlier scientific achievements and writings are often forgotten. But in Sweden the scientist-turned-mystic continues to be honored for his works on such prosaic subjects as docks and locks, coastal erosion, salt pans, and iron smelting. He designed a safety-lamp for miners, an air-pump, and a mechanical piano, and he drew designs for a submarine and an airplane.

Carl Linnaeus, Sweden's only other international figure famous both in science and literature, did the bulk of his great work in botany in this Period of Peace. His school of natural science at Uppsala attracted students and scholars from afar.

Among the other scientists of the period were Anders Celsius, the astronomer, who perfected the centigrade thermometer, Johan Wallerius, the mineralogist, and Torben Bergman, the chemist. Altogether this was the great age of science in Sweden; and, in 1739, the Academy of Science was founded after the model of the famous English society established in the reign of Charles II.

During his thirty-one years on the Swedish throne the German Frederic did nothing of any great significance himself, but at his death in March, 1751, the country was in good order and relatively prosperous. He was succeeded by his son Adolphus Frederic, whose wife Louisa Ulrica was the vivid sister of Frederick the Great of Prussia. The queen was far keener than her amiable husband. Influenced by the brilliant court of her learning-loving brother, she was eager to make changes in Sweden's society, and at the same time to secure more power for the Crown. But the queen met stout opposition to her ambitions on every hand—even the tutors for the crown prince and his brothers were chosen by the Council. The royal prerogative was reduced to little more than a formality.

The queen, denied political power, salved her wounded pride by turning to culture, and, under her patronage, an Academy of Belles Lettres was established in 1753. But in June of 1756 she attempted to engineer an insurrection to restore the dignity of the Crown. Her coup ended abortively, with executions of several high officers, including the premier nobleman of the land, Count Erik Brahe.

After the thorough squelching of the court party, stimulation of manufacture and foreign trade became Parliament's major interests. The Swedish East India Company alone was soon making annual profits of "three barrels of gold"—approximately $300,000.

In 1776 Sweden established freedom of the press by legislation, thus becoming the first European monarchy after the English to have an uncensored press. But during the sixties, because there was no outstanding strong man in the Government, a constant struggle ensued between political parties for control of the Riksdag. Confidence in the Government's abilities sharply waned, as money was wasted and a new fear of Russia's menace was added to general uneasiness. Conditions became so bad in the house divided against itself that it was feared Sweden's independence might be lost through the influence of scheming foreign powers. The captivating young Crown Prince Gustav, who was only twenty-three, now asserted himself and became the leading spirit in the court party. It was his strong intention to bring about restoration of royal power. He encouraged his father to threaten abdication if the Riksdag did not convene at an extraordinary session called by the king. When the king's desire and threat were brushed aside, the crown prince in person went to the various officers of State and announced his father's abdication. As perturbed conservatives began to give him their support and talked of changing the constitution, there were wholesale resignations in high circles.

With everything at sixes and sevens, one night in February, 1771, the self-indulgent Adolphus Frederic, who had not really abdicated after all, supped so greedily on seafood, sauerkraut, and champagne, that he died of acute indigestion.

Crown Prince Gustav was not at his father's deathbed. The young man had gone to Paris on a private mission, endeavoring to get France to back a coup amplifying the royal power. Gustav was in high favor in Paris. He had received his education there and, like his illustrious uncle Frederick the Great, he was an ardent admirer of French culture. Both Marie Antoinette and her husband, who was shortly to become King Louis XVI, were fond of the Swedish prince. Old Louis XV gave him some farewell advice: "First reconcile the opposing parties in Sweden."

9.

The Period of Glamour

*What shall I do to be forever known
And make the age to come my own?*

—COWLEY

LIKE THE Emperor Augustus Caesar in Rome, Gustav III is honored by having an historical period named for him. In Swedish annals the Gustavian Era is reckoned from his accession in 1771 to the establishment of the Bernadotte dynasty in 1818, though Gustav himself did not live beyond 1792. While not an extensive period, its early years achieved a brilliance never reached before or since. Perhaps no sovereign of either sex ever wore ermine with more natural grace than did Gustav III. He is the "Roi Charmeur" and, by all odds, Sweden's foremost royal patron of the arts. But besides his cultural interests, he possessed remarkable political astuteness, and in national crises he could act with fierce energy and force.

When the twenty-five-year-old Gustav appeared before the new Riksdag, he made an immediate stir with his eloquent oratory. For a Swedish monarch to possess the combination of personal charm, perfect manners, keen intelligence, and an extraordinary gift for speech was a new excitement indeed.

But party enmity and struggle for privilege between the commons and the nobles still raged so bitterly that the commonweal was virtually disregarded. Party rule had become rampantly lawless, while a famine undermined the national morale, the treasury remained bare, and Russia, through a new alliance, became a real threat to Sweden's independence.

The young king did his persuasive utmost to bring peace between the contending political factions. Then, convinced that no concilia-

151

tion of the rival parties would restore health to Sweden, he secretly determined on a *coup d'état*. With a Finnish colonel as his key friend in insurrection in outlying strongholds, Gustav won the officers in Stockholm by an impassioned and moving speech. The officers promptly arrested the members of the Council, who were in session in the royal palace. Then, with a white ribbon wound about his arm as an identification badge, the king rode out to face the citizens and let them know what was happening. Inspired by his charm and daring and his promise of a better order, the populace acclaimed him lustily. The navy, as well as the army, went over to Gustav with enthusiasm. At the end of one hot August day— it was the nineteenth, in 1772—the coup was an accomplished fact, and no one had lost a drop of blood.

Two days later, when Gustav called the Riksdag to the guarded Assembly Hall, he appeared before the members resplendent and regal, very much a king. In a brilliant speech of restrained invective, he censored them roundly and pointedly for the sad state of affairs to which their selfish and ignoble strife had reduced the fatherland. He told them with conviction that he would bring happier days to the land by the security of law. When he had won his audience and reached his climax, he dramatically drew forth the draft of a new constitution he had prepared. He read it, and it was straightway adopted.

The young king had achieved one of the most striking political victories in Swedish history. The ease with which he made himself virtually absolute monarch amazed the other nations. Russia, who had looked to "guaranteeing" Swedish liberty, was constricted with resentment; but she had to swallow her disappointment because her armies were too busy now in Turkey and Poland. Frederick of Prussia was not only astounded at the daring of his nephew, but joined with Denmark in a threat to make him relinquish his absolute power. England hardly knew how to react to the extraordinary news. But France backed Gustav stoutly, and informed the Russians, the Prussians, and the Danes that if Sweden was attacked, France would move against her aggressors.

The king proceeded to set his house in order. He appointed the proved best men of former Governments to the high offices. The use of the disturbing party names of the preceding decades was taboo. Slates were wiped clean; all was forgiven. Conciliation and moderation were the qualities to be cultivated. Henceforth torture was never to be employed; and whatever torture rooms still existed in the kingdom were promptly destroyed on the king's personal order. Shortly, the death penalty for several serious offenses was abrogated.

As political wrangling ceased, all factions took renewed heart. State finances were put on a firmer basis. Once more foreign trade became vigorous. As Sweden had virtually a world monopoly on exported iron, she could demand high prices.

As soon as political harmony and commercial prosperity seemed well established, the national defenses rehabilitated, and the navy reorganized, the king turned his attention to Russia. In June of 1777, in the interest of maintaining peace, he paid a courtesy visit to Catherine the Great at St. Petersburg, accompanied by a refulgent entourage. Gustav's charm of manner quite captivated the full-blown czarina, and, for a few years afterwards, they carried on a warm correspondence.

With Russia rendered unhostile by his friendly gesture, and with home affairs restored to health, Gustav was free to devote his major energy to his heart's desire: the cultural development of the Swedes. At home Gustav was indeed more than the glass of fashion and the mold of form. He had learned manners at the French court and now he introduced into Swedish life the so-called French refinements, currently so admired by the world at large. He knew that mere literacy is not the criterion of culture, but that what counts is the use of it. From the various provinces he invited the talented and the beautiful, as well as the most intelligent and amiable of the nobility, to abide at his court. Court life had never before played such a significant role in Swedish civilization, and never had good manners and courtesy been so highly regarded.

The king was a born actor. He had not only the courtiers to applaud his dramatic performances in the theaters he built at Drottningholm and Gripsholm castles, but he had the whole Swedish population for his audience. His grace of movement and his purity of diction made him a natural for romantic parts. He possessed that sense of timing so essential to a star performer, and he knew just when to make his public appearances. He could assume the most easy grace in an elaborate form of etiquette. Fortunately he had a keen sense of humor, and on the actual stage he could convulse his audience in comic roles of plays he had written. At the same time that he was amusing himself, Gustav looked upon court life and the theater as excellent schools for social behavior and as means of influencing public opinion.

In 1773, his second year on the throne, he had given the Swedish people their first grand opera, and in the subsequent years he imported numerous foreign conductors and stars. In 1782 the Royal Swedish Opera House was opened with great brilliance. Its fine reputation, established almost immediately, has never lost its sheen.

The Royal Palace in Stockholm, so nobly conceived by the Tessins, father and son, and finished when Gustav was a little boy, now became a nursery of the arts. Sculptors, painters, poets, and architects were warmly welcomed and stimulated to develop their talents under the kingly patronage.

In architecture Gustav's predilection for the style known as Louis XVI, modified by the classical Italian, led to the evolution of a Swedish style called Gustavian—of which the Royal Opera House was an example. As buildings arose, their façades of the new materials, pastel and rose sandstone and subdued red granite, gave an unwonted soft radiance to the capital's somber thoroughfares.

Carl Gustav Pilo, in painting, and Johan Tobias Sergel, in sculpture, surpassed all predecessors, and became the first Swedes to be compared favorably with the contemporary great artists of Europe. Sergel, who remains the foremost sculptor Sweden produced before the present day, was a warm friend of the king. The statue of Gustav III that stands below the Royal Palace, opposite the National Art Gallery, is one of the finest examples of his work.

This was also a period of music-making. The lyrist, Carl Michael Bellman, who depicted the life of the lower classes in a kind of graceful rococo, was the most popular of the ballad-singers. This Swedish Robert Burns of the city was a composer as well as versemaker. Today his evocative songs are still sung with delight.

For all Gustav's passion for French literature, he became the champion of a national Swedish literature. The Swedish language was now brought "to a new pitch of elegance" by Johan Henrik Kellgren, who sometimes collaborated with the king on librettos.

In 1786, to encourage genius and to promote "the purity, strength, and ennoblement" of the Swedish language, Gustav founded the Swedish Academy after the model he had known in France. Today election to it is yet the highest honor that can come to a literary Swede. Its eighteen members are elected by the Academy itself, which also awards the Nobel Prize for Literature.

Superbly attuned to the sophisticated world, Gustav took little interest in religion as such. He was nothing of a mystic or an emotionalist, but completely "rational" in his thinking. Yet in religious matters he would abide no intolerance. Though the State religion was Lutheran, "Let every man follow his individual faith" was Gustav's decree. Under his regime Christian nonconformists were granted complete freedom of worship. Jews were permitted to settle in the cities and practice orthodoxy as they inclined.

When the American War of Independence broke out in 1776, the royal Gustav watched its progress with interest. Though he was a neutral and anything but a republican, his expressed sympathies were all with the Colonies, on whose side more than eighty Swedish officers fought. He was the first neutral monarch to recognize the new nation and voluntarily to offer friendship.

On the reverse side of the medal of this enlightened king were two notable faults: he was a spendthrift and he found it difficult to conclude reforms. Though he was by no means licentious or dissipated, his nerves required constant relaxation and many of his administrative duties suffered in consequence. His extravagance led his Councilors to devise wrong ways to raise money.

The worst error of Gustav's reign was denying the people the time-honored privilege of distilling their own gin. Instead of adding to the Crown's exchequer and reducing drunkenness by making gin a royal monopoly, the new decree brought about a defiant bootlegging, an increase in intoxication, little money to the treasury, and unpopularity for the monarch.

Gustav took the bitter grumbling of the populace very much to heart. To regain popular affection, he turned his eye to playing a part in foreign affairs.

It had always been his dream to get Norway away from Denmark, annex it to Sweden, and so make the entire Scandinavian peninsula his domain. In 1784, when he had failed to secure a nonaggression pact with the wary Czarina Catherine, who was now allied with Denmark, he paid a visit to France, the country dear to his heart. There in the midst of glittering festivities in his honor, he arranged an alliance, with a large cash subsidy for Sweden's defenses. But Louis XVI, who was unaware of the catastrophe approaching his own throne, gave the Swede some gentle advice that has since been often quoted. "Peace, that kind of glory which is after your Majesty's heart," he said with gracious tact, "is much to be preferred to the deceptive splendor which invests princes who yearn for conquest."

Despite an implied threat of a now cool Catherine and a verbal warning of a cordial Louis, the younger monarch inwardly refused to relinquish deceptive dreams of splendor.

But on his return home Gustav was beset with troubles on every side. The nobles and certain high military officers, who had been his warm supporters, were now cold to him and on occasion even disdainful. Some of the prominent Finns were talking of withdrawing from Sweden and forming an independent principality. They felt they could rely on Russia's protection, because Catherine was determined to attack Sweden at the most favorable opportunity and overthrow the Government of her former friend.

But luckily for Gustav, Turkey again declared war on Russia in September, 1787. Giving up his plan for Norwegian conquest, the king rushed to Copenhagen to persuade the Danes to break their Russian alliance and give him leave to attack the great eastern neighbor. But the Danes did not trust the intentions of Gustav. He now approached England and Prussia with diplomatic overtures, painting up Russia as a dangerous menace to the balance of power. He arranged a treaty with Turkey that provided a subsidy for Swedish defense. He infected the Swedes with excitement of a potential war, and every day he made an appearance on the wharves to encourage the workers and the ships' officers in their preparations.

Then, with his dramatic sense of timing, in May of 1788, he appeared dressed like the portrait of the greatest of Swedes, Gustavus Adolphus, and, to the clamorous salutes of the navy's cannon, boarded his flagship and sailed out of Stockholm harbor—presumably to take the Russian capital.

That Gustav had so bravely set sail without a tangible pretext did not trouble him greatly. In Russian uniforms sneaked from the Royal Opera's costume wardrobes, a handful of Swedish soldiers were sent to burn and loot a Finnish village just this side of the Russian frontier. War was then declared. The Swedish fleet engaged the Russian in the Gulf of Finland. St. Petersburg was thrown into a state of unreasonable fright.

The aging czarina, never dreaming the Swede capable of such a daring gesture, had left her capital virtually without defense. But the naval encounter proved such a doubtful Swedish victory that Gustav's land forces scheduled to advance on the capital hesitated to proceed. Some of the officers resigned on the spot. The Finnish soldiers had no desire to bring the wrath of Russia down on themselves.

But Gustav with his eloquence persuaded the soldiers to march on Fredrikshamn under his leadership. No strategist like his illustrious predecessor whose costume he had copied, he failed in his campaign. When the rehabilitated Russian fleet bottled up the Swedish ships at Sveaborg, prominent Swedish and Finnish officers appealed to Catherine herself to open peace negotiations, and begged the pestered king to listen to her proposals.

Desperate now, with even friends opposing him, Gustav sulked in his tent like Achilles and bewailed the sad fate of kings like that other actor-king, England's Richard II. For a few days he even toyed with the idea of abdication. When his personal ruin seemed imminent, the czarina made the error of urging the Finns to form their independent state, under her protection. This suggestion opened the eyes of the Swedish officers to the real danger from Russia, just as Denmark, seizing the opportunity of the crisis, sent troops into Swedish territory. Gustav snapped out of melancholy with the cry, "I am saved." Leaving his army gazing, he rushed back to Sweden, changed to peasant dress and, following the historical example of the first Gustav, the Vasa, he proceeded to Dalarna to exhort the peasants to help him save Sweden from the Danes. The peasants, moved by his patriotic zeal, laid down their implements of harvest, seized their arms, and marched off with the king. Everywhere he appeared, Gustav now excited fervent allegiance.

When he turned up in Göteborg to save the city from a threatening Danish-Norwegian force, the national patriotism rose to a frenzy. But the war did not proceed, for England intervened and persuaded Denmark to withdraw her troops.

Gustav's popular esteem was again elevated. With tables turned, basking in his new prestige, and enthusiastically supported by the commons, the king called Parliament and set about to curtail the power of the unfriendly nobles. The Finnish people declared they had no taste for Russian protection. The top conspiring officers were arrested, brought to Stockholm, tried for treason, and condemned to death. But with his usual moderation the king asked for the reprieve of all but one ringleader, who was executed as an example.

On February 17, 1789, in an electrically charged meeting before the assembled Four Estates, Gustav upbraided the nobles in scorching language for their defection and irresponsibility. Then with a resounding crack of his jeweled scepter on the table by his throne, he ordered them out of the room to meditate on their sins. For some breathless moments the infuriated nobles hesitated and cast menacing glances at the crown itself lying on the table beside the sovereign. Then one of the more temperate of them rose and quietly obeyed the royal command. After a tense pause the rest of the noblemen followed. For the first time in history a Swedish king was left in session with commoners only.

After a flattering speech Gustav presented a brief supplement to the constitution which he called an "Act of Union and Security." The Act gave the commons special benefits and leveled the difference in privileges: henceforth appointments to high offices were to be made not on birth, but on merit and "proved civil virtue." It also put all legislative power in the king's hand and gave him the power to declare an aggressive war without consulting Council or Riksdag.

One of the enemy nobles was moved to pay Gustav an ironic tribute: "There he was, with Russia and Denmark and even his own country against him, and he without money, with an incapacitated navy and a half-mutinous army. And suddenly the Danish attack is frustrated, Russia still on the defensive, and Sweden in chains at his feet."

In the flush of his single-handed triumphs, though hampered by a precarious economic situation, Gustav then proceeded to declare each of his proposals accepted, regardless of the voting in the Parliament. The nobles seethed with indignation and rage, without legal recourse.

After a brief resumption of naval fighting in an effort to weaken the Russian fleet, Gustav attempted once more to charm the czarina and to make a reasonable peace. When her terms were not acceptable, he attempted to frighten her by bringing the entire Swedish navy into the Gulf of Viborg, close to St. Petersburg. By closing in on the harbor mouth, the Russian fleet again bottled up the Swedish ships, with the king himself and thirty thousand soldiers aboard. Week after week, with western winds persistently against them, the Swedes remained trapped, while the Russians licked their chops over the haul of prisoners they were to bring to the czarina. In early July when the Swedish situation seemed utterly hopeless, the wind suddenly shifted to the east, and the resilient Gustav ordered a running of the gauntlet. The escape was brilliantly executed and, despite heavy losses, the fleet got through the Russian cannonading. Gustav ordered retirement to the Svensksund to lick wounds and prepare for final decisive action. He would gamble on a winner-take-all throw.

The stronger Russians prepared to make the crushing of the Swedes more historically memorable by scheduling the event for the anniversary of Catherine's coronation, July ninth. They chose badly, for Gustav's stars were in most propitious aspect that day.

With an illuminated presence and glory words, Gustav put inspired vigor into his men. The attacking Russians were met with such precise and withering volleys that after two hours they sought to retire. But now, as if the heavens themselves were allied with Gustav, the skies darkened ominously and high winds arose and blocked retreat. In trying to escape, Russian ships ran aground. Others sank or surrendered to the Swedes.

At Catherine's court, while the chilled champagne was waiting to be uncorked to celebrate the Swedish annihilation, the staggering news was brought that the Russian fleet had lost a third of its ships and half its men.

Gustav returned to Stockholm a conquering hero. Mighty Russia was no more to be feared. The Swedes once again lauded to the skies their dazzling, dramatic king. Though they did not know it, they were celebrating the last great victory in Swedish history.

With his personal prestige at its apotheosis, Gustav turned his attention to the French Revolution, which had imprisoned his friend Louis XVI. Foreseeing the danger to all royalty, he proposed a coalition of European powers that would send a force headed by himself into France to restore the monarchy. Envisioning himself as champion of the old order, he entertained little doubt that he could win the French people. But of the various European monarchs, he could attract none to his scheme except, oddly enough, the Czarina Catherine.

While Gustav now spent most of his days alone working with his secretaries, he occasionally allowed himself the relaxation of the theater. On March 16, 1792, he was persuaded to attend a masquerade ball at the Opera House. He was completely unaware that three conspirators, two young noblemen and a swashbuckling army captain, had plotted his assassination for two months.

The king did not arrive until just before supper was served. Dressed simply in a black robe of Venetian silk, unlike the rest he wore a white mask rather than a black one. During the meal a note warning him of grave danger was slipped into his hands. He chose to ignore it. And after supper, while the orchestra played, he walked onto the stage with his favorite, Count von Essen, the field marshal. As a group of masked figures circled about him, one touched him on the shoulder and called out a Judas greeting. A pistol shot electrified the assembly. The king cried out: "I am hurt. Arrest the man." Then he dropped into a chair, removed his mask, and remained perfectly calm.

The maskers began crying "Fire!" and started rushing away. But, as in the last scene of *Hamlet,* von Essen yelled, "Let the doors be locked," and few escaped.

Most of the king's enemies were as shocked and distressed by the shooting as his friends, and sincerely hoped for his recovery. But the bullet proved too deeply lodged to be removed. Gangrene began its painful and mortal corrosion. As death approached, the suffering Gustav received the leading noblemen who had fought him, and reconciliations were effected. The king was not concerned that punishment should be meted out to the captain who had shot him. He even stopped his ears to keep from hearing the names of the other apprehended and confessed conspirators. His death was as gracious as possible under the circumstances—his last hours were concerned only with his country's welfare and the immediate comfort of those who came to say good-by.

When he died at the age of forty-six, after a reign of twenty-one years, Gustav had just reached his prime. For all his sheer histrionic displays, his master dissimulations and subtle deceits, and his occasional errors in judgment, Gustav's credits far outweighed his debits. The nation was infinitely better off domestically when the actor-king made his exit than when he ascended the throne. And internationally Sweden was highly respected. While he unquestionably relished playing the stellar role in the Swedish drama, much of which he himself created, he was never unmindful of the commonweal. He loved Sweden with a romantic ardor. It has often been quoted: "Gustav dared to think greatly of the fatherland."

The reign of Gustav III is the period of Swedish history touched with glamour. Rays of influence from those courtly days still sift into Swedish culture today and give it a pleasing glow. After his passing, Swedish art and architecture went into a decline, and for almost a century no first-rate native artist appeared.

10.

Bernadotte Comes

Society waits unformed and is between things ended and things begun.

—WALT WHITMAN

THE YEARS BETWEEN the death of Gustav III, 1792, and the establishment of the new Bernadotte dynasty, 1810, shed no luster on Sweden. No man so strong or politically so astute as the late king appeared on the scene to guide the national destiny. Not one of the disaffected nobles revealed any marked ability in the critical years of Napoleon's meteoric rise.

At the king's death, the heir who became Gustav IV Adolf was an uninteresting, obstinate boy of thirteen, who had inherited none of his father's charm or tact. Duke Charles, his uncle, ruled as regent. But Charles, too, was lacking both in force and in judgment, and his Councilors were ill-chosen and unpopular. When Gustav Adolf reached his majority, however, he cleaned out these bad advisers, most of whom had been his father's enemies. At first there was some internal prosperity. But Napoleon's rising power, together with English prowess and piracies at sea, made the period more than critical. Sweden joined Russia and Denmark in a pact of armed neutrality and attempted to close the Baltic to hostile fleets. Admiral Nelson promptly brought the British navy against the Danish fleet and bombarded Copenhagen. Russia broke her alliance and offered to treat with England. Sweden naturally had to subscribe to the new convention, and she made a new commercial trade treaty, to Napoleon's great displeasure. When the Corsican crowned himself emperor, Gustav Adolf foolishly broke off all diplomatic relations.

In 1805, on the promise of an enormous war subsidy, Sweden

162

joined Russia and Austria in coalition with England against France. It proved a disastrous error. Shortly Napoleon crushed the coalition forces at Austerlitz. The defeat of Prussia at Jena followed in October, 1806; and the next spring, at Tilsit, the young Czar Alexander I formed an alliance with Napoleon. Sweden had lost Pomerania, her last territory on the Continent. But the French commander magnanimously allowed her to bring her troops home without reprisals.

Gustav Adolf, who hated Napoleon with venomous passion, persisted in sticking by England. He refused to close Swedish ports to British trading vessels, although the emperor threatened Sweden with a Russian occupation of Finland. In February, 1808, Russia presented the Swedish ambassador in St. Petersburg with an ultimatum that Sweden join Russia and Denmark immediately in their cause against England. The same day Russian troops crossed the Finnish frontier. The Finns fought with great valor against the invaders, but the Swedish general staff seemed to consider the war lost as soon as it began. To the amazement and disgust of the patriotic Finns, the commander-in-chief did little but order pell-mell retreat. Then the Swedish admiral who commanded the impregnable fortress of Sveaborg was tricked into the ignominious surrender of the fortress, with the entire Archipelago fleet.

On May 3, 1808, the disgraceful capitulation to an inferior Russian force took place. When the Swedish flag was lowered, soldiers wept and cursed and threatened to murder the admiral, as the Russians sang anthems of joy.

Never in all the chronicles had Swedish officers displayed such weak and cowardly spirits as in this war of defense of their Finnish province. The valiant Finns were finally forced to accept Russian domination, which was to last a century and nine years. Finland was declared an autonomous Grand Duchy of Russia; Sweden had lost a third of her kingdom, which she had possessed since the twelfth century, and descended to the all-time nadir of her fortunes.

With Danes attacking in the south and Russia preparing to pounce from the north, in his agony of misadventure, the king was ready to break with England, too, and stand at bay against the world. Fearing the next move of the desperate Gustav Adolf, the Council felt the only possible salvation was to get rid of him. A revolution was hatched. On March 7, 1809, Colonel Adlersparre declared it openly in Värmland, and started with his soldiers on the march to Stockholm to arrest the king. Gustav Adolf attempted escape, and the palace rang with a furious game of cops-and-robbers. At last he was overpowered and taken under guard to imprisonment in one of the summer castles. Again a Swedish revolution had been accomplished without a death.

A new constitution, which forms the basis of the present democratic state of Sweden, was drawn up and signed on June 6, 1809. The document clearly defined the different functions and authorities of the ruling monarch and the Riksdag. On the same day Duke Charles ascended the throne as Charles XIII.

Since the old king was without legitimate offspring, Sweden had to look for a successor who would establish a new dynasty; for Parliament had renounced not only Gustav Adolf, but his little son and heir, "and all his family."

The deposed king was condemned to exile. In secluded poverty in Switzerland, he lived out the dregs of his unfortunate life until 1837, hearing repeatedly of the manifold improvements in Sweden under the chosen king, that French parvenu named Bernadotte.

The election of the great French field marshal, Jean Baptiste Bernadotte, as the heir apparent of aging Charles XIII, proved extremely happy. But he had not been the first choice. A Danish prince, Christian August, had been first selected. Arriving early in 1810, the prince won immediate popularity because of his natural amiability and graciousness. Secretly, he hoped in time to bring about a restoration of the old union of the three Scandinavian countries—under one head, not his own, but the current king of Denmark.

In the late spring, however, the crown prince fell off his horse and died, presumably of a stroke. Rumors of poisoning threw the capital in a turmoil. Enemies of the aristocratic Axel von Fersen, the gallant admirer and intimate friend of the late beheaded Marie Antoinette, whispered suspicions of him and his sister. When the State funeral procession passed through the streets of Stockholm on June 20, 1810, the populace was in a state of muttering agitation. Feelings ran high, as inflaming reports spread, aided by a free dispensing of liquor.

In the rioting that ensued, Fersen was dragged from his carriage by the angry drunken mob, tortured, and then brutally trampled to death in plain sight of the marching troops, who lifted not one protecting finger in his behalf. This bloody killing in bright daylight of a distinguished citizen is perhaps the most shocking incident of unseemly behavior in all the reasonable Swedes' history.

The nation was obviously sick, and needed a transfusion of invigorating new blood. The remedy was supplied by Marshal Bernadotte, who had been elevated by Napoleon to the title of Prince of Ponte Corvo. Bernadotte had originally won the gratitude and admiration of the Swedes by his consideration in allowing their forces to withdraw unmolested from Pomerania in 1806. But his election to the throne was effected in an extraordinary way. An aristocratic young lieutenant named Karl Otto Mörner was obsessed with the idea that only the French field marshal could restore Swedish prestige. In his zeal, he betook himself to Paris, laid his self-created mission before Bernadotte, who, believing the lieutenant to be the representative of the Swedish nation, consented to be candidate for the succession.

The jubilant young emissary rushed home to present the wonderful news of his diplomatic conquest to the august Council. The high dignitaries were flabbergasted. Young Mörner was officially spanked for his astounding presumption by being placed under guard in his barracks. The slow-moving Swedes, including even those who had already suggested the candidacy of Bernadotte, were not geared to such sudden moves. The situation was extremely embarrassing, for the majority had decided to elect Prince Frederic Christian, the late crown prince's unimpressive younger brother, whose candidacy Napoleon was backing.

As the idea of becoming King of Sweden grew more alluring to the former sergeant from Pau, he had a French agent at the Swedish court drop a strong hint that, if he were elected, France would offer certain economic advantages to the financially depressed Swedes. This suggestion was interpreted as originating with the emperor. So the Government made a last-minute switch in their decision to elect the Danish prince, and formally offered the heir-apparency to the Frenchman on August 21, 1810.

The announcement proved tremendously popular, because the Swedish people looked to the renowned general to regain from Russia all that had been lost, and perhaps more.

Many of the noble families, however, anticipated no joy in bowing before the one-time provincial non-com. The election brought no elation either to Napoleon, who had already perceptibly cooled—though the Swedes knew it not—to his friend, whom he had reason to fear as a possible rival at home. It still rankled, too, that Bernadotte had won for his bride Desirée Clary, the Marseilles merchant's beauteous daughter, who had once been engaged to the young Napoleon. Her older sister had married his brother Joseph Bonaparte and he had made her Queen of Naples. Now his former sweetheart would become a queen without his elevating her to such rank. However, after ruminating on the idea of squashing the Bernadotte election, the emperor let destiny have its way.

On his arrival in October, Bernadotte won golden opinions by his commanding forceful presence and his charming manners. Almost immediately, as Crown Prince Charles John, he began making policy. Soon he let it be known that he had no intention of trying to regain Finland. But to make up for the loss of Finland, he purposed (as had Gustav III) to bring Norway into a union with his newly adopted country and thus place the Scandinavian peninsula under one rule. Secretly, he made friends with England, because he did not dare risk trouble with British seapower. Realizing that Russia's nonintervention would be essential if the union of Norway with Sweden was to be effected, he made friendly overtures to Czar Alexander, who was delighted, because Napoleon was now preparing a fresh offensive against him.

July of 1813 found Charles John allied with Napoleon's enemies. His was the most astute advice in the war council planning the campaign against his former master. Following Napoleon's defeat at Leipzig, the fighting prince seized the opportunity to attack the Danish army in Holstein, where he won a decisive victory. In January of 1814, by the Treaty of Kiel, Denmark ceded Norway to Sweden.

What Swedish kings had been desiring since the days of Charles XII had been achieved. Presumably. For the Norwegians were yet to speak. On May 17, 1814, they declared their national independence, drew up a constitution, and elected the Danish Prince Frederic Christian king.

Charles John promptly marched his now well-trained soldiers to the border, and urged the Norwegians to accept him as their future sovereign. On August 14, Christian capitulated when Sweden agreed to recognize the Norwegian constitution. So Norway was brought into forced union with her sister country under one ruling head, but internally remaining an independent commonwealth. Aging Charles XIII, who had been a figurehead since Bernadotte's arrival, found himself, on November 4, 1814, twice a king. He lived on for four more years, each season becoming more convinced, as was the world at large, that Lieutenant Mörner's exciting visit to Paris had been inspired by Sweden's guardian angels. In his four years on Swedish soil Bernadotte had lifted Sweden from a slough of despond by his astuteness and force of character.

After the Peace Congress in Vienna in 1815, which really ended the career of the great Napoleon, Sweden settled down to improving conditions at home. And unlike the rest of Europe, Sweden has ever since followed the declared Bernadotte policy of peace and neutrality. Never, since 1814, has Sweden become directly involved in any kind of war.

After his coronation as King Charles XIV John in 1818, to the disappointment of numerous imperialistic-minded Swedes, Bernadotte, the brilliant campaigner, became a most peace-loving monarch. Many sighed to think on the illustrious two preceding centuries, when Sweden had cut such a swath in European affairs, and when her ambitious soldiers brought home stores of loot from foreign conquests. But the king turned his energies resolutely to internal reorganization and to economic expansion.

In matters of domestic policy, however, because of his lack of understanding of Swedish tradition, and because of his own impetuous nature, he often encountered stout opposition. Having been well acquainted with French intrigue, Charles John was apprehensive that latent Swedish revolutionaries might endanger his throne—especially partisans of the deposed Gustav IV. One of his ministers calmly reassured him: "Sire," he said, "the only danger to which you are exposed in Sweden is a cold, and that you may avoid by wearing galoshes."

Once the king's formidable temper got completely out of hand. He became very angry with a Swedish general. He spoke harsh words, and finally tore an epaulette from the general's shoulder, and threw it on the ground. The general drew himself up and said, with quiet fury: "Sir, I am a Swedish count and I will not permit a king to do this to me." With that, he tore off the other epaulette. The king came to himself and regretted his rashness. "No," he said, "let us be friends." After a pause the general said, "I will pick up one epaulette, if you will pick up the other." The king said, "All right, let us do so." The general picked up one; Bernadotte picked up the other. They smiled, they shook hands, and were friends.

Desirée, a gay-hearted and naturally friendly woman, might have made things easier for her impetuous husband if she had accompanied him to Sweden. But, deeply absorbed in the sophisticated and exciting society of Paris, she refused to go to that wild north country. Finally, after her husband had been king for ten years, her curiosity got the better of her, and she set out for Stockholm to see what the place could hold for him. She was amazed to find the Swedes so civilized. In fact, she was so delighted with what she discovered, she decided to remain and be the queen. She demanded another coronation ceremony just for herself, with all the trappings, and got it. Though she was an incorrigibly unconventional woman, the dignified Swedes put up with her vagaries because of her charm, even when she wandered about the streets at night unattended to see how other people behaved. She outlived her husband by many years, and continued to stay in a wing of the royal palace after her son was king. In her eighties she still prowled at night when the notion struck her; and one chilly dawn the dowager queen was found sitting in an obscure doorway, dead, with an enigmatic smile on her old French lips.

After a comparatively quiet but productive reign of twenty-six years, King Charles XIV John died in 1844. He was succeeded by his son Oscar, whose wife was Napoleon's step-granddaughter, Josephine Beauharnais. Like his father, the new sovereign concentrated on peace and internal improvements, and avoided war, although England attempted to stir up bad blood between Sweden and her mighty neighbor Russia.

In 1842 compulsory education had been introduced under Charles

John, and in 1845 women were granted the same property rights with men. The guild system was abolished in 1846, though not until 1864 was choice of trade made completely free. In 1855 work was begun on the Swedish State Railways, which were Government-owned from the beginning.

Having barely avoided embroilment in struggles between the Great Powers, King Oscar died in 1859, and was succeeded first by his eldest son, who became Charles XV, and then by a second son, Oscar II, who lived until 1907.

In the reigns of both grandsons of the first Bernadotte, one serious war-threatening crisis occurred. The first one came in 1864, when Prussia, aided by Austria, invaded Denmark to capture the German-speaking provinces of Schleswig and Holstein. King Charles was eager to go to Denmark's aid and called for troop mobilization. But the Swedish prime minister knew the cause against Bismarck's combined forces was hopeless, and sympathetic Sweden was forced to remain idle and watch the defeat of the brave outnumbered Danes. After the loss of their provinces, the Danes did not love greatly either the Swedes or Norwegians, who had also abstained. So recurring hopes for a real Scandinavian union were shattered.

In 1866 the Riksdag underwent drastic reorganization. The Four Estates were abolished, and a democratic bicameral system on the American model was introduced. From this year forward the nobility as a group has played no important role in Swedish politics._

When Oscar II came to the throne in 1872, he reiterated his grandfather's policy of neutrality and isolation, and Sweden was kept clear of entangling alliances. During his reign marked progress was made in industry. The beginning of the rise is often traced to the perfection of the Bessemer process for making steel, in 1858. (The final experiments on the great English invention were made on Swedish soil.) In its quantities of high-grade iron ore, Sweden had an asset of prime value, which, together with its vast tracts of timber, was the foundation of the new prosperity that came towards the end of the century. By the thousands families began moving from the agricultural districts, where many barely subsisted, to the ironworks and the sawmill communities.

But the birth rate was increasing so rapidly in the nineteenth century that after 1845 shiploads of Swedes had been emigrating to

America. Before the Civil War many had already taken up homesteads in the West, and after a series of Swedish crop failures in the sixties, came a large-scale emigration of farm workers, who could not find employment in the Swedish mills or mines. The peak year was reached in 1882, when over sixty-four thousand Swedes sailed from their native shores to settle in the Promised Land.

During the time of the emigrations the Swede best known throughout the world was a woman: an enchanting singer named Jenny Lind, who was billed in the metropolitan concert halls as "the Swedish Nightingale." Wherever she appeared she was a sensation; and in the silver purity of her thrilling voice she was without an equal in her day. The admirable propaganda she made for Sweden was supplemented by that of another internationally famous opera star, Christina Nilsson, born the daughter of a Småland laborer, who retired at the height of her career in 1887, the year Jenny Lind died. This Swedish prima donna was signally honored by being chosen to open the Metropolitan Opera in New York on October 22, 1883, the night of its dedication. She sang Marguerite in Gounod's *Faust,* a role she had created at the opera's *première* in Paris.

Except for these two women blessed with marvelous voices, and a brilliant playwright named August Strindberg (1849-1912), Sweden was little heard of abroad during the reigns of the second, third, and fourth Bernadottes.

But at home, in the last quarter of the century, were happening events that were to have momentous significance, though at the time they created little attention. In 1881 the first public address on socialism in Sweden was given by a tailor named August Palm, who had come in contact with the doctrine while working in Germany and Denmark. In the following years socialistic societies sprang up in various industrial towns. The ideology of "social democracy" came to hold more meaning and hope for industrial employees than "liberalism." By 1889 enough men had been won to the cause to found the Social Democratic Labor party.

The first Swedish trade union, in the modern sense, that of typesetters, was founded in 1886. Twelve years later, when the extension of the organization system of the trade unions had become fairly widespread, the majority of unions formed a general federation for the entire country. The creation of *Landsorganisationen,* or L.O., as it is called, makes the year 1898 an emphatically significant one in Swedish modern history. Without the Labor Federation, Sweden would by no means have achieved the admirable state of general well-being she boasts today.

In the tag end of the century two other events of ultimate importance occurred. In 1899 the Cooperative Union was formed as a central contact point for the small local consumers' cooperatives and as a medium of cooperative propaganda. In 1896 Hjalmar Branting, the upper-class leader of the rising Social Democrats and a former schoolmate of the Crown Prince Gustav, was the first one of his party ever to be elected to the Riksdag. While the event passed with little notice in Sweden at the time, twenty-four years later, in 1920, King Gustav was forced to greet a cabinet made up entirely of Social Democrats.

Hjalmar Branting proved to be the man of his time whom the Swedish people could least have spared. The son of a well-to-do professor, Branting played a dominant part in the Labor movement even before the party came into existence. At Uppsala University Branting was studying the stars, with some idea of becoming a professor of astronomy. But he would continually turn from his observations of the heavens to speculate on the plight of some of his fellow-beings on earth. On his twenty-first birthday, to show where his heart interest lay, the young idealist gave 3,000 kronor to the new Labor Institute.

Branting believed in a democratic form of socialism. But he insisted any change in the state of society should be brought about gradually by parliamentary means only. He steadfastly opposed those members who urged a more violent policy. Never, he said, must social revolution come about through bloodshed. "It will take longer by evolution, but not so long as it would take to undo the destruction both of property and spirit a revolution would bring." And except for an anarchistic few, he persuaded those who needed persuasion to aim to bring about the revolution by lawful evolutionary methods. A man of impeccable integrity and first-rate social position, Branting's influence in promulgating the Social Democratic views, and in gaining friends in State and municipal administration, was invaluable. Yet three times he suffered imprisonment for propaganda. The jail sentences, however, only made him more an idol of the people.

Branting sought first to effect changes in suffrage regulations so that persons of humble income could express themselves forcibly in public affairs. When the Government continued to deny the right of ballot to the low income groups, the Social Democrats resorted to extreme measures. On May 15, 1902, the party declared a general strike. Quietly, in most orderly fashion, a hundred and twenty thousand employees stopped work. They let the lawmakers and the incensed industrialists ruminate for three days. It was a new experience in Sweden, and the Government realized it had a powerful force to deal with. Some suffrage reformation was granted by the Riksdag, and after the next elections Hjalmar Branting had three new members to sit with him: a shoemaker, a bricklayer, and a machine-shop assistant. Branting continued his dynamic but equitable leadership of the party into the next reign, and in 1920 he formed the first purely Social Democratic Government.

The disturbing war crisis of Oscar II's long reign of thirty-five years came in 1905, when Norway determined to withdraw from the union with Sweden. The Norwegians had never been reconciled to their definitely second-fiddle position. As the decades passed, they had become more restive. Three times the Articles of Union had been revised in an attempt to satisfy them. And, in 1884, the king had recognized a separate parliamentary government in Norway, headed by a Norwegian prime minister. But still Norway was not content. She wanted to work out her own foreign policy entirely independent of Sweden. On June 7, 1905, the Norwegian Parliament met in an implacable mood. An Address to the Throne was read, in which the union with Sweden was declared dissolved. But to prove that there was "no ill will towards either the Swedish people or the royal family," Norway asked for a prince of the ruling house of Bernadotte to be offered for election as her king.

The seventy-six-year-old Oscar was strongly opposed to letting the Norwegians get away with such revolutionary procedure. As both sides began to mobilize along the border, where Norway had been constructing fortifications for the last decade, war seemed unavoidable. The majority of the working people in Sweden, however, believed in letting the Norwegians have their complete independence if they desired it. So the trade unions threatened a paralyzing general strike if Sweden attacked Norway.

With high tension in the air, the Riksdag was called in extraordinary session. A committee drew up Swedish requirements that were to be satisfied before secession was allowed to proceed peacefully. First a plebiscite of the Norwegian population was demanded. If the vote went against the union, then as a safeguard to future amity all fortifications along the common border were to be razed.

When the plebiscite proved the Norwegians to be virtually unanimous for dissolution, delegates from both countries met at Karlstad in western Sweden in September of 1905. The momentous meeting was conducted with typical Swedish moderation and reasonableness. The Act of Union of 1814 was voided and the old king was authorized to recognize the sovereignty of independent Norway. It was the bitterest hour of his long reign, and he could not bring himself to consent to one of his tall sons accepting the new crown of Norway.

So the Norwegians elected Prince Karl, brother to Denmark's King Christian. He was crowned as Haakon VII, and his wife, a daughter of England's Edward VII, became Queen Maude.

Two years after the separation from Norway, Crown Prince Gustav followed his father to the throne in 1907. His reign was destined to be the longest and by far the most progressive in Swedish history.

II.

Gustav V and the New Social Order

Often do the spirits
Of great events stride on before the events
And in today already walks tomorrow.

—COLERIDGE

WHEN GUSTAV SUCCEEDED to the throne in 1907, the people had their doubts about him. Although he had had an excellent democratic education at home, and had spent much time observing foreign affairs as guest of various royal families, his potentialities were not at all clear. As a young man he had been decidedly unpopular. He was considered coolly indifferent, and interested chiefly in the society of officers, with whom he hunted and played cards for high stakes. But from the day he declined to be crowned in the cathedral by the archbishop to save the state the expense of a coronation, and at the same time shrewdly giving up the old claim to "divine right," the tide in his popularity turned. His first address from the throne was considered very fine. For his official motto, he chose "With the people, for the fatherland." His subsequent actions seemed to bear out his later statement that at the bottom of his heart he "always placed first the honor, the happiness, the prosperity of Sweden."

The king's task was not always an easy one, for in the following decades two world conflagrations swept close to Sweden's shores, and within the kingdom momentous social and political changes took place. A new era evolved which brought to Sweden some of the blessings of Utopia. A social revolution occurred by the most orderly of evolutionary processes.

The year of Gustav's accession, 1907, fell in a general period of optimism and confidence throughout the world. Edward VII was setting the bright tone of Edwardian society in England. In Austria, a certain splendor still clung to the decaying Hapsburg empire of old Francis Joseph. Kaiser Wilhelm was on seeming good terms with his British cousins. In the United States, the dynamic Theodore Roosevelt was breaking trusts and at the same time stimulating a greater prosperity. Only a very few statesmen discerned the shape of a gathering war cloud. But soon, through various ententes, alliances, and rapprochements, Europe seemed to be divided in two great rivalries: with England, France and Russia on one side; and Germany, Austria-Hungary, and Italy on the other.

In 1913 Sweden found herself in a most uncomfortable position. Germany was now in command of the Baltic, and the upsurging of Pan-Slavism in Russia had made Sweden's traditional enemy loom up as something to be feared tomorrow. National defense became a burning issue. Cold water was consistently thrown on the question by the Swedish labor movement which was demanding extensive social benefits. The Conservatives, while urgently advocating military defense, were timid about antagonizing the Labor party that shouted "peace, peace" to every proposal for armament appropriations, and even demanded reductions. Hjalmar Branting, the Social Democrats' leader, however, stood with the king, his old schoolmate, in realizing the critical necessity for defense measures. Yet nothing but talk occurred until the February of 1914, when rumbling rumors of likely war grew alarming. Then thirty thousand farmers, by prearrangement, marched to the Royal Palace to assure the king of their loyal support and their willingness to assume their proportion of the tax burden necessary for defensive armaments.

In a fervent speech of gratitude the king said he agreed fully with the farmers on the necessity of immediate action. On his own initiative he had gone against his dilly-dallying prime minister and Parliament. The farmers then trooped to the various buildings of state and told the officials what they and the king thought.

A few days later the industrial workers created their own demonstration. They asked for reduction of military appropriations and severely criticized the king for his unorthodox intervention.

For some months Sweden was a house divided. But in August, when the dreaded war did break, the rift was quickly healed. In speaking for the Labor party, Branting was now able to assure the king and the Government of "the full confidence of a united people."

It was peculiarly distressing and disturbing to the Swedes that Russia was allied with the Western Democracies. Some feared the old-time foe would attempt passage through Sweden by way of the north. Few indeed could look with jubilation to the destruction of Germany, for a strong Germany served as protection against Russian depredations.

Sweden promptly declared her neutrality, and almost immediately Denmark and Norway did likewise. King Gustav then invited the other two Scandinavian kings, with their prime ministers and foreign ministers, to a conference at Malmö. Here the three nations agreed to remain firmly united in efforts to maintain neutrality, and to refrain under every circumstance from fighting each other. The assembly marked perhaps the most cordial relations between "the brother peoples" that had existed since the early years of the Kalmar Union in the fourteenth century. In 1917 King Gustav paid the first official visit to Oslo since the dissolution of 1905, and in a speech of deep sincerity begged that friendship between Norway and his country be made permanent. Since 1917 no important move in matters of foreign policy has been made by one of the Scandinavian nations without consulting the others.

To live, during the war's progress, Sweden had to trade both with England and Germany, though each country made traffic with the other excessively difficult and hazardous. The Liberals and the Social Democrats, who suspected the Conservatives of having too strong German sympathies, formed a coalition against them in 1917, and won. With the new groups in power, for the first time the king's Cabinet embodied socialistic elements. This same year the Bolshevik revolution in Russia relieved Sweden of the menace of czarist encroachment. She could now look forward to a German defeat without grave misgivings.

Virtually each sequent year after his accession the popularity of the king increased. During the first World War, however, with much suffering due to shortages and inflationary prices, the people had to blame someone for their distress. Some put the blame on the king. So the king called the socialist leader Hjalmar Branting and said, "Do you want me to go? If it is better for the people, I'll go to England and buy a castle, and the Crown Prince will come and live near me in another little castle." Branting said, "No—if you go, there will be a clash between classes. If you stay, there may be hard words from the Reds; but don't let them reach your ears." So the king remained.

Politically the years from 1907 to 1920 are looked upon as a transitional period in Swedish history, out of which emerged a thoroughly democratic constitution, universal equal suffrage (in 1918), and a completely parliamentary Government, which meant that the prime minister rather than the king became the chief executive.

Throughout the eighteenth century the nobility held predominance in government. During the reigns of Charles John and Oscar I, the bourgeoisie were the most powerful class. After 1868 the farmers, with their Agrarian party, rose to the top and directed affairs for over twenty years. In 1920, the Labor party came to dominate, and it has won the highest vote in most election years since.

In 1920 King Gustav became the first monarch ever to be presented with an all-Socialist cabinet. For the first time in world history, a socialist Government came into power without bloodshed. Perhaps one reason that the transition was made so smoothly was that the king was as equable in temper as the new prime minister, his old classmate Hjalmar Branting. While conservative in his own thinking, King Gustav found he could get on as harmoniously with a Cabinet made up of journalists, small farmers, and one-time laborers, as with former Cabinets consisting largely of titled estate-owners.

When Hjalmar Branting died in 1925, Sweden had perhaps never known such profound grief at an individual's passing. He was not only beloved, but to the masses he was a kind of god. His influence in Swedish political thought and on the course of the general welfare was more far-reaching in effect than that of any Swede in the two centuries his life touched. Since Jean Baptiste Bernadotte, who was elected heir to the Swedish throne in 1810, Branting was the man Sweden needed most. There was no one in the kingdom capable of taking his place as the idol of the people.

But in 1932, after a sweeping victory, the Social Democrats chose for their prime minister another man of marked abilities, Per Albin Hansson, who remained in power until his death in 1946. The king and this son of a Malmö laborer developed a mutual admiration and often played cards together at the palace when the day's work was done.

In many important issues Gustav and his new prime minister saw pretty much eye to eye. The king was aware that the best safeguard against growth of domestic Communism was to provide security and well-being for the masses through enlightened social legislation. And when he did not believe in certain advanced reforms, he was always prudent enough to bow to the inevitable with good will.

When the Second World War came in 1939, King Gustav and Per Albin Hansson were equally determined to preserve and protect Sweden's national independence, peace and liberty. In expressing the stand for neutrality, the prime minister declared, "This policy implies neither isolation nor indifference to what is going on around us. But we decline to participate in rival combinations of powers, and we desire to avoid everything that can give rise to doubt regarding the seriousness of our intention to remain free in all respects."

Like the other Scandinavian countries, Sweden had looked with great hope to the success of the League of Nations and its ability to prevent future wars. So from 1920 to 1936 she had spent the smallest amount possible to maintain reasonable peacetime armament, while allocating large sums for social services.

In the crisis, this time, no one questioned the necessity of strong military defense. All Swedes were resolved to make the greatest possible resistance to any attempt at depriving them of their external and internal freedom. The military budget which annually had averaged less than $30,000,000 for the decade before 1936 was now hiked to more than $300,000,000 in 1939-40. During the remainder of the war years it was set at something above $500,000,000.

As the whole country was mobilized for defense, conscription proved the Swedes to have no peer in physical and mental fitness, for of all the conscript material called for enrollment, less than five per cent were declared unfit for military service. And unlike the American army, wisely, by careful examinations, the Swedish command placed each conscript in the place he was best suited to fill by experience, physique, and temperament. During the progress of the war over a million Swedish women enrolled in the various auxiliary services.

Fortunately Sweden possessed an important armament and ordnance factory at Bofors, together with a plentiful supply of iron and steel. And most luckily the Nazis did not attempt invasion at the time they took over Denmark and Norway in April, 1940, when Sweden was most inadequately prepared to resist a mighty force. After the invasion of the other Scandinavian countries, Sweden's defenses grew stronger month by month.

The king, who had met Hitler some years before and had once at a luncheon openly criticized him for his attitude towards the Jews, now took it upon himself to communicate with the Nazi leader directly, and without instructions from the Riksdag. He said to him, "Sweden will resist without delay and with all her power any invasion of her neutrality, especially any attempt to cross her borders militarily." Later he spoke to this effect, "Look here, now, it will be too costly for you to try to invade us, for we shall fight you with everything we possess. In the meantime we desperately need German coal."

Because of the German blockade of the North Sea, Sweden's maritime communications with the West were severed, and she had to trade within the blockade. At one stroke, one-half of Sweden's merchant marine had been cut off from home ports. With the supply of coal and coke from England completely stopped, Sweden had to obtain coal from Germany to exist.

Since 1934 Sweden and Germany had engaged in barter trade, under which system Germany had to deliver goods to Sweden in order to obtain goods in return, as well as to finance shipping services and service charges on prewar debts. Thus Sweden was able to get from Germany more goods than she delivered. After the blockade a direct balance was set up between Swedish iron ore and the coal so essential to Sweden's industry. At no time during the war were foodstuffs, munitions, or any finished war materials shipped by Sweden to Germany. In the fall of 1944, having got herself in a relatively strong defense position, Sweden broke off commercial relations with Germany, and gambled on an early end of the war and the probability of securing indispensable imports elsewhere.

Compared to her occupied neighbors, Sweden, like neutral Switzerland, suffered no real hardship during the war. To the average Swede the absence of gasoline was the first specific consequence of the outbreak of the war, and next was the prohibition by law of hot water in apartment houses. To the cattle, it was the substitution of cellulose for seed cake and fodder. By the end of the third year of war, some seventy per cent of Sweden's food consumption was rationed. To prevent profiteering, price controls were set on everything. And to prevent suffering in the working classes, as had happened in the first World War, the Labor Federation got the Employers' Association to agree to compensate wage-earners for increases in the cost of living by comparative raises in wage scale.

In some newspapers of allied countries Sweden's avoidance of being forced into the war was severely resented. Some even chose to forget that Norway, Denmark, Holland, and Belgium got involved only because they were actually invaded, and that it took the Japanese attack on Pearl Harbor and a German declaration of war to move the United States to fight.

Now, it is universally admitted that it was an inestimable boon to Norway and Denmark, as well as to Finland and the Baltic States, that Sweden was able to maintain her official neutrality. Sweden proved a welcoming sanctuary for all the Danish Jews—except the few that were captured and taken to the miseries of a Nazi concentration camp. Sweden was a haven for thousands of refugees from the Baltic States, escaping first the Germans, and then the Russians. She succored thousands of escaped Norwegians, and offered homes to tens of thousands of Finnish children orphaned by the war. For relief in devastated countries Sweden contributed enormous sums by private contributions, as well as by Government appropriation. Without the relief of Swedish food and clothes and medicines, life in Norway under the Germans would have been far more distressing. During the war Sweden prepared thousands of prefabricated houses to be sent as gifts into Norway and Finland to replace dwellings destroyed by the enemies. As soon as the war ended, Sweden was ready to take care of trainloads of ill persons, rescued from concentration camps.

If Sweden had antagonized Germany beyond the endurance point, or had refused to exchange iron ore for coal, she would have been in no position to offer either asylum or relief to her neighbors. She played a touch-and-go game of avoiding war, giving in to the very minimum of Germany's requests and demands, in order to maintain her neutrality. In the meantime half her merchant fleet was sailing in the Allied cause—much of it sunk by the Nazis—and planes were secretly flying ball bearings to Britain. It was an inestimable advantage to the Allies to have Sweden represented diplomatically in Berlin, where she maintained a well-organized secret service and could inform of German plans.

Though Sweden was able to preserve her official neutrality throughout the war, there was little attempt to conceal the sympathies of the people for the Allied cause. It is estimated that ninety-five per cent of the population were with the Democracies, while the five per cent for Germany were motivated either by a belief in the German army's invincibility, or by a fear that a destruction of the German forces would leave Sweden at the mercy of Red Russia. The only Swede of prominence to declare openly his pro-German sympathy was the aging explorer, Sven Hedin, the last man ever to be ennobled before the law of the land forbade further aristocratic distinctions. For all of his strain of Jewish blood, Hedin looked upon Germany as the only check against the westward surge of Communism. Twice on his own initiative he went in person to Hitler and urged him not to violate Sweden's neutrality. Though he became terribly unpopular with the Swedes because of his German sympathies, many now believe that Hedin's self-appointed diplomacy may have helped to save Sweden from planned attack.

Though the king and the crown prince kept discreet silence in public, as was their duty, Prince Wilhelm, the king's younger son, did not hesitate to express broadly his intense anti-Nazi sentiments. Perhaps the most vehemently outspoken of all Swedes in his opposition to Nazism was Torgny Karl Segerstedt of the Göteborg *Handels- och Sjöfarts-Tidning,* "Trade and Shipping News," one of the most influential dailies in the land. He never let up, though the army high command warned him that his stinging editorials might infuriate Hitler to an invasion before Sweden was prepared to meet it. While a few of the papers did temper their antagonism for prudence's sake, all of them were unquestionably pro-Ally.

In his private diary Goebbels complains bitterly of the anti-Nazi sentiment of the Swedish newspapers. He refers half a dozen times to the "provocative and insolent attitude of the Swedish press." On December 11, 1942, he writes resentfully: "The better we hold our own on the Eastern Front, the more impudent the Swedish press becomes. . . . If the Anglo-Saxon nations achieve only mediocre victories, the Swedes regard themselves as on the top of the world."

There was nothing the Germans could do to make the Swedes friendly or to stop the free expression of their democratic sympathies. From the beginning Per Albin Hansson had played a most shrewd diplomatic game with the Nazis, and won several times by the narrowest margins. But the Swedes were not at all comfortable about being forced by circumstances to trade with the Nazis and to let German troops on their vacation leaves pass through their land in sealed trains under Swedish guard. As a famous Norwegian woman novelist said to me, "Though it is well for us that the Swedes are not in this war, I am sure they must feel a little cold in their bottoms."

With the cessation of fighting in Europe, the Swedish Government could return to the business of trying to provide a more abundant life for the citizens. The recovery of peace-time economy was naturally quick in Sweden, which, despite shortages and rationing, had suffered comparatively little disruption. Building increased at a great pace. Foreign trade boomed. Swedish air transport spread to the other hemispheres. The advancement in social services that had been halted during the war was resumed with energy.

For the forty-first year, on January 13, 1948, King Gustav formally opened the Riksdag in the royal palace, and made his traditional speech from the throne. His forty years of sovereignty made his reign the longest in Swedish history. Under his symbolic leadership, Sweden had enjoyed her happiest, if not most exciting, era. The extraordinary improvement in the general welfare had excited the world's admiration. During the last two decades the king's popularity with his subjects had steadily increased. On one occasion the Socialist party's organ went so far as to say, "The Swedes simply love him. . . . They know how well and how smoothly he cooperates with the representatives of the people in the Government. . . . They like 'Mr. G.' for his sportsmanship, for his love of the open-air life, and for his simple manners."

Only once—shortly after the death of Branting—had there been a mildly expressed inclination to dissolve the monarchy. Some of the radical element went to the new socialist leader Per Albin Hansson and said, "It is not the fashion any more to have kings. Let's have a republic. We can make Crown Prince Gustav Adolf president." Hansson replied, "Suppose I go to the Crown Prince and say, 'Your Royal Highness, I beg you to be president of this nation,' and suppose the Crown Prince says, 'I do not care to be president. If you do not want me as king, then I will leave the country.' Then what shall I say? I shall have a silly face. So I beg you do not put me in such a position."

Constitutional monarchy in Sweden is much like that of Great Britain. The king reigns but does not govern. Whereas England still clings to her House of Lords, Sweden gave up her House of Nobles eighty years ago. The cost to the State of maintaining the Swedish royal family is remarkably modest: less than $200,000 a year for all of them, and not one-fifteenth part of the British royal family's allowances. The Swedes consider their monarchy an excellent investment, symbolizing the dignity of the State and supplying the color and distinction human nature craves.

On June 16, 1948, when King Gustav celebrated his ninetieth birthday spontaneous rejoicing filled the land. The king and the royal family had never been more popular. When the Bernadotte clan gathered the old monarch could look about him contentedly at a large and loving immediate family with numerous great-grandchildren and great-nieces and nephews as well as octogenarian brothers. His brother Prince Oscar, father of Count Folke Bernadotte, was almost eighty-nine, while Prince Carl, father of Martha, Crown Princess of Norway and the late Queen Astrid of Belgium, was eighty-five. (His youngest brother, Prince Eugen, the bachelor artist, had been eighty-two at the time of his death in 1947). Prominent at the birthday festivities was his only granddaughter Ingrid, daughter of Crown Prince Gustav Adolf, who had become Queen of Denmark in 1946.

Since the death of his wife eighteen years before, King Gustav had known only one crushing sorrow. In January, 1947, his eldest grandson, the hereditary Prince Gustav Adolf, had been killed in a plane crash. The next heir-apparent to the throne after the sixty-five-year-old crown prince was a baby only a few months old, Prince Carl Gustav. But on June 16, 1948, at the birthday jubilee the boy was big enough to ride with his great-grandfather through the streets and be applauded by the crowd.

While the princeling was put to bed extra early, the old king was in such splendid health that for fifteen hours he was active on the job of accepting congratulations. Besides driving slowly through the festive streets behind aging horses that had pulled his carriage on his eightieth birthday, he spent hours receiving foreign sovereigns and distinguished visitors. He attended a state dinner in his honor. Again and again during the evening he was forced to show himself on the palace balcony to accept the plaudits of his subjects. After a last balcony appearance at eleven o'clock at night, when his daughter-in-law, Crown Princess Louise, solicitously tried to get him to go to bed, he protested, "But I feel fine—only my legs are a little weak."

Gustav was now not only the oldest king in the world and the tallest—still holding himself erect as he stepped into his tenth decade—but he had lived longer than any king of recorded age. His longevity could be attributed to his regular habits, his sparse eating, his out-of-doors exercise, and his determination from youth never to let himself be upset by the corroding emotions of anger.

Six feet four inches tall and precariously thin, the king has always enjoyed remarkably fine health. Rarely did he go to bed before midnight, and he was always up by eight o'clock, or six, if going hunting. The hunters admire him because he never wastes his shots. In his time he has killed perhaps a thousand moose. One of his private apartments in the royal palace is most extraordinary. Its high walls are studded with hundreds of pairs of horns and antlers of wild animals he has shot, arranged in striking vertical patterns from floor to ceiling. As a sportsman, the king became a record-breaker by playing tennis until his eighty-eighth year, when his physicians stopped him. Then he took up embroidery, specializing in altar cloths, which he presents to churches.

The physicians did not forbid his shooting, however, and when he was duck hunting at eighty-eight on a wintry December day and his car skidded into a lake, the old gentleman waded out of waist-deep water without even catching a cold. At eighty-nine when he began to find it tiring to stand for a long time while waiting for moose to pass, the king consented to shoot from a chair.

Though inclined to bolt his food, he has always been a light eater. At ninety he could still eat anything—his favorite dishes being wild game and lobster in brandy sauce—and smoke twenty or thirty cigarettes a day.

For the first time, when he opened the Riksdag on January 11, 1949, for the forty-second year, did the ceremony visibly tire him. His physicians feared that it would tax his strength too much to make his customary winter trip to the French Riviera. But on February 2 they reversed their earlier opinion and decided he might go, as it has been his custom for seventy-nine winters.

As his happy reign was drawing to an inevitable close, King Gustav could look with rare satisfaction on the modern Sweden that had evolved since his accession. He could say with modesty and assurance, "Though we are a small nation, I think our people are everywhere esteemed."

III

COOPERATIVES FOR BETTER LIVING

12.

Consumers' and Producers' Cooperatives

The problem is to find a form of association which will defend and protect with the whole common force the person and goods of each associate, and in which each, while uniting himself with all, may still obey himself alone, and remain as free as before. This is the fundamental problem of which the Social Contract provides the solution.

—JEAN JACQUES ROUSSEAU

THE MERE MENTION of the word "cooperative," with an agreeable inflection, often arouses a controlled, and sometimes uncontrolled, fury in the average American businessman. Where Harold Laski finds this American businessman the villain in the democratic drama and capitalism the evil principle, the American is inclined to look upon the cooperative as a snake-in-the-grass to be crushed with a booted heel. Yet Swedish capitalists today freely admit that the cooperatives have been an indispensable factor in improving the general welfare of Sweden and in elevating the tone of the country. It is largely due to the material benefits and the moral influence of the cooperatives that there are no slums, no sordid poverty, and even no population group that can rightfully be designated the proletariat.

As many school children now know, the modern cooperative society had its origin in 1844 among the English weavers of Rochdale, who, to relieve the miserable conditions under which they lived, formed an association on a nonprofit basis. Danes were among the first Europeans to follow after the Rochdale experiment, and Danish cooperatives were functioning successfully a long time before they achieved any significance in Sweden.

Though the cooperative movement in Sweden has made its great headway during the last thirty years, contemporaneously with the rise of trade unionism, the beginnings date to the decade 1860-70, when a few faltering attempts were made to establish consumer societies. However, it was as early as 1825 that the word "cooperative," used in regard to economic functioning, first appeared in Swedish. After studying the miserable social conditions in the industrial regions of England, Erik Gustaf Geijer, the Värmland historian and poet, wrote, "Cooperation is a new social order provoked by necessity in the present wilderness of civilization."

About 1865 a few university professors, lawyers, and journalists attempted to promulgate the theory of cooperation as a means whereby the masses might improve their economic conditions. But all the scattering little cooperative societies begun in the sixties and seventies succumbed, except that at Trollhättan founded in 1867 and today possessing almost three thousand members.

In the 1880's an attempt to reduce the cost of living for workers was originated by a wealthy industrialist named L. O. Smith, who inspired the establishment of "Workers' Rings." These associations were to receive discounts from private merchants and wholesalers to whom they gave their custom. Hundreds of rings among laborers were eagerly formed, but in the end they were dissolved, because the merchants did not play fair. For some years afterwards cooperation in Sweden was looked upon by once hopeful consumers as a snare and a delusion.

The significant turning point came on September 4, 1899, when the Kooperativa Förbundet (Cooperative Association or Union) was established as a central organization. The assembly which achieved the foundation of K.F., as the Union is generally called, was anything but impressive; for only forty-one of the three hundred consumers' cooperatives sent delegates. By the beginning of the new year 1900, no more than thirty societies, with a total membership of 7,300 members, had seen fit to join K.F. By the meeting in 1903 the growth of the organization was still far from encouraging. A great depression lay upon the assembly. But a few devoted pioneers kept zealously at the work, gave their leisure time, made sacrifices, and on occasion spent their own money for the cause.

In the critical years before 1910 the movement might have collapsed, but for the infectious enthusiasm and brilliant eloquence of a poetic-looking young man named Martin Sundell. Blessed with brains and a splendid voice, he also possessed that astute, practical sense that appeals to Swedes. Sundell realized that promotion propaganda was necessary to save the movement; and so he went about the country, expounding the ideas of cooperation and winning converts by his convincing logic and the charm of his address. Soon he was forced to combat attacks that began to come from aroused business interests. By threatening boycott the retailers tried to force certain firms to break their contracts with K.F. This move led to the Union's renting a warehouse in Malmö in 1904, and beginning to purchase commodities in wholesale lots for its branch societies. Early in 1908 the merchants, becoming more alarmed, established a National Union of Retailers, whose chief immediate objective was eradication of cooperative wholesaling. They tried to get legislation passed to make it illegal for banks to give credit to cooperative societies. By various pressures they hoped to rout the whole cooperative movement.

Sundell, in his acknowledged leadership, was forced to redouble his efforts to teach individual managers how to build up their businesses and make their shops more attractive. He spoke tirelessly, confidently, persuasively to the members and potential members. And, though half-exhausted, he entered the fray against the retailers' combine with all his remaining strength. The general public began to take the first real interest in the fight when it reached a little crisis in 1909, because the Swedish margarine cartel refused to sell this most needful commodity to the Cooperative Union at the usual wholesale discount. Sundell and his stanch supporters in the executive committee had to meet this challenge in a way to inspire confidence among the members. This they did by buying a small independent margarine factory and announcing their own boycott of the leading manufacturers in the cartel. The surprised cartel heads immediately lowered the price of margarine—to the benefit of all Swedish households.

In the midst of the struggle Martin Sundell, the fighting idealist, died in 1910 at the age of thirty. But at his passing he felt assured that the cooperative movement would survive and spread and that because of it the Swedish underprivileged would enjoy a more abundant life. It may be doubted, however, if he envisioned such rapid growth as the movement was to have. In 1935, a quarter century after Sundell's death, almost 600,000 households were members of some cooperative society, which meant about a third of the entire Swedish population.

By the middle of 1948 membership in the Cooperative Union had passed 870,000. Branch societies numbered 706. There were altogether 7,177 cooperative shops, including 700 in Stockholm, serving 125,000 members or households.

In the years between the death of Sundell and the end of World War I the waxing cooperative movement won a succession of victories over the Swedish cartels and international monopolies. Often a threat to establish a factory proved sufficient to bring prices down. But more and more K.F. had to go into manufacturing business to get certain products at reasonable prices, if at all.

Shortly after the margarine boycott the Union was faced with no soap and no chocolate for its members. By the time these little blockades were broken, the trust that handled Swedish-produced sugar made conditions so difficult for K.F. that the Union was forced to break the blockade by importing German sugar, which could be sold at a lower price than Swedish sugar. In the end the Swedish trust was forced to readjust its prices to the world market —again to the benefit of all Swedish households.

The results of the big interests' various efforts to quash or restrain the consumers' cooperatives made good propaganda and elicited increasing public interest. World War I, with its attendant economic difficulties and profiteering, proved an enormous boon to the cooperative movement, for it turned the attention of thousands of hitherto disinterested persons to more effective means of meeting the increased cost of living. Membership grew steadily, and, as the cooperatives accumulated cash reserves, they were better able to bargain with certain combines or to fight them when necessary.

One of the struggles that attracted the greatest national attention after the war was that of the rubber-overshoe or galosh business. The outcome affected every man, woman, and child in Sweden, except the permanently bedridden; for in a climate like Sweden's overshoes are a prime necessity. The profits made by the galosh cartel had long been a national scandal. On an initial capital of 4,000,-

000 kronor, it had paid dividends amounting to 15,000,000 kronor in the fifteen years preceding 1926; and in one single year it paid as high as seventy-seven per cent a share. Dignified protests in Parliament and railing in the press had no effect whatever on the smug monopolists.

After the Cooperative Union had done its utmost to persuade the combine to lower prices substantially, it made plans to build its own factory. Then the executives of one of the combine's factories at Gislaved became frightened and sold a controlling interest to K.F. Within a short time the price of ordinary overshoes dropped from $2.00 a pair to $1.00.

My own first purchase in Sweden in 1939 was a pair of Gislaved overshoes, not at a cooperative, but at a regular shop on fashionable Norrmalmstorg. For them I paid eighty cents. The quality was so good that they were still in excellent condition when I lost them seven years later. This personal experience had its effect in impressing me with the value of cooperatives.

An annual saving on overshoes is not an inconsiderable thing in a Swedish household with growing children. And to low-waged timber workers and dirt farmers it meant a lot to be able to get a pair of high rubber boots for $3.00 instead of $8.00. Since nearly six million persons profited by the breaking of the galosh cartel, the general public rejoiced when K.F. bought a second rubber factory, and began the manufacture of bicycle tires and tubes, highly essential items in cycling Sweden.

The citizens had already benefited greatly when K.F. stepped in and influenced the price policy of the Swedish Flour Mills Association. Here again, K.F. had achieved what Parliament and the press had been unable to do by criticism or pleading. In 1922 the Cooperative Union bought Sweden's largest flour mill, Three Crowns, splendidly situated on the island Kvarnholmen at Stockholm's harbor entrance. Remodeling the plant in the most up-to-date manner throughout, K.F. was prepared for production in mid-1924. The margin of profit in flour shortly dropped by more than half, and the Swedish people had a good saving on their bakery bread and cake, as well as household flour.

K.F. further strengthened its position by shortly buying another large mill, Three Lions, in Göteborg. And in 1938 the Union built the largest grain elevator in all Europe. By modernizing their own mills, the Cooperative Union forced the other mills to do likewise. At Kvarnholmen, where the Three Crowns Flour Mill and a co-operative macaroni factory are situated, K.F. has erected pleasant dwellings arranged in terraced tiers along a hillside, so that each house has a free view over the inlet to Stockholm. These structures are simple models of modern construction and convenience, each with a large *perspectiv* window. Situated on a green island, the mills and the apartments add their own ordered beauty to that of the harbor entrance. And by the construction of attractive, airy homes for its own workers, the Cooperative Union encouraged private industry to follow its example, which it has been doing on a large scale.

Perhaps the most spectacular achievement of K.F. was the defeat of the international cartel that controlled the manufacture and sale of electric lamp bulbs. In 1930 an ordinary little 25-watt bulb cost the citizen about thirty-three cents. K.F. believed that twenty cents was a fair and reasonable price. From its headquarters in Switzerland the electric-bulb combine flouted the idea. Because of the great expense of building such a factory the combine's executives believed their position to be impregnable. But the Swedish Cooperative Union tried a new tack by inviting the Danish, Norwegian, and Finnish cooperative centrals to join forces with the Swedish in the manufacturing venture. This they did, founding the first international cooperative business organization. It was called North European LUMA Cooperative Society. Just outside of Stockholm, the huge LUMA plant was erected. In 1931 the first Luma bulbs were put on the market in the four countries. The annual saving to the Swedish people who use an estimated twelve million bulbs a year is reckoned at considerably more than $1,000,000.

For two decades after its founding K.F. entered the manufacturing field only when big interests, local or international, made it necessary by boycott or by refusal to make prices reasonable, as in the case of cash registers. In the latter instance, for the first time K.F. went beyond the manufacture of household necessities and into that of shop supplies. Soon K.F. was able to sell its own make of ʀash registers at half the price asked by the National Cash Register

Company. And now Sweden exports registers to cooperative organizations in thirty-six other countries.

In the 1920's, however, K.F. began to manufacture several items in constant demand by consumers. Among these were shoes, artificial silk material, chinaware, and wall boards. It built an oatmeal factory, established several coffee-roasting centers, and bought a partnership in one of Stockholm's established coal-importing companies.

In the thirties Stockholm's local cooperative, known as "Konsum," acquired one of the city's two great department stores, long known as P.U.B. because it had been owned by Paul U. Bergström. Situated in the heart of the city, facing the flower market and the Concert House, it is a kind of Macy's, and serves the people well. American tourists are interested in it chiefly because here Greta Garbo once clerked in the hat department.

Stockholm's "Konsum" owns and operates a chain of attractive restaurants. Originally built for workingmen, they are now patronized by their respective neighborhoods and passers-by. Charmingly situated on the water close by the royal palace and dominated by Carl Milles's famous statue of the Sun Singer is a cooperative out-of-doors café.

For twenty-four years K.F. has maintained its own staff of first-rate architects to design retail shops and factories, and for more than a decade it has owned the largest architect's office in Scandinavia. The architectural creations have invariably been on advanced but discreet modern lines.

K.F. also controls three insurance companies: one for life, and two for fire, accident, automobile, and burglary. The year before World War II funds in the life-insurance company amounted to more than 300,000,000 kronor. And to assist and encourage members to be thrifty, K.F. established a savings bank, in which deposits and withdrawals are handled through the consumers' cooperative shops.

One of the most wholesome effects of cooperation is that it releases many an industrial worker and farmer from a vicious kind of credit buying. In former days a poor man was virtually in debtor's thrall to the company stores or the merchants in his vicinity. Nowadays he pays cash for his groceries.

Besides the prime function of wholesale buying (including manufacture of certain products) K.F. deals in education, in the training of cooperative employees and the dissemination of adult education through study circles.*

For instructing administrative officers and personnel an intensive course is conducted by K.F. at Saltsjöbaden, the fashionable seaside resort half-an-hour from Stockholm. At this center special courses are offered for general managers, shop managers, shop assistants, and auditors. Since the school's inauguration in 1925 some 20,000 persons have received instruction in cooperative work, while enjoying the delights of one of Europe's most charming vacation spots.

K.F. also trains cooperative employees by correspondence courses, giving instruction in arithmetic, accounting, and languages. The Letter School, as it is called, has about 35,000 enrolled annually.

By means of local study circles K.F. encourages adult or continuance education. Groups formed in various communities are provided with study guides and occasional lectures. In 1947 there were 4,000 groups with 50,000 students. K.F. publishes a journal called *Vi* (We), which in the early thirties achieved the largest circulation of any publication in Sweden, and by 1938 more than 550,000 copies, approximately a subscription for every third family in Sweden.

Consumer cooperation in Sweden is a voluntary popular movement in which true democracy is the cornerstone; any citizen rich or poor who buys a 100-kronor share may become a full member. The basic principle of the cooperative movement is radically democratic in that the number of shares owned by a member is not significant in voting power. A man who owns one share has as much authority in voting as a man who owns a hundred shares. With each purchase a cash check is handed the customer, and at the end of the year he turns the checks in. The total amount of the year's purchases determines the individual's dividend. Generally this amounts to no more than three per cent of his purchases. The rest of the profits is put to the reserve fund or devoted to education and propaganda. The member may take out his full dividend in cash or leave it in the savings department to draw interest or buy more shares with it.

* See section on Informal Education.

Though the cooperative movement's original objective was to relieve the poverty of the underprivileged, persons of any social group may join any consumers' cooperative society in Sweden. Industrial workers, handicraft workers, and the poorer-paid white-collar employees comprise some sixty-one per cent, farmers and independent workers account for twenty-one per cent, while professional men, teachers, and better-paid white-collar workers make up about eighteen per cent. Some members of the royal family, as well as a number of estate-owners and many retail merchants, belong to a cooperative.

In size the numerous consumer societies vary greatly, some with a hundred thousand members, and some with no more than thirty. In Sweden (as in Finland, though not in Denmark or Norway) nonmembers and foreign tourists may buy at cooperative shops as freely as members. More than half of the Swedish population is estimated to do some trading at cooperative shops.

The living man to whom most credit is due for the remarkable achievements of the consumers' cooperative movement is Albin Johansson. Like certain brilliantly successful businessmen, he has something of the dreamer in his make-up. Despite his dynamic drive, in appearance he more resembles a homely, wide-eyed poet than he does a top business executive. His career began at the age of thirteen, when he got a job as a department-store errandboy. Then he was a traveling salesman. In 1907, at the age of twenty-one, he was made office manager of K.F. During his six years in this position Johansson continued his education and he even managed to study for some months in Germany. In 1924 he became president of K.F., and for the past quarter-century he has been the recognized leader of Sweden's cooperative movement. In 1915 it was Johansson who, at twenty-nine, brought about the amalgamation of three separate consumers' cooperative societies in the capital to form the Stockholm Cooperative Society, which by 1939 was operating over four hundred different shops in the city. Because of his administrative gifts and his commercial acumen, Johansson has naturally been offered some of the best-paying executive jobs in Swedish industry. But for the good of the commonwealth he prefers to work for less than a tenth of the salary he could easily command. On $5,000 a year he and his family cannot afford to live luxuriously, but they live comfortably in a small cottage and drive a somewhat ancient American-make car. His chief extravagance is music. For seven years (1933-40) he served as chairman of the board of the Stockholm Opera. Albin Johansson is highly esteemed by his competitors in private enterprise.

A more recent growth of cooperative organization is that of the producers' association formed by agriculturists for the purpose of marketing their own products to the best advantage. Although in 1905 a farmers' cooperative was begun on a national scale for the purchasing of seeds, fertilizers, and cattle feed, it was not until the 1930's that Swedish farmers really took an enthusiastic interest in cooperatives. Now farmers with ten-acre places and titled estate-owners with fifteen thousand, and even the royal princes who live in the country, belong to the producers' creamery cooperative. By 1937 approximately ninety per cent of all milk to be separated was processed by the cooperative creameries, and more than ninety per cent of the creamery butter was produced by the cooperative.

The new impetus in agricultural cooperation was largely due to the forming of the National Federation of Creameries in 1932. At this same time a central organization called the Swedish Slaughter-house Association was founded to facilitate the slaughtering and marketing of hogs and beef cattle. At the outbreak of World War II some seventy per cent of the national butchering was handled by the association. In 1932, also, was established the Swedish Egg Cooperative Federation; and in 1934 a National Fruit Union brought together the various associations of fruit-growers.

The cooperative purchasing society has grown tremendously since 1905. Besides procuring supplies at wholesale prices, it has bought a factory for manufacturing farm implements, acquired a shipping line to transport its foreign purchases, opened a real-estate office for handling sale and rent of farms, and established its own bank. The farmers now have their own credit societies for supplying members with necessary operating loans.

In all, over three hundred thousand members belong to one or more of the producers' cooperatives. And many of these farmers also belong to their nearest consumers' cooperative society.

The general difference between the two types of cooperatives is this: the consumer cooperates in order to buy the necessities at low prices, the farmer-producer to sell his products to the best advantage, with the greatest economy in marketing and delivery.

To keep relations mutually advantageous between consumers' and producers' societies, a permanent joint committee was arranged in 1936. The producers' cooperatives are pledged not to engage in retail distribution, while the consumers' cooperatives promise to keep hands off the wholesale-creamery and the slaughterhouse business.

So far the Cooperative Union has crushed all attempts of powerful business interests to prevent the societies from obtaining the goods they need for their shops at reasonable prices. It has served not only to curb monopolistic combines of big business, but it has acted as a powerful check against inflation, and benefited the general consuming public, as well as its own members, by keeping down prices of essential commodities. Besides, it has influenced businesses large and small to mind the quality of their wares and the services of their salesmen. Though the cooperative trade lies mainly in the staple necessities of life, not in the luxuries, the competition between free enterprise and cooperation is stimulating and works to the advantage of the buying public.

While the consumers' cooperatives are most highly esteemed for their contribution to the wholesome prosperity of the nation, they have never received any financial assistance whatever from the State. And they pay taxes on their retail and wholesale business precisely as private shops and industries do.

Visiting American businessmen, who are tremendously impressed by the admirable conditions of Sweden's lowest income group and yet shudder at the mention of the word "cooperative," are somewhat reassured to learn that only fifteen per cent of the total retail turnover passes through the cooperatives. Eighty-five per cent of the nation's retail business, including all of the so-called luxury trade, is conducted through regular free-enterprise channels. One-fourth of the country's food, however, is sold through the cooperative shops and the total sum spent in the cooperative food departments provides nourishment for the third of the population in the lowest income bracket.

My own experience may be unique, but I have never yet talked with a Swedish industrialist, banker, or lawyer, who would desire to see cooperatives abolished. Many of these men who fought the idea twenty years ago are not only reconciled to cooperation, but heartily appreciate its indubitable contribution to the general welfare.

Today in Sweden the Consumers' Cooperative Union is in a most wholesome and energetic state. Like the trade union and the sick-benefit movements, the cooperative societies are still primarily an expression of the workers and the low-incomed middle class to improve their economic conditions through mutual help and solidarity.

13.

Cooperation for Better Housing

"The latter glory of this house shall be greater than the former, saith Jehovah."

—HAGGAI 2: 9

THE COOPERATIVE BUILDERS' movement has had a most salubrious effect on housing conditions in Sweden these last two decades. The largest cooperative building society in the world today is the Swedish central organization called Tenants' Savings and Building Society. It is generally spoken of as HSB from the initials of its Swedish name. Its objective is to provide new dwelling units on the basis of organized cooperation of tenants. Formed as recently as 1923, within a little more than a decade it had become the most important single construction enterprise in Sweden.

On the theory that the homeowner makes a better citizen than the tenant, Sweden encourages every family to own its home, whether it is city apartment or cottage in the country. The Swedish ideal is to house families of every income group comfortably in attractive surroundings.

When the industrial era began in Sweden in the 1880's, the country was emphatically rural, with Stockholm as the only city of more than a hundred thousand inhabitants. The comparatively recent period of urban growth is a leading reason for the new and up-to-date appearance of Sweden's municipalities. No more than twenty per cent of the dwellings in the cities are sixty years old. Though her capital has often been overcrowded, and without adequate housing facilities, Sweden has never had a real slum problem, as have some other countries where the industrial development came earlier. But even early in this century, the city of Stockholm began

201

buying outlying tracts and encouraging worthy occupants of un-hygienic, cramped apartments to build cottages in the suburbs. The municipality gave loans up to ninety per cent of the value of the completed house and the landscaping, and lost no money in the process.

In 1905, as an inducement to stop rural people from flocking to the cities, Parliament launched an "Own Your Home" movement and financed it with a State loan fund. Since the rapid industrial expansion after 1880 had been regarded with apprehension by certain groups as a social maladjustment, an increase in the number of rural landholders, particularly those who would establish new agricultural holdings on virgin land, was considered excellent for the health of the commonwealth. Between 1905 and 1935 some 80,000 new houses in the country districts were built with State aid, and it is estimated that one-tenth of the rural population has had its housing problem solved by these State loans. Those receiving home-ownership loans had to meet the simple requirements of being "able-bodied, thrifty, sober and respectable, in need of help, but not destitute."

In addition, to make rural living more attractive, and as a relief of unemployment during the 1933 depression, a grant of 40,000,000 kronor was made for the purpose of repairing and improving dwellings already in existence. As a result more than 32,000 houses were renovated, and unemployment was considerably reduced.

Already before the outbreak of the first World War, the demand for good, small apartments in Stockholm far exceeded the supply, and rentals were extraordinarily high. To remedy the critical situation, in June of 1916 the Social Welfare Association of the city formed what was called the Stockholm Cooperative Housing Society. Its declared intention was "to secure for its members high-grade, moderately priced homes, either in the city of Stockholm or in the suburbs on property already owned by the city, or to be bought, and to construct multiple dwelling houses and rent out apartments as required."

To have the privilege of renting a new apartment at a figure considerably below the market and for a virtually unlimited lease, the prospective member had to invest ten per cent of the cost of his apartment. The Society really functioned, and still does, as a rental agency, whereas from the start HSB has been a sales organization.

The Stockholm Society, which entered the housing business as a social measure, gradually emerged into one of the city's foremost real-estate owners. At the end of its second decade its renter-members numbered 2,429.

The mild success of the Stockholm Cooperative Housing Society's first half-dozen years inspired the formation of Tenants' Savings and Building Society (HSB) in 1923. The first year's achievement of HSB was the construction of four blocks of apartment houses, consisting of one hundred and fifty-four apartments and eight shops. The three years following were marked with extraordinary progress, with societies springing up in Göteborg and Malmö and several industrial centers in various parts of the land. After the formation of a National HSB in 1926, cooperative building flourished like the proverbial watered garden.

But HSB is no temporary body created to meet a crisis. It is a permanent organization with "a technical and financially sound backbone" for the purpose of constructing more and better houses for the citizens. The Stockholm HSB is ever the head of the house, with branch societies in other cities, which in turn have smaller individual societies under their supervision. But the financial obligations of each separate society are in each case its own concern. So no society can suffer in any way from the financial difficulties of any other. The soundness of the financial structure of each organization depends entirely on the responsibility and sense of order of its own members.

To become associated with HSB is extremely simple. A group of persons who want new and better places to live in form a society, generally with the help of HSB. The prospective tenants furnish ten per cent of the value of the apartments they wish to build. In the case of the cheaper type of apartments, it is only necessary to put up five per cent of the cost. Plans are drawn by expert architects for practical, efficient, and attractive apartments that utilize the available space in the most economical manner. Since risk margins and speculation do not exist in HSB projects, the tenants who build and occupy the houses take their profits in the form of lower rents or monthly payments. Because HSB has a unified purchasing agency that procures materials at lowest possible wholesale prices, there is a great saving in costs. And, if needed, Government credit at most advantageous rates is available to HSB.

The building operations of HSB are mainly financed by cooperative funds paid in by members, through first and second mortgages taken by banks and insurance companies (especially cooperative insurance companies), and through third mortgages used as security for loans from the Government or municipality. Because HSB construction is such a good risk, sometimes the contractor himself furnishes the loan.

The City of Stockholm lends money to the organization at low interest, usually about three per cent, on up to eighty-five per cent of the property value, with twenty-five years in which to pay. The Government allocates to HSB a share of its authorized funds set aside for its social program. Both the Government and the municipalities are glad to lend money on HSB mortgages, not only because the organization helps vitally in relieving housing shortages and thus improving the social welfare, but because it is a wholesome regulator of the real-estate market.

For his pleasant new apartment the prospective owner pays an annual sum lower than he used to pay as rental. Each year the fee decreases in amount until the total is paid up. The householder who is his own landlord has no fear of eviction or an unreasonable advance in rent. This is a consummation to be cherished, and those who fail to meet their obligation are few indeed. Less than one per cent of the annual fees due are recorded as unpaid.

The regular HSB city apartments vary according to the pocketbooks and desires of its individual members. In the best or A-grade houses the size of the apartment ranges from two rooms and bath to six rooms. The equipment, fixtures, and decorations are naturally more expensive in the A-grade apartment houses, which are generally located in the most desirable parts of the city.

In constructing apartments, HSB gives thoughtful consideration to the sites. Two of the largest housing projects built in 1937 are situated on a bluff that gives on a superb view of Stockholm, which is unflaggingly exciting winter and summer. One of the most attractive rows of apartments is built in the center of the city along a narrow branch of Lake Mälaren, with a view of Town Hall Tower at one end. By night the lights from the hundreds of apartment windows reflected in the canalized water makes a fascinating sight. The color of paint on the stucco and wood is invariably pastel and harmonious. Some of the houses are cream with beige trimming, some are painted the soft pale green of white grapes. An occasional white building will have blue balconies or rust-colored awnings.

In the least expensive apartment buildings certain amenities are not lacking. Each is so situated as to provide the greatest amount of sunshine and open air possible for every apartment. The balcony and the picture window have come to be standard features of an HSB modern apartment house. Each group of buildings has green spaces between them, embellished with flowering shrubs.

The Swedish improvements in designs for city living, in which there are no ugly alleys and no unsightly backyards, but landscaped gardens and green areas for children's play, are due, in considerable measure, to the cooperative-housing movement.

In the kitchens equipped with stainless steel sinks, smooth-faced cupboard doors, and glass brick walls, everything is made as convenient and pleasant for the housewife as possible. A garbage-disposal chute is conveniently located, and beside it a laundry chute. In the basements are washing machines and drying rooms, where the housewife may do the family laundry without messing up her own place. In some of the HSB houses, rug-cleaning rooms are provided with sound-proof walls, vacuum cleaners, and dust-sucking electric fans.

For the menfolk there are workshops, where fathers and sons may build bookcases, repair skis, carve wood, and tinker to their hearts' content.

Many blocks are equipped with public dining rooms, in which the tenants may eat what meals they choose. Some are arranged so that the housewife or the bachelor has merely to order dinner from the ground-floor restaurant to be sent up on the dumb-waiter. One may entertain ten at dinner in his own home and have no cooking or dishwashing.

To help the members furnish their apartments in good taste, HSB puts on display in its new houses samples of carefully selected modern furniture, rugs, and hangings from designs by some of Sweden's leading artists. Modern pieces and units of bookcases and chests of drawers in blond wood can be bought from the Tenants' Furniture Company on easy terms. In regard to vases, lamps, ornaments, and tableware, HSB encourages following the slogan of the Swedish Society of Arts and Crafts, which urges, "More beautiful things for everyday use." Since half of the owners of cooperative apartments are manual laborers, this guidance in discrimination and economy has had its effect on the good taste of the whole nation.

To harassed American mothers, in these servantless days, the item of HSB cooperative building that appeals most strikingly is that of the apartment-house nursery. Here infants and children under school age of widower fathers or mothers who work may be left all day from seven o'clock until six under the care of child specialists. The little ones are given three meals a day, put to bed for naps on a sun balcony, bathed, and entertained. For a baby's all-day care the charge is only twenty-five cents. The nursery is located on the ground floor or the top floor, where the flat roofs are utilized for sun baths and games. If on the ground floor, the green out-of-doors is provided with sand piles, see-saws, swings, and wading pools. The indoor playrooms for different-aged children are equipped with diminutive furniture and toys and educational games suitable for their years. In the respective playrooms each child has his own drawer for his private belongings, blocks, paints, and picturebooks, marked with his individual "sign," say an elephant, a polar bear, a rose, or a Pierrot.

The tots get training in table manners as well as fair play in games and consideration for one's fellows. School children, on returning to apartments while both mother and father are at work, may spend their time playing under supervision or do their homework in one of the quiet rooms.

In one nursery, I particularly remember talking with a charming little girl of ten whom I found reading in a window nook. On a school holiday she had been left for the day, not because her mother worked, but because she had had to attend the funeral of a relative in another town.

In the evenings there is no baby-sitter problem for HSB apartment dwellers. Parents merely take the offspring down or up the elevator to the nursery and leave it at a cost of about twelve cents an hour. And arrangements can be made for leaving children all night.

HSB has evolved a further convenience for parents: a Children's Hotel at Kungsklippan, Stockholm. Here children may be sent for a fortnight's stay, say, while house guests are in the apartment, or when the parents are called out-of-town, or because of a mother's illness, or the birth of a new brother or sister. The charge for the child's board and dormitory bed is only seventy-five cents a day, no more than that for a small dog's board in an American city.

Since it is quite common in Sweden for the wife as well as the husband to hold a paying position, these special services to be had in the cooperative apartments are more than blessed conveniences.

HSB has its own seminary for training nurses and playroom supervisors with an aptitude for and love of child-welfare work. Many of Sweden's foremost authorities in child-training work serve on the faculty or lecture during the twenty months' course.

Besides the construction of city apartments, of which over 20,000 had been completed by 1939, HSB launched into a small house-building program in 1936. (The City of Stockholm had already erected, under municipal financing, some 4,000 small houses in suburban subdivisions.) At the edges of Swedish cities HSB bought large tracts of land as suitable sites for groups of cottages. The ground is sold to the prospective homeowners at cost plus the outlay for roads, sewers, grading. The smaller types of cottage are delivered in such a convenient and uncomplicated state that the owner himself, with the help of his son and a couple of neighbors, can erect the house. He needs to call for the professional services only of the electrician and the plumber.

To facilitate the erection of private homes, HSB owns a large lumber company with its mills and its equipment for prefabricating houses. It has acquired a factory for making parquet floors and wood trim. It has created its own plant for mixing mortar and stucco. The architects of HSB designed fourteen standard models of cottages, some one-story, some two-story, consisting of from three to six rooms. The prospective owners must choose from one of the fourteen models. There are wide choices in the colors of paint, which has been carefully selected so that there will be no color clashes.

Monotony is avoided by the rolling terrain, the special character of each plot, the grading, and the set of the house.

Between 1939 and 1949 a tremendous amount of cooperative building was done in the suburban areas about Stockholm. The planting of fruit trees, flowering shrubs, climbing roses and clematis, together with the use of white gates and fences, has given some of the new districts an idyllic aspect. One of the most attractive of the cottages I visited belonged to a taxi driver, with whom I became acquainted in 1946. His near neighbors included office workers, factory workers, lesser Government officials, a lawyer, and an opera singer.

To provide the lower-salaried city worker with vacation cottages on the Archipelago, HSB bought a tract at Årsta thirty miles from Stockholm, and there built small houses among the rocks and pines, together with community piers and a summer hotel. The whole project is managed by a special unit of the Stockholm HSB known as the HSB Summer Home Society.

Building construction in the style sometimes called "Swedish Modern" has perhaps been the most notable outward sign of progress in Sweden these past two decades. In the seven years preceding World War II Sweden enjoyed an unprecedented building boom. During the depression years following 1932 virtually full employment was achieved because of the steady activity of construction industries. In 1939 some 45,000 units were constructed. Then, because of the war, new construction dropped within two years to one-fourth of its 1939 mark. To stimulate new building and to hold down rents, the Government appropriated 60,000,000 kronor in 1941 to be lent at three and one-half per cent. Immediately construction work picked up. It more than doubled in 1942; and by 1945 it surpassed the high mark of 1939. Since 1942 HSB has been averaging more than thirteen per cent of the annual construction of dwellings in Swedish towns.

Through 1945 to 1949 Stockholm spread farther and farther into the countryside in the form of planned garden cities, with modern flats and villas and cottages attractively spaced and arranged. Some houses were built by private persons, some by real-estate concerns, and some by the cooperative-housing societies, but all with municipality's blessings and within its rules and regulations, and ninety per cent with the aid of public credit.

Although general housing in Swedish cities is of such high standards today, overcrowding is still something of a problem, for a large proportion of the apartments need another bedroom. But Swedish authorities have a thorough understanding of the psychical as well as physical risks of overcrowding, and they are promulgating the idea of extra floor space and more rooms, and trying to devise means to meet the extra expense.

In 1935 the Government made a radical move to encourage a higher birth rate by voting funds for the construction of special apartments for large families in the cities. The Government provided the building loans, the municipalities contributed the sites. For the new, efficient, roomy apartments, the Parliament undertook to pay a proportion of the family rent, scaled according to the number of children. A bonus was offered for having more than two children. For a family with three children, the reduction in rent was thirty per cent, forty per cent for four children, and up to seventy per cent reduction for seven children. Today for the same rental, parents with eight children—a rarity indeed in Sweden —may have as commodious a dwelling place for their brood as parents with an only child. These many-roomed apartment houses, called Children's Houses, or Sunshine Houses, have been built under the management of the municipalities themselves or by cooperative-building societies.

The municipalities pay merited tribute to the good work of the cooperative-housing societies, which have helped to relieve them of large responsibilities. And in serving to raise the living standards of the common man, the work of HSB has proved as significantly effective as that of the more publicized consumers' cooperatives. The world's admiration for the state of the general welfare in Sweden these last fifteen years is indubitably due in considerable measure to the success of these two great movements.

IV

FOR THE GENERAL WELFARE

Let the assemblies be annual . . . the representation equal . . . He that will promote discord under a government as equally formed as this would have joined Lucifer in his revolt.

—THOMAS PAINE

14.

Mr. Möller Remembers

THE CHIEF CAPITAL ASSET of the four Northern Countries lies in the health, energy, and talent of their people. While for centuries the Scandinavians have been esteemed as a sturdy and honorable people, it is notably since the first World War that they have made such spectacular progress in improving the general welfare. In Sweden there are four outstanding men to whom uncommon credit is due for the excellent state of well-being achieved since 1920. These four were all born of humble parentage within two years of each other. They are as follows: Gustav Möller, Minister of Social Welfare, born in 1884; August Lindberg, head of the Labor Federation, and Per Albin Hansson, the late Prime Minister, both born in 1885; and Albin Johansson, the leader of the cooperative movement, born in 1886.

In 1939 I was received by Prime Minister Hansson, and I had long talks with August Lindberg and Gustav Möller, both in 1939 and 1946.

It was Mr. Möller particularly who made me realize the magnitude of the humanitarian achievements of recent decades and the contrast between the state of the underprivileged at the turn of the century and at the present time.

Since his youth the ruling principle of Gustav Möller's life has been to work for the day when no citizen should suffer from want. Some such ideal is infused into the Swedish social-welfare legislation. This does not mean that a man may shirk his responsibility to his family; but because of circumstances like illness, old age, unemployment, or sudden disaster over which the best-intentioned of individuals may have no control, he may find himself powerless to fulfill that responsibility.

213

"Perhaps the most important factor in improving general conditions," Mr. Möller said to me in April, 1939, "has been the trade unions. The general standard of living is determined largely by the wages of union workers. Before the Social Democrats came into power, employees did not have their rightful share. When economy was necessary—when industrialists had to cut production costs to meet competition—naturally the first thing that occurred to them was to cut wages. The industrialists were rarely willing to increase wages except under pressure. But in the 1930's they underwent a change in point of view. And today, I believe, the general standard of living in Sweden is the highest in the world. But shall I tell something of conditions in my childhood a half-century ago?"

I urged him to go on, and from time to time I interrupted him with specific questions.

He smiled a bit grimly and began. "I was born in Malmö the year before Prime Minister Hansson and only a couple of miles from his birthplace in the suburbs. I was only three months old when my father died. He was a metalworker, something like a blacksmith, as his father had been before him." Mr. Möller took up a long pair of keen desk shears and began to toy with them idly.

"My mother was left a widow at twenty-seven, with me a baby and my brother three years old. To support us she became a general cleaning woman. She would go with her scrub brushes and pails and mops from house to house. She made one krona a day, first at one house, then at another. Six kronor a week in all—about a dollar and a half in your money—though, of course, things were cheaper then. As a child I saw my mother only on Sundays. I was still asleep when she left in the mornings, and again asleep when she returned in the evenings. My grandmother looked after me. My mother had also to support my grandmother. We paid six kronor a month for our miserable lodgings."

He opened and closed the shears twice and began to talk without looking at me. "My mother worked so hard that after eleven years she became very ill and was taken to the hospital. After she was on her feet again, she set up a little bread and milk shop in a half-basement place, and we lived in the dark room behind the shop. One day the doctor came to collect his money, because my mother had not been able to pay his bill though it was only ten kronor. He saw that the walls of our place were all damp and moldy. He said, 'You must move. You can't live in such a hole. It will kill you.' The doctor was kind and did not press his own claim. Within two years my mother did die." Möller laid the shears aside and looked at me again. "It was poverty and hard work that killed her, for she was a woman of strong constitution."

After a moment he went on. "I was fourteen when she died, in 1898, the year the Labor Federation was organized. I had had the full six years of primary school and almost two years of secondary school when my formal education stopped and I had to make my living. I was now on my own, for my brother, who had become a baker, soon went off to America. I got a job as officeboy in a cement plant. The owner was a great industrial builder. He took a fancy to me and lent me books. I studied by myself in all my spare time. At sixteen, I became his private secretary."

As he reached into a drawer, I said, "But you must have been unusually clever and bright."

The minister smiled with modest pride. "At school," he said, "I did stand at the top of my class." He offered me cigarettes. "Do you want to hear more?"

I pressed him to go on.

"In 1904 my employer suggested that I enter a commercial school to improve myself. I did, and studied business for two years, while I was still working for him. There I became a member of the Youth Movement of the Social Democrats. When my employer heard about it, he said, 'You cannot belong to that organization and work for me. I am very fond of you, but we cannot be together any more. You will be forced to give Labor our secrets.' I told him I could not give up the Youth Movement. So I lost my position and had to give up my studies at the commercial school.

"But my employer still seemed fond of me. He was a candidate for the Riksdag, and he said, 'If I get elected to Parliament, I shall take you back anyhow.' He lost the election, however."

Mr. Möller smiled, and then his expression became grave. "I owe much to that man. From working as private secretary to the cement-plant owner I had got many lessons about business and industry. A man can have few secrets from his private secretary. So I learned the ways and methods of businessmen. I noted the tricks." He paused, and then looked fixedly at me. "I realized it was completely unnecessary that my mother had worked herself to death."

A tone more of sorrow than of bitterness had come into his voice. After a moment he said with quiet emphasis, "I determined to do all in my power to bring about better conditions for working-class Swedes. But first I had to earn my living. At twenty-two, I became a journalist. Then I was manager of a publishing concern for a few years. In 1916, when I was thirty-two, I was made secretary of the Social Democratic party. The next year I was elected to Parliament. In 1920 I was elected Social Democratic leader in First Chamber; and in 1924 I was made Minister of Social Welfare."

As we talked about numerous current phases of his work, I could sense Mr. Möller's profound gratification in knowing that no Swedish woman would ever again have to exist in such wretched circumstances as had his valiant mother. I felt somehow that the privations of Mrs. Möller had not been in vain. Her heroic struggles had inspired the son to urge the passage of bill after bill to guarantee a certain amount of decent living to every Swedish citizen.

When I was received by the minister again in mid-July of 1946, I saw that the strain of the war years had told on him, for he had aged more than a man should in seven years. But though he was tired, he seemed in excellent spirits. On June 29 the New National Pensions Act, which was something very close to his heart, had been passed.

Mr. Möller looked upon the passage of this pensions act—it went into operation on New Year's Day, 1948—as the crowning achievement of his life's work. It substantially increased the existing old-age benefits, and provided certain new forms of pension, such as sick benefit, "wife's allowance," and "widow's pension." Today, on reaching the age of sixty-seven, every Swede is entitled to a pension, irrespective of private income. The base pay is 1,000 kronor a year for a single person, or 1,600 kronor for a married couple. Besides, there is a housing allowance up to 600 kronor for a single person and 800 kronor for a married couple, depending on the local cost of living. But a person whose private income is above a certain amount may not receive the housing supplement.

Anyone whom ill health forces to give up work before he reaches sixty-seven is entitled to the same amount as the old-age pension with the housing supplement. A blind person who has lost his sight before the age of sixty is granted an extra allowance, regardless of his private income. The wife of a man who is entitled to a full old-age pension is granted a wife's allowance after she has reached the age of sixty. A widow who is fifty-five or more at the time of her husband's death is entitled to a widow's pension of 600 kronor a year and a housing supplement, depending on her income.

Pensioners who are still gainfully employed at sixty-seven may continue to work as long as they are able and receive their full annual pension at the same time. In a nation with a shortage of manpower there is no penalty for industriousness. I met several workers well in their seventies, who held factory jobs and drew their Government pensions, which they were laying by for a still more comfortable old age.

Mr. Möller was also much gratified by recent emendations to the Holiday Laws. Strongly believing that the morale and health of the people required generous vacation periods, the minister had worked hard for his objectives. Before 1936 the mighty labor unions had not been able to get more than a four to six days' vacation with pay incorporated in collective agreements. Mr. Möller appointed a committee to draw up proposals requiring that industrial workers be granted a fortnight's vacation with pay. The Riksdag passed the law in 1938. Later it was made to include seasonal workers like lumberjacks. Now, in 1946, all employees under eighteen years of age and men doing especially heavy industrial work were granted an extra week, which they might take in winter, for skiing, or as they chose. And the Government grants for free vacations for city children of low-income families had been extended to children living in the country.

As I rose to leave, Mr. Möller leaned back in his chair with a glow in his eyes of one who has labored faithfully and is now assured of the harvest. "When you were here in 1939," he said, "Sweden was being given too high praise for its social standards. As I told you then, it was my ambition to try to make the saga a reality. By 1950, in regard to social welfare, Sweden will be a model we can be proud to display before the world."

15.

Better Babies and Public Health

AN EXCELLENT TEST of the social ideals of a nation is the interest shown in child welfare. It is a major concern in Sweden, as Mr. Möller had said to me.

During the first third of this century the decline in birth rate in Sweden was marked. By 1934 it was the lowest of any nation in the world. A well-documented book called *The Re-population Crisis,* by Gunnar Myrdal and his wife Alva, caused something of a sensation. Responsible citizens were duly disturbed. The Government ordered a comprehensive study of the problem, with recommendations for legislative enactments that might lead to an increased birth rate. In relatively short order financial aid was given in maternity cases, low-rate loans for house improvements were offered, and low-rate loans to newly married couples for household furniture. With Government aid municipalities began the construction of large-family apartment houses for low-income groups, with rebates in rent for every child beyond the first two.* "Four Kids to Every House" was a patriotic slogan that appeared in the press repeatedly from 1935 to 1939. While it is impossible to prove the direct effect of these inducements, it seems significant that after certain laws went into effect in 1935, the birth rate began to rise. By 1945 it was greater than it had been since the 1880's; births numbered 204 per thousand inhabitants, approximately the same as in the United States.

To produce better babies, free prenatal care is offered at clinics, where examinations of expectant mothers are given, and treatments administered when necessary. In special cases certain protective foods are provided, along with adjustments and advice. Even travel

* See section on Cooperative Housing.

218

expenses of prospective mothers from rural districts are paid by the State. Each prenatal clinic is directed by a gynecologist or an obstetrician, assisted by midwives and trained nurses. Child delivery is free to the poor and costs next to nothing for those who can afford to pay. Expectant employed mothers are not allowed to work for a certain number of weeks before and after delivery, and their wages are paid in full. The Swedish Government believes that low-income women should spend their confinement in conditions as relatively comfortable as those of women of means.

Since 1937 the free service of examination and advice has extended to a postnatal period for mother and child. And if a mother is in need of special financial assistance at the time of childbirth or within nine months thereafter, she may apply for it, and receive help either as a gift or as a loan without interest. Generally the assistance is given in the form of orders for clothing or food or the payment of rent. Sometimes it is given in cash. In no case does it exceed 400 kronor or some $120.

The Mothers' Aid Council advises on the merits of each case. If a mother is delicate, domestic help is provided to look after the house and the other children until she recovers her vigor. In 1947 the salaries of some two thousand "home-assistants" were paid by the Government.

As to whether or not the maternity and pediatric care of Government-employed physicians is appreciated, one need only note that seventy per cent of all expectant mothers avail themselves of this free medical service for prenatal care; while eighty-two per cent of all newborn babies are registered at the child-health centers, where they may be periodically examined and treated. In 1939 the gynecologic clinic of Göteborg, Sweden's second city, looked after eighty-five per cent of the city's births. The cost to the patient was about thirty cents a day. For a week's confinement the charge was around $2.00 for all services. The excellent work of the State clinics is proved by comparing the infant mortality rate in 1920 with that of a quarter-century later after the new services had been instituted. In 1920 about 60 infants per 1,000 births died; in 1945, only 26.3. In the United States in 1945, 38 infants out of 1,000 did not survive.

Child Welfare Centers constitute an effective system for medical supervision until a child reaches school age, and then the School

Health Service takes on the job of guarding the health of children between the ages of seven and fourteen. Each child is examined on entering school, and facts are noted on his health card, which follows him up through the grades. Even the most robust child must have a thorough examination at least three times during his elementary-school years.

In 1939 Government-supported dental clinics for children were established. Parents pay a smallish fee regardless of income and their children receive annual examinations and compulsory treatment. The fee is still smaller for the second child of a family, and after the third child, the others are treated without cost. Completely free treatment is given to children of parents too poor to pay anything. Some dental clinics go on wheels into the backwoods to save the children's teeth, and some go in boats among the skerries where fisherfolk live.

Since 1945 a mental-health service for children, with trained psychiatrists, has been facilitated by State support. These mental health clinics for young persons work in cooperation with child-welfare institutions, public schools, and city and country hospitals, which must earmark a certain number of beds for mental cases. Parents are also greatly assisted in bringing up problem children by trained child psychologists.

The Swedes carry their health program for children into recreation facilities not only by providing well-equipped playgrounds in the towns, but by sending the children for free holidays to the country. The grants for children's holidays are given to those whose family income is below a certain level and the value of property less than $6,000.

Holiday camps with sports fields for young people are supported largely by the Public Inheritance Fund, which accrues from persons dying intestate and leaving no known close relatives. Approximately $300,000 annually is paid from this fund to run the open-air camps, where the children's play is supervised by well-trained specialists, who teach them good manners, as well as principles of healthy living.

Housewives who have the care of two children are given free transportation for their own holidays. The maximum length of a free trip is 360 miles, except in the more sparsely settled far north, where it is 720 miles. In order to get the proper benefit from these trips, a child is required to remain away four weeks and a housewife at least ten days. To ease expense problems of vacationing housewives, Government stipends up to fifty kronor are granted.

A measure considered of special import to the national health is that which aims to provide all school children with free lunches, including one nourishing hot dish containing a goodly supply of proteins and vitamins, besides ample quantities of milk and bread. For a family with three or four children of school age, the saving on these hot luncheons is not inconsiderable. The measure was only partially in effect in 1946; but in 1950 it is scheduled to go into full force throughout the land, from the metropolitan schools to remote Lapland villages.

As one extra inducement for larger families, the Government decreed in 1948 that each child between one year and sixteen should receive an annual grant of 260 kronor, approximately $75. These grants for children go to the rich as well as the poor. This measure takes the place of former tax reductions for each dependent child, which did not help those with numerous children and virtually no taxable income. The Swedes believe that childless couples and unmarried persons should contribute their share to the health and well-being of the nation's future men and women.

A most impressive commentary on all these social measures for the benefit of children is that from the beginning the conservative elements in Parliament have supported them as heartily as the radical. And since World War II the majority of all welfare reforms passed by the Riksdag have been supported with virtual unanimity by all political parties.

For more than two decades the trend in general public-health work has been towards equalization of advantages, through municipal services and health benefits offered by the public authorities. As early as 1720 the Swedish Government required district physicians to note the living habits of the people and to correct unsanitary conditions, besides attending the sick.

In public-health administration today doctors and nurses have charge of medical care as well as public-health work and preventive medicine. There are some four hundred different health districts in Sweden. Public-health officers may also be private practicing physicians. The district physician is always a Government official. His fees are fixed. Consultation costs something less than a dollar. All preventive medical work, together with treatment of venereal diseases and tuberculosis, is given absolutely free of charge. The fight against tuberculosis in a quarter-century has reduced the number of fatalities from 165 per thousand deaths in 1920 to 50 in 1945.

In 1918 Sweden was the first nation to pass a law making it compulsory for all persons infected with a venereal disease to report to a health officer and receive free treatment. Not to reveal the affliction is a criminal offense, and one may be sent to prison for refusing to confess the source of infection. By 1939 syphilis was virtually wiped out. But during the war, when so many refugees were received, the figure rose to almost 1 case among 5,000 persons.

A doctor makes his own choice as to private practice or Government employ. But because of the assured salary at the beginning of a medical career, the majority of young doctors apply for Government positions. Some devote their entire time to "socialized" practice—either in hospitals or in the field. Some work half-time on Government salary and half-time in private practice. And there are those physicians whose practice is entirely private and who may charge as large fees as their clientele will stand for. No one is forced to go to a State-paid physician. But the majority of citizens seem happy and grateful to do so. Those who take advantage of the socialized services may choose from a number of doctors, and change if they are not pleased.

A foreigner has only to spend a week in a Swedish hospital in the provinces to realize the high standards that are maintained. The cost is extremely low. Complete care in a ward is less than $1.00 a day. In a private room it may be as high as $3.00 a day plus a fixed nominal fee to the hospital physician. A ward patient can be operated on for appendicitis and remain six days in hospital for as little as $5.00.

I met a diplomat from Holland who had just been released from a hospital after an appendectomy and eight days in a private room. His entire bill was $70. He said similar services in his country would have cost at least four times that figure.

To keep its people healthy the Swedish Government appropriates large sums. But more than a third of the entire population already holds private sickness-insurance policies, which include hospitalization, operations, everything. In 1950, instead of the present system of voluntary insurance, all Sweden is to have compulsory health insurance with medical care and cash benefits. Then much of the financial burden for keeping the public health at a high standard will be taken from the Government.

Though the Swedes are assured of excellent care at small expense in their illness, they do not fail to do their part in keeping themselves fit. They are passionately devoted to out-of-doors sports. No people indulge more in gymnastic exercises for health's sake. The father and inventor of modern physical exercises was a Swede, Pehr Henrik Ling, who was born in 1776, and whose first gymnastic hall was in an old Stockholm gun-foundry with a floor of stamped clay. Today gymnastics is a compulsory course in all Swedish schools. The Swedish Union of Gymnastics currently numbers almost 170,-000 active members, with over 2,000 different associations spread throughout the country.

Swedish proficiency in athletics was strikingly demonstrated in the 1948 Olympic Games held in London. In the sum of points Sweden ranked second only to the United States, whose population outnumbers hers more than twenty to one. The Swedes won seventeen Olympic championships, and 353 points against the Americans' 662 points.

In the Modern Penthalon, again, the gold medal went to Sweden, as it has every time except one since it was first introduced at the Olympic Games in 1912. A young captain in the Swedish army named Wille Grut came out first, and a Swedish lieutenant was third. In Graeco-Roman wrestling the Swedes won five of the eight gold medals. They were first in the shooting contests and won the first victory in the equestrian events. In the Winter Games held in Switzerland in February, 1948, Sweden took first place, followed by Switzerland, and then the United States.

Those who may have questioned if a hundred and thirty years of peace had made the Swedes soft, or whether they had been enervated by so much social coddling this last quarter-century, could find a resounding answer in the 1948 Olympics.*

* The total score of the four Northern Countries—Sweden, Norway, Denmark, and Finland—with a combined population of 17,000,000 was 719 points, which the press compared with the 662 points won by the United States with its 140,000,000 persons.

16.

Enlightenment

TREATMENT OF PRISONERS

SWEDEN'S SOLICITUDE for its people does not stop with care of the aged, the children, the physically handicapped, and the mentally sick. It extends to malefactors and asocial beings who have run afoul of the law. Compared with most countries, Sweden has no great problem with criminals. There has been no execution since 1910, and in 1921 the death penalty was abolished by law. In 1946 the total number of prisoners serving sentences in all the nation's prisons never passed two thousand. Of these only six were serving life sentences, and less than sixty were women.

On July 1, 1946, a new penal law went into effect, with the basic principle that a prisoner shall always be treated with regard for his dignity as a human being. Though about half of the male prisoners are sentenced to hard labor, no further severity in correction is deemed advisable. Loss of liberty is considered in itself sufficient punishment. The old idea of society taking its revenge by making incarceration needlessly unpleasant is a thing of the past in Sweden.

Prisoners are not crowded into one huge building, but divided more or less according to types and dispersed among thirty walled and barred institutions and twenty open ones. The largest prison in the city of Stockholm, with its population of almost 700,000, accommodates only three hundred prisoners, and it is quite beautifully situated on an island in Lake Mälaren.

The open prisons devoid of window bars and restraining outer walls are for the most part in agricultural districts. To these, some five hundred of the lesser offenders are sent. Some of these open institutions, which resemble large farms, house no more than thirty.

224

Many of the normal amenities of life, like writing desks and flowering potted plants, are permitted, especially to prisoners who show a sincere desire to reform. The men work in the fields or the forests, or at handicraft and mechanical shopwork, as do the city prisoners. All prisoners are paid small fees for their productive work. They may spend up to half of their earnings on sweets, fruit, cigarettes, magazines. Part is sent to dependents, and part must be saved for the time of their release.

In Sweden they do not try to break a prisoner's spirit, but work to restore his self-confidence. Prisoners are encouraged to keep in touch with their families and old friends. By the Penal Act of 1946 furloughs to visit their families and attend to private affairs are granted as often as four times a year to men who have proved themselves well behaved.

Before a man is committed to prison, he is examined by a psychiatrist. A number of convicts, including murderers, are sent to mental hospitals instead of to prison.

Children under fifteen, who have committed a crime, are regarded as delinquents. First they are warned, and then placed in special schools run by the Child Welfare Board of the Ministry of Social Affairs. Sentences passed on youths under twenty-one generally differ from those passed on adults. The motivating principle in dealing with the young is to substitute care and training for punishment, and to create conditions inspiring better future behavior.

Delegations from foreign nations come to Sweden to examine its penal system and the workings of its humane program. They express special interest in the open prisons, where guards are not armed, windows not barred, and where nothing prevents a prisoner from quietly strolling away over the fields. It may be doubted if for a long time to come many other countries will be in a position to adopt the Swedish penal ways. The regeneration program, with its emphasis on leniency, is easier to put over among a homogeneous people, with relatively good living standards for all, in a nation where personal decency, honesty, and law-abiding attitudes are in such general high repute.

HONORING THE DEAD

It is not only governmental agencies that work for the social welfare in Sweden. Numerous private associations and scores of public-spirited individuals devote much time to good works. One such person who started a movement that has spread to foreign countries is Alma Hedin, the spinster sister of Sweden's famous explorer Sven Hedin. The great work, which has made the declining years of tens of thousands comfortable and happy, bears the gentle name of The Flower Fund.

In May, 1921, Alma Hedin founded in Stockholm what she called Blomster Fonden for the purpose of honoring the dead "in a more worthy and lasting way." To her, it seemed sinfully wasteful to spend hundreds of dollars in ephemeral flowers at a funeral, when that money could go to relieve the distresses of genteel old persons who still had to endure the business of living. She proposed that instead of sending expensive wreaths to a funeral, friends and admirers of the deceased should remit checks to be applied to building apartment houses for old people in straitened circumstances.

The first membership roll was signed by Archbishop Söderblom, by several provincial governors, by writers and artists, and by some political leaders. Naturally a howl of opposition rose from the florists, and their protests fanned the publicity campaign.

At first the gifts came in slowly. But three and a half years after the first donation was received, construction work was begun on a large apartment house on a site donated by the City of Stockholm. Then another rose beside it. Within a few years six more were built in another part of the city. The idea spread to other municipalities in Sweden, and to Denmark, Norway, and Finland.

Today in death announcements in Swedish papers one often reads the lines "Remember the Flower Fund," which means that the family of the deceased requests "no flowers," but would be grateful for a check sent "In memory of ———." The Flower Fund office accepts any gift above 5 kronor. Cards bearing the information that one has contributed are sent to the family of the deceased, but the amount of the check is not revealed.

The people who live in these Flower Fund apartments pay a very low rent. The apartments are all conveniently modern and there is nothing whatever institutional about them, though the occupants receive a certain amount of nursing if they are ill. On the ground floor there is a nonprofit restaurant, where those who do not care to cook their meals may eat good nourishing food at small expense. In 1939 a tasty, adequate meal could be had for twenty-five cents.

At my request Miss Hedin took me to luncheon at one of the houses, and after we had had coffee on the common sun veranda on the roof, we called on some of the old persons she knew personally. Two of the couples were surrounded by heirloom furniture and family portraits. All we met seemed not only contented, but grateful not to have to live with their children, or in an old folks' home in the country. For they had been city dwellers, and they still relished the bright lights and the advantages of urban life.

Except for inheritance taxes on estates beyond a certain value, dying is little more expensive than being born in Sweden. In the cities the majority of the dead are cremated for a small fee at the municipal crematories, which have been designed by first rate architects. Since the coffins are to be quickly consumed by flames, there is no point in having any but the simplest wooden caskets, which are generally concealed by a simple blanket of flowers.

MORE SWEETNESS AND LIGHT

THE SWEDES do not expect the lowliest man to live by bread alone. Besides their efforts to provide the material blessings of solid social security, better public health, and better housing, they are not unmindful of the hyacinths that nourish the national soul. The State Railways have gradually developed a garden that is the largest in Europe. It covers more than ten thousand acres of beautifully planted ground. This is the total area of all the flower gardens and parks that have been laid out above the railway stations from the fertile South to stops far above the Polar Circle. When one descends from a railway carriage in Sweden he steps into a flower garden, varying in aspect according to seasons and latitudes. Extensive or diminutive, each has been designed by expert landscape gardeners according to the immediate terrain and local climatic conditions. In some, evergreen shrubs and bulbs have special emphasis, in others, annuals. Tulips and daffodils in early spring are followed by larkspur and snapdragons and then dahlias and chrysanthemums. Some stations specialize in roses. In the farthest north the fuchsias and begonias and anemones that bloom out-of-doors in summer must be taken up and conserved in hothouses in the nine winter months. Americans who are accustomed to views of concrete, grime, and ugliness when they arrive at a railway terminal, often find the station gardens of Sweden the most impressive of all the admirable Scandinavian innovations.

As long ago as the 1860's the Swedish State Railways began to lay out these welcoming, verdant plots. Since 1939, approximately half a million new perennials, a hundred thousand hedge plants, twenty thousand fruit trees and a hundred and fifty thousand rose bushes have been planted. Though a million kronor is spent annually on the maintenance of the gardens and though the horticultural department of the State Railways includes a regular staff of more than fifty expert gardeners, the splendid result is largely achieved by the voluntary work of the railway personnel in spare hours, from the humblest workman to the station-master himself. These employees cheerfully give their time to cultivating, pruning, mowing, entirely without recompense, simply for the pleasure of adding brightness to their spot of the world.

The Swedes themselves look upon the Government's appropriations to the horticultural department of its State Railways as a most rewarding investment. Now the fame of the Swedish garden is spreading to an international public in Europe. In August, 1948, at a meeting of world master gardeners in London, Gösta Reuterswärd, the head of the Swedish Railways garden development, was asked to exhibit photographs of various types of gardens and parks in hamlets, towns, and cities.

Other Government ventures into the realm of sweetness and light range from recent grants for works of art in the common schools to the long-time subsidies for opera and drama. The excellence of the Swedish dramatic training is obvious to Americans who have seen our two top female cinema stars, Greta Garbo and Ingrid Bergman, as well as Signe Hasso, who is perhaps a still better actress.* All three got their training on scholarships at the State-supported

---

* See section on Stockholm, City of Space and Grace.

Royal Dramatic Theater in Stockholm. Six of the Metropolitan Opera stars, including the leading lyric tenor, Jussi Björling, came direct from the Swedish Royal Opera.

That Sweden, with a population approximately that of the state of Ohio, can maintain such high standards in its theatrical and operatic productions is due in great measure to Government appropriations of some $650,000 a year. This sum is divided among the Royal Opera and the Royal Dramatic Theater in Stockholm, the Lyric and Dramatic Theaters in Göteborg, and the Municipal Theaters in Malmö and Norrköping-Linköping. Because the Swedes believe that opera and high-class dramatic productions should be made available at moderate prices for the general public, one pays approximately a third or fourth of what one does in the United States for the same class of entertainment.

A People's Park Organization was established in 1905 to advise on the creation and maintenance of recreation and amusement parks "for the people by the people." Now there are some 160 of these parks distributed throughout Sweden. The popular theater movement is under the organization's direction. More than thirty different theatrical companies, with a personnel of over eight hundred actors and actresses, tour the country and present classical and modern plays as well as musical comedies. The Government began contributing to the improvement of the People's Recreation Parks in 1931. In 1939 the total attendance at the park theaters was more than four million. Men and women living in remote towns occasionally have the opportunity to see Sweden's foremost actors as special guest stars of these park theaters.

In 1947 a new national association called Art in the Schools was founded, with Crown Prince Gustav Adolf as honorary president, to acquire paintings and sculpture to adorn schoolhouses devoid of artistic embellishments. Two hundred schools in different parts of the country are to benefit from an allotment of some $2,500 worth of pictures and statuary for each school. The purpose is to stimulate appreciation of art in children, teachers, and citizens of the community. The Government has been asked for grants amounting to 2,000,000 kronor extending over a ten years' period.

A bulletin from Sweden dated May 1, 1949, comments on the noise abatement campaign. Sweden is considered a pioneer country in the battle against noise in the cities. It is the only country that has a special "anti-noise statute" incorporated in the building code. The statute was made a law two years ago, and American authorities recently have asked for a copy of the ordinance so that it can be used as a pattern for a similar regulation in the United States. The Swedish law, however, is now regarded as ripe for a revision. For that reason, five hundred dwellings in Stockholm and other cities will be subjected to a careful examination. The buildings, of every conceivable type and house plan, will be visited by medical experts and specialists in acoustics who will interrogate the inhabitants about the exact kind of disturbances they are suffering from, if any, and will take careful measurements of the so-called "objective disturbance level" in the homes.

One recent service which serves to make it less strained for families to have large families is known as Domestic Assistant Service. Since 1946 the Government has set aside funds to provide home-assistants to act as housewives in critical situations, in case of a mother's illness, for instance, or a compelling absence from the home. For families with three children or more the service is free. Families with less children pay for it. In 1948, the salaries of some 2,000 home-assistants were paid for by the Government.

INFORMAL EDUCATION

THE ADVANCED and wholesome state of the general welfare could not have been achieved except for intensification of democratic education. Little need be said of formal education in Sweden, except that it is extremely good, with excellent facilities on the whole. Like the other Scandinavians, the Swedes are one hundred per cent literate. For a century (since 1842) school attendance has been compulsory by law. Since the coming into power of the Social Democratic Party in 1924, more and more opportunities for higher education have opened for the less well-to-do. The cleverest sons of workingmen find available numerous scholarships at the universities of Uppsala, Lund, and Stockholm. Adult or continuation education is almost a passion in Sweden. The great popular movements, like the Labor Federation, the cooperatives, and the temperance orders, have taken the initiative and original responsibility for continuance education. While in most countries adult education is promoted for the people as a kind of philanthropic gesture, in Scandinavia it has been developed by the people themselves for the people through the people's organizations.

The study circle as a phase of adult education originated in 1902 in the university town of Lund. The man responsible for its creation was Oscar Olsson, a temperance leader undergraduate. By lectures and printed articles Dr. Olsson, who is sometimes called "the father of the study circle," became also the chief stimulator of its early development. Today the study circles in Sweden exist on a scale that no other nation approaches. In 1946 there was a total of 22,915 different study groups functioning in Sweden, with an active enrollment of 263,217 persons. The members were studying everything from Swedish literature and foreign languages to political science, psychology, and higher arithmetic. Enrolled in various courses were lumberjacks, industrial workers, dairymen, stenographers, and farmers' wives.

The lecture method of imparting knowledge also plays a significant part in Swedish adult education. The first modern lecture institute was organized in 1880 as the Stockholm Working Men's Institute. Today some 600 different societies about the country arrange approximately 8,500 public lectures a year.

Correspondence schools of many categories do a flourishing business in Sweden. About 300,000 persons subscribe annually to a variety of correspondence courses.

The Swedish Broadcasting Corporation conducts educational courses by radio, selling what is known as Listeners' Letters to subscribers to assist them in keeping up with the lessons. In 1945 some 70,000 families subscribed for letters prepared for a first year course in English.

Long before the study circle, the correspondence course, the public lecture, and the radio became educational innovations, the Folk High School, adopted from Denmark, was raising the cultural sights of farmers' sons and daughters.

In 1868 three Folk High Schools were established by farmers' associations in the south of Sweden. The avowed purpose was "to give education for the soul and useful schooling for life." In 1949 over sixty of these schools exist in various parts of the country almost invariably situated in the rural districts in attractive surroundings.* The aim is still to "awaken, kindle, and enlighten" the minds of young men and women, and the emphasis is laid on instruction "which inspires and fosters personal thinking and integrity of character." Though at first these schools were exclusively for farmers' sons and daughters, now less than sixty per cent of the students come from farms, while over thirty per cent are young industrial workers. One of the most famous of the schools, Brunnsvik in Dalarna, specializes in training future labor leaders. Its best-known teacher was Rickard Sandler, who brought into being The Workers' Education Association in 1912 and who later became foreign minister.

Six thousand students, ranging in age from about eighteen to twenty-four, are received each year, and yet there is always a long waiting list of applicants. Most of the students have been working at some job for two to six years before returning for the continuance education. All the Folk High Schools receive financial support from the Government, which regards them as an excellent investment, paying rich dividends in imponderables. For young people who attend come away not only enriched with certain facts but presumably with qualities of "sense and discernment, poise and politeness."

For many years the Swedes have carried their message and desire for peace into the schools and the Swedish Department of Education charges the teachers thus in its publication, *Municipal School Tasks:*

Teaching in history must be so planned and performed that its guiding theme is the development of peaceful culture and social order through the ages. . . . Its aim is to give a true picture of past times, and narratives and descriptions of war history must therefore be included. In such cases it should always be stressed that the conviction has been growing ever stronger as culture advances, that war is an evil and a curse and attention should be drawn to the sufferings that have always followed in the wake of war. The difference between wars waged in defense of a country's independence and just cause and wars prompted by the desire to conquer or other similar motives, should also be impressed upon the pupils.

The teacher shall take pains to counteract hate and hostility against other peoples and further the knowledge that peace and mutual understanding between all countries is a basic condition for the common advancement of human-

---

* See section "The Spell of Värmland."

ity. The children should be made to feel very strongly that there are heroes also in peace work and that these have also shown courage and self-sacrifice and made themselves deserving of the gratefulness and admiration of their people by contributing to its advancement.

In the common school history teaching should be concentrated to the lives of important personalities and significant facts and events, in the first place, such that have served advancement and culture.

Where the Swedes once learned French or German as their foreign language, now English is the compulsory foreign language taught in the schools.

TAXES AND A CERTAIN MEASURE OF PUBLIC OWNERSHIP

NATURALLY IN A COUNTRY where social services have been developed as they have in Sweden taxes are high. In 1939 Swedish taxes were considerably higher than they were in the United States. A man with an income of $6,000 paid approximately one-fourth of his net to the Government and the city in taxes. During the war taxes rose. A new tax law passed since the cessation of war grants reductions to ninety-eight per cent of the population. By the new law, all real and personal property assessed at 30,000 kronor or less is exempt from Government tax. Both inheritance and corporation taxes are slightly increased.

The major tax burden is on the rich, who naturally do a certain amount of grumbling, but on the whole they assume an attitude of patriotic resignation and console themselves with the old homely Swedish saying: "If a thing tastes extra good it costs something." And they do not speak viciously against the Government's ventures into business, for the profits accruing to the State help to keep income taxes from being higher than they are, and most of the State businesses or partnerships were implemented when the Conservatives were in control.

A certain measure of public ownership exists in Sweden and functions without criticism. Not only the postal, but the telegraph and telephone services are run by the Government, and the most conservative Swede cannot see why the two latter should be considered more socialistic than the first. Both the telegraph and telephone systems are highly efficient, and though moderate rates are charged, the Government makes an annual profit that is relatively high on its capital investment.

Because Sweden's industrialization came late, several public utilities were begun as Government enterprises during Conservative regimes, because private initiative did not possess the necessary capital or did not care to take the risks involved. Thus the Swedish Government built all the main railroad lines, though a few of the feeders are still owned and operated by private corporations.

Some of the electric power stations are owned by private interests, and some of them are owned by the Government. As a rule waterworks and gas plants are municipally owned, as are local bus and streetcar lines. The great majority of the timber lands and the mines are privately owned, but in some developments the Government is a partner. Occasionally, to provide employment in depressed areas, the Government runs ironworks and sawmills. Recently it has completed a large Government-owned steel mill in Luleå.

The Government holds a monopoly on the importation and manufacture of tobacco, while the retail distribution remains in private hands. The Government likewise holds a monopoly in both the importation and distribution of alcoholic beverages, though local breweries and distilleries are in private hands. All profits, however, above the fixed rate of return on capital go to the State. This is also true of wines and liquors sold in hotels and restaurants. (There are no saloons or bars in Sweden. One buys his household supplies at regular Government liquor stores.) The large Government revenue which accrues from the tobacco and alcohol monopolies goes a long way towards meeting the costs of the various social services.

The Government owns the radio facilities, while a private concern controlled by the combined press of the various political parties arranges the programs. One of the delectable features of daily living in Sweden is the complete absence of commercials on the radio. All advertising by radio is prohibited. The expenses of broadcasting are taken care of by annual license fees of $2.50 for each receiving set. In 1948 the number of licensed radios reached the 2,000,000 mark.

Except, however, for public utilities, tobacco, and alcoholic beverages, the Government has not ventured far in public ownership, though in the last few years there has been some agitation for making the sale of gasoline a Government business. The Conservatives strongly oppose any further participation of the State in business. But few indeed are they who claim that private enterprise could do any of the existing public-ownership jobs better than the Government does them, and no one advocates a return to private ownership.

Because of the very high taxes on large incomes and because the State has a small stake in industry, the number of individual Swedish millionaires is on the decrease. Judged according to tax valuations, in 1947 there were only 809 millionaires (a million kronor amounted to $278,000 in 1947) as against 1,018 the previous year. Persons with half a million crowns also were becoming fewer; but all the smaller categories of fortunes from 300,000 crowns down to 20,000 had become considerably more numerous. To most economists the gentle redistribution of wealth was healthy and sound. Some rich men of their own accord gave away property and sizeable sums for charity and worthwhile institutions that took them out of the millionaire class. Some others divided their holdings among their heirs to avoid the heavy death duties that would have to be paid out at their decease.

While the number of millionaires decreased, in 1948 Sweden's industrial production, most of which is privately owned, was forty-three per cent above that of the peace-time year of 1937, which was considered a very good one.

At the end of 1948, the Swedish treasury was in healthy condition. More than 437,000,000 kronor were collected in taxes from tobacco alone that year, and this amount went a considerable way in helping to pay for the increased social welfare services. Almost double the amount for defense was earmarked for the Ministry of Social Welfare: for old-age pensions, sickness insurance societies, maternity aid, free vacation travel for children, etc. So Sweden was still looking hopefully forward into 1950 and beyond to a peaceful solution for the Great Powers' contention.

When the budget estimates for the fiscal year running from July 1, 1949, were prepared, they showed a surplus of 721,000,000 kronor or about $200,000,000, while taxes remained unchanged. Some of the surplus is to be used to finance public capital investments, unless the strong probability of war necessitates its use for armament.

Many of the Conservatives are firmly opposed to the State's going further into industry, though they have been urging the Government to go into the hotel business, as the Finnish Government did before 1939, by building more hotels at the tourist centers, which private capital considers too great a risk.

While the cooperatives, which are really stock companies owned by a mass of individuals, have been of invaluable benefit to the Swedish general welfare, by no means have they driven private business out of any given field. There are more than 125,000 small producing concerns which, together with the small retailers, provide a living for a fourth of the Swedish people. The privately owned shops still do some eighty per cent of the retail business. The individualistic Swedes have such a goodly regard for private enterprise that few have any desire to set up an all-cooperative State.

Swedes seem to have arrived at just about the right mixture of socialism with their capitalism to suit the needs and tastes of the people. They have achieved a golden mean between free enterprise and State control, between what holds the most good for the individual working on his own and the most good for the general welfare.

17.

Labor and Capital

THE CORDIAL RELATIONS and mutual respect that exist between capital and labor struck me forcibly in 1939 and again in the postwar period of 1946. It was Crown Prince Gustav Adolf who arranged my first interview with the head of the Swedish Labor Federation. In the course of our conversation, when he received me at the Royal Palace, he expressed surprise that I had not yet met August Lindberg. "But that should be remedied at once," he said. "Lindberg is one of our finest and ablest men. The King and I both admire him very much. He and his wife dined with my father here at the palace last Thursday. Would it be convenient to call on him tomorrow?" The Crown Prince straightway rang for his equerry, who telephoned Mr. Lindberg and made the appointment.

"While the motive force of the Swedish labor movement has always been the benefiting of the working class," the Crown Prince said, "as it grew in power its leaders recognized more clearly their mighty responsibilities to the whole nation. There has been no taint of 'class-interest fanaticism' in their leadership. By their prudence and moderation the trade unions have really been a wonderfully stabilizing agency in the labor market. And many Swedish employers have come to esteem the good faith, the fair-dealing, and the constructive ideas of the union leaders."

August Lindberg received me at labor headquarters the next day. He was a tall, handsome, reddish-blond man in his middle fifties. His splendid lumberjack physique and his sympathetic way of speaking both inspired confidence. Trustworthiness and compassion were qualities that seemed ingrained in his make-up. As the hour went by, the words "integrity" and "nobility" came to mind along with "strength" and "modesty."

When I asked him about his education, Lindberg smiled and said, "Like a character I remember in a Jack London novel, I hardly knew what the inside of a school looked like."

August Lindberg was largely self-educated with the help of the labor study circles. But in his childhood he had attended a short-term backwoods school until he was ten, when he began to work twelve hours a day at a sawmill. His job was to fetch timber and pile it. "You must be very strong for that kind of work," he said reminiscently.

Born on October 16, 1885, Lindberg had inherited his good constitution from his father and his grandfather, who had both been employed in an ironworks. Now, for his health's sake, because of his present sedentary life, he walked four miles to his office instead of taking a bus. He could not afford an automobile, since his salary was only $2,000 a year. Though he was head of a powerful federation, with large capital reserves and over 1,000,000 dues-paying members in a nation of less than 7,000,000 persons, he himself did not think it odd that a labor leader should be paid no more than a shop foreman. In 1939 $2,000 was also the standard annual salary for labor federation heads in the other two Scandinavian countries. I could not help but compare the figure with the salaries of such union leaders as John L. Lewis and Petrillo.

During our conversation I said to Mr. Lindberg that some Conservatives claimed that so much social service would make the people stale, take away dynamic qualities, and undermine the spiritual well-being of the nation.

Mr. Lindberg reacted with a mild how-can-that-be expression. "But," he protested politely, "an improved economic standard of the working class increases the cultural standard too, and with that the spiritual. Certainly the Swedish people are better off spiritually than they were forty years ago. For instance, when I was a youth, the working classes bought alcohol, now it's books. Oh, no, I assure you, the rise in real wages has not resulted in lack of spiritual growth—in fact, quite the contrary."

As the Crown Prince had sent me to the head of the Swedish Labor Federation, so Mr. Lindberg in turn telephoned and arranged an interview with Gustav Söderlund, head of the Swedish Employers' Association. "But you will only know the half of it, unless you talk with him," Lindberg said with a frank smile. "Söderlund is an able fellow and most personable. We are good friends. We spent a lot of time at Saltsjöbaden together last year."

In the United States the bulk of employers have not yet organized to treat effectively with labor. But in Sweden, back in 1902, only four years after the founding of the Labor Federation (LO), the Swedish Employers' Association came into existence to offset the workers' waxing power. Shortly the employers began their counter-attacks by declaring several lockouts against union members. In 1909, when the Labor Federation tested its strength by declaring a general strike in response to a number of lockouts, a tremendous battle between the forces was fought. After considerable suffering to the laborers and great financial losses on both sides, the employers finally won. It was not until after the boom years of 1919-20 that labor began to feel its full might. From 1919 to 1929 union membership rose from 200,000 to more than 500,000, and collective agreements increased by three hundred per cent. Since 1931 employers have made no attempts at strikebreaking. By the outbreak of World War II more workers in proportion to population belonged to trade unions in Sweden than in any other country in the world. In 1941 trade union membership passed the 1,000,000 mark. Yet, today, if the Labor Federation moves against a single industry, it knows it must face the combined forces of the Employers' Association.

Gustav Söderlund was an affable man, who might have doubled for Spencer Tracy, the cinema actor. Though his salary from the industrialists was exactly six times that of Lindberg's from the unions, he had much the same background as his opposite number in labor. He grew up as a small boy in Dalarna, where his father worked in the same sawmill with August Lindberg. But he had received considerably more formal education than had the labor leader.

"In Sweden," Söderlund said, "labor has far more potential power than in the United States. It has the advantage of not being split into two jealous camps like A. F. of L. and C. I. O. It is all under one federation. It possesses its own press with thirty-four daily labor papers and a circulation of more than half a million copies. Swedish labor has its own political party, the Social Democratic, and does not divide its votes between Democrats and Republicans. The Social

Democratic party is almost as large as all the other political parties combined. So you can see the employers have a mighty opposite, and we have to be wary of our procedures." He paused, and then said, with the knowing smile of one born in a workman's family, "You have to treat workers very carefully. 'Give, give,' they keep asking. We might give them the factory and they wouldn't be satisfied. So we have to make them feel they've earned what we give."

In 1938, when the leaders of both sides got together and talked things over for several weeks at the seaside resort near Stockholm, the result was known as the Saltsjöbaden Basic Agreement.

"You see," said Söderlund, "we know each other well enough to call one another by first names, and that makes argument easier. We might argue around the council table all the working hours of the day, but at night we dined together and played cards or billiards."

This peace treaty between capital and labor, which was signed five days before Christmas in 1938, provides guarantees to the public against interruption of essential services and delaying strikes and lockouts—all without Government interference.

"Labor wage contracts," Söderlund explained, "are automatically renewed unless they are denounced three months in advance of their termination date. All factory-owners in Sweden stick together. If a labor union should make utterly unfair or unreasonable demands, the whole bunch could be fired."

Both Swedish employers and employees, I learned, prefer to keep Government out of their dealings if possible. Swedes like to try things out privately and then, if they work successfully, to confirm them by law.

By 1928, following Denmark and Norway, Sweden had set up a Labor Court. The function of this court is not to prohibit strikes or to settle disputes over wages, but to interpret labor contracts, of which more than 11,000 exist today. While a contract is in force, both lockouts and strikes are forbidden by law. The Swedish Labor Court has absolute jurisdiction over labor relations based on written contracts. The seven judges are appointed by the Government, as are all judges in Sweden. One judge must have had experience in labor mediation and two must be lawyers with some judicial experience. Two are nominated by the employers, two by the Labor Federation.

During its first ten years this court decided 1,650 cases brought before it by trade unions or individual workers, and 309 cases brought up by employers. Rarely do the proceedings in each case take more than an hour, and final decisions are announced within ten days at most. Up to the present time some two-thirds of all decisions have been unanimous. Both labor and capital must accept the validity of the court without question, for there is no appeal.

Though employers have the theoretical prerogative to employ and dismiss as they deem fit, the demand for a closed shop has no point, because labor in Sweden is virtually one hundred per cent organized. This high percentage of organization disposes of picketing. Swedish labor does not indulge in "sit-down" strikes. The American practice of "feather-bedding," that is forcing employers to hire more workers than are needed, is completely unknown and would be looked upon as unprincipled. Since 1938, except for one ill-advised serious strike in the metalworkers' union, which was engineered by the Communists and which ended in defeat for the workers, Sweden has enjoyed remarkable industrial peace.

"Since 1936," in August Lindberg's words, "the trade union movement has a range which does not allow it to act without consideration for the justified interests of other social groups. In consequence, the trade union movement must work for the healthy development and strengthening of Swedish economic life in general. Only in this way can the working class hope to secure better economic and social conditions."

A great difference in intention between Swedish Social Democracy and Soviet Communism was sharply pointed up to me in 1946 by Gunnar Andersson, who had been selected to succeed August Lindberg as head of the Labor Federation, but whose untimely death came before he could take office. When a commission of Soviet labor "experts" visited Sweden and examined conditions of the workers in their homes and in the factories, their summing-up comment to Mr. Andersson was as astonishing to him as it was disturbing. With a slight trace of menace the Communists declared, "The standard of living of the Swedish worker is far too high. It must come down."

The comparative harmony that exists between theoretically opposing political forces in Sweden was never more strikingly illuminated for me than in New York at a supper in August, 1948, when the brilliant political scientist and Uppsala University lecturer, Dr. Gunnar Hecksher, who has always voted the Conservative ticket, told me he would be happy to see August Lindberg, the long-time labor leader, made prime minister.

On August 7 and 8, 1948, the Swedish Labor Federation celebrated its fiftieth anniversary with representatives from twelve foreign nations attending the festivities. From the founding in 1898 it has grown to a membership of 1,200,000, which means that more than one person out of six of the total population, including children and the aged, belongs to the federation. Today there is no country in the world where labor holds such power, since it has control of the Government and possesses large cash reserves in its banks. Yet labor has not been guilty of taking unfair advantage of its strong position. It has been scrupulously careful not to injure the capitalistic goose that lays golden eggs for the masses as well as for the privileged. While wages have gradually risen with the years, in no form of activity has the scale gone to such extreme heights as in the United States. Where a bricklayer in New York now gets $23 a day, in Stockholm he earns about $8. Workers in Sweden do not feel that they must own automobiles. Very few of them do. They ride bicycles to work or take a bus or a streetcar, as did Prime Minister Hansson for ten years. Swedish workers like first to own their own homes and furnish them well. And then they may save up for a little boat.

The laborites in the Government are level-headed fellows, who for the most part have grown more conservative as they have become more powerful. When Norman Thomas and other Socialist leaders visit Sweden, where the power is in labor's hands, and find so little socialization of industry, they ask reprovingly, "Why don't you socialize?" But the labor Cabinet just smiles with quiet assurance and replies that it is socializing just as fast and as much as is good for the commonwealth. The Social Democratic party is committed to an ideal of socialism, but only to the extent that "the satisfaction of needs is thereby furthered in a systematic manner." As practiced in Sweden, socialism means little more than social security, a good standard of living for the workers, an opportunity for the clever of any background to rise, and a social structure where ability and achievement supersede financial rating as criteria. In other words, the Swedish Social Democrats practice what citizens of the United States like the world at large to think they believe in.

V

SWEDISH CHARACTER AND TEMPERAMENT

18.

The Swedes Themselves

*If of the long life
one single day was left me
Then I would seek
the most beautiful thing in the world.
The most beautiful thing in the world
is just integrity,
But without that life is not life
or reality.*

—KARIN BOYE

WHEN I WAS first received by the Crown Prince Gustav Adolf in March of 1939, he said to me, "If you should ever write about us, please don't merely praise us. Do point out our faults as a foreign observer like yourself may see them. We know we still have plenty wrong with us and we really don't want to become smug."

The day before I flew from Stockholm in September of 1946, after a summer of gathering postwar impressions, at a press conference with reporters from six Swedish newspapers I was urged to point out flaws. I did so, to my regret, for some of the papers played up the minor criticisms rather than the major admirations. I should have recalled the experience of a noted American journalist, who, after waxing eloquent on Sweden's manifold virtues, finally confessed, on being pressed to say something derogatory, that Swedes did not know how to make a good cup of tea. The next morning he was astounded to see his long adulatory interview headlined in one paper: "Swedes have abominable tea."

It is always hazardous to make judgments on an alien people, and it may seem ungracious to speak anything but praise of the Swedes, who have created such an admirable design for living. But

247

because I so greatly admire what they have achieved, I have the temerity to look critically, as well as sympathetically, at the Swedes, who have the natural defects of their qualities.

Though they are not easy to analyze, the Swedes are relatively an uncomplex people, largely because of their remarkable homogeneity. The best Swedish virtues are deeply ingrained. Many of their seeming blemishes might be eradicated within a generation or two, as their ancient national vice, intemperance, was considerably curbed in a short space of years.

From Viking days foreigners have expressed respect for the Swedish people. In 1857 Bayard Taylor, that shrewd American observer of other lands, wrote: "The more I see of the Swedes, the more I am convinced that there is no kinder, simpler, and honester people in the world." Of the Swedes of West Bothnia especially, he went on to say, "The people of this region are noble specimens of the physical man—tall, broad-shouldered, large-limbed, ruddy and powerful. . . . It is exhilarating to see such people, whose digestion is sound, whose nerves are tough as whip cord, whose blood runs in a strong full stream, whose impulses are perfectly natural, who are good without knowing it, and who are happy without trying to be so."

In the 1930's Cicely Hamilton, the British author, was surprised to find that despite generations of excessive drinking among their forebears the Swedes were "indeed an exceptionally fine race physically." "Taken all around, in all ages and stations of life," she considered them "the best-looking people" she had ever met in her extensive travels.

Physically the Swedes are tall and athletic in build—as a race the tallest people in Europe, with the longest heads. For the most part they are fair-haired and blue-eyed, and they possess an innate dignity of bearing that is to be remarked even in the children. Their little boys are among the handsomest in the world, though the women say, "So rarely do our men live up to the wonderful promise of our little boys!" Yet perhaps there are proportionately more fine-looking men of all classes to be seen in Sweden than in any other land. And those who are homely generally possess what Prince Wilhelm calls "honest, dependable features." Multiple Ingrid Bergmans and Greta Garbos without make-up or dramatic talent are to be observed among shop assistants, schoolteachers, airline stewardesses, ladies of title, and factory workers.

Disputing Lord Byron's belief that "the cold in clime are the cold in blood," Bayard Taylor declared that Swedes are "only cold through superior self-control." While many Swedes, as well as many foreigners, would agree with Byron, none would fail to admit that self-control is perhaps the most significant common denominator of the Swedish people.

Not a passionate or mercurial people, they are yet much too sensitive to be called stolid. In temperament the Swede is the very opposite of the excitable Latin. He cannot bear scenes. In moments of exasperation he generally remains quiet. If someone's action is boorish, a Swede commonly chides him with the utterly devastating rebuke, "Perhaps you left school too early."

Swedes are well aware of the dividends a controlled temper pays. The ninety-year-old King Gustav himself is a fine example of self-discipline. He does not attribute his longevity and vitality so much to his tennis playing as to a rule he has followed for seven decades. Since his youth, every morning when he gets out of bed the King says to himself, "Man, do not get angry." This maxim he tries to apply the rest of the day, regardless of all the annoyances and stupidities he may encounter. He firmly believes that his long training in not allowing himself to become cross or excited has helped to keep him mentally and spiritually young, and has had a most happy effect on his constitution.

Moderation, then, is a prime quality in this land where hotheads and ruthlessly rugged individualists do not prosper, and where a high respect is maintained for the dignity of the individual in all classes.

The Swede is an extremely practical fellow, who knows how to reckon with the hard, cold facts of life and to make the best of them. He thinks first and speaks afterwards. But when a Swede does speak, he can generally be depended upon to keep his word. A handshake over a transaction may mean just as much as a document signed in triplicate. A Swede who breaks his word is never forgiven, but always held despicable.

As Swedish voices are well modulated, Swedish gestures are few. Naturally patient and taciturn, the Swede can yet become eloquent, as well as indignant. He cannot bear to see injustice. He will not stand for cruelty to a dumb beast. And while ordinarily the most peaceable of men, he will fight tenaciously for a principle, and not lose his discretion either. Like Hamlet, though he is not splenitive and rash, there is something dangerous in a Swede that is not to be trifled with too far. Gustavus Vasa once remarked that the Swedes are "a sluggish people full of hot impulses."

While that primordial beast that lurks in the human animal's breast has been pretty well subdued in the Swede, the self-taming process has by no means degenerated him. He is not soft or in any sense effeminate. He is something like a rangey thoroughbred dog of gentle disposition, that will resort to fight only on extreme provocation, and then give a fine account of himself.

Though the virile Swedes have courage aplenty—I have personally witnessed Swedes risking their own lives to save the lives of both men and beasts—they have an especial horror and hatred of war as a thing unworthy of civilized man. True, in the seventeenth and eighteenth centuries Sweden was involved in wars of her own making, as well as in those forced upon her; but since 1814 she has been at peace and managed to stave off invasion and to retain her official neutrality when world conflagrations raged on every side.

Swedes have contempt or distrust for anything that smacks of old German military strut and swagger. And many deplore American motion pictures with gangster protagonists. Unlike American small-fry, Swedish boys are not likely to find toy swords or toy revolvers in their Christmas stockings. Such antisocial playthings are not manufactured in this country noted for its production of antiaircraft guns and other armaments. This lack of toy weapons for little boys does not mean that the Swedish youth is not trained to be expert in the forest with hunting rifles and knives, when he is old enough to use them properly. But it does have significance in the blessed fact that there is no serious problem of juvenile delinquency in Sweden.

Their championship records in Olympic games year after year are well known. In athletics Swedish taste runs to field sports, in which they excel. Perhaps no people spend more time in the development and care of their bodies than Swedes. They well know the value of gymnastics for the systematic development of muscular power. Its inventor, Pehr Henrik Ling, was famous long before Bayard Taylor visited Sweden in 1856. But the health-conscious Swedes never look upon work-outs in a gymnasium as a proper substitute for the exhilaration of exercise out-of-doors.

The Swede has a devotion to nature. He feels especially close to the forest. This does not mean the same thing as "closeness to the soil," though Swedes are good farmers and sixty-five per cent of the population live in the country or small towns. Something more than earth is involved in this attunement with the dark and silent forests. A Swede seems to come into harmony with himself in the woods, and here he is at his best, whether companioned or alone, whether he is hiking, camping, shooting, collecting specimens for his herbarium, or merely meditating. Lumberjacks spend most of their lives in the forest, and these steadfast men, tall, silent, strong like the trees, contribute a special quota of stamina to the national health and character. On holidays city laborers hike or cycle to the woods. Business and professional men have lodges or shacks in the forests, and periodically retire there for refreshment of soul as well as body. It is, I think, this ready and close communion with nature that keeps the sophisticated, well-to-do Swede from becoming effete.

The Swede has a great love for the sea, too. He makes an excellent sailor, and has a natural knack for handling boats. To know the real Swede behind the conventional society mask, go sailing with him in summer, if you can't go with him on skis through a wintry wood.

A Swede is not ashamed to confess his pleasure in flowers. Many business executives keep fresh cut flowers on their desks in winter as well as summer, though it may be only a single rosebud or a small bunch of violets. Virtually every worker's cottage has flowering plants on the window sills. School children know the botanical, as well as the common, names of hundreds of field and wood flowers, for botany is not only a required course in Swedish schools, but a favorite one.

Besides a predilection for botany and forestry, Swedes have an uncommon aptitude for mechanics and science. They are gifted in invention as well as construction and possess remarkable manual dexterity. There is a common saying that every second Swede is an engineer. The loss of a hand would be peculiarly tragic to a Swede, because he makes such excellent use of his hands, whether wielding a surgeon's scalpel or a woodman's saw, or holding a delicate crystal vase against an emery engraving wheel.

Whatever his profession or trade, the Swede is more than apt to do a good honest job. He almost never attempts what he cannot do well. He may be slow and deliberate, but he is thorough, oh, how thorough! and he refuses to get in a swivet.

At dinner one evening an American representative of an internationally known firm handed me a slip on which he had traced a Swedish worker's day. It ran as follows:

> Gets to work at 7:30.
> At 9:00 knocks off for short breakfast of eggs, mush, and fish.
> At 11:30 goes to lunch: roast beef, potatoes, coffee and milk.
> Returns at 12:00 and works until 2:00.
> From 2:00 to 2:15 stops for coffee and cake.
> At 3:30 goes out to smoke.
> At 4:30 stops work and goes home.

Not all employers concede so many intervals for refreshment, but all do give considerable attention to the prevention of industrial fatigue.

Yet with a Labor Government in power now for many years, there is no worship of the worker in Sweden, and there never has been. Even in most tense periods the Swedish leftist intellectuals never made a fetish of the working class. A clear-eyed people, Swedes know their union workers for what they are—good, careful workmen who have a full sense of their rights and duties, who love their homes, and who have about the same aggregation of virtues and vices as the average professional or white-collar man. Swedes do not believe in some mystical goodness in the laboring class any more than does the realistic high bureaucracy of Soviet Russia.

"The Swedish man," observed an English correspondent friend of mine, "knows only what he has been taught. If he has to do a simple thing, he takes a six months' correspondence course. Swedes are often 'over qualified' for their jobs. A man whose job is merely to install telephone cables is expected to know how to build the George Washington Bridge single-handed."

The Swedish housewife is certainly well trained for her work. There is no better housewife in the world than the Swedish, though she is not the *Hausfrau* type of woman. To prepare herself for running a household after marriage, the Swedish girl of good family, even of noble blood, sometimes takes employment in first-class restaurant kitchens, in hotels, in private households, or in nursery schools, and prepares herself thoroughly for the job of being a good wife.

No man or woman can get a degree in agriculture until he has completed two years' service on a farm besides passing his examinations. Young Count Bonde,* who inherited one of the finest castles and estates in Skåne, had to work as laborer for two years on someone else's farm before obtaining his degree from an agricultural college. The young Countess Wachtmeister served two years as a dairy maid before receiving her degree.

By nature Swedes are industrious, and everyone works in Sweden. Even members of the royal family have paying jobs. Prince Wilhelm, the King's second son, is a writer, a book-reviewer, and a photographer, besides owning a large dairy farm on which he lives. His son, Lennart Bernadotte (whose mother was the Grand Duchess Marie of Russia), is in the motion-picture business and also has a profitable small farm. One of Crown Prince Gustav Adolf's sons designs silverware and stage settings. A gentleman in Sweden who has no useful occupation is apt to be looked upon as something of a blackguard.

As a people, Swedes are more law-abiding than any I have met in four continents. "One thing these Swedes won't do," a Georgia college boy on scholarship said to me my first week in Sweden, "and that is break the law." The same justice is meted out to the rich and the powerful in Sweden as to the most humble. Take the case of driving while drinking. It is against the law to drive a car if one has imbibed as much as a glass of sherry. If an accident occurs, the driver is immediately taken to a police station, where a doctor is sent for to test his blood for alcohol. If a millionaire manufacturer or titled estate-owner is found guilty, he goes to jail and serves his sentence just the same as the laborer or the student. A few years ago the socialite wife of a prominent cabinet minister was sentenced to prison for criminal libel in a preface she had

* See section "Skåne, Sweden's Most Opulent Province."

written to a book attacking the prison system and falsely accusing the warden of certain practices of which he was proved innocent. She served her full term.

There is far less need for lawyers in Sweden than in the United States. For the law there is comparatively simple, direct, and without equivocation. All the laws are to be found in one book, clearly codified and indexed. Virtually every rural household possesses a copy, as American households possess copies of a Sears, Roebuck catalogue. A small farmer can read the law for himself, as well as a miner or a corporation board chairman or a countess seeking divorce. One has merely to turn to the proper page and see what concerns his case. Often he can see immediately that the suit would go against him, in which case he does not waste his money on a lawyer's fee. Remarkably full of common sense, these Swedes. No lawyer's shenanigans, no silly technicalities can get around honest interpretations of just laws.

A Swede is proud of his reputation for integrity. He cannot bear the ignominy of being looked down on as a cheat. Cheats are hard to find in Sweden, despite the famous case of Ivar Kreuger, who committed suicide when his global manipulations went awry and were discovered. As businessmen, though honest, Swedes are shrewd. They know values and they demand good value for their money. A Swede does not often get rooked in a business deal. He is conservative and yet progressive, both cautious and far-seeing. He can drive a hard bargain, and he may be exceedingly ungenerous if one fails to meet his obligations. Yet there are no high-pressure, go-getting salesmen in the American huckster sense. Swedes scorn trying to make people buy what they do not need or want, and they despise ballyhoo as much as they do vulgarity.

While not a greedy people, Swedes set considerable store on material wealth, as the Roman historian Tacitus mentioned as early as the year 100, when he wrote: "They are powerful by reason not only of their men and weapons but also of their fleets. Among them wealth enjoys an especial esteem."

Though they are not grasping, by their own admission jealousy is a common vice—not sexual jealousy, but envy of one's neighbor rising high in estate or reputation. They refer to it with ironical self-mockery as "the royal Swedish jealousy," because it is so prevalent. This jealousy is not only professional, where successful colleagues are sometimes damned with faint praise, if not disparaged, but it extends to everyday affairs. Yet envy may have its value in that it stimulates the citizenry to high qualities of performance. One of less ability struggles hard to equal the ability of the more proficient. Envy of a beautiful garden may inspire the neighbors to create better gardens of their own. Jealousy of good breeding makes the less well-bred take on the good manners of their betters.

The Swede is much concerned with making a good appearance. The Swedish proletariat on Sunday makes the best appearance of any laboring class in the world. I remember running into a crowd of workers coming from a football match in a sewing-machine-factory suburb of Jönköping and my delighted surprise at the uniform good cut and quality of the men's topcoats and the smartness with which they wore their fedoras. The chambermaid on Stockholm streets dresses so nearly like the lady that sometimes the only way you can tell the difference is to look at her hands. It would be difficult for a hussy to dress like a hussy in Sweden, for no hussified clothes are to be found in the shops.

The young clerk who goes about in what is called "society" has his clothes made by first-class tailors, just like the banker or industrialist. And not in London is better custom tailoring for both men and women to be found than in Stockholm or Göteborg. A chap who earns a small salary will not hesitate to pay $125 for a suit, and skimp for months to pay for it.

A Swede cannot bear not to conform, and therein lies some of his strength and some of his weakness. Almost a century ago Bayard Taylor noted this pattern of Swedish conformity. "You might stick all the men you see into pasteboard cards, like a row of pins," he wrote, "so precisely are they clothed upon the same model."

This correctness of dress may derive from a strong motive force in a Swede's life: fear of criticism. Swedes care tremendously what their fellows think of them. Far too much so, I think; for fear of disapproval has an obviously constraining effect on these somewhat introverted people. From birth a Swede is trained in doing the right thing, obeying the code, making that proper appearance. He is often so engrossed with the thought of what kind of impression he himself is making that he is only vaguely aware of what his companion is like, even if she is a charming woman. The foreigner often finds this withholding of attention either chilling or disconcerting.

Swedes cannot tolerate any taking of liberties with themselves by their own countrymen or foreigners. At a Rotary Club luncheon in Stockholm there are no nickname-bearing tags and no back-slappings. A Swede is apt to conceal his first name as long as possible. In signing his name he generally prefers to use only initials.

The Swedes say their reserve comes from shyness. And by nature they are shy. (Garbo's shrinking from publicity is no publicity pose. She is painfully shy.) But their reserve also comes from their education. "These poor chaps are bludgeoned with discipline from birth," my English correspondent friend said. "You may live here for years and never get beyond a certain reserve with Swedes." A Kansan born of Swedish parents said on her return from Sweden, "I am glad I went for one thing: I discovered that my father wasn't really queer, he was just Swedish."

Not in England or in the best houses of Boston or Madrid should one mind his manners more than in Sweden. Punctuality is revered as something next to cleanliness. If one is invited to dinner for as early as six o'clock, it is better to ring the doorbell at a minute before the hour rather than a minute after.

In Sweden politeness is a science or an art, as you choose. After meals little boys bow and little girls curtsy and thank their parents for the food. At the end of a dinner party the hostess goes and stands by the drawing-room mantel or piano; each lady guest in turn comes to thank her for the dinner, and to kiss her on the cheek if they are old friends; the gentlemen line up to kiss her hand.

Even the dogs have their code in Sweden. At N.K., the great Stockholm department store, which provides resting mats, leashes, and red drinking bowls in its vestibules for the dogs of shoppers, I saw a dachshund begin to whimper when he discovered his mistress had left him. At first the other chained dogs ignored him, and then, when he did not subside, they turned such a weight of canine disapproval upon him that his whimpering was cut short and the wretched little beast took on an expression of humble, though dignified, contrition. Whereas a Danish dog will make friends with you at once, a Swedish dog is apt to put you coolly in your place if you attempt to pat him on too short an acquaintance.

Though Swedes do take themselves seriously, often they laugh at their own correctness, and tell of Mr. Carlson, who was traveling by himself in a railway compartment facing two Swedes who were friends. One of the men told his companion such a side-splitting story that they both laughed with un-Swedish gusto. Finally Mr. Carlson, in pain at suppressing his mirth, rose, extended his card, and said, "I beg to introduce myself. I could not help but overhear. May I be permitted to join the laughter?"

The formality of Swedish address, always using a title like Herr Director or Herr Consul or Herr Chief Engineer or Herr Book Publisher sounds more than a bit stiff to an American ear. Even the women get the feminine counterpart of their husbands' titles— the admiral's wife becoming Amiralinnan Johansson and the bishop's wife, Biskopinnan Nilsson. In the shops the wife of a consul general expects to be addressed by shopkeepers as Generalkonsulinnan This-or-That. Successful Swedish businessmen, who are not born Baron or Count, and who have no profession like that of architecture or engineering, will often go to no end of trouble and expense to get themselves made consul of, say, Costa Rica or Albania, in order to have "Konsul" engraved on their cards. The distinguished and charming owner of a world-famous manufactory continues in 1948 to have "Konsul" on his cards, because thirty years ago, before he had "arrived," he was appointed Austrian consul at Göteborg; and, though he long ago gave up the office, he still retains the title.

In democratic Sweden where the well-to-do and the humble are so much alike in ideals and physical appearance, such fervor about bourgeois distinctions seems incredible. If you chaff Swedes about such silly devices to gain prestige, they may relate an anecdote of a coastal town where so many shopkeepers got themselves made consuls that there was little distinction for anyone, until the shoemaker got ahead of them by becoming consul for two countries and having to be addressed as "Mr. Double-Consul."

Letters of introduction and recommendation from the right people carry mighty weight in Sweden. Scarcely anywhere else does an important name casually dropped have more effect. Swedes are not particularly good psychologists and do not trust their own casual judgments. Danes seem able to tell instinctively who and what you are, while Norwegians don't give a tinker's damn, any more than Texans do, if they happen to like you. But the Swede moves cautiously, and may entertain you in the degree your connections or attainments merit, after he has made inquiries into who you are and into what households you have already been received.

In one respect only are the Swedes like the Latins. They like to entertain with splendor. Formal dinner parties are taken quite seriously. In the winter season diplomatic circles and high society are booked for invitations six months in advance. To maintain prime social position in Stockholm, a Swedish family must give three large dinners a year. Sometimes the host can ill afford the lavish feasts; and then, of necessity, the family must dine privately for weeks on herring and potatoes to pay for the rich abundance and the imported wines served at the prestige dinner.

Paradoxically, the careful, disciplined Swedes today are not thrifty in the German sense or tight-fisted in the French sense. They spend their money freely, though not thoughtlessly. They live in the best possible manner, eat the best possible food, surround themselves with furniture and pictures of the best taste. The Swede gets excellent value for his cash, demands first-rate quality, and despises shoddy. Some are inclined to live a fraction above their incomes. But Swedes do not squander money on gaudy jewelry, special-bodied automobiles, polo ponies, or gold-plated bathroom fixtures. Style and quality are essentials in their purchases, rather than current fashion.

A Hungarian woman, who has preferred to live in Stockholm long after her divorce from a Swedish husband, was delighted to express her opinion of the Swedes. "Good is the Swedish peasant," she affirmed. 'Good is the aristocracy. In other countries today many aristocrats are apt to be degenerated idiots—in Hungary, France, Austria, anywhere—and a few of them in England are unspeakable! But the Swedish aristocrat is generally an intelligent man, often a man of charm, and one aware of his responsibilities. Here the only man you can really talk to, besides the artist, is the traveled aristocrat. The snobs are those who have made money in the last fifty years. It is they who are terrified of not doing the right thing. Often they are gentlemen in so far as it pays, if somebody important is looking at them. They have no *natural* desire to please. It never occurs to them to try to please a woman. A man will hold the coat for a lady if he *must,* if somebody is looking, or if she simply stands and waits and looks expectant. Otherwise he will never think of it."

Despite his fear of not doing the right thing, the Swede, like the English public school boy, seems to take his superiority for granted. This gives him confidence in dealing with the other Scandinavians, with Continentals, and with Americans, with everyone except the English, who have been nurtured on more generations of belief in their own superiority. This inner assurance, paradoxically, gives the Swede a becoming modesty, for "where merit is acknowledged there is no need to proclaim it."

The Swedish male feels decidedly superior to the Swedish female. This is due, in part, to the women themselves, who make a great fuss over their little boys at the expense of their little girls. In most Swedish households the boy gets the best of everything. But there is no "Mom worship," so deplored by Philip Wylie as a fetish that keeps the American male eternally juvenile. Nor is the Swedish husband ever a "sap," as the American husband is reputed to be, unless he marries an American woman, in which case he often does become henpecked.

Sweden is a man's country where the women have equal rights, but the men most of the fun. It is more of a man's country even than England. The Swedes are men's men, but never in the vaunted, cinematic version of the two-fisted, hairy-chested American. A Swede merely prefers the company of men. He most enjoys stag affairs. Unlike the Dane, he does not automatically take his girl or his wife out with him for a diverting evening. A Stockholm friend of mine, recently married, met some other men who proposed going out for an evening. "Shall we take the women with us?" he asked. The others replied, "Good heavens, no—we want to have fun." Fun did not mean picking up attractive loose women. It simply meant being alone with men, so they could talk and drink as much as they pleased. And if they had their wives or sweethearts with them they would feel under obligation to make some conversation with the poor women, and they did not want to be bothered.

Though the well-brought-up Swede knows how to kiss a lady's hand correctly and even with masculine grace, he is the least romantic of men. Feminine coquetry is wasted on a Swede. The word "flirt" has no counterpart in the language, and the act of flirting is something the average Swedish man would be ashamed to be caught doing. He might not hesitate to proposition a girl, but he would not belittle himself by flirting. If a foreign girl attempts to charm him, she is often quietly squelched. I heard a glamorous, vivacious Polish girl cry out with despair at a party, "Oh, you Swedes! I am frozen here twenty times a day."

Courtly love of the pre-Chaucerian era can hardly have existed in Sweden. In the Norse sagas love for a woman is little touched upon. The woman often fights side by side with the men, but it is her heroism that is extolled, rather than her personal attraction. The one really exciting romance in Swedish history is that of Count von Fersen's devotion to Marie Antoinette, a tale full of daring and idealism. But for all his admirable parts, Fersen's detractors claim that the queenly state of his beloved inspired much of the gallantry. The only widely known romantic male in Swedish literature is Selma Lagerlöf's Gösta Berling, and he is more a spinster's valentine of an heroic lover than a man of flesh and blood.

Today a young Swede treats his girl somewhat like another fellow, a less clever fellow, naturally, but one who is expected to do her full share of the work on a camping trip. Before a man marries in Sweden he must ski with the girl in winter and swim with her in summer and then think it over. Often he looks up her father's financial rating before he proposes or accepts her proposal. The girls say the Swedish young man holds himself at high price. They must strive for his favors. In Stockholm, where females outnumber the males by sixty thousand, it is often the girl who makes the advances. Watch the couples in the park. It is the girl who reaches for the boy's hand or puts her arm about him or leans her cheek against his. "Swedish boys aren't so bad after we have given them a few drinks," an American girl student said to me. "Then they become quite lively and rather sweet." The man's reticence may be largely due to his self-consciousness, for the Swedish male is more shy than the female, as he is more vain.

Until recent years Swedes were reared under a strong Puritanical tradition. The moral restraints of fifty years ago were too stringent. With the growth of the Socialist party and the advocacy of free love by some of its more radical leaders, much restraint was thrown off after the first decade of this century. But though recent modern Swedish fiction has a strong sexy tinge, the Swedes are uncommonly clean-minded, and regard sex without English hypocrisy or French prurience. They are realistic about illegitimacy and have most enlightened and humanitarian laws concerning it. Some Swedish girls deliberately invite pregnancies to induce marriages. And many give in to a man on the first or second date as a means of holding him.

The laws for women are very fair, none in the world fairer, and, on the whole, Swedish women have been treated well in the courts since before the Middle Ages. Legally the Swedish woman is completely emancipated. Spiritually she often seems hampered, both by man's assumption of superiority and his indifference. Some Swedish women of beautiful features have blank expressions of the unloved. And because her affections are starved, a Swedish wife may indulge in extramarital affairs, which mean little or nothing to her emotionally.

Swedish women sigh and say, "Oh, these Swedish men!" And they may hint that they aren't a bit enthusiastic about them as husbands. "We really prefer Austrians or Italians, but, because we value security, we marry Swedes."

A delightful Swedish woman who is happily married to a Norwegian chemical engineer tells me she believes the Swedes' indifference to women is due to the fact that they work very hard, not only at their professions, but in fulfilling numerous civic duties. "They are often too tired," she says, "to remark the charms of women."

How much of this lack of appreciation is the Swedish woman's fault, it is impossible to say. I know three Swedish women whom I consider unsurpassed in charm in any land. It is a charm that goes beyond that of most attractive women, because it seems so utterly unstudied, and beneath it lies an integrity and a sincerity that add to the radiance. But these three women are properly appreciated and admired by their husbands.

I am inclined to agree with Marcus Wallenburg, the banker, that the Swedish woman is really a finer human being than the Swedish man. Yet the off-beat, unspoiled Swedish male, one who yet possesses the dependable Swedish virtues, without a trace of Swedish stuffiness, is about as pleasing a specimen of humanity as contemporary civilization has produced.

A forthright Norwegian woman, divorced from a noted Swedish publisher after a rocky marriage, said to me, "I have lived in Sweden twenty-one years and I think I know these people. To a Norwegian, Swedes are overpolite, correct, and stiff. But once you have got through that iron thing around them, you will find them the most wonderful friends who will go through fire for you." And she is indeed right, as I have proved for myself.

Many foreigners, however, seem to have difficulty in penetrating "that iron thing around them"; and, consequently, I have heard discriminating persons exclaim, "There is everything to admire in Sweden, and so little to love."

Because Sweden is so obviously a superior nation, so smoothly functioning in its progressive ways, so remarkably harmonious in its various manifestations of living, perhaps one comes to expect too much of perfection in the people themselves, who are too reserved to be casually heart-warming. What Sweden needs, I think, to confirm the impression that it is the nearest to any Utopia yet achieved in this earthy world, is more smiling faces and less logic, less manner and more heart. A favorite text on which the Swedish character seems formed is one I heard the minister use at Leksand in Dalarna: "And he that is of a cool spirit is a man of understanding." It would be blessed indeed if these steadfast and most fortunate people could recall without embarrassment I John 4:11: "Beloved, if God so loves us, we ought to love one another."

19.

My Most Unforgettable Swede

For the understanding of the soul's defencelessness, of the conflict between the two poles, is not the source of the greatest song. The source of the greatest song is sympathy.

—HALDÓR LAXNESS

ONE SWEDE TO WHOM the gentle admonition of the apostle seems to come as naturally as breathing is Hedvig Hamilton. It was some eighteen years after her misfortune that Thérèse and I first met the Countess Hamilton at a small dinner to which we had been invited through her daughter Madeleine, who had sat at table with us on the *Drottningholm,* when we crossed in '39. She was then manager of the large "repose" hotel at Saltsjöbaden, the fashionable seaside resort in the Archipelago near Stockholm. The last time I saw her, in 1946, she was working eighteen hours a day managing refugee camps for sick Polish women whom Count Folke Bernadotte had rescued from Auschwitz and Belsen.

When we first met her we knew nothing of her story except that she was a countess who worked for her living. Good-looking, with hazel eyes and chestnut hair, she was a woman in her early fifties, but seeming a decade younger because of her slim, girlish figure and perfect grooming. As a guest, she was rather deprecating in manner, and while I liked her at once, there was nothing striking about her until it was her turn to perform a Swedish folk dance. She did it with such abandon and flashing spirit that she made the performance of her own virile eighteen-year-old son and the other Swedes seem pallid.

A month later, as a quiet place in which to do some writing, I spent a week at the Saltsjöbaden hotel—Sanatoria och Badanstalt—

designed for convalescents and for business and professional persons desiring a holiday of rest.

Here Countess Hamilton was something quite beyond a pleasant lady I had met at dinner and much more than the manager of a hotel. In her own milieu a kind of radiance emanated from her. I remember her vividly the first morning as she stepped from the elevator into the lobby. She was dressed simply in a well-tailored gray skirt with an immaculate soft white blouse and a smart crimson jacket. Several depressed, bored guests sat drooping in window seats, staring glumly at the March snow, or in armchairs, idling with magazines. She took them all in with her smile like a simple benediction. Then she went to greet each person with a Swedish "good morning" that made the morning seem blessed. With some she shook hands. With each she exchanged a pleasant word or two. She made a couple of introductions. Then she turned to sympathize with a very nervous woman who rushed up to complain that the porter had rudely banged her baggage. She calmed the woman; spoke a gentle word of reproof to the porter. Within five minutes the whole atmosphere had changed, as if a bright lamp had been brought into a gloom-shadowed room.

As she approached me, half hidden by a column, a mélange of words came to me: chic, vibrant, heart-warming, and thoroughly sweet. It was not that she was merely a charming hostess greeting an alien guest, but as if my happiness was her heart's special desire. The attitude was in no sense professional, but the quintessence of sincerity. There were no barriers to break down. It was as if I were an old and dear friend of the family, instead of an American who had happened to sit at table by her daughter on an ocean voyage.

Before two days had gone by, I had much of Countess Hamilton's story. Part I drew out from her, and part from other Swedish guests who had known her long, especially from Elsbeth Funch, the writer, whose husband had been the king's chamberlain.

Countess Hamilton was the first lady of title in Sweden ever to work for her living, and thereby to stimulate a new independence for Swedish women of like birth and breeding. In 1923 in conventional, code-circumscribed Swedish aristocracy this meant enduring humiliations and it took exceptional courage. While today in Sweden it is not uncommon for a lady of the nobility to take a paying position, just a quarter-century ago it was taboo. Not because she was a feminist or desired a career did Countess Hamilton defy tradition, but out of absolute necessity, when her husband lost their estate.

The Hamilton manor, Tågerups säteri, lay in Skåne, that beautiful southern province of castles and fertile soil, with almost five hundred acres in productive agriculture. Most of the Countess's dowry and the money she later inherited from her father had gone into improving the estate. Her rose garden was her special responsibility and joy, and the house, as well as the garden, overflowed with roses. She had a talent for flower arrangements and those for her "big dinner parties" were famous among the gentry. Because she just naturally attracted people, the house was always full of guests. Among them often was her aunt, the Countess Lewenhaupt, who for thirty years was first lady of the Swedish court. During the summer months the family members came in succession with rows of children. The Hamiltons seldom sat down to a meal with less than ten to fifteen.

When conditions became bad after World War I, to keep the place going Count Hamilton borrowed money several times and was paying as much as twelve per cent interest. Educated as an army officer he knew little of business, though he loved the land and farming. His wife, seeing him look worried, would ask—as she expressed it—"Have you sorrow?" But he would smile and reassure her. Then one day the director of a bank came to tell her all was finished, that the entire estate belonged to the bank, and that she must leave as soon as she could get packed. When she reproached her husband for not warning her of the impending disaster, he said he could not bear to frighten her and kept hoping for a miracle. She rushed to Stockholm to her wealthy relatives and pled for help. They were loath to give it. She came home and began packing. "I can ask once," she said, "but I cannot ask twice."

The loss of everything, her son's and daughter's patrimony, all the devoted work she had put into making the manor a beautiful home, was hard to endure. But she suffered most for her husband, who was too crushed to remain in Sweden. They went to Munich and took a small apartment for themselves, the two children, and the nurse, who refused to leave even though wages had ceased.

The Count inquired about positions, with no result. After a year and a half the Hamiltons approached the absolute end of their vanishing resources. In her desperate unhappiness Countess Hamilton said to herself, "It would be better for me to die, for there is nothing else." Then she turned to the New Testament for help. She was struck particularly by the verse from Romans 12:2, "Be ye transformed by the renewing of your mind." To her, it was like a sudden shaft of illumination.

The very next day a friend suggested that, with her good taste in dress, she might take a collection of clothes from Munich couturières to Sweden. Her husband was appalled by the idea. "Hamilton is one of the distinguished names of Sweden," he said. "Society will not stand for your working." When her mother learned of the plan, she telegraphed, "It is utterly impossible. Ladies cannot do such things."

In spite of them all, Countess Hamilton got a collection of frocks and exhibited them in Stockholm. Many of her old friends came to look and to buy. But some would not shake her hand. For now she was different, she was a workingwoman.

She was unprepared for this hurt. Yet she accepted the cuts along with the patronage. And she was doing an extra-fine business on the fourth day of the showing, when a burly man burst into her hotel showroom and demanded gruffly: "Do you call yourself the Countess Hamilton?" She admitted she was the Countess. He pulled back his coat and revealed a police badge. "You are committing a crime. You have no license for selling clothes."

Countess Hamilton protested; her lawyer in Göteborg had arranged about the license. "He has not arranged," the man said. "You will come with me to the police station." The lady customers cast looks at each other as she got her coat.

The police station adjoined the prison. To her, it was a horrible place. (This was in 1923. It is very different now.) Miserable, degraded-looking people were sitting about awaiting examination. One of the officers was talking over the telephone in a loud voice and using unprintable words. When the examiner called her to him, he said sarcastically, "Why do you sell, *Countess* Hamilton?"

"Good heavens," she replied, "do you think I do it for my pleasure? I have a husband who is not well. I have two children. I must provide a place for them and food. Their existence is my life. My lawyer was supposed to have arranged my permission."

"So you are a countess," the inquisitor mocked. "Have you references?"

She began to name some people, while he contemptuously wrote them down. Then she named her aunt, Countess Lewenhaupt, first lady at the court and the King's official hostess when the Queen was ill.

With a cat-torturing-mouse expression, the man reached for the telephone and called the royal palace. It is well known that King Gustav sometimes answers the telephone himself. His Majesty happened to answer that day. The police officer turned strangely red. When he rose from his desk, he began bowing and begging pardon. He insisted on showing her out the private way, so she would not have to go through the prison waiting room, where the common people sat.

"No," she said. "When you thought I was not a countess you had me brought that other way among those unfortunate people. I am no different now from what I was a quarter of an hour past. I go out the way I came in!"

But in the taxi she realized she could not go through this kind of ordeal again. She determined to get a regular wage-earning job. She told the driver to take her, not to her hotel, but to Nordiska Kompaniet, the department store.

At N.K. she went to the manager's office. "Would you please give me some position?" she said. "I have good taste in clothes." He asked for a reference, some businessman. Because business affairs were quite another circle from that she had been used to, she knew only one—the husband of a girlhood friend. He chanced to be a director of the company, though she had not known it. Over the telephone the director said, "Give her a position." She became *dame de réception.*

Within one hour Countess Hamilton had been arrested, released, had applied for a salaried job, and been hired.

Excitedly she called her husband in Göteborg. "Impossible," he cried. "A Countess Hamilton cannot work that way."

"I'm sorry," she said, "but she must."

During the first weeks the company and her relatives decided that she must work under some other than a noble name. Her mother had been born a countess, a Lewenhaupt, but her father had no title, so she used his name. Then people would say, "What, are you now divorced?" Explanations were troublesome. She stood it for one month. Then she announced firmly, "I'm taking my name back. Let everybody know: the Countess Hamilton is working."

Like Southern women of the ruined antebellum homes who were more enterprising than their defeated men, Countess Hamilton could face a new life better than her husband. He tried the insurance business for two years. "He wanted so much to work," said his wife. "But he could not ask. He would go to call, but he could not ask. So he would sit at home all day and try to read. It grieved him terribly to see me working." After two years grief turned into a cancer. Then, in six months he was dead.

Soon Countess Hamilton was traveling abroad for the firm, buying clothes in Paris, London, Munich; and also designing costumes for some of Sweden's noted actresses and for Gertrud Pålsson-Wettergren, who sang Carmen at the Metropolitan.

She remained at N.K. for ten years, lighting everything she did with her peculiar radiance. She became deeply interested in the misfortunes of the girls who worked in the store. When in trouble of any kind they would turn to her. She would visit in prison those who stole, comfort them, encourage them. And after they were released from prison, she would keep up with them, help them to find a new life and peace of mind.

"I would tell them," she said, "that instead of rehearsing the negative things in my mind that belong to yesterday, the first thing I do on awakening is to thank God for life and the fresh start."

"Hedvig refound her life by giving it up," Mrs. Funch said to me, "by becoming selfless and thinking only of others' good. Out of her own suffering came her extraordinary perception and that quality the Bible calls lovingkindness. So the shy talk easily with her, and those carrying a sense of guilt, for she never condemns."

In 1932 when Marcus Wallenburg, the banker, asked Countess Hamilton to take over the management of the "repose" hotel at Saltsjöbaden, she accepted. It gave her a wider scope for helping people whose lives were disharmonious.

She who had run a manorhouse found easy enough the management of a hotel that accommodated 130 guests and a staff numbering 110, including masseurs and electrotherapists. All the servants belonged to the union. "I simply follow this little book of rules called *Kollektivaltal*," she said, handing me a copy one day while we were having tea in her sitting room.

That room had its own characteristic charm. It was furnished with a few beautiful pieces she had saved from the wreckage of her home. The polished mahogany surfaces had a satin sheen that comes only from years of devoted polishing, and seemed to reflect the glow of the crystal bowls of yellow daffodils. Distinctive and simply elegant, the room was yet homey, comfortable, and contenting. I remembered her daughter telling me how her mother had often lived in the humblest circumstances to keep her and her brother in good boarding schools. "Once she had just a tiny room without even a stick of her own furniture. But coming into that room was coming into *her* room. Having dinner there with her on a rickety table with the simplest food and a single rose became a festive occasion."

I asked Countess Hamilton if she ever longed for the old way of life in Skåne. She glanced towards the windows that faced south. After a moment she shook her head and smiled. "Not for anything would I give up knowing what I know now. What I went through has made me understand people. That is why I can tell the character of my personnel here in the hotel. Why, when I engage a woman, I am so sure she will be right. If any of the staff ever gets angry and flares up, I do not say anything. I just look at them quietly and try to see the perfect person behind the distorted image. I wait until they come to me later and say they are sorry. I know they will come. They always do."

As we were finishing tea, a former kitchenmaid of the hotel came to call, to thank the Countess again and tell her she was to be married. "See!" she said ecstatically, taking off her hat and running her hands through a mass of short curly honey-colored hair. "It is too wonderful." It seems that the Countess had discovered the girl had no hair, and that she was wretched and withdrawn over her affliction. She took the shamed girl to an expensive specialist in Stockholm and got virtually free treatment for her. The hair grew.

The girl had a much better job and a completely new outlook, as well as the promise of a husband.

"It is easier to make hair grow," Countess Hamilton said, thoughtfully, after the girl was gone, "than to get persons to give up a corroding sense of fear or resentment. The people who come here, except those who really just need a rest, are mostly ill through fear. And fear, I think, is almost invariably the villain in the human tragedy. A young violinist from Holland—see, here is her letter that came today." She got the letter from a desk and handed it to me. It was in French. "She was here for six months with rheumatism and thought she could never give another concert. When baths and massages did not seem to help, I would talk with her in the evenings and listen with her to music on her gramophone. She needed reassurance, to forget herself, and—to love life. When an offer of an engagement came from Helsinki, I said, 'You must accept and play.' Last week as she was to take the boat to Finland, she said, 'I cannot go. I am too ill. I will not be able to play.' I said, 'Yes. You must go. We go together. You there—I here. But I am with you throughout the concert. You shall play well. It will be a success.' . . . See the letter and the newspaper notices. It was a success. I think now she must know she is cured.

"Many of the guests here are half-starved for affection," she said, as she rose to get her coat, for we were going for a walk in the snow. "Mankind devotes energies to seeking money, fame, power, but the deepest need of the human heart is for understanding love, and Swedes, alas, are not always gifted in such understanding."

In a leopardskin coat and a tailored brown felt hat, with walking boots and stick, she looked extremely smart and little enough like the "self-made, self-immolating sister-of-mercy incognito," that Mrs. Funch called her.

When we started out, she handed me her stick and picked up a bowl of daffodils from a table. She rapped on a door down the corridor and disappeared for a moment. When she came out, her eyes were shining. "It's a Jewish scientist whom we knew in Munich. He's a dear old man recovering from melancholia. Though he won't leave his room yet, he is much, much better. I get some of our distinguished guests to call on him in the evenings."

As we passed through one of the drawing rooms, a large, handsome woman, who carried her problems in her face, turned to speak. The severe self-centered expression seemed to melt as Countess Hamilton smiled lovingly at her and said something in Swedish. "She was one of those aristocratic friends who bought my clothes, but refused to shake my hand. Long ago she came to me for forgiveness, and now she comes to me for comfort. The poor woman is very rich and much weighted down with the superfluities of life. Because I shed them long ago, she finds me consoling. She is like the others who are absorbed in their own egos, their own pleasure. I once told her she would be healed if she could realize that the goal of life is not personal pleasure, but growth in spirit."

In my week at Saltsjöbaden I never ceased to marvel at how many unhappy people with every luxury at home depended on Hedvig, who had nothing to offer except the spirit of love and life. Night after night I would watch her come into one of the drawing rooms, radiating health and lovingkindness as naturally as if she were a center of divine energy. She did not have to speak a word. Haggard lines of self-pity or apprehension would disappear from grave faces. Men would stop coughing. A woman who complained of shortness of breath would stop fanning herself with the evening paper. Color would come into cheeks and eyes would glow as if by reflection. The mere presence of this harmonious woman seemed to bring individuals into some harmony with themselves.

The last time I saw her was after the war in mid-August of 1946. While managing two refugee camps at the same time, one at Rättvik and one at Vikarbyn, she was sent to Göteborg to organize the departure of 333 recovered *repatriandi* from different nations, and at the same time to receive 275 undernourished children from Czechoslovakia, to be placed in Swedish private families. It was a tremendous job of organization and execution, for it had to be done very quickly.

The day it was finished, she passed through Stockholm on her way back to the camps in Dalarna, and lunched with me. "But I can't go to a very fine restaurant in these camp clothes," she said. "Some simple place, please." She was wearing beige slacks, a jersey sweater, and well-cut brown jacket. With her slim girlish figure she looked casually smart and incredibly young. It was her sixtieth birthday. Though she had gone to bed after midnight and arisen at five to take the train, now at noon she was soignée and fresh.

When I again reproached her for working too hard, she smiled reassuringly. "But, Hudson, I do not know what it is to be tired. Heaven must approve of my work these last few years, for I am certainly sustained."

After a decade of ministering to spiritually depressed well-to-do, she had resigned to care for sick and broken-hearted refugees. She had helped organize and manage several different camps. Among them was Stratenbo, with 450 Jewish and Catholic Polish girls and women, some from the upper classes, some factory workers, some prostitutes. They were suffering variously from tuberculosis, nervous disorders, and venereal disease. At first a few were temperamentally difficult to manage and, caring little how they might infect Swedish citizens, would break bounds and go to fairs. But Countess Hamilton persuaded them to have consideration and she made life as cheering as possible with limited means. At the camp near Rättvik, which I had visited, I had noted the added touch of bright-yellow curtains at windows, the vases of field flowers on the dining-room tables, the spotless order, the smiling service. I had watched her as girls came to her office and when she went to visit the sick-in-bed. She would look at each in that absorbed manner, as if she was more interested in this one's happiness than in anything in life, and at the moment she was. Though there were adequate physicians and remedies in the camps, I saw that Love was the divine specific with which Hedvig wrought her own cures. It was selfless devotion that gave her strength to work so many arduous hours a day, to endure having her rest broken by some nightmare-ridden girl risen in the night.

I remembered what someone had said of her, "I have never seen her discriminate in any way with any person. To her, a human being is just a human being. If help is needed, she gives it to all alike, the dull and the brilliant, the poor and the privileged, with no other thought than to do the helping. That is something for which I admire her no end."

I admired her, too, for this incarnated vision that could discern the true person behind any façade of circumstance, as much as I admired her for turning her early defeat into such a victory by making her life a blessing to others.

As she boarded the train that was taking her back to the refugee camp, I remember her standing on the platform so full of vitality and sympathy. When a station newsboy called out some potential new atomic horror, she only smiled, a little sadly, at man's foolishness. "I hope life has taught me," she said, "not to be dismayed at anything."

20.

Prince Wilhelm at Home in the Country

But we do not therefore shut ourselves in. On the contrary, we prefer to maintain and extend our contacts with other lands and their affairs, whether they be spiritual or material. No one is too old to learn, or learned enough to live in an ivory tower.

—PRINCE WILHELM

THE FIRST WEEK in August, 1946, Prince Wilhelm invited me to spend a day in the country at Stenhammar, his manor in Södermanland sixty miles southwest from Stockholm. I had had the honor of meeting His Highness in 1939. Shortly before our arrival in Sweden early in that fateful year, he had reviewed a Swedish translation of a book of mine on South America, a continent he knew well. The review appeared in *Svenska Dagbladet* and was uncommonly favorable, and I was extremely grateful. But I did not meet the Prince in person until many months later at a small informal dinner of Swedish writers given in honor of H. G. Wells a week after World War II had begun. "I hope you liked my review," was the first thing he said to me. I saw at once why the young Swedish writers, with whom he periodically met for dinner and talk, were so genuinely fond of their author prince. "We criticize each other's work," one of the young novelists had told me, "and the Prince lets us exchange the familiar 'du' [thou] with him."

Prince Wilhelm was a rather extraordinary-looking person, making one think of both eagle and grayhound. Towering tall as his father King Gustav, he was slim like a hay-drying pole. Considered almost theatrically handsome in his youth, now his ascetically thin face had barely enough sun-tanned skin to cover the distinguished bony structure. Deeply entrenched lines ran from his eyes and his

274

mouth. A long strand of dark hair streamed unruly across his strange gray eyes which drooped intriguingly. His left eye sparkled with wit and charm and kindness and the devil. While the right eye maintained the royal dignity, the fun-loving left eye faintly mocked at conventions. Little puffs under both eyes betrayed his recent sleeplessness because of distress over the new world tragedy just begun.

But he talked with unconstrained ease, warm, frank, engaging, moving his hands about eloquently. His face was extremely mobile, with sudden changes from eaglelike gravity to debonair charm. He seemed a man who had savored life with curiosity, and with his active nature and wide interests, he had found it diverting on the whole, while for the rest he had devised a private philosophy.

As the second son, Prince Wilhelm had had more freedom to range and indulge his hobbies than had his brother the Crown Prince Gustav Adolf. So a good deal of his young manhood had been spent in big-game hunting and in world travel, about which he has written several books. In various parts of the globe he had served as both official and unofficial good-will ambassador for Sweden. And in 1927 and 1928, on extensive lecture tours through the United States, talking of his African hunts and his archaeological exploits, he had made many American friends. Another hobby, photography, both stills and motion pictures, had proved a profitable avocation. While he lived on a five-thousand-acre productive estate, which supported a hundred families to work the fields and tend the cattle, he held a position as literary critic on one of the Stockholm papers.

Now, in 1946, I was very happy to be seeing him again after the war years, during which he had been passionately anti-Nazi and had dared to speak his mind freely. Instead of taking the early-morning train from Stockholm to Flen, where Prince Wilhelm said he would have his car meet me, I telephoned the night before and asked if I might drive down and bring with me Gunnar Rosvall, a young Swedish friend who was helping me with some research.

On a hill near Lake Valdemaren spreads the oyster-white château with its black metal roof. The foundations of Stenhammar date to the seventeenth century, but the present structure was erected only in the 1880's. Its last owner bequeathed the property to the State on the condition that it should be given to one of the royal princes as a residence. It naturally fell to Prince Wilhelm, because he holds the title of Duke of Södermanland. Stenhammar was the favorite residence of the gay-hearted Grand Duchess Marie of Russia during her six years of marriage with Prince Wilhelm. She could hardly abide the stuffy stiff court life in Stockholm in the first decade of King Gustav's reign, but at Stenhammar she could breathe and be herself.

The drive within the grounds winds up through a wood and approaches the manor from the back and then half encircles it. The chauffeur stopped the car on a wide terrace between the broad stone staircases, one leading up to the porch, the other down into the rose garden.

The August morning had turned quite warm, and Prince Wilhelm received us in shirt sleeves at the entrance to the reception hall, which bristled with antlers from royal hunts. He had been working on an essay in his study beyond the right-hand drawing room. The strain of the war years had aged him somewhat. He looked even more attenuated, his hair was gray now, and I could not discern so much devilishness lurking in his left eye. But his informal charm of manner was just as I remembered it.

On his study desk were new volumes in French and Danish, as well as Swedish. A newspaper clipping of a review lay conspicuously spread beside them. "I was looking in my files," he said, smiling, "to see what I wrote about you. I am glad it wasn't uncomplimentary."

I apologized for bringing a chauffeur along with Rosvall and me. "Don't worry," the Prince said, "we'll see that he gets some grub." I wondered where he had picked up that Southern slang. The use of the word "grub" by His Highness established an immediate ease before he invited us to sit down.

Big comfortable chairs and sofas made the study a pleasant place for talk and lounging as well as work. In the window nearest his desk stood framed photographs of his son, Lennart Bernadotte, and his daughter-in-law and each of their four children. Over his desk hung an original drawing of his grandfather, King Oscar II. On the walls were two paintings of scenes of Pau, the birthplace of his great-great-grandfather, Marshal Bernadotte, who established the present dynasty. On a bookshelf stood a striking bust of the Prince done in bronze by Väinö Aaltonen, Finland's foremost sculptor. A vaulted archway divided the long study into two parts, each with its fireplace. The back one was lined with high bookshelves and about them stretched a series of weird banners—ferocious human faces painted on squares of cloth. They were like primitives from some unfamiliar savage race. Prince Wilhelm said they were *"lapptyg"* pictures. "Lapp trick" paintings on cloth, used in olden times on wolf hunts.

"The pictures took the place of men or beaters in the round-up," he said; "they would be strung on ropes to prevent the animals from breaking through. These specimens date from 1780. The custom of using painted faces for real men in hunts is virtually extinct. But my father still makes use of them for moose shooting in Västergötland, when he takes only a few persons with him."

On our stroll through the lower-floor rooms I noted some jeweled ikons and several chandeliers with the Russian double-eagle, which I knew the Grand Duchess Marie had brought when she came as a bride to Stenhammar. In the large drawing room on the left of the reception hall was an arresting portrait of the Prince by Beskow, the Swedish artist, and a scenic painting by his uncle Prince Eugen. There were some pieces of sculpture by Christian Eriksson, the second most famous Swedish sculptor of the present reign. These had been brought to the château by Eriksson's widow, who was born Jeanne Trancourt in Paris, and who for many years had been Prince Wilhelm's hostess.

When we came back from looking at the empty cow barns, for the cows were all grazing in the meadows, a petite lady was awaiting us at the top of the stairs. "Ah, there is our hostess," the Prince said, and presented us as we came up the stairs. She wore a black and white print silk and a band of blue chiffon knotted about her dark hair. She had style and a gracious charm, but she looked a trifle concerned.

"The soufflé—" she spoke in French—"alas, I fear. You are five minutes late—and minutes may be ruinous to a soufflé."

As we went into the dining room, the Prince said, "It is really hot today. Don't you want to take your coat off?"

But I demurred, for I could not quite bring myself to lunch with the King's son and his hostess in my shirt sleeves. Besides, compared to Alabama or New York heat, the temperature seemed almost moderate.

The soufflé had not suffered by our tardiness. After this first course, which the butler served, we helped ourselves from chafing dishes on the buffet. Madame Jeanne herself had prepared chicken "a la nègre"—sliced breast of chicken in a chocolate-colored sauce, French and delicious. With this entrée came little new potatoes from the garden. Almost everything they ate, except sugar and sea foods, was produced on the estate.

When Prince Wilhelm asked me what I would have to drink, wine or beer, he was much surprised when I said, "Milk."

He glanced at me obliquely, as if one never knew what to expect from an American. When the Swedish Rosvall, who never touched anything alcoholic, also took milk, it was almost too much for His Highness. He leaned his coatless elbows on the table and looked quizzically from one to the other of us.

"But," I protested, "I really like milk. We are in the country. You have hundreds of cows. I want to test their quality."

Prince Wilhelm turned to the butler and said, "Bring two jugs of our best milk."

Madame Jeanne said, "I try so hard to get the Prince to drink milk, but he refuses."

"If he would drink six glasses of rich milk at intervals every day besides his regular meals," I said, regarding the elongated concave of his middle as he leaned forward, "I guarantee that he would gain fifteen pounds in six weeks. I was once skinnier than the Prince. I proved that the prescription works and I've put flesh on hundreds by the simple remedy."

"Oh," Madame Jeanne said hopefully, "if he could only be persuaded to drink milk! He is so very, very thin." She held up her hand in curving profile. "His little stomach goes in like this."

Prince Wilhelm smiled wryly, sat up straight, and asked for beer. During the meal he said, "By the way, how is that milk? You know, though we sell plenty of it, I don't recall ever tasting it." I assured him it was more than first rate, and I knew his customers must be pleased. Rosvall bore me out.

For dessert we had the choice of jellied purée of red currants, which Madame Jeanne had made herself, or *filbunke,* which is nothing more elegant than clabber. "I *know* our clabber is first-rate," the Prince said. The *filbunke* was served in beautiful deep silver dishes, each embossed with the royal initial *W* in gold. The status of lowly clabber, which is hardly considered a *delicatesse* in the United States, seemed surprisingly elevated by being presented in such style at a royal table. But in Scandinavia clabber is as much esteemed in the manor as in the crofter's cot. Prince Wilhelm confessed that clabber was his favorite luncheon dessert. I took the red-currant dish and could praise Madame Jeanne's skill with sincere enthusiasm.

Our hostess ate very little, but spent much time daintily breaking bread into tiny bits, until she had a neat little mound of crumbs on the cloth. *"Pour le petit oiseau,"* she said. When we went down onto the grass terrace for coffee, she brought the crumbs in a saucer. A manservant fetched a cage with a single lovebird and set it on the grass. Madame kneeled and slipped out the floor of the cage, so that the parakeet could enjoy picking the crumbs out of the grass.

"His name is Philippe," Madame explained, looking up. "But he is not French; he is a Stockholmer and speaks Swedish. Because he has no mate, we try to make up to him by giving him a lot of attention."

"Why don't you get him a mate?" I suggested.

"Ah," said Madame, "then he would not sing. Lovebirds in pairs are too contented to sing."

Philippe began to flutter his iridescent blue feathers delightedly as he pecked among the grass blades.

Since the terrace was in full sun, the butler brought Madame a coquettish little Chinese hat, which she put on to pour the coffee. Every move she made held instinctive grace, whether she handed me a demitasse or pointed out a certain drawing in *L'Illustration* or knelt to drop crumbs in the grass for the bird.

I remarked her closely in the strong sunlight. There were few traces of gray in her dark-brown hair. There was no rouge on her olive cheeks, only on her lips. She was delicately made, and her figure was girlish. The silhouette from chin to neck held little clue to age. Only her forearms and wrists hinted that she was perhaps more than fifty. Later the twenty-six-year-old Rosvall said he had felt the same, and he was the more baffled, because he knew that her late husband, the sculptor Christian Eriksson, was born the same year as the King, who was eighty-eight in 1946.

The next day in Stockholm I learned Madame Jeanne's real age. Her seventieth birthday had been celebrated at Stenhammar the previous December. So she was eight years older than Prince Wilhelm. She was the most remarkable woman for her age that I had ever seen in any land.

"As beautiful as an angel, she was," an old gentleman told me, "when she came to Sweden as the seventeen-year-old French bride of Christian Eriksson. And when her children were small and she would take them walking in the afternoons, people would casually line up to see her pass, she was so dainty and exquisite."

As I was shortly to go on a trip into the southern provinces of Småland and Skåne, Prince Wilhelm fetched some maps to help with advice about the journey. And he presented me with an inscribed copy of his latest book called *This Land of Sweden,* which Norstedt, his publisher, had got out in a handsome format to coincide with the meeting of the International Pen Club Congress in Stockholm the first week in June, with the author-prince as chief host.

Though the boundaries of Småland and Skåne march together, I knew that few provinces differed more in physical and temperamental characteristics. While the Prince answered my questions about which castles to visit in luxuriant Skåne, he seemed more interested in the Småland countryside far from the main roads, and, since I was motoring with a Swedish friend, he suggested our taking to the byways when we could.

"You know," he said with a twinkle in his left eye, "while Our Lord was busy making refulgent Skåne, He left the creation of Småland to Saint Peter. But Peter did not build very well. He just jumbled a pile of rocks together helter-skelter. There was no order or system. When Our Lord saw what a confused mess His assistant architect had made of things, He decided that He Himself would create the inhabitants of Småland. That's why the people of Småland have such sterling qualities, why they have been able to make the utmost out of what Saint Peter amateurishly knocked together."

"But, oh," exclaimed Madame Jeanne in gentle dismay, "those dark little back roads in Småland! You will think you have lost your way forever."

She took the book from me, turned to a passage, and handed it to Prince Wilhelm to read.

"But such excursions over the small roads can be really quite captivating," the Prince said, "if you are not in a hurry." At my urging he put on his glasses and began to read his own words:

The roads twine capriciously, one moment turning aside for a rock or a marshy piece of land and the next climbing friskily straight up to heaven, and no sooner have they done this than they fall forward down the other side towards a river whose bridge, from a distance, appears barely able to support the weight of a baby-carriage. Not satisfied with this, they make an uncalled-for swing or an abrupt breathtaking turn around some old and long since abandoned building which happens to stand in their way. It is like returning a few hundred years into the past. One forgets the callousness of the twentieth century, and leaves it to get along as best it can on the main thoroughfares. One forgets there is a place called the big world where, for the moment, people are doing their best to kill one another. Forgets that there exists something decadent which aspires to be called civilization and progress, reason and human dignity. Instead one finds here a neighborhood redolent of ancient tradition and sound peasant sense. It does you a lot of good—as though you had exchanged a city suit for the everyday patched clothes worn in the country.

Later when I was driving along a back way through Småland to get to the glass factory at Orrefors, I could appreciate the discernment and the accuracy of Prince Wilhelm's observation. And as I read at my leisure his measured confession of love for various provinces, it was clear that this son of the King had very deep roots in the best national characteristics of Sweden.

VI

SOUTH SWEDEN

21.

Orrefors, Industrial Idyl

If you are a weaver of fine cloth, weave as if the goods were to embrace the limbs of your beloved. If you are a blower of glass, fashion the cup as if it were to be touched by the lips of your beloved.

From the Hindu

IN SWEDEN the word "industry" often has unfamiliar connotations. Factory towns may have a special beauty of their own, for the esthetic has a place of emphasis in Swedish gainful calculations. Some industries happen to be located in settings that are idyllic of themselves. One such is the glassworks at Orrefors, where the world-famous decorative crystal is produced, deep in the woods of Små-land. In Swedish the concern is known as *Orrefors Bruk.* The word *bruk* is untranslatable, as Holger Lundbergh, the Swedish-American journalist and poet, once explained to me, and "factory" is not a synonym. "A *bruk* is a kind of oasis of industry surrounded by miles of forest or iron-bearing mountains, as the case may be." It means something more than small plant or workshop. The owners, the foremen, the artisans, and the apprentices, with their families, all abide within the close radius of the *bruk,* like a great, self-suffi-cient family. They have their community singing, their amateur theatricals, their study circles, their sports field. This harmonious set-up may seem a strange feudal anomaly in a Social Democratic country where the Labor party is dominant and where the local workers all belong to unions and are members of consumers' co-operatives.

The *bruk* in the Småland woods were originally evolved from material necessity. Unlike the fertile provinces with the manor

285

houses that border it on the south, Småland possesses grudging, rocky soil. Through the centuries the Smålanders knew sparse fare, and only the strong survived. Their chief resource was timber. As a hedge against starvation, to supplement the income from timber, to make better use of the surplus wood, glass factories as well as ironworks came into being. The wood made the hot fires that melted the sand that was transformed into window glass and tableware, just as charcoal was used to smelt the bog ore obtained from lake bottoms.

Orrefors Bruk dates back to 1726, when the estate's owner set up a small foundry to make use of surplus firewood. Not until 1898 was a glassworks established. And for seventeen years nothing more imaginative than inkbottles and windowpanes was produced. But in 1913 the acres and the plant at Orrefors came into the possession of Johan Ekman of Göteborg. A businessman of vision, he began the manufacture of a high-quality glassware and specialized first in cut crystal. Then in 1916-17 he was inspired to engage two first-rate artists, Simon Gate and Edward Hald, as designers. He gave them carte blanche to ply their talents. A revolution in glass resulted. At the Paris Exposition in 1925 the specimens of engraved glass from the remote little works at Orrefors captured the Grand Prix. "Here," said the judges, "is something really distinctive and new in glass since the days of the Phoenicians." Ever since, at all other world expositions, Orrefors glass has won a top award, and "Orrefors" has become a kind of an international trademark for the general high quality of Swedish industrial art, architecture, and way of life.

Though Orrefors glass as an international product is the best-known of the products of Småland, the factory's rural setting, far from the madding crowd, is not exceptional. In densely wooded Småland, within a radius of thirty-five miles, there are thirty other *bruk* actively producing glass. The Kosta works, next most famous after Orrefors, has been making glass since 1742, when it was founded by Baron Koskull, an army officer under King Charles XII, who imported glass blowers from Bohemia.

With Allan Kastrup, my Swedish friend from New York, I paid a visit to Orrefors in late August. We drove from Malmö, on the southwest coast, through verdant Skåne, his native province, and traversed the flowery, fruit-rich Blekinge bordering on the Baltic Sea. Then we ascended to the pine-thick, granite levels of eastern Småland. For mile after mile there was no sign of human habitation—only the dark woods with shadows like heavy purplish wine staining the moss-covered rocks, among which trolls are fabled to gather after sunset.

Occasionally we emerged into stretches of violet-colored heather, with honeybees hovering near a lonely crofter's cottage. Now and again there was a hamlet with weathered gray houses and a little white church with a steep, black roof. Just after six we drove into a crossroads village with half a dozen buildings, including a modernistic barbershop and an inviting general store with "Konsum" painted above its long plate-glass front. We knew "Konsum" meant the cooperative shop where the people of Orrefors bought groceries, clothes, drugs, hardware. Attractive houses of the workers stretched in four directions. These more recently built ones were modern in design, but those along the road running directly to the glassworks were early-nineteenth-century cottages, painted dark red, with white-trimmed casement windows lined with blossoming plants.

Orrefors lies along a willow-bordered stream studded with white and yellow water lilies. On the other side of the little river with the long name, Vapenbäcksån, the great forest marches back into the hinterland with its thousands of acres of growing trees. The workers' picturesque cottages are set along a hard-packed dirt road bordered with clipped lime trees.

At Orrefors the phlox and the rose trees grow tall like the men of Sweden, and all summer there is flower fragrance in the air. Most of the hundred and fifteen industrial workers live near enough to walk to work. They use their bicycles chiefly for week-end excursions to historic Kalmar on the Baltic or deeper into the countryside. Some of the employees have passed their seventieth birthday. Yet these men continue to work largely for the joy of producing, since every Swede on reaching sixty-seven receives a pension from the State. Some of the over-age artisans were born at Orrefors, and their sons and grandsons work today under the same roof with them.

The factory workers of Småland have ever abided close to trees and water, and in their leisure hours they may cultivate their gardens, when they are not indulging in athletic sports or canoeing on the river. The factory personnel has the privilege of hunting in the woods and fishing in both the near stream and the lake two kilometers away. So no one need suffer from industrial fatigue. For men who constantly create new designs and for the varied skilled craftsmen who take the raw materials and turn out the finished products, this familiar association with earth and natural beauty is regarded as essential nourishment, an imponderable supplement to the tasty and substantial Swedish diet.

When we arrived, it was the hour before supper. Men were pottering about their yards. One fellow stopped his raking to direct us to the company guest house, next to the home of the factory owner, Henning Beyer. It was through Mrs. Beyer's niece, whom I had known in Stockholm, that we had been invited to spend the night here, instead of staying in Nybro, the nearest town with a hotel.

My upstairs room spread along the back, opening on an uncovered gallery that faced the river. Across the stream the fringe of forest stopped just at the water's edge. On the dark-green water beneath me a young workman with fair hair was paddling a sky-blue Eskimo kayak, guiding it expertly among the water lily pads. There was no sound except the faint, clean cut of the double-bladed paddle and the birds settling themselves for the evening. There was no savor of industry in the air that held only the aromatic odor of burning birch wood, phlox, and petunias.

At seven our host was waiting for us in the drawing room. Mr. Beyer was a handsome man in his middle sixties, with fresh coloring, gray eyes, and dark hair only slightly touched with gray. A gentleman of cultivation and wide travel like so many Swedish industrialists, he had been educated as a lawyer and had served as a judge in Göteborg and a consul of a foreign country. He had come into glass manufacture not through training but by marriage and inheritance, for he had married a daughter of the deceased Johan Ekman. Now he and his wife were—since March, 1946—the sole owners of Orrefors Glasbruk, though not of the twenty-four thousand acres of the Orrefors estate, which had been separated from the glassworks in 1938 and assigned to other heirs.

In a many-windowed dining room with white Swedish eighteenth-century furniture we dined well and leisurely, served by the housekeeper, Fröken Bergkvist, whose old father was the chief glass blower of the *bruk*. Just as we started back into the drawing room for coffee, the sunset above the trees approached its glory. Mr. Beyer did not know that for three months Mark Twain had once lived in Småland and had praised the sunsets of Sweden above any in the world. While we remained in the dining room and had our coffee before the open west windows, I told him of Mark Twain's visit, which I first read about in the *American-Swedish Monthly*.

In 1899, the year after glassmaking was added to the ironworks at Orrefors, Mark Twain and his family sojourned at the small village of Sanna from early July to October. The Clemenses had gone there seeking a cure for the epilepsy of their younger daughter Jean at the sanatorium of Dr. Kellgren, a noted Swedish physician famed as the discoverer of osteopathy.

In the author's letters to friends he was as eloquently enthusiastic over the sunsets of Småland as he was over the new therapeutical science, osteopathy, which he urged upon everyone as "the great curative certain to restore universal health." About the sunsets, in a letter to his friend Twichell, dated September 6, 1899, he wrote characteristically:

Dear Joe, I've no business in here—I ought to be outside. I shall never see such another sunset to begin with this side of heaven. Venice? Land, what a poor interest that is! This is the place to be. I have seen about 60 sunsets here; & a good 40 of them were away & beyond anything that I have ever imagined before for dainty & exquisite & marvelous beauty & infinite change & variety. America? Italy? The Tropics? They have no notion of what a sunset ought to be. And this one—this unspeakable wonder! It discounts all the rest. It brings the tears, it is so unutterably beautiful!

As we looked now at the luminosity in the west, I thought how wise Mark Twain had been not to attempt to describe a Småland sunset, but merely to record the ineffable wonder. It was not the intensity of flame and lemon that made the glory, but a kind of super-refinement of those colors. The illumination made a golden fretwork of the forest roof and turned the silvery leaves of the near willows into quivering tongues of candle flame. There were no boats on the stream now, and under the mystic lemon light the water lilies gleamed softly as if endowed with the properties of fireflies.

The sunset seemed to try to atone for the austerity of the province, where Clara Clemens had found the "only form of decorative life to consist in brilliant sunsets and the performance of Swedish dances" in which she and her little sister would take part in the village square.

It was eighteen years after Mark Twain's sojourn in Småland that the community of Orrefors began to create "a form of decorative life" in glass that has brought distinguished beauty into many homes about the globe, as well as into palaces and museums.

I asked to see the plant by night, and so about half-past nine we strolled down the road that ran parallel with the river between the officials' white houses and the red cottages of the workers. Though the cottages possessed radios, if any were in use they were turned so low that no sound escaped into the street to disturb the twilit serenity of late evening.

There was nothing unusual about the physicality of the factory outside. The river ran behind it, and before it on a private track stood some freight cars with sand and one loaded with boxed glass to be sent to the port of Göteborg for transshipment to various world ports. As we traversed dimly lit corridors, the place seemed entirely uninhabited. We heard nothing except our own voices and footfalls. When we were almost into the middle of the vast first-floor room where the firing and blowing are done, a heavy-set figure carrying an iron implement emerged from behind a furnace. Dressed only in undershirt, trousers, and wooden sandals, the man was masked by enormous black goggles. It was he who kept the furnace fires going through the night. "He is most essential," Mr. Beyer said, smiling, as he introduced us to Mr. Linderberg, "equal to a whole troop of vestal virgins."

After a minute or two, as if he bore a compelling time mechanism within him, Mr. Linderberg moved to a furnace, opened a heavy iron door, and fed the fiery maw with birch logs.

There were some ten furnaces to be kept going, Mr. Beyer told us, and a heat of some 700° or 800° centigrade to be maintained for the molten sand mass. All night the single fire-keeper would walk from furnace to furnace, feeding, testing.

Twice Mr. Linderberg took a long iron shovel and scooped from a pile of broken glass, cuttings and trimmings from vases, discarded wineglasses, and other pieces that had not turned out to be perfect. The sound of the crackling fire, as the logs fed the flames, was varied now and then by the ringing out of fractured crystal, as the pieces cascaded from the iron shovel into the whirlpool of viscous glass.

"Isn't this rather lonely work?" I asked the fire-keeper in one of his pauses.

"In summer I am mostly alone. But in winter generally I have some company."

Mr. Beyer explained: "In winter it is an old custom here to let travelers, passing foresters, men temporarily out of work, spend the nights close to the fires. And in the morning we always provide a warm breakfast to cheer them on their way. Sometimes the passing guest takes a hand and helps Mr. Linderberg with the stoking."

I remarked the raw materials: bins of white sand, boxes of soda, pieces of lead, the fires, and the cooling water, out of which simple ingredients, touched by breath from a man's lungs, came the output of beautiful objects. I asked to be shown samples of finished work.

We stopped before thin wooden double doors, which a man might smash with his shoulder if he had a mind to. Kastrup struck a match in the dusky corridor, and on the second trial Mr. Beyer found the right key. The showroom was faintly lit by the northern sky that still retained some blue at ten o'clock. Mr. Beyer manipulated a wall switch and the room was flooded with light.

It was like being plunged into a vast subterranean ice cave with glittering stalagmites rising in fantastic forms on frosty ledges. Scores of white-clothed tables, as long as those used for palace banquets, were set with pieces of translucent crystal, like wedding presents at the nuptials of some fabulous potentate.

Thousands of different objects were on display, but each piece bore a half-thumbnail shield of gilt-embossed blue paper with the bird called *orre* and the magic name of Orrefors. I recalled aloud Mark Twain's remark about the sunset: "This unspeakable wonder! It discounts all the rest."

Some of the pieces were as coolly classic as a Doric column. Others were romantic in conception and exciting in color. The objects on the nearest tables were all of engraved crystal, but on tables beyond there were swirled bowls in sea-green, and table glass in topaz, and specimens of extraordinary Graal and Ariel glass, with their iridescent colors and designs embedded deep and covered with clear or colored glass like a thick veil.

Two vases in engraved glass on the nearest table caught my fancy. Upon the wide front facet of one was engraved the exquisite nude figure of a girl rising in the water along with twelve ascending bubbles. Not more than nine inches in height, the figure was so perfectly conceived and executed as to reveal each curve of the lovely young body. Even the nails of her toes held their own perfection. On the same table stood a tall slender oval-shaped vase with an ethereal high-breasted girl in soft summery attire standing in a demure pose of consummate natural grace. The latter piece was signed by Sven Palmqvist, one of the younger designers, whose sculptures, drawings, and engraved glass were already in museums, and whose decorative windows adorned hospitals, crematoriums, and luxury ships.

I walked to the corner of another table, attracted by a thick elliptical vase more like an egg in shape than a globe. In color tone it suggested dark-violet water through which a strong light shone mysteriously—and in its depths among the swaying seaweed and frail anemones swam strange finny fish veined like Portuguese men-of-war. At the base the color deepened until it took on the purplish-brown tints of iodine. It was unbelievably heavy to lift. This was a specimen of the famous Graal glass, so named after the Holy Grail which Christ used at the Last Supper. The piece was scratch-signed on the bottom by Edward Hald, the chief designer and begetter of Graal glass.

"In later years," Mr. Beyer said, "the tendency has been towards heavier glass, more bulky proportions. Hald's early designs leaned to the faëry, to tenuous sea serpents, crowns and constellations, exquisite maidens and athletic youths. But he too now creates thicker pieces with ancestral patterns made sophisticate."

The variety of color and kind of glass was as impressive as the multiplicity of designs. Some unadorned pieces in icy blue were an inch thick, others though intricately engraved seemed bubble-thin. In shape and form there was everything from amber-colored liqueur glasses to frost-white funeral urns. I remarked the blending of audacity and perfect taste, high sophistication with classical simplicity.

I noted the use of prehistoric figures found on stone ledges in Sweden, and a stylization of almost everything that lives and moves in water from the nude human figure to seahorses and starfish.

"So glass is made from sand by fire and air," Kastrup commented, "and in the end it looks like water."

"One of the designers," said Mr. Beyer, "always thinks of glass as solid water."

I stood a long time before a large pedestaled bowl or fruit dish in crystal. It depicted some festival in Elysium, with hundreds of engraved figures, beautiful to the smallest detail of sandal or blossoming branch. Before the war its retail price was $3,000, and none just like it has been made since.

As my eye roved among the thousands of pieces—no two alike on the floor and ranging in price from fifty cents to $5,000—Mr. Beyer said, "Each year some three hundred new designs are created. A few of the earliest ones we still retain—those for which the designers or the buying public have special affection. Some originals bought by museums are never repeated, nor are special pieces made for, say, persons like Queen Mary of England or the late Franklin D. Roosevelt. But any of these on the floor may be purchased by dealers—only in most limited quantities, of course."

He smiled reminiscently. "Occasionally when American industrialists pass this way, some of them say, 'But, man, man, why don't you expand?'" He made a deprecating gesture. "What should I answer? I shrug politely and let them interpret the shrug as lack of dynamic American drive. I doubt if I could make some of them understand that what we strive for is distinction—distinction created under harmonious conditions. Frankly, I don't want to harass my own brains. And our designers must take all the time they want, let the springs fill up before they begin to create something new. Our workmen are good and steady, but they must not be hurried. They are loyal and do not take advantage, and they seem to enjoy living here. Tomorrow you may see them at their various jobs, if you care to."

When we left the private showing, the night sky still held a trace of blue as we strolled back to the guest house. The lights in the workers' cottages were all out now. The sun would rise at about three, and at six the work day would begin, gently, without any factory whistle to grate on the summer air.

Just after five I was waked by children's voices coming through the thick curtains I had drawn tight to keep out the early morning. Wondering, I went to the window. Three flaxen-haired youngsters were fishing at the edge of the stream between the guest house and Mr. Beyer's dwelling. They were excited over a diminutive fish hardly five inches long. Just as I was about to call out in a subdued voice to urge them to go away and let us sleep, I heard Mr. Beyer speak pleasantly from his window, "What have you caught?"

The surprised boys turned and held up the fish.

"Is it for your cat?" the boss said teasingly.

"No, for us!" the boys answered, their pride a bit deflated.

"It won't be but one good bite."

"But it will be good—and we'll make it three bites."

"Good appetite!"

Beyer laughed, and apparently went back to bed. No stern reproof, no demanding what they meant by disturbing him in his own garden at such an hour. Just a pleasant reminder for them to make no more noise. I crept back to bed, self-rebuked by the incident. The boys did not make another sound, and it was breakfast time before I waked again.

After breakfast we went to see the men at work. The glass blowers sat on old-fashioned buggy seats set low on the floor. A helper would dip an iron blowing pipe into the readied molten glass and carry it with a great blob of the glowing mass coagulated on the end. He would rest the blowing pipe on a wooden support before the master blower, who would take the clean end of the pipe in his mouth and send his breath down the shaft. As the glass began to expand into a shape, with a stick or some primitive instrument the blower would pat, punch, shape. Then he would blow again. At last the bowl, the vase, or whatever the design called for, would emerge. Then with a pair of metal shears the blower would cut away the superfluous glass. Another helper now received the shaped object on a shovel and slid it into the bake-oven. The apprentice would carry the blowing pipe back again to dip up more molten glass, and the act would be repeated.

It was like a pantomime or a ballet, in which coordination and teamwork were essential. The grace of movement, the balance and the timing, were pleasant to watch. All was done in silence, never a word exchanged. Sometimes a slight nod, like that an unsmiling concert singer gives to an accompanist as a signal, would be perceptible. When a helper did not come immediately, the blower merely knocked lightly on the floor or on the edge of his buggy seat with a piece of wood.

"The blower never deigns to look around to see what causes the delay, if there is one," Mr. Beyer said. "He merely knocks again peremptorily."

He spoke in a hushed voice as in a church. Then he said, even more *sotto voce:* "I want you to meet our master blower, Mr. Bergkvist. He is seventy-one. I would appreciate it if you would shake hands with him."

"But I should be honored."

When Mr. Bergkvist had finished blowing a large vase with an outer covering of colorless crystal and a *décor* of opaque yellow and transparent dark purple, Mr. Beyer introduced us. The old gentleman rose from his buggy seat and smiled pleasurably when I asked if he would be so good as to sign a piece I wanted to buy and which Mr. Beyer told me he had blown.

I spoke to his helper, a blond young man of twenty-three, with a sensitive, refined face, and a body like a sprinter. He had been born in Orrefors, he said, and attended school until he was seventeen, and had been working here ever since his army service. There was a second helper so un-Swedish looking—somber black eyes and black curly hair partly hidden by a gray linen cap—that I inquired about him. He was a Polish Jewish refugee who had worked with glass in Poland. "He is as deft and assured as our old-timers," Mr. Beyer said, "though I think he is a little homesick, poor lad." I did not have time to speak with him, for Mr. Bergkvist knocked gently on the floor, and we moved on to watch another man shape a fluted dish on a whirling wheel.

In the engraving room upstairs a score of men sat or stood before long tables facing long windows. With small pen-and-ink designs before them, they pressed pieces of glass against whirring emery wheels. We stopped by an engraver who was etching a stylized royal coat-of-arms on a wine glass. The two men on either side of him were working with the same design on goblets and champagne glasses. "These are for the Emperor of Abyssinia," said Mr. Beyer.

Haile Selassie had ordered eighty-two pieces of each kind and twenty-eight different kinds and sizes of table glass. Three engravers would be working for weeks on this one order.

I moved to where a man was completing a fragile figure of a woman on a tall slender vase. "It is like a modern Botticelli," I said.

"But that is what it is," said Mr. Beyer, pleased. "It's a much-admired old design by Simon Gate who died in '45. Gate was sometimes called 'the Botticelli of today.' This special engraver worked for Gate, and he still gets the artist's spirit into his creations."

In the studio where the new pieces are conceived, we met three of the six foremost designers. Gate was dead. Edward Hald, now sixty-four and the artistic head of the *bruk,* was on vacation. Vicke Lindstrand, who did the spectacular six-ton fountain in glass for the Swedish pavilion at the New York World's Fair in 1939, now lived in Stockholm. But Edvin Öhrström and Nils Landberg and Sven Palmqvist were there before their tilted drawing boards. These men, whose names were already well known in Sweden and by connoisseurs in other countries, belonged to the second generation of designers. In August, 1946, all three were thirty-nine years old. Touseled, tow-headed Landberg had come to Orrefors when he was eighteen and had worked first in the engraving room. Edvin Öhrström had specialized in sculpture at the Royal Academy of Arts and the Government had paid for his further studies in France, Italy, Belgium, and Germany. Thin, sensitive, high-foreheaded Palmqvist was also a product of the Royal Academy of Arts, and for two years he had studied painting in Paris and later in Holland and Belgium.

Besides these renowned artists, there were other younger designers at work—men who had not yet reached the goal where their names might be signed to pieces, but who were allowed to make their own experiments unrestrained as long as they did not violate Swedish good taste.

Before a heavy paper, hung man-high on the wall, one young designer was limning in banners, which soldiers were bearing up a winding road to a medieval castle. It was to be a decorative window for an office building.

Another chap was designing a group of light fixtures for small apartments. Another was creating a flared modern cocktail glass with a thick wide base. Palmqvist was drawing a stylized tree with exotic fruit. Öhrström, who was painting an Ethiopian head in profile, said, "We designers study the process of manufacture from the initial mixing of the sand and soda to the engraving. We are well aware of the snares and caprices of our material. And sometimes we have catastrophes. Making Ariel glass is always a breath-holding process. We can never be sure until the firing and the cooling how it is going to turn out."

It was eleven o'clock, the hour when all work stopped for a filling old-fashioned Swedish breakfast. After what we would call luncheon, the men would work until three or four, depending upon the job, and then they would have the rest of the long summer afternoon to amuse themselves.

On our way out, as we looked in again at the display room, we met two brisk dealers from South Africa, who had made the trip from Cape Town by air. They were quite excited that they had been allowed to buy such a quantity of the glass.

"It's an odd thing," said one, "not only can an expert recognize an Orrefors vase at sight, but a top expert can tell you which of the six designers created it."

Though designers get the chief credit, the trick is done by the perfect cooperation of the blowers, the engravers, and those who bake and cool, and even the man who keeps the night fires going. It is the harmonious teamwork that turns out the quality product, like those dramatic productions Stanislavsky used to direct at the Moscow Art Theater where the smallest role was as perfectly portrayed as the stellar. From the first, Ekman and his chief designers, Hald and Gate, and the master blowers and technicians worked on the principle "that only the best that can be achieved is good enough."

"My function," said Henning Beyer,* as we strolled back along the shady road past the workmen's cottages, "is merely to strive to maintain the character of Orrefors and its artistic conscientiousness, and, if I may use the expression, its commercial integrity."

In world marts today Orrefors glass is looked upon as a seal and symbol of Swedish quality in commerce as well as in modern culture.

* On September 21, 1948, Henning Beyer died. His son Johan Beyer became director of Orrefors Glassworks.

22.

Skåne, Sweden's Most Opulent Province

*Their minds had the calm of this very plain where
their ancestors had lived and toiled for thousands of
years. Their life was ordered and stable. Many of the
old farms had gone down as inheritance from father
to son through generations. And as a Scanian farmer
could stand at the gate of his house and look around
for miles across the level plain, so in his youth he
could look ahead in life and know with reasonable
certainty what it would be like. His life would be
much like his father's—much as his son's life would
be after him. This knowledge put its imprint on him
and gave him assurance. And when a man can take
such a long-range view of his life, how can he find
reason for hurry?*

—GÖSTA LARSSON of Skåne

MILK AND HONEY

SKÅNE IS Sweden's most opulent province. Its gently rolling contours
are delighting to the eye; its soil, which has been cultivated for four
thousand years, is uncommonly fertile. The atmosphere of abundance and well-being is strikingly obvious, in the bright-eyed people,
the sleek cattle, the tremendous barns, the endless fields of growing
crops. But the quality of this southernmost province takes special
tone from the old castles, where private families still carry on their
daily routines, as naturally as the swans that skim the surface of the
lily-studded moats. In resplendent Skåne the aristocratic tradition
yet abides and enriches the texture of the whole region. The culture
of the manor is as emphatically reflected in Skåne as the sturdy
peasant culture is marked in Dalarna. Both attitudes are of high
significance in their contributions to what is meant by "Swedish."

298

In Sweden's program to uplift the so-called common man, the aristocracy has fallen in line and at the same time continued more or less in its accustomed way. The nobility has survived through today, because its members acknowledge their responsibilities. The great families of Skåne have always been active agriculturists, and they have been alert to take advantage of the improved methods of scientific farming. They are not absentee landlords residing on the Riviera. Though they may retain small apartments in Stockholm for "the season," they really live on their land and have close knowledge of everything that goes on. In these latter years of increased wages and almost confiscatory taxes, many estate-owners have found it hard to retain their places, and most of them have had to curtail the casual sumptuousness of former living. But the last sacrifice to be made is in the parks and gardens. For the estate-owners acknowledge a patriotic duty to keep their gardens and parks in splendid condition for the public which is privileged to visit them. Call it esthetic feeling or mere pride, well-ordered beauty has a special place of emphasis in the thought and energy of the Swedish aristocrat.

Skåne possesses a patina not often discerned in other Swedish provinces. Though each of the castles is distinctive in itself, they are little different from those of Denmark, for Danes built the majority of them. Until February, 1658, Skåne was Denmark's most "resplendent jewel in her treasury of provinces," when, by the Treaty of Roskilde, the territory passed into Sweden's possession.

When one comes to Skåne by way of Denmark, as I did the first time, the province seems an extension or continuation of Danish life, despite the fact that it has been Swedish for almost three centuries. The beech forests are like those of Denmark, the boxwood hedges, the grouping of fruit trees about the white cottages. The people one meets often have Danish figures and physiognomies rather than Swedish. They smile more readily than most Swedes, are less shy and have more engaging ways. These Scanians have been consistently well-fed through the ages, and they like to eat, drink, and make merry almost as much as their cousins across the narrow water of the Öresund. Only when one reaches Småland, where farmhouses are red and fir trees grow somber among rocks and the men are tall and lank, does he know he is in Sweden.

Because of the munificence of its farm produce, the epithet commonly applied to Skåne is "the Granary of Sweden." Eighty per cent of its fields are under cultivation. Seasonal cascades of silver-green oats and golden wheat spill gently down the slopes to meet the endless flat acres of juicy sugar beets. Bees make honey in a mellifluous bee paradise of fruit blossoms and clover. Cows abide in succulent grasses and give such quantities of creamy milk as to have their private histories recorded in international dairy journals.

Skåne's wealth originally came not from the soil but from the sea. In the Middle Ages its coastal fish marts attracted merchants from all North Europe. And unlike the typical rocky coasts of most of Sweden, Skåne is rich in beaches, not just occasional pockets, but mile after mile of soft sea sand and dunes of stirring beauty.

The garden of Skåne is even blessed with coal. Ten miles northeast of Hälsingborg begins the coal-mining region, and here again nature has conferred special dispensations, for the mines are screened by beautiful beech woods, and that loveliest of the castles, Vrams-Gunnarstorp, lies close by the coal mines of Bjuf.

Skåne is by no means all rural and agricultural. In a statistical sense it is an urban as well as a rural province, for it contains one-fourth of all Sweden's towns numbering more than 10,000 inhabitants, while Malmö, its capital, is the kingdom's third city, and Hälsingborg ranks fifth. Most of the region's prosperous industries cluster around these two seaports.

Lest one surmise that mankind decays in this munificent region where wealth accumulates, it must be known that Skåne is reputed to produce Sweden's cleverest men. Per Albin Hansson, the most able prime minister since Hjalmar Branting, was born in Malmö. So was Gustav Möller, Minister of Social Welfare and one of the most important Cabinet members of this century. Citizens of all degrees of estate and breeding take a special pride in their Scanian birth, as Virginians do in the United States. Though they do it disarmingly, they do not hesitate to admit to feeling a bit superior. Once in Stockholm a group of Swedes were asking each other what they would prefer to be, if they had not been born in the province of their birth. A Stockholmer said he would rather have been a Värmlander. A Laplander confessed he would rather have been a Dalecarlian. When one turned to the man from Skåne and asked,

"If you were not born in Skåne, what would you be?" he answered gravely, "I would be ashamed."

A HOTEL, A GARDEN AND A PRIVATE SHOWING

If one enters the peninsula of Skåne from the north, either from Göteborg or Stockholm, he gets the first flavor of the province at Båstad, the idyllic seaside resort situated at the tiptop northwestern corner on the Kattegat. Here on the *en tout cas* courts of Båstad, renowned for its tennis matches, King Gustav V played his much-publicized game every summer, until his physician stopped him in 1946, as he entered his eighty-eighth year. Båstad boasts Sweden's favorite southern hotel, patronized by Swedish and European royalty, as well as discriminating persons from both hemispheres. Called Skånegården, the hotel was built as a hobby by Ludvig Nobel, nephew to Alfred, inventor of dynamite and bequeather of the Nobel Prizes. Architecturally it is designed on medieval monastic lines with porticos, arcades, and cloistered courtyards, graced with fountains and flowers. The heavy oak furniture, the textiles and rugs, have been especially designed to accord with the style of the building. The color tones are masculine and mellow, autumn oakleaf, faded orange, burgundy, and old saddle-leather. The place is run much like an English country house. Tea is served in the English manner about lily pools in a high-walled garden. Breakfast is brought to the bedrooms. Luncheon and dinner are taken in a large dining pavilion at the sea's edge, a two minutes' walk down from the hotel, where the western windows open directly upon the Kattegat and the sunset.

Ludvig Nobel, who lavished such taste and expense in creating a hostelry of simple elegance, is recently dead and the present director is his son, Olof Nobel, an ingratiating young man who shares his father's devotion to public-spiritedness and gracious traditions. By American standards, prices are reasonable.

One could not have a better introduction to Skåne than a few days' stay at Skånegården, whether his interest lies in sport or sea bathing or the mere luxury of rest in charming surroundings. The salubrious climate of Båstad is so remarkably mild that tropical, as well as subtropical, plants have been acclimatized in the famous

Norrviken garden a few miles south. Like Ludvig Nobel, another man with a passion for bringing more beauty into contemporary civilization was Rudolph Abelin, who devoted his substance and his last twenty-five years to creating series of gardens in the manner of different periods of time and different nations. At Norrviken are to be seen a Hindu garden, a Medieval garden, a Renaissance garden, a Romantic garden, and a water garden, each distinctive, imaginative, and evocative. But for me and for Dagmar Abelin, the Diana-like daughter who has inherited her father's work, and who dresses in beige coveralls, the climax is the Japanese garden. As it slopes from a high ridge down the winding flagstone steps and paths to the blue sea, every few yards a new enchantment unfolds. Japanese red maples, weeping beeches, Swedish silver willows, and fantastic dragon spruce trees are placed with such artistry among rills and cascades, little bridges, and stylized Oriental ornaments in stone, that you ask, Can there be anything more lovely in Japan itself?

Though King Gustav comes as a fortnight guest of Skånegården each summer, the chief celebrity who lives the year round in Båstad is Ossian Elgström, one of Sweden's strangest geniuses and most original artists.

As Olof Nobel and I were taking a walk one night, I mentioned that an etching of a reindeer round-up by Elgström hung on our wall in Alabama and elicited much admiration. "Would you like to meet him now?" Nobel asked. "I know him well."

"Of course," I said, "if you would dare call at this hour."

But there was a light in one of the front rooms of his cottage, and when Nobel knocked, a woman came to the door and sent us around to the artist's bedroom entrance at the back. I could not blame her if she resented our intrusion, for she was serving coffee to a male caller, whom we could see through the open window. As we went around the house, Nobel told me that the woman had been Elgström's cook, but was his new wife. The artist was divorced from the charming wife I had met in Stockholm in 1939, when I had visited a small temporary museum provided by the city to house Elgström's collection of panels interpreting Norse mythology.

I remembered his wife's saying somewhat wryly that her husband was one who lived in communion with sea storms, snow, stars, and strange gods of his own creation. And the lovely sixteen-year-old daughter told us of her father's accumulation of toy soldiers and miniature ship models of all times and countries. A Hungarian lady art-dealer had given me other hints of Elgström and his unconventional predilections. As a young man, he found affinity with the rough-hewn, archaic world of Greenland and Swedish Lapland. In West Greenland he enjoyed the pagan feasts of the Eskimos, eating their blubbery fare with relish and taking as much pleasure in their coarse habits and customs as in the exciting mystery of the polar nights. Ethnography became a passion with him, and when he painted, his picturesque details and decorations were as authentic as they were fascinating. He cultivated an "at-one-ment" with the heroes of mythology, and took as major themes the struggle of primitive man against the elements and good against evil.

It was natural that such an individualist would break completely with both the sentimental Swedish tradition of painting and the more realistic Norwegian. I had been impressed by the daring and originality of his imagination and techniques. As it suited his purposes, he had skillfully employed water color, Chinese ink, gouache, and lithography. When I had looked upon a large canvas celebrating a bear hunt in Lapland, with hundreds of intricate figures of men and beasts in tense movement, I had thought Elgström seemed to paint by the illumination of lightning flashes. I had hoped some day to see this unorthodox artist, who felt impelled to live within sound of what he called "his friend and counselor, the sea."

When Nobel knocked on the artist's back door, I wondered what tempest we might stir up in this unpredictable man. Though the light was burning in the room and it was not yet ten o'clock, Elgström had gone to sleep in his clothes, but with his shoes off. When Nobel told him an admirer from America desired to meet him, he roused himself. Instead of howling like an Arctic bear, in a sleepy voice he sent us back around to the front to the studio that adjoined the living room. When we entered at his bidding, there, under the glare of an unshaded hanging electric bulb, the close-cropped white-haired artist stood blinking and teetering, with one black-socked foot set protectively over the other. As he shifted for better balance, I saw he was hiding a great hole in his left sock, from which his white big toe protruded like a terrapin's head.

Canvases stood thick against the walls. Elgström would reach out for a picture quickly, and then hold it before him like a shield. With the good-sock-foot again protectively set over the abashed, undarned one, he would stand as if on one leg like an ibis, and wait for the reaction. And as he clutched at his loose unbelted trousers, whenever he set a canvas down and took a new one up, he resembled one of his own Minor Prophets about to lose his pants. From Lapland themes and interpretations of the Edda, he had turned recently to Biblical subjects, with saints and sinners and prophets in unorthodox attitudes. Though his poetic and dramatic vision was entirely his own, I found in his work some kinship with William Blake, with Oriental painting, and the Bayeux Tapestry.

Elgström's eyes held the guarded fire of genius, yet his smile was shy and almost childlike. He seemed the gentlest-disposed of creatures, and when we apologized again for disturbing him, he reassured us by asking what was an old man's dozing worth anyhow. When Nobel invited him to tea with us next afternoon, Ossian Elgström declined with a wide grin, on the grounds that Nobel's fine guests might not care for the unfashionable cut of his garments.

PRINCESS IN THE PARK

Some of the guests in the hotel garden the next afternoon were fine indeed. Crown Princess Louise and her English mother, the Dowager Marchioness of Milford-Haven had driven up from Sofiero, the summer home of the Crown Prince, to have tea under the garden willows with their cousins, the Earl and Countess of Athlone, who were staying at Skånegården.

I had not yet met the Crown Princess, though I had been presented by letter from her brother-in-law Prince Wilhelm, who had written her I was coming to Skåne. The next morning she received me at Sofiero, and I learned that she, as well as her husband, who was absent on a fishing trip in the far north, was an admirer of Elgström's paintings of primitive Lapland.

On the drive from Båstad to Sofiero a series of pastoral scenes unfolded in steady succession. The heavy rains of the night had endowed the landscape with an enhancing dewy quality. The clover fields shimmered in the sunlight and the hides of the Friesian cattle glistened as they grazed, each in its own tethered orbit, making a stylized pattern of variegated black and white ovals on a rich green fabric. Windmills twirled briskly in the breeze from the Sound and the bearded barley rippled like a wind-stirred lake. Vacationists on bicycles pedaled energetically, as if to beat the next shower to their destinations.

At the gates of Sofiero uniformed guards told us we were to drive within the park up to the villa door. Though splendidly situated in its park, the house was neither medieval palace nor Renaissance manor. It was just a big, ugly structure built in the tasteless last quarter of the nineteenth century by a greatuncle of the Crown Prince.

At the foot of the stairs we were greeted by an equerry, who said Princess Louise was expected back at any moment. She had had to take her mother on some medical mission to Hälsingborg twenty minutes away, and she had asked the head gardener to show us about the gardens against her return. With the white-mustached old gardener leading the way, we strolled down into the vale that lay between the villa and the sea. The trunks of towering beeches, like polished olive-gray columns, supported the fretted roof of beechen green and azure. Rhododendrons and gigantic ferns crowded the slopes, and flowering shrubs along the winding walks reflected the dappling half-light. It was all so well done it looked as if nature had created a masterpiece unaided by man. But it was the Crown Prince's first wife, Princess Margaret, who had laid out the plan of the garden many years before. She, too, was an Englishwoman, the daughter of the Duke of Connaught and thus a granddaughter of Queen Victoria. The gardener told me that the present Crown Princess shared her cousin's passion for nature. "Her Highness," he said, "regards nature as something not just to be looked at, but lived."

We had paused at some rare shrub with great white blossoms before which the gardener swelled with pride. I remembered the place as it had been in May of 1939, when the beeches had just unfolded and the wild honeysuckles were coming into bud along the brook. Deep in the pale-green shadows of a dell Thérèse and I had stood silent. "Even Denmark cannot surpass this," we said. "It is like some haunt in Paradise."

When we came up to sea level again, rain clouds had blotted out the sun and turned the Öresund from blue to green-gray. Through the back gateway we reached the beach and the water reeds growing around a plain wooden structure that was as simple as a royal bathing pavilion could possibly be. The narrow strip of sand between the park and the sea belongs to the public, and on the sandy bridle path a young equestrian was cantering on a spirited mare.

As we traced a different curving path back up through the vale, the place seemed even more enchanting under a sunless sky. Through the thick damp foliage a figure appeared above, coming down to meet us. In some surprise, the gardener said, "It is Her Highness."

Princess Louise greeted me with a warming smile. "I'm just back," she said, "and I guessed you might be coming this way." She was wearing a gray tailored suit and a small cream-colored panama with a gray band. In her hand she carried a rolled umbrella like a walking stick. "We had a shower in Hälsingborg," she said. "And I am still British enough to carry an umbrella when it looks like rain." She shifted the umbrella and gave me her ringless right hand.

This great-granddaughter of England's Victoria was a good-looking woman, quite slim, and casually smart. She faintly resembled her glamorous younger brother, Lord Mountbatten, who at the time was making a farewell gesture in history as India's last viceroy. And something in the chiseling of her sensitive aristocratic features, her deep-set violet eyes, the spring in her step, made me think of Virginia Woolf, the late English novelist.

We stopped to look at new small plantings the Princess had made to replace the magnificent boxwood killed by the unprecedented freeze of 1945, which, she told me, had ruined much of Skåne's century-old shrubbery.

When we came into a walled space with espaliered apple trees wired to the bricks, I told her how much my wife and I had admired this spot in mid-May of '39 when the blossoms were in full flower. "What is more lovely," she said, "than flowering fruit sprays spread against a sunny wall? But, alas, my husband and I are almost never here in May to see the blossoms."

Princess Louise was somewhat reluctant to show the house. "It is really nothing at all," she said, "built at a bad period. But we've arranged a sun room that looks to the sea, where the view is rewarding in all weathers."

The glassed-in room was bright and cozy, done in a silvery green. The sun had burst forth again, so we could see Hamlet's castle of Elsinore in visible splendor on the Danish coast. If the royal summer residence of Sofiero was commonplace, it was blessed with magic casements, as well as a superlative park. The water of the Öresund was now a sparkling blue, almost identical with the iridescent blue of the lovebirds in a gilt cage that swayed slightly on suspended springs. "But you have a pair," I said; "not a lone bachelor like Philippe at Prince Wilhelm's, who is denied a mate so that he will sing."

Princess Louise smiled. "I'd rather they would be happy than vocal," she said. "And the grounds abound in thrushes and nightingales. We have only to open the windows for a chorus of bird song."

"A REVEREND ESTEEM OF ALL"

Between Denmark's Kronborg Castle and the Swedish port of Hälsingborg pass merchant ships to and from the port of Stockholm, Baltic harbors, and northern Germany, as well as Finland and Russia. Of great strategic importance, Sweden's third port, Hälsingborg, is older than Stockholm. But its charm and beauty are due more to its situation than to antiquity. It is built on three levels: along the edges of the Öresund, on the plateau, and on the higher ridge. A fountain by Carl Milles graces the harbor front not far from the spot where Marshal Bernadotte first set foot on Swedish soil on October 20, 1810. The twelfth-century defensive tower called Kärnan rises impressively to dominate the whole landscape and looks across the Sound to Renaissance Kronborg, hardly three miles away. Sailors of many nations enliven the city's busy streets and pleasant parks, and also the near-by fashionable spa of Ramlösa, from whence comes the mineral water served in every restaurant in Sweden. Hälsingborg is one of the focal points for visiting the privately owned castles.

Through Allan Kastrup I had been invited to tea at near-by medieval Borgeby, a former residence of the archbishops of Lund. Its present owner, Ernst Norlind, is not a baron or a count, but a genial minor poet and a painter, who in his youth had entered the baron's house as an art-teacher, and who had married the spinster heiress and in time become the master himself.

Kastrup, who was born and bred in Lund, told me how much Norlind was beloved in the province. Because he sang with unflagging rapture of the charm of the region, he was often called "the spirit of Skåne." Regarded as an embodiment of the Renaissance, Squire Norlind seemed more a legend than a man connected with the modern world of bartering actuality. And it was his eighty-year-old wife, who, despite her stone-deafness, discussed husbandry with the bailiff and the farm workers and managed the main business of the estate.

When Kastrup's car drove through a great arch in the masonry into a court studded with ancient trees and a group of medieval buildings, Norlind himself bounded out of the castle to greet us. His welcome was as overflowing as if we were returned prodigals or Eastern philosophers bringing him tidings from afar. His expansive smile held no trace of Swedish reserve. And Norlind looked more a Dane than a Swede. He was shortish, with plump pink cheeks, a close-cropped white beard, and blue eyes that sparkled with merriment.

Before entering the house, we walked this way and that about the court. Our host would point to a tower, a heavy oak door, a high window. He would give a date, name some noted person of the past. In a garden we stopped before the tomb of a baron set in a wall, with his wives buried upright on either side of him, their replicas in bronze bas-relief, one fair, one plain. "Which do you think brought him the greater happiness?" Norlind asked. "Why, the homely one, of course."

At the end of a walk bordered with hazelnut trees he called my attention to a medieval inscription chiseled in old Swedish, and translated it for me:

> O cold marble,
> Guard the memory
> Of a warm heart.

From an arbor he snipped two bunches of grapes and presented them to us to eat as we strolled. When I admired an especially magnificent yellow rose, he drew out his knife and cut it quickly. But I restrained him from cutting a whole bouquet, saying they were too beautiful to disturb and explaining that we were motoring.

"Here, under this magnolia," Norlind said, "the young Austrian poet, Rainer Maria Rilke, and I would sit and talk poetry, when I had finished giving the Baroness her art lesson. Then Rilke came again for a long visit after we were married. Poor fellow, such a genius—but he did not manage his life well. How could he, though, with that bizarre mother who would dress him in girl's clothes because she had wanted a daughter? I have so many fascinating letters from Rilke. I will show you after tea.

"And that amazing Ellen Key," he went on, "who clutched at people and clasped their hands fervently all the time she talked with them. But a brilliant and big-hearted woman, whose frank books had mighty influence in female emancipation. She liked to watch me paint and chattered without ceasing."

For his studio Norlind used a great upper hall of one of the medieval outbuildings. It was crowded with stuffed owls, long-legged storks, spreading eagles on pedestals, a variety of gorgeous-plumaged birds, and a collection of white herons that had not lost their immaculate sheen. "These are my models," he said affectionately. "They have served me well, living and dead." I knew they had; for Norlind's bird paintings were in museums and galleries and countless private homes.

Amid the piles of discarded castle furniture, scores of canvases lay about, some half-finished, others only begun. When the mood was on, Norlind would paint in the poor light of the narrow windows, and then he would write verses out-of-doors down by the river that ran through the estate. Often he would sit and meditate by the marble tombs in the garden, or stroll about sniffing one rose tree after another in the small back court.

Since his early twenties, except for three monastic years, the seventy-year-old Norlind seemed to have existed in an almost perpetual state of esthetic enjoyment and creative activity. During the decades innumerable famous and interesting people had been guests to Borgeby. Since Norlind had nothing pressing to do but entertain them, the visitors enjoyed themselves hugely, for he had a gift for savoring life and he could communicate his delight in the flight of a bee, the color of old brick, the illuminations in the margin of an ancient book of devotion. He smiled almost continually, and he was witty in his speech, though his most common expression, as we strolled, was, "Isn't it lovely? It is so very, very beautiful, I think."

When we finally entered the castle itself, it was through a cellar scullery. The underground kitchen was a vast room with mammoth squat stone pillars supporting the main floor. A banquet for a conquering army could have been cooked here. But now, amid the great copper pots and iron spits and baronial bake-ovens, two pretty shy maids were daintily preparing tea for four.

Up some circular stairs we wound into a hall, and then passed through a drawing room hung with Norlind bird paintings to a small library where tea was laid on a round table. The Baroness, who was awaiting us, looked much younger than her eighty years. A strong-featured woman, with an aristocrat's bearing, a rough-weather complexion, and a husky voice, she talked little because of her deafness. But her kind dark eyes were alert, as she gave attention to my English, a language she had never studied. As we lingered over tea, I got the feeling that the lady had gladly given over her life to relieving her younger husband of burdens that might keep him from entertaining his friends and indulging his hobbies.

Once Norlind had renounced Borgeby and strayed from the Baroness and their only child to take up an even more sheltered existence, but this one rigidly austere. In his search for Truth, he had entered a monastery in Italy, and for three years at Assisi he read the metaphysicians and did the religious disciplines. The monastic routine calmed his troubled mind, gave him reassurance in himself and the world of active man; and he returned to Sweden with renewed zest for living. The volumes on the shelves behind Norlind attested to his spiritual studies: Ansari of Herat, St. John of the Cross, Nicholas of Cusa, Ruysbroeck, St. Anselm, Thomas Traherne. My fingers touched a little volume of Traherne. As I took it from the shelf, it fell open at a page with a marked passage: "Your enjoyment of the world is never right till every morning you awake in Heaven; see yourself in your Father's palace; and look upon the skies, the earth and the air as celestial joys, having such a reverend esteem of all, as if you were among the angels."

"Oh, yes," Norlind said. "It is so true, so true! And in the monastery I learned to appreciate Skåne and the world."

As we finished tea, I could not help but think: "All this—a manor, a medieval atmosphere, cloistered gardens, acres of income-bringing produce, a wife to handle the tiresome routine details—for one genial gentleman's pleasure." This indeed was superprivilege for one not born to baronial inheritance. And, besides, Ernst Norlind had troops of admiring friends to cheer his tag end of life. For Norlind accepted manifold gifts from life only to give them back transformed to others. He was as eager to share his experiences and enthusiasms as to break his bread with strangers and friends.

I looked at this gracious, dynamic man, who had become a kind of living legend, as I might regard one of the last of a species at the verge of extinction. I felt somehow as if I were being entertained by a breathing museum piece.

The dominant factor of Ernst Norlind's attraction was his infectious response to life. After seven decades the old gentleman savored familiar experiences with delighted surprise, as if he had never before tasted a hazelnut, or smelt a rose, or seen the afternoon sun turn his wheat fields to shimmering gold. His gift for life was such, I felt, that if he had been destined to a hall bedroom, he would have yet responded happily to Fortune's alms, or what the Norwegians call "the Poor Fates."

When we had made our farewells to the Baroness, our host asked if he might ride with us to Lund, the university-cathedral town seven miles away. He said he had a late-afternoon appointment there. His small bag was ready by the front door. Of course we were more than delighted to have his company; but I could not help but notice that on the drive his conversation lost much of its sparkle, and occasionally his manner became distrait. By the time we reached the ancient town on the rise above the plain, he was visibly agitated. But when we let him out at the hotel, he once more assumed his jaunty air, and with the most cheery countenance imaginable bade us good-by.

As we drove away, Kastrup told me what the appointment meant. The Norlinds' only son and heir was in a hotel room with an attendant, ill with an old nerve malady. He had been sent back that morning to Lund after "taking a cure" somewhere without improvement. The father and mother were naturally extremely apprehensive. But they had had the son kept in Lund, so as not to mar the pleasure of the American's visit, and they had been careful not to let any of their concern reveal itself. I recalled that during tea our host was twice wanted over the long-distance telephone, and that he and his wife had exchanged strange looks over a telegram that had inadvertently been left face up on a desk. I was touched indeed by the brave gesture to keep the glowing hospitality undimmed by a hint of their own agony of spirit.

So with all the cotton wool of privilege, I said to Kastrup, one has no more assurance of escaping the griefs and pitfalls of this earthly world than a stevedore. The episode of the son-and-heir's illness merely underscored some handwriting that I thought I had discerned on the medieval walls.

AN ANCIENT UNIVERSITY AND A THEATER OF TOMORROW

At the beginning of the tenth century chroniclers were treating the place called Lund (a wood) with respect; and, according to an anonymous rhapsodic poet, the town already "stood in fairest growth, when Jesus the Christ let Himself be born." Like Visby and Uppsala, Lund gives out a pleasant aura of antiquity. In pagan times temples to Norse gods were centered here. It was the Danish Canute, King of England, who sent the first missionaries to bring the Christian faith to Skåne, and about 1085 Lund was made the seat of a bishopric.

It was this same Canute who founded a cathedral school here, reputedly the first school in the Scandinavian peninsula. The massive Romanesque cathedral itself was begun in the last quarter of the eleventh century; and in 1163 Lund's archbishopric was granted primacy over all Scandinavia. The cathedral possesses a famous many-pillared crypt, where Danes of great lineage lie entombed; but its fourteenth-century astronomical clock is the chief source of tourist delight and wonder. Marking not only hours, half- and quarter-hours, but equinoctial hours, and the movements of the sun and moon and the fixed stars of the zodiac, the clock puts on a special show each midday, and has for over five hundred years. Just before noon, watchers gather to behold a pageant in miniature. At the stroke of twelve, warriors on horseback brandish swords and robot trumpeters emerge to sound a Christmas jubilation hymn. Then gates open and diminutive mechanical figures, the Wise Men of the East, move across the stage to worship the new-born Christ.

Kings have been crowned in Lund cathedral and royal weddings and christenings have been celebrated before the high altar with lavish splendor. Here, in 1405, Princess Philippa, the brilliant sister of Henry V of England, was wed to that stupid Erik of Pomerania, who became king of all the Scandinavians.

At the time of the Reformation, Lund still held high significance as a religious center of the North, boasting seven convents and twenty-two churches. But after the State religion was made Lutheran, Lund's importance waned sharply. With the founding of the university in 1668 by the Swedish Charles XI to help reconcile the former Danish citizens to Swedish nationality, the place began to assume some of its former prestige. Today, because of the university, Lund is recognized as the cultural center of southern Sweden.

In this pleasant residential town of comfortable size (32,000 inhabitants plus 4,000 university students), numerous old houses from the Danish period still exist, along with half a dozen museums containing everything from prehistoric utensils to ornate ecclesiastical vestments. Just behind the cathedral stands the one-story home of Esaias Tegnér, poet-bishop of the first quarter of the nineteenth century, whom Longfellow admired and translated. This is perhaps the most visited of the museums, doubtless because Tegnér is considered Sweden's national poet. But the Cultural Historical Museum in the Lundagård, where the various buildings trace the whole history and cultural life of Skåne, is one of the finest of its kind in Europe.

Tegnér received his degree from the university in 1802, and stayed on to teach Greek and write poetry until he was made a bishop. While Tegnér was lecturing in the classics, Pehr Henrik Ling, the inventor of systematic gymnastics, was teaching fencing to the students to pay for his own medical education. Though Dr. Ling has no house preserved as a memorial, the message of his system of body culture for health and esthetics has made his name far better known about the globe than that of the epic poet.

Ten and a half miles southwest of the old university town is Malmö, the capital of Skåne, dating from 1319. Sweden's third city and second seaport is beautifully situated on the ship-stirred Öresund, opposite Copenhagen's copper spires sixteen miles across the water. Malmö is a railway and air-transport center, as well as a seaport. All the international trains to Germany and the Continent pass here on their way to the ferry station of Trälleborg on the Baltic. From Malmö passenger trains to Denmark are ferried across the Sound; and at frequent intervals planes make the ten minutes' hop to the Danish capital. Within the city itself one is scarcely aware of railways, ferries, or airports. But he notes that the old part, with its medieval mansions, is surrounded by picturesque canals that were once defensive moats. Malmö is particularly impressive for three features: its sixteenth-century great square, its garden apartments, and its splendid municipal theater, which is hardly to be equaled in any metropolis of several millions, though Malmö has little more than 150,000 inhabitants.

As viewed from the Kramer Hotel on the west side, the great square is memorably mellow and attractive. In the center stands the fine equestrian statue of Charles X by Börjeson, one of the best since the Renaissance. The north side is occupied by the governor's mansion. Facing the hotel stands the town hall in a modified Renaissance style, and behind it rises the Gothic spire of the Petri church, dating to the early fourteenth century. In the town hall is a magnificently proportioned council chamber of St. Knut's Guild, a medieval commercial organization, which gave the Malmö branch its charter in 1360.

While a brisk air of prosperity pervades this active business center, in the summer afternoons the city streets are virtually deserted. Drive to the parks and there will be found citizens basking in the sun or strolling under the trees or dallying in the alfresco cafés. The lovely Kungspark, with its extensive summer restaurant, lies north of the town. Just beyond is the castle called Malmöhus, where Bothwell, third husband of Mary of Scotland, was kept prisoner, in comparatively agreeable incarceration, for the six years following 1567.

In its design for living, Malmö has one feature that holds an especial appeal for home-lovers—a series of garden apartments. Instead of living above or below neighbors, one lives beside them in rows of story-and-a-half cottages linked together in attractive lines and angles by tiled roofs and soundproof interior walls. Only the two front houses of a unit are on the street. The rest curve away down flagstone walks bordered by flowers and facing a common green belt. To avoid uniformity, the houses are staggered, every other one in the row turns its back and faces another unit. The only entrances are on the fronts, and the projecting backs of the alternate houses on either side form walls of a private flagstoned terrace, where one cannot be seen by either of his next-door neighbors. The living rooms have two exposures with plate-glass windows to bring in as much of the out-of-doors as is structurally reasonable. The common gardens and lawns are tended by professional gardeners, so that the whole effect is harmonious. No householder has to tend his furnace, for the apartments are all heated from a central plant. And besides garbage disposal, such community conveniences as a nursery and a laundry are provided, and also domestic help when desired. With each series of apartments goes a community center with recreation rooms, garage, and shops. Instead of elevators, concrete pavements, and city noise, one may have a charming six-room cottage of white painted brick, with lawns and shrubs and country air, and all for a modest rental of $600 a year.

This "Open Air City" is a practical and esthetic answer to the desire for the pleasant atmosphere of a private home with all the conveniences of a town apartment. To create more of these bright living quarters for city folk, surrounding meadows are being purchased. The creator of the Friluftstaden is country-born Eric Sigfrid Persson, a former brick mason and an architect without benefit of a degree in architecture. Because of the exigencies of business, Mr. Persson himself lives in a city apartment house of his own design facing the sea. His drawing room of pale wood and glass is furnished with inviting long chairs and decorated in festoons of growing vines with great heart-shaped leaves. The apartment seemed to reflect his own genial, expansive personality, his love of light and a sea view, and his belief in luxurious ease after the long day's work.

The Malmö Municipal Theater exemplifies the new tone of the age even more strikingly than Eric Persson's two types of apartments. The theater was only begun when I first saw the spot in 1939 and it was not completed until the fall of 1944. In the best sense of the word, it is municipal, built from voluntary contributions of the townsfolk, who paid in 8,500,000 kronor before the cornerstone was laid. For operating revenue today the theater receives 200,000 kronor annually from the city lottery and 80,000 kronor from the municipal treasury.

For four decades the idea had been taking shape, and at last a collaboration of modern architects and designers achieved the splendid whole. A motivating force in the interior design was renunciation of the old "court theater," where the important and wealthy sat in the best seats. An auditorium for a classless, democratic society has been devised, and from any of the sixteen hundred seats in the house a spectator can see and hear equally well. The rows of seats are arranged in a fanwise spread up from the apron of the stage at a moderately steep angle. Members of the royal family can sit in no more conspicuous places than the butcher or the baker's wife. For all comers, the price of admission is the same, 1 krona 50 ore. For forty cents one can see the best Swedish actor play *Hamlet* or a troupe do *Oklahoma*.

The interior decoration is quite different from the gilt and velvet of the old-fashioned theater. Ceiling and walls are pure expanses of blond linden veneer, and the lighting fixtures are of chaste crystal glass. The only obvious opulence lies in the upholstery of the sixteen hundred seats, in which the material is a handsome woven stuff with an original design in white on a rusty-red background.

By means of an ingenious innovation the auditorium can be scaled to seat as few as four hundred. Sliding wall panels of blond wood are suspended from concealed steel tracks in the ceiling to make four different-sized auditoriums, according to the type of performance. And the sixty-foot-wide stage can be diminished by folding walls to a suitable size for an intimate closet drama.

If standing room is required for a spectacle, the entire back walls of the auditorium may be removed to provide ample space for five hundred standees in the great curve of the foyer's upper level.

Gracious double staircases connect the two levels of the white marble foyer. Gossamerlike but substantial balustrades of platinum-colored metal make the only decoration besides the twenty chandeliers of Orrefors glass. These hanging lamps light the foyer at night, but in the day the illumination comes through outside walls of glass that bring the green or white or autumnal season within doors. The whole effect of the theater's interior is both clarifying and esthetically exciting.

The two-story functional façade is constructed of plate glass and square white columns, about nine parts glass to one of stone. From the outside, with Orrefors crystal illuminating the white marble stretches of the foyer, the theater looks like a pleasure pavilion of some future age or a structure on another planet. Before the façade spreads a great paved court, and on one side is a long low wing with a restaurant. On summer nights the theater-goers dine at small tables on terraces under the sunlit sky.

Only in one detail is there a jarring note. In the center of the lower foyer between the opposite sweeps of stairs, a statue stands larger than life, a beefy-armed, big-breasted, big-bottomed Thalia, with frizzed hair and a swirling floor-length skirt. In choosing the Muse of Comedy and Bucolic Poetry for his subject, the sculptor Marklund was justified in making the figure blooming and buxom, as the name Thalia implies, but he has committed an error in taste in dressing up the country gal like bad Hollywood. In this beautiful and inspiring structure this silly statue is as offensive as a calliope set before a church's high altar to play *Te Deums* on steam pipes. Except for Thalia, the Municipal Theater of Malmö is an ideal embodiment of a people's aspiration for the utopian age of a classless society, where culture and democracy do not clash, but mingle in creative concord.

VISION AND THE CLEANLY PIGS

While modernity has fused happily with the patina and tradition of Malmö, there is one much-visited town in Skåne that outwardly seems virtually untouched by modern temper. Ystad, the southernmost town in Sweden, spreads along the open Baltic Sea in its old-world picturesqueness and claims to rival Visby in charm.

Though it was never so important as the Gotland capital in its heyday, it, too, was a prosperous mart and a religious center, as half-ruined medieval monasteries and churches attest. The narrow labyrinthine streets add a special allure to the well-preserved examples of pre-Reformation domestic architecture. The epithet "quaint" is most readily applied to Ystad today. But its half-timbered mansions from the fifteenth and sixteenth centuries, with their galleried courtyards and richly colored plaster, are too splendid for such a word. While Ystad now thrives largely on fish and tourist trade, it retains its atmosphere of sunny serenity and old-fashioned urbanity.

Beyond the eastern edges of town lie commodious resort hotels which have been erected to take advantage of the beaches that stretch for mile after mile. Besides the diversions of boating and sea bathing, there are the varied attractions of fishing villages, Viking graves, bridle paths through forests, the grim stronghold of Glimmingehus, and a half-dozen of Sweden's famous castles lived in by their owners.

Twenty miles inland from Ystad the grandfather of Charles Augustus Lindbergh was born in a one-story stone house, with stone barns and stables forming a courtyard. The farm is still called Gårdlösa. But the real name of Colonel Lindbergh's grandfather was Ola Månsson. He was not only a prosperous farmer, but a friend of the king, and four times he was elected to the Swedish Parliament. When he lost his seat in 1858, because of his ardent advocacy of building newfangled railways in Skåne, he was so exasperated at the lack of vision among his constituents that he sold his place, emigrated with his family to Minnesota, and changed his name to Lindbergh. His Swedish-born infant son grew up to become a representative in the United States Congress and the father of Charles Augustus, who, inheriting some of old Ola's vision, immortalized the adopted family name by his daring achievement in aviation. In 1933 when the famous flyer and his wife, Anne Morrow, visited the acres once owned by his ancestors, their tour through Skåne was like an heroic progress, and they were forced to drink gallons of coffee in the various households of country cousins. As a fitting souvenir of the visit, Colonel Lindbergh was presented with his far-sighted grandsire's spectacles.

Roughly, there are four types of landowners in Skåne: the small holder, the average-size farmer like Lindbergh's grandfather, the great farmer with a thousand or more acres, and the titled owner of a castle with an estate of several thousand acres.

In 1939 I was taken to see Bergsjöholm, a prosperous big-scale farm of the third category, with a beautiful beech forest, perhaps the oldest beech woods in Sweden. The active proprietor, Mr. Hageman, was born a Dane, short, plump, and genial, with some of the manner of an American business executive, tempered by Danish grace. His father had made a fortune in sugar in the Virgin Islands, and both father and son had ardently encouraged the raising of sugar beets in Sweden. Mr. Hageman took us about the place himself, and in every phase of big farming from beet-culture to pig-raising we could see his shrewd ability behind the order and prosperity. His pigs could not have been sleeker, cleaner, or more contented. Each sow and her farrow had their own four-room apartment on the concrete floor of the long piggery—feeding room, living room, nursery, and toilet at the back, where the animals were trained to perform their natural duties. The narrow nursery retreat in front was protected by short spaced bars so that the pigs could slip through and sleep in peace without danger of being mashed by their mother. "Hogs," Mr. Hageman said, "do not like filth and mud, as some people assume. They don't like to foul their nests any more than larks do. My hogs prefer to go to the back compartment when they need to." We witnessed the proof of his contention.

Mr. Hageman told us that though there are fewer persons engaged in agriculture in Skåne than there were in 1900, production has increased three hundred per cent. This increase is due to scientific methods and cooperative dealings, by which the owners of entailed estates benefit as much proportionately as the small holder. Cheap electric power provided by the Government has made threshing and wood-cutting easy. And on most places cows are milked by electricity.

On Mr. von Pappen's large farm, however, the gentleman proprietor did not believe in milking by electricity. He claimed he got 1,500 liters a cow more a year by having them milked by human hands. For the purpose he had imported a score of Finnish girls, whom we went out into the fields to watch at work. There twenty golden-haired milkmaids in fresh blue linen sat on three-legged stools, beside a line of black and white Friesian cows staked on a green carpet of meadow grass. The native pastoral scene made a picture easier to recall in sharp focus than that of most of the castles, which are Skåne's number-one attraction.

HOW LONG WILL THE CASTLES STAND?

For all Sweden's Labor Government and democratic institutions, interest in the aristocratic traditions is still strong. Often factory workers from distant districts take their vacations in Skåne and cycle from one nobleman's domain to another to gaze upon the castles and wander about the parks.

No area of ground on the globe has proportionately more private castles and parks worth the visiting than has Skåne. Maps of the province are printed with little facsimile pictures of the great houses in red or white, depending on the brick or stone of the building material. On these maps the castles look as thick as the fixed stars of heaven, and it is often difficult to make selections from such richness.

Unless one has friends to introduce him to the province and arrange special visits to the castles, the most agreeable procedure for covering the château country is to radiate by car or bus from four centers: Hälsingborg and Malmö on the Öresund in the west, Ystad on the Baltic in the south, and Kristianstad, the chief town in the east.

Among the noted places reached from Hälsingborg, two are peculiarly rewarding. One is moated Krapperup, which lies in the extreme northwest of Skåne on that thumblike peninsula that shoots protectively towards the Danish coast. With Krapperup goes one of the largest private estates in Skåne—fifteen thousand acres. It is the seat of the Gyllenstjernas, whose family name of "Golden Star" is memorialized on the castle walls, embossed with great six-pointed stars in white stone that gleam like white gold by moonlight.

At the foot of a range of beech-covered hills ten miles to the northeast of Hälsingborg is Vrams-Gunnarstorp, the most charming of all Swedish castles. Built in a graceful Dutch Renaissance style, it has attractive awnings over the first-floor windows, which gives the castle a surprisingly homelike quality that none of the other great houses possesses. Its romantic gardens are set with the most magnificent boxwood in North Europe. Because of the special charm that exudes from the happy combination of gay architecture, splendid gardens, and surrounding beech forests, King Duncan's lines come naturally to mind:

> This castle hath a pleasant seat; the air
> Nimbly and sweetly recommends itself
> Unto our gentle senses.

Southeast from Vrams-Gunnarstorp stands austere Knutstorp, famous as the birthplace of the great Danish astronomer Tycho Brahe in 1546. And southeast of Knutstorp rises the fabulous, five-storied, U-shaped Trolleholm, with five round towers crowned with high peaked caps of black metal, and altogether looking as if it had been designed after an illustration in a book of fairytales.

From Ystad one visits Marvinsholm with its ghost-haunted halls, Svaneholm with its eight-hundred-year-old oaks, and the moat-bound Tosterup, where Tycho Brahe built his astronomical tower for studying the language of the stars. Some fifteen miles directly north of Ystad is the eighteenth-century white-walled, red-roofed Övedskloster, which King Gustav III resented as "far too regal for a subject."

As the Danish Brahes in the sixteenth century owned many estate with castles, so do the Swedish Counts of Wachtmeister to-day possess several great properties. Within the orbit of Kristianstad various Wachtmeisters hold five large estates, including two of Sweden's finest castles, Trolle-Ljungby and Vittskövle. The latter, built by the Brahes in 1551 and sometimes called "The Red Castle," is generally considered the most magnificent private castle in the land.

The geometry of the design makes Vittskövle unforgettable. Its moat lies square in a wooded park with two stone causeways connecting the square of island with the mainland. Constructed in four parts around a square court, the castle walls do not rise sheer from water, but from green terraces bordered at the moats' edges with spaced boxwood bushes standing like a guard of honor. At diagonal corners are two thick round towers, more strikingly different in design than those of Chartres' heaven-pointing spires. One is topped with a stony crown of crenelated battlements. The other terminates in tiers of narrowing bulbous domes, each covered with black metal. Somewhere near its top a slender octagonal belvedere, suggesting a Byzantine minaret, breaks the bulging motif, and the tower's tip ends in a kind of black exclamation mark against the sky's blue slate.

The builder of Vittskövle indeed expressed himself and his age in creating this castle for defense and gracious living. The architectural language from 1551 is as eloquent in its way as an old poem of technical perfection, stirring rhythms, and surprising delights. Superbly conceived for a special breed of men and executed with enduring material, Vittskövle today is something concrete to point to as a product of a culture, when men were originally ennobled for bravery or some distinguished service to the State.

If a hundred guests are no longer housed at a time at Vittskövle, a score or more sit at table at certain seasons of the year. And, as in past centuries, guests appreciate the spacious halls to walk in when the storms blow, and the flowering courts to meditate in when the sun shines. To guests returning from a hunt or a picnic on the Baltic shore, the romantic spectacle of the castle itself never fails to be exciting.

Persons who are privileged to stay in Skåne's illustrious houses, but who have none of the responsibility in keeping them, may hope that the way of the castle would flourish forever. But few are the male guests, come for the fall shooting or the Christmas parties, who would covet stepping into the shoes of the master of the place. Few are the ladies who would desire to manage such households, planning meals and directing the laundering of the thousand pairs of linen sheets that must be washed and ironed and lavendered twice a year to keep them from yellowing. In these days of staggering inheritance taxes and domestic-servant scarcity, the younger generation of counts and barons growing to adulthood do not seem eager to come into possession of the family castle. Some say frankly that they doubt if the struggle will be worth the golden candlestick. Only the most incorrigibly patrician may want to give over their energies to ordering the lives of retainers and to the grooming of parks for the delight of the populace.

Two of the Skåne castles already stand uninhabited: Bollerup and Örup. Another has been metamorphosed into an agricultural school. Within the last decade two noblemen have turned their castles into museums. One of these is the pearly-white castle of Ellinge. Set in its olive-green moat, it is as luminous as the smooth-feathered swans that skim the reflecting mirrors of the water. Ellinge is now a museum, because its owner can no longer afford the domestic staff necessary to maintain it. He lives in a small manor near-by and watches over his castle like the anxious guardian of a beloved ghost. However, the proud gardeners who tend the grounds have no desire to change their way of life, for they consider themselves peculiarly fortunate to work always within the boundaries of beauty.

About twenty of the Skåne nobility endeavor to keep their places running in some approximation of former grandeur. Among them is the wealthy Baroness Henriette Coyet, who lives in Torup, the most admired castle situated within twenty miles of Malmö. Like Vittskövle, Torup's two great towers are at diagonal corners; but two sides of the extra-large moat have been filled in and turned into gardens, while the other two sides retain their traditional swans and water lilies. The formal garden with clipped boxwood in circular patterns is one of the most noted in Sweden. The widowed Baroness Coyet revels in the daily life of her castle, where she often entertains members of the royal family, as well as distinguished foreign celebrities and experts from the agricultural experiment station at Svalöv. An energetic, witty woman, she is an able estate-manager, as well as a famous hostess. Though she herself never attended an agricultural college, she is well versed in agronomy. Her special hobby, however, is her herb garden with varieties collected from all corners of the globe.

Some enterprising spirits like the Baroness von Schwerin have devised original ways of meeting the pressure of taxes and increased household expenses. She is the youngish chatelaine of Skarhult, a formidably magnificent castle from the sixteenth century, with ivy-mantled towers reaching to impressive heights. Set in a regal park, with gardens walled with stockades of clipped boxwood, Skarhult breathes antiquity from every reddish-orange brick. But the Baroness herself, who invited Allan Kastrup and me to luncheon, is very much of the present. An affable, handsome, well-dressed woman in her middle thirties, she gives the impression of one able to cope with the times on any terms.

If half of the castle is like a museum, there is nothing of the dry custodian about the lady herself, though she appreciates her husband's treasures and knows their stories as well as the Baron, who has devoted his spare time to writing histories of the great houses of Skåne. Among the *objets d'art* and bric-a-brac in one of the drawing rooms, I was attracted to a cabinet of eighteenth-century snuffboxes, perhaps because the trinkets seemed peculiarly archaic in the 1940's. When I picked up a strikingly handsome one of plain gold, I was told that King Gustav IV had given it to an ancestor. I was surprised to find brown powder in the box. Since I had never sniffed snuff, I was invited to a pinch. I snuffed deeply, but failed to sneeze, and had to make four tries before I got a worth-while reaction. As I thanked the hostess for the treat of clearing my head in the eighteenth-century manner, I wondered how often the Baroness secretly replenished the receptacle with fresh powder. When she assured me it had certainly not been refilled since her husband had inherited the place, I felt somewhat relieved about my own gauche failure to respond sensitively to the elegant custom.

There was nothing particularly memorable about the drawing rooms of Skarhult, for they were more or less like those of any castle where generations of varying tastes had accumulated and discarded. But one whole long wing of the castle was original. The Baroness had transformed it into a school for household management. Cooking and sewing and weaving and baby care were taught to thirty resident girls at a time. They learned everything about housekeeping, from making beds and laundering fine linens to designing homespun fabrics, arranging flowers, and preparing canapés for cocktails. The Baroness, who was chief executive and daily on the job for eight months of the year, gave instruction in the art of gracious living, while skilled instructors taught weaving and plain and fancy cooking.

Housewifery is taken very seriously in Sweden, where virtually all girls take some course in home economics. The classes at Skarhult Castle are mostly for girls from upper income groups, but some of the neighboring farmers who have special aspirations for their daughters send them to the castle school to learn more about the amenities. Students come from the Continent too, and occasionally from the United States.

Now it was the vacation period between semesters, so we did not see the school in session. But we saw the looms and the electric cook-stoves in great halls, as well as the bedrooms, where knights and ladies were once domiciled for the shooting parties, now made cozy for the students with fresh hand-woven fabrics. The profits help to keep the castle running, and the school's future success seems assured by the long waiting list of applicants.

Down in a bright flowered-chintz morning room, where British and French and American magazines lay on tables, we had dry martinis in a windowed nook that gave on the blood beeches of the park. The Baroness' army officer brother and his wife were the only other guests. The appetizers were new to me: cubic inches of bread covered thickly with a rich cheese like the icing on little cakes and served piping hot. The hostess confessed they were not her origination, that she had just brought the idea back from Iceland.

When I asked Baroness von Schwerin if she really enjoyed living in a castle, she smiled and said, "What else are we to do? My husband inherited the place. We have people working here whose ancestors have been on the estate for centuries. Their living and ours comes from this soil. They are as attached to the place as we. Their roots are fixed even more firmly. And we feel we have an obligation to the State to keep the park and the gardens trim and open to the public certain hours each day. It's all part of the tradition. How long? Who knows? In the meantime, we carry on. We work and we have fun. There are generally house guests, and we play about with the people on neighboring estates. Doubtless we shall keep the thing going as long as we can, and if it comes to an end, we shall content ourselves in some simpler way of life."

When Thérèse and I had visited Bosjökloster Castle a few miles northeast of Skarhult, in 1939, we had then sensed the strain of possessing a castle and making an estate pay off in this industrial age. Bosjökloster lies almost in the center of Skåne, on a stretch of land that divides Ringsjön, Skåne's largest lake. Some of its masonry dates to the twelfth century, when a Benedictine convent was established here. Since the seventeenth century the place has been possessed by the Bondes. The present Count Bonde of Bosjökloster is a hard-working, youngish man, who prepared for his job by taking his degree in agriculture, which entailed his hiring out as a farm laborer for two years on someone else's place in another part of the country. So he knows thoroughly every branch of the estate business, from fruit culture and forestry to scientific silage and the proper spreading of manure. If a laborer should become ill during a pressing seasonal job, the master could fill his place, where he would not hesitate to work side by side with his men.

In an oak-paneled library with dark-red hangings we were entertained to sherry and Swedish biscuit. Count Bonde told us of the rare giant aspen which the famous Professor Nilsson-Ehle had discovered recently deep in his forests and which he was propagating at the experiment station of Svalöv. Since match stems are made from aspen and match-making is one of Sweden's important industries, bigger aspen trees will add to Sweden's revenue. He told, too, how the crossing of winter-hardy Swedish wheats with pure-bred, high-yielding varieties from western Europe had increased the mean yield in Skåne between forty and fifty per cent. He explained the difference in quality and habit of Star oats and the variety known as Golden Rain II. When the present apple orchard of four thousand trees plays out, Count Bonde said he expected to replant with some breed of extraordinary new apples that Nilsson-Ehle was propagating at Svalöv.

Because it was late in the forenoon, the nightingales of Bosjökloster were silent in the hedgerows. But at night, Count Bonde said, when they sang their plaintive songs, the farm laborers told their small children that the ghosts of the friars were chanting their even-songs.

Count Bonde was an attractive and modest young man. In tweed plus fours, his legs showed strong and shapely, not only from the constant walking about his lands, but as an inheritance from ancestors who once had need of calves and thighs to set off court knee breeches. The noble shoulders, however, seemed none too broad for his double job in this high-taxed semisocialistic present. It was a big responsibility for any man to keep his helpers happy and to wrest

from the soil cash to maintain a medieval castle in some semblance of the manner to which it had been accustomed.

When we left Bosjökloster, I remarked that Burton's dictum that "idleness is an appendix to nobility" would certainly not apply in Skåne in the twentieth century.

As the Swedish writer, the Countess Posse-Brazdova, said to me at dinner one night, those from the outside who see only the romantic trappings have little conception that the master and the mistress of a castle are working at something from early morning to evening. They can hardly conceive that this way of life, which undoubtedly has elements of the fabulous, is yet radically real and resolutely earnest. The swans, the boxwood, the art collections, the family jewels, the tapestries are dispensable; but absolutely essential are the fields, the forests, the tractors, the milk cans, and the fattening pigs. The sale price of butter and grain are of more significance to the estate than the espaliered pears, the crested wineglasses, the pheasants, and the liveried footmen.

The cult of the manor house is a product of centuries of cultivation and refinement. Its way of thinking is characteristic of all old land societies with traditional heritages and special responsibilities. Its seasoned attitude towards life and human relationships is something that no new millionaire industrialist knows anything about. There is a genuineness about these gentlefolk and their adherence to inherited ways and objects that cannot be imitated. And in modern Sweden, with its advanced social consciousness, the aristocracy is not unappreciated, because it helps keep high the tone of what is called Swedish culture.

VII

LAST WEEK-END

23.

A Crayfish Party and a Barn Dance

I ask you for white blossoms.
I offer you memories and people.
I offer you a fire zigzag over the green and marching
  vines.
I bring a concertina after supper under the home-like
  apple trees.

— CARL SANDBURG

I MEET LENNART BERNADOTTE

JUST AS I was leaving Stockholm on a three-day motor trip, the manager for Europa Film called and said Lennart Bernadotte, the son of Prince Wilhelm, was completing a film on Sweden to be exhibited in the United States, and he would like me to be the voice that accompanied the sequence. The Europa man said the American Embassy had suggested me, and asked if I could discuss the matter with Mr. Bernadotte on my return from Dalarna. A dinner engagement was arranged.

The evening of my return to Stockholm the telephone rang at six o'clock. It was Lennart Bernadotte saying he believed I was dining with him at seven and what did I think about motoring into the country and having dinner at Drottningholm in a pleasant little restaurant across from his favorite castle.

I liked his friendly voice immediately, as I had liked his face in the newspapers that told of some of his recent cinematic work. And I recalled a magazine article at the time of his marriage fourteen years before, when he was twenty-two, by which he lost his possible succession to the throne because his bride was a Swedish girl instead of a foreign princess. For under the Constitution a prince of

331

the blood who marries a Swede is no longer ranked as a Prince of Sweden and he is deprived of all support from Government funds. From her best seller, *Education of a Princess,* I knew that his mother the Grand Duchess Marie of Russia had left his father when Lennart was six years old. With pleasure and a certain curiosity I looked forward to meeting this independent-minded prince whose blood was half Romanov, with that best of the Russian czars, Alexander II, for a great great-grandfather.

If Lennart Bernadotte's natural warmth was Russian, his punctuality was Swedish. At two minutes to seven I was in the upper lobby of Hotel Stockholm facing the elevators. And at one minute to seven out stepped Mr. Bernadotte, hatless, and tall as his grandfather, King Gustav. His horn-rimmed spectacles gave him something of a combination businessman-student appearance. His engaging smile and responsive manner cut straight through the formalities of self-introductions. He seemed a very youthful thirty-six, and, though almost all his life had been spent in Sweden, he was certainly not typically Swedish.

On the drive through the blue summer's evening we found we had many points of agreement besides our preference for the hydramatic Olds in cars. (His was a brand-new model, the first 1946 that had arrived in Sweden.) We both liked living in the country. We disliked cocktail parties and had an aversion to radios. "I see," he said, using the radio term, as he parked the car near the castle gate, "we are on the same wave length."

In the restaurant he had reserved a small private upstairs room with eighteenth-century furniture and a large window facing the lake and a segment of the castle. The table was already spread with smörgåsbord: salads, caviar, cold lobster, smoked salmon, foie gras. A middle-aged large-bosomed waitress, who had known the prince since his babyhood, took orders for the rest of the dinner. "Broiled chicken, if it's very tender?" Mr. Bernadotte suggested. The waitress said she was not sure. "Excuse me, I shall go feel." She returned with good report. She had felt carefully and there was a very tender plump young chicken.

We began with the ritualistic Swedish schnapps, and had a small bottle of champagne with the dinner. My host was careful to drink with great moderation, because of the Swedish law against driving under the influence of alcohol.

The dinner went with the Continental grace of leisure. Bernadotte told of his motion picture of Swedish scenes, and we set a time for trying out my voice at the Europa studios. He found his job most congenial, but because he did not care greatly for city life, he spent every day possible on his farm eighty miles from Stockholm, when he was not working on a picture.

He confessed to a fondness for Drottningholm Castle across the way, and after coffee we took a stroll in the grounds. "The King always comes here for Christmas," he said, "and commands the presence of the entire family. With all the grandchildren and great-grandchildren and great-grandnieces and nephews we make a sizable gathering. Of course there is a huge Christmas tree, and the park is very beautiful in the snow. Continuous children's parties create a lot of noise and confusion. My grandfather loves it."

As we approached the Hercules Fountain in the French garden, Bernadotte stopped and laid a warning hand on my arm. "Look," he said softly, "rabbits dancing on the lawn! I wish my little boy were here."

I counted more than a dozen rabbits in the ten o'clock twilight, frisking about the fountain that had been brought back from the Wallenstein palace in 1648 in the time of Gustavus Adolphus.

As if playing a game, the rabbits let us come very close to them and then shot off into the shadows of the English park, which began where the French garden left off. We looked back at the silhouette of the castle that had been rebuilt after a fire in 1661. Queen Hedvig Eleonora had commissioned Sweden's greatest architects, the Tessins, father and son, to design the structure and she had brought in foreign artists to decorate it.

"Drottningholm has been a favorite residence with the royal families ever since," Lennart Bernadotte said. "The theater is my favorite part. That was built by Queen Louisa Ulrica, the blue-stocking sister of Frederick the Great. But it was her son Gustav III, our most glamorous king, who made the theater the center of Sweden's artistic life. After his assassination at a masked ball in 1792 the theater remained closed for a hundred and thirty years. It was used as a storeroom when it was rediscovered in 1921—with all its white and gold *décor* intact, its pewter footlights and chests of costumes. This and the one at Gripsholm are the only two palace theaters left in the world that preserve the eighteenth-century scenery and mechanical devices. Since its reopening as a museum exhibit in 1922, we often have performances there with people from the Opera or the Dramatic Theater in Stockholm. Some of the performances are private, some open to the public. In my youth I loved the smell of the old theater. I still do. Probably it had something to do with my being in the motion-picture business."

It was growing darker, and we turned back at the beginning of the park. "When my mother left, and my father was away on his big-game hunts and world travels, my grandmother took charge of me. I learned punctuality from her. Victoria was a Hohenzollern, and could be very stern. But my father was the complete opposite, unconventional and indulgent. When he was home, he taught me to love the out-of-doors, sports and fishing. Between them they brought me up. Perhaps they weren't a bad combination for me. But I married to suit myself, and I wouldn't swap my little farm for twenty castles like this. Wait until you meet my wife."

My first evening with Lennart Bernadotte was a pleasant prelude to a real friendship, and I spent my last week end in Sweden with him and his wife at *Hornet* in the country.

THE FARM

He had warned me not to expect a manor like his father's Stenhammar. It was only a simple farm, he said, and his wife would do the cooking, because their cook had been established in the town apartment to look after the two older girls, who had started back to school.

I had just snapped the locks on my suitcase when the hall porter telephoned and said, "The Prince is here in the lobby."

I looked at my watch. It was precisely two o'clock. The scrupulous promptness of Swedes never failed to impress me despite the countless times I had noted it.

In the front seat of the car outside was Karin, Lennart's wife, looking cool and lovely, with a yellow wool sports coat thrown about a blue summery dress, underscoring the clear Swedish blue of her eyes and the gold of her hair. She had such a girlish freshness that it seemed incredible she was the mother of four children. But it was easy to believe that she was a favorite with the King. Half of the back seat and floor of the Olds was piled with baskets of food and bags of imported fruit and boxes from the bakery.

The early afternoon was green-gold when we drove out into the country, where the reaped wheat fields were now carpets of gilt-bronze stubble spread over rolling plains. Here and there sprays of silver birches were touched with the first autumnal gold. The last ten miles lay through rugged country on a twisting narrow dirt road, far from the châteaux and spruce parks.

Lennart's farm is twenty miles deeper in the country than his father's place. It has been known for two generations as *Hornet,* which is Swedish for "The Horn," because its acres stretch like a horn-shaped peninsula into a lake, with the master's house near the tip.

As we drove into the property, Lennart indicated on a rise of ground to the left the red barn and the three neat cottages, in which his farmer and his helpers lived.

"My farmer is celebrating his fortieth birthday tonight, and we are going to a dance in the barn after my father's dinner."

By coincidence the farmer's birthday fell on August 31, the day of the year on which Prince Wilhelm entertains some of his literary friends at a crayfish dinner, an annual celebration known as *Röda Dagen,* the "Red Day," which closes the crayfish season. I had been invited to make the fourteenth at table.

Around a curve in the road we came to a short driveway of clipped lime trees leading to the house. Headed directly for the car came running a sturdy-legged youngster, with a blackish blue-gray dog leaping and barking excitedly at his side. The boy wore a coverall playsuit of blue duvetyn and a beret to match. It was the six-year-old son Carl Johan, whom they called John. He had a broad brow and enormous dark-blue eyes, dark-gold hair, and a generous full-lipped mouth. Radiating health and high spirits, he was as handsome a child as I have ever seen. With a shout of joy he climbed up into his father's lap, kissed both his parents with big smacking kisses, gave me a glowing welcome, and laughingly commanded Blackie, the ecstatic Reisenschnautzer bitch to get down.

Taking the wheel from his father, who held him in his lap, John steered the car, and we crept the last distance between two idyllic-looking long low red houses that flanked the drive—one for the gardener's family, one for the washing and storage. In a small courtlike space between multicolored gardens, we drew up before the steps of a porch so festooned with enormous heart-shaped vine leaves that we could just barely see the white door of the timbered house painted the characteristic red of the countryside.

Two pink-cheeked maids in white uniforms came down to help with the luggage, while the youngest Bernadotte daughter, a two-year-old, stepped forward gravely to greet her parents and to curtsy sedately and unsmilingly to the stranger. She was as reserved as her brother was impulsive and responsive. John had already broken into one of the confectioner's boxes. With a cry of delight he seized upon a glazed meringue and began devouring it with gusto, asking his mother's permission after his mouth was crammed full.

We entered at the back of the house, for the kitchen was at the left of the entrance. At the end of the hall was the dining room furnished with peasant antiques. Beyond was the living room, with great windows in the three walls, looking respectively upon a flower garden, a terraced lawn, and a rambling apple orchard that descended to the rock-edged lake.

Lennart and I stepped through the French windows of the living room to the veranda and out onto the lawn. Spaced white hydrangeas grew like small umbrella-shaped trees and surrounded a flagstone terrace set with white garden tables and yellow deck chairs. The water of the lake was green-gray and stirring. The variegated distant shores were edged with spruce and rock. It looked like a lake more accustomed to wild life than human beings.

In the rural stillness I gazed admiringly in four directions. I could not help comparing this secluded farm with the magnificent Castle Mainau on Lake Constance, which Lennart's German grandmother, Queen Victoria, had left to him and his father and which some 275,000 tourists paid admission to see in 1938. Lennart stood looking first at the lake and then back towards his rolling grain fields. On his face was an expression of ultimate satisfaction. "This," he said with a sweeping gesture, "is the perfect antidote for the city and my other job. Do you know, if Heaven were to offer me any plot on earth, I wouldn't want to swap it for this."

Because we were to be at Prince Wilhelm's at six o'clock, we had tea in the drawing room instead of the garden. John had cambric tea with us and consumed several more meringues with relish. Then he ate a bowl of clabber. He would stretch his mouth wide to meet the dessert spoon and stretch his eyes, too, with gusto. Twice he paused to kiss his mother's hand out of respect and gratitude. "Yes, John eats life with a large spoon," his father commented. "And he has kissed hands since the age of three. No one ever taught him to kiss hands. I suppose it's the Russian coming out in him."

"Why is his left ear so red?" I said.

"Excitement over our homecoming and the cakes. Whenever he's excited or enjoying himself very much, blood runs to his left ear. He gets it from me—mine did that way when I was a child."

In Karin's flower garden the ear cooled down to a healthy pink, as John walked beside his long-legged father, taking exaggerated manly strides to keep in step with him. On this last day of August the flower garden was still at its height. Sweet peas grew to such sizes as I had seen equaled only in Edinburgh. In this land of short summer, spring flowers like sweet peas and delphinium bloomed at the same time with dahlias, asters, snapdragon and gladioli, while the drooping birch branches by the lake were already touched with fall.

While we walked among the flower beds, the afternoon turned cool, and I declined the dip in the lake Lennart offered. As he was splashing naked in the chilling water, I had a hot bath and cold shower in the house. When I was wrapping myself to dry in a vast luxurious bath towel, my eye was caught by an embroidered monogram. A diadem with nine stars made a half-circle about a great flourishing letter M, three or four inches across the hem. Below the initial there was embroidered a date, *1906*. The linen pillowslips and the sheets on my bed had the same monogram, with the M under the starred crown, and the same date. I realized that this linen had been brought by the Grand Duchess Marie when she came to Sweden as Prince Wilhelm's bride. When the marriage ended in annulment, she had left everything she brought from Russia to the four-year-old Lennart, as well as the little palace she had built in Djurgården in Stockholm, which he had later sold to the Italian legation in order to buy *Hornet*.

THE CRAYFISH PARTY

We arrived at Stenhammar at one minute to six, and Prince Wilhelm himself came to the door to receive us. When the two tallest living princes greeted each other, the six-foot-four son kissed the six-foot-four father on the cheek.

All the nine male house guests but one had arrived and were down in the right-hand drawing room, with Madame Jeanne and Anita Nerman, Madame's pretty twenty-year-old granddaughter just returned from a season in New York. The only one I had met before was Karl Ragnar Gierow, the young dramatist who wrote plays in verse. There were novelists and poets, an art critic, two publishers, and a newspaper editor who had fought the Nazis in strong editorials throughout the war. The youngest of the men was Olof Lagercrantz, a brilliant young satirist of thirty-three, who hardly looked twenty-five.

I went over to Madame Jeanne seated on a divan and inquired after Philippe's health. "Let us go see him," she said, rising and taking my arm lightly. In the drawing room across the hall Philippe's cage sat on a front window ledge beside a fluted bowl of gray-blue Orrefors glass, almost exactly the color of Madame Jeanne's chiffon evening dress. The lovebird was at his supper. I remarked that he had been eating the last time I saw him. *"Philippe mange beaucoup,"* Madame said.

Just then Prince Wilhelm's motor car, which had gone to meet the last Stockholm train at Flen, drew up on the lower terrace. A gentleman got out and the chauffeur followed with his bag. "Pär Lagerqvist," said Madame Jeanne. *"Very* distinguished poet. A member of the Swedish Academy."

When Pär Lagerqvist came back downstairs, a cocktail was served, and we went out to dinner. We passed through the large dining hall into a long narrow room which may have been a sun parlor. But now the high windows were blacked out with long red shades, and in the wall spaces between the windows were fixed enormous crayfish made of glazed red cardboard. The room was lit by red candles in red lacquered candlesticks and wall sconces. Silver platters were piled high with great mounds of red crayfish bearing tendrils of feathery dill. From across the table Prince Wilhelm asked Gierow, on my right, and Karl Asplund, the art critic, on my left, to instruct me in the Swedish technique of eating crayfish. "Be sure to select females for Professor Strode," he said. "They are more tender and delectable."

"How can you tell the females?" I asked.

Prince Wilhelm smiled and leaned slightly towards me as if imparting a secret: "By the soft expression in their eyes."

Fortunately I had eaten crayfish before, in Finland in 1939, and I knew something of the ritual of breaking the crustacean in two, and first sucking the juice from the front half and then the back half before getting at the flesh. At a crayfish party given by Sibelius' daughter Eva, her husband had made a great to-do by having all the ladies remove their rings, bracelets, and necklaces, and the men their wrist watches to protect them from the juices.

The gay Danes say that the formal Swedes really relax only in the crayfish season, largely because of the heroic injunction "a glass of schnapps for every claw." Since a man may easily consume a score of two-clawed crayfish, the hardiest Viking would soon land under the table if he followed the letter of the prescription. On the way to the party Karin had warned me that her father-in-law's schnapps glasses were double-sized. But though I remarked the crystal schnapps bottles set between each two guests, I completely forgot the warning about the size of the glasses.

It is Prince Wilhelm's nature to enjoy seeing persons in his presence happy, and he would raise his long-stemmed glass with a flourish and say, "Skål!" in a disarming way that warmed the heart as much as the alcohol warmed the inwards. Now and again he would nod to Gierow and indicate that my glass was empty.

As shells were cracked and discreet sucking noises were made, facets of raised glasses of aquavit reflected the myriad candle flames, while fragments of conversation blended in a pleasant mélange. I could readily agree with the Swedes that there is no taste to surpass that of the northern crayfish, which is so enticing that each bite creates new appetite.

As we ate, I noticed that Gierow and I shared also a waterless golden finger bowl to which he would contribute tiny claws and legs too small to eat. He explained that I, too, was expected to contribute, and that the alms-bowls of cast-off parts were to be collected and used the next day for a potage "beyond description and wild fame."

When our plates were littered with empty shells, Prince Wilhelm went about the table with a great round silver platter, and we would empty the red debris onto something that resembled the full moon. Then we would start afresh.

The conversation may have been brilliant. I don't remember anything special after Karl Asplund had reassured me about my enthusiasm for the Lappland paintings of Helmer Osslund, and Gierow had given up and said, "I just can't discuss verse drama while I eat crayfish."

For almost two hours we lingered over the crayfish and the skåling. At last we rose to join Prince Wilhelm in wishes for each other's happiness in the year to follow the Red Day. Then the eleven men lined up behind the three ladies, and we washed our fingers in silver basins at a long buffet.

Back in the dining room where a chicken course was then served, the fourteen now sat about a round table with a centerpiece of dark-red roses. Here Prince Wilhelm put me next to him with Anita Nerman at my left.

I gazed across the table where Madame Jeanne was smiling at the man at her right, holding a slim wineglass gracefully as she skåled. I shook my head incredulously at her youthfulness and paid tribute with my eyes at the same time.

"Is she really seventy?" I asked Anita Nerman.

"We celebrated her seventieth birthday in this room last December."

"How *does* she do it?"

"Charm, I think, is her only formula for keeping young," her granddaughter replied after a moment. "And of course she has just never thought of herself as growing old. Perhaps living in the country away from society and city excitements has much to do with it."

When we came from the dining room Philippe was flitting in festive freedom back and forth through the drawing rooms and the hall. He would light on a faïence jar, then on a piece of sculpture, then on a balustrade, and then on the shoulder of Madame Jeanne. To make up for denying the lovebird a consort, his mistress said Philippe was privileged to fly about the château at certain hours each day.

But he did not fly into the library off from Prince Wilhelm's study, where I found myself with Olof Lagercrantz, the young satirist. As we sat down to drink coffee and sip brandy, we got into an argument over English poetry. Lagercrantz, also flushed with copious schnapps, was a stimulating opponent, and it was fun to fight with him. In the thick of the fray Madame Jeanne glided in to join us, with Philippe atop her hair like an exotic blue-jeweled ornament.

"He does not like the chiffon of this gown, so he takes to my head," Madame explained, as we rose, and she seated herself very erect in an armchair.

Like Marchbanks in *Candida,* young Lagercrantz threw himself on the floor at Madame's feet and kissed her right hand. Not to be outdone, I, sitting in the corner of the davenport by her chair, raised her left hand to my lips. Then we went on with the argument in English, little of which Madame understood. But when Olof became heated, she would extend her hand, like a cooling draught, for him to kiss, and when I was too sharply emphatic she would lift her left hand, with gracious warning, and I would bend over it. Philippe would stretch his pretty neck and peer at Lagercrantz when he made a point vehemently, and then at me when I answered in underscored words. His yellow eyes glistened and his feathers ruffled and smoothed as our voices rose and fell. With superb tact and grace, Madame played the role of silent moderator, while Lagercrantz and I debated, now turning her head down to right and then over to the left, granting first one hand to be kissed and then the other. I am sure that the three of us were quite aware that we were indulging in impromptu play-acting and being a bit silly, with the lovebird an audience of one in the balcony of Madame's dark hair.

Prince Wilhelm found the situation highly amusing when he came and joined us, and he laughed when the irresistible young Lagercrantz had the effrontery to tell the sixty-two-year-old Prince that his chief charm was that he had never lost his youth.

It was near midnight and drizzling when Karin and Lennart and

I signed our names in the guest book on a page headed Röda Dagen, August 31, 1946.

In the cool night air, winding away from Stenhammar, I suddenly remembered the warning about the extra-large size of the schnapps glasses. Lennart only laughed and said, "Too late now, and you'll have to take one more small one at my farmer's party."

A BARN DANCE AND A QUIET SUNDAY

The farmer's house was jammed. Countryfolk from miles about had come to the birthday celebration. The little front stoop was so crowded that some of the men had to step out into the yard so that we could get to the door. The small sitting room was crammed with women, and the center table was loaded with sandwiches and cakes and bottles. After we had greeted the farmer and his wife, Lennart and I went upstairs to a large room under the roof, which was filled with males from fourteen to eighty-odd. Lennart went around shaking hands with everyone present, and I followed suit. Again downstairs, we drank the farmer's health with schnapps, and then set off to the barn whence the music came. It had begun to rain. Karin, escorted by the farmer, walked across the muddy yard in her white evening slippers, as unperturbed as if she were treading the royal palace's parqueted ballroom.

The illumination of the barn came from a dozen old-fashioned lanterns, which the neighbors had brought and carefully hung on hooks here and there. Towering up to the roof beams, tons of wheat, that had just been reaped and stored in open compartments to await threshing, gave off a wonderful odor, clean, sweet, and inspiriting. On a head-high platform above the tallow-slicked wooden floor was the musician's stand. The music was made by a single, comical-looking, carrot-headed Swede, who was marvelously adept at squeezing melody out of an accordion. As he played, he sang words to infectious dance tunes in a rasping tenor. "He is the one-man orchestra of the region," Karin said. "He can play all night. He never tires because he does not drink or smoke."

Lennart was already dancing with a sedate, plump farm wife. A tall, white-haired old man in a black suit came up and bowed be-

fore Karin, and they were off in a whirl. I turned to a buxom young milkmaid with braided red hair and apple cheeks, and we were in the thick of the crowd, dancing I know not what.

The singing accordion-player shouted out a command and everyone changed partners. In the midst of the jollity I realized that I was witnessing another of the manifold unpublicized manifestations of Swedish democracy. And I saw why people said Lennart Bernadotte had done more than his share to make the royal family so popular. And the next day I saw that his wife could be as much at home in her kitchen as in her parlor.

When we left the barn at half-past two, the party was in full swing. "They'll dance on till milking time," Lennart said.

It was still raining the next morning, and I was grateful to have the children's nurse bring breakfast to my room. Later, between showers, I tramped the fields with Lennart and the farmer. We looked at cows in the meadows and at pigs in their concrete houses. The two agreed on plans for crop rotation, for increased silage, and for repairs to fences. I knew enough about farming to know that Lennart had a real feel for the soil and was quite knowledgeable in husbandry. I had noticed the cooperative farm journal on his table. The farmer looked weary, for he had not been to bed at all, and Lennart urged him to spend the afternoon sleeping.

Karin herself cooked the Sunday dinner—the main course was wild duck with cauliflower and rice. Like most upper-class Swedish women, she was an expert cook, and we dined extremely well. But she had to wait until the gardener's wife had cooked her own family's meal on the Bernadottes' electric stove, since the gardener's cottage kitchen was torn up in the process of being modernized.

Because the rain still poured that afternoon, Prince Wilhelm telephoned to say that he would not bring his ten house guests for tea, as he had promised. Twice twenty miles over country roads in the rain was a trifle too much. We were somewhat relieved to have an afternoon of quiet, and Karin was spared a lot of work.

Before a fire of birch logs we lounged and talked. Lennart read me a short historical drama he had written and produced at a commemorative celebration in one of the northern provinces. He showed some pictures he and his mother, an ardent amateur photographer, had taken and developed themselves the summer before at Mainau. The Grand Duchess Marie had come from Buenos Aires to visit her son at the castle on Lake Constance shortly after the war's end, and they found that French soldiers had done a vigorous looting job. The looters had even taken away souvenirs of Lennart's last exciting visit to St. Petersburg at the three hundredth anniversary of the Romanov dynasty, when he was five. He had promised those mementos and little gifts from Romanov uncles and greataunts, including the murdered Czar and Czarina, to John. He told me about his dream of creating a sort of international institute for the Y.M.C.A. at Mainau. He planned to give the castle for the purpose, and he hoped it would become a kind of university for young men from all over the world.*

After supper Karin asked Lennart to play to us on his lute. "Then I must first make you extremely comfortable," he said. He put Karin on one divan and threw a light robe over her. He indicated that I should stretch out on the opposite matching divan with pillows piled behind my back. He set small tables with brandy glasses beside us and opened a bottle of Heering's Cherry Brandy. "To make you less critical of my singing," he said.

With his natural gift for music, he had taught himself to play the lute. He had an agreeable deep baritone and a good memory for folk songs in Russian, Swedish, French, and English. In the flickering glow of birch logs, while the rain beat softly against the

---

* In January, 1949, it was announced that the ancient castle of Mainau on the Swiss border in the French Zone of Germany had been given to the International Y.M.C.A. and would become a school for Youth leaders from all over the world. Lennart Bernadotte became chairman of the school board and Dr. Hugo Cedergren, secretary-general of the International Y.M.C.A., vice-chairman. The Swedish Government contributed an initial grant of 100,000 kronor to the maintenance of the new institution, which will be open to members of all groups in the world working for democratic instruction.

In a letter to the author from Lennart Bernadotte from Castle Mainau dated July 3, 1949, he wrote: "We are down at our castle in the lake of Constance with all our children and my father, and I must say we are having a grand time. The other day we opened the international institute for world youth leaders here in the castle. Y.M.C.A. will have courses almost all the year, and we hope that this may bring world-wide contacts with the German youth who need it badly. Just in these days the world committee of the Y.M.C.A. holds its annual meeting at Mainau, and the castle is full of international and inspiring life."

curtain-drawn windows, Karin and I lay propped up luxuriously with pillows, sipping brandy and listening to Lennart's varied music. I was surprised to like him best in melancholy, brooding songs touched with foreboding.

John in his pajamas had crept downstairs and stood hesitating in the doorway. Then he ran and cuddled beside his mother and lay there, with wide wondering eyes, watching his father's fingers move over the lute strings. The mellow mood of the hour was peculiarly contenting. When Lennart began an old love ballad from Robert Greene, he sang it directly to Karin.

> Ah, what is love? It is a pretty thing,
> As sweet unto a shepherd as a king—
> And sweeter too,—

He paused and came with lute in hand and bent down to kiss his wife on the forehead. Then as he went on with the words that made the shepherd's carefree lot more desirable than that of a king, I thought how Karin's and Lennart's union had been a kind of idyl in itself.

I could not have spent a last week-end in Scandinavia under happier or more heart-warming conditions. I admired Karin and Lennart for their understanding of true values, for their common sense, and for their lovingkindness not only within the home, but in their general attitude. And I thought how remarkable in this northern social democracy that still maintained a monarchy was the harmony and mutual respect and sympathy between all classes and kinds of men.

VIII

AFTERWORD

BECAUSE ON September second the Stockholm sky was overcast, Europa Film canceled the out-of-door shots that Lennart Bernadotte was scheduled to make that afternoon, so he and his wife drove me to the Bromma Airport to take the Transatlantic plane. I had come by American Overseas Airways, and now I was returning by the Scandinavian Airline System, which had inaugurated its first regular overseas flight* a fortnight before—an amalgamation of Danish, Norwegian, and Swedish lines, another evidence of Scandinavian cooperation and harmony. Some other friends had come down to say good-by, among them Hjalmar Procopé, the former Finnish minister to the United States, who had been forced to leave Washington through Soviet pressure in the days when the Administration was trying hard to believe in Russia's good-will and fair intentions. Now exiled from his native land by more Soviet pressure in Finland, Procopé was in Sweden, a refugee without passport.

The preliminaries of ticket-taking and baggage-weighing over, we stood in a group looking out on the field, when a plane from the U.S.S.R. dropped out of the eastern sky. I remarked the alert, grave glances of my friends. Though the Scandinavians do not talk much about it, the menace of communistic Russia shadows their thoughts to a degree and touches them with natural anxiety. Just across the narrow Baltic stretches the Soviet Union with all its mortal potentiality. For centuries the Swedes had good cause to be apprehensive of imperial Russia's might. And now that Soviet Russia had swept into her freedomless orbit one after the other of the Eastern European states, Swedes fully realized the baleful threat to all they hold dear. At the moment of the plane's landing I recalled what a recent visiting Soviet commission had said to Gunnar

* By May 16, 1949, regular service was established to fifty-one cities in twenty-seven countries, including nine flights weekly to New York and two to Buenos Aires.

Andersson, the labor leader. "The Swedish living standards for workers are far too high; they must come down." Whether inadvertently or not, the Russian spokesman had had the effrontery to use the sinister word "must."

As early as the summer of 1946 there was a general worry all over Denmark, Norway, and Sweden that something even worse than a Nazi invasion of Scandinavia might come. There was the feeling, particularly in Denmark, that the United States had saved Europe from one ravaging foe only to leave the small countries at the mercy of a still more disrupting and destructive one.

When my own plane was called it was with some unexpressed apprehensive heartburning that I said good-by to my Northern friends. As we rose from the field and I looked down on the city of Stockholm, an involuntary swelling of affection and gratitude for its existence surged within me, followed by a sharp sense of concern for its near future.

The only serious flaw in the happy state of well-ordered Scandinavia is her geographic nearness to Russia. Social democracies that manage their commonwealths with such justice and fair division, and with such respect for the dignity of the individual are, by contrast, sharper thorns in the flesh of communistic regimes than the more capitalistic and imperialistic states. It is not difficult for the Communists to point out abuses in countries with mighty concentrations of industry and capital like the United States, but very hard indeed to find honest fault in social democracies where responsible Labor is in control and the well-being of the general citizenry has been a main objective for three decades.

As long as Russia bends her chief efforts at expansion or the reducing of other countries to subservience to Moscow, instead of concentrating on improving home conditions as the Scandinavians have done, there is no security in the North.

As our plane headed towards Norway, I recalled Mr. H. G. Wells' speech at a dinner given for him in Stockholm by Swedish writers in mid-September of 1939 after the war had begun. He emphasized his fervent hope that Sweden would not allow herself to become involved in what he then called "this aimless war." He urged the Swedes to hold to their traditional neutral policy, to keep their country intact as a model of democracy in order to point the way for the confused and broken people of strife-torn nations after the war was over. By maintaining her own peace, he said, the country could be a haven of refuge and assist materially in reconstruction.

Though Sweden did manage to escape virtually unscathed during the five years of destructive strife, and though she afforded a refuge for hundreds of thousands, including ninety per cent of Denmark's Jews, and helped tremendously in the rehabilitation work, World War II proved to the Swedes that minding one's own business is no guarantee of safety, as was too evident in the case of peace-loving but unprotected Denmark and Norway.

I had learned from many prominent sources during the summer of 1946 that the realistic Swedes were quite aware that, in a third world war, they might disappear as a nation. But I had also learned that the vast majority believed their best bet was still to stay clear of any Great Power alliances, a policy that had served them well for a hundred and thirty-odd years. "We are determined," Foreign Minister Undén had said to me, "to make sure that we have not challenged any of the mighty or offered anyone the slightest provocation for attack." (There is of course, it should go without saying, no question of "spiritual neutrality" in democratic Sweden, for no people could be more opposed to libertyless Communism.)

I had learned too that, having not too much faith in the United Nations' ability to maintain world peace, Sweden, instead of disarming, had methodically gone about strengthening her defenses since the victory celebrations. If an attempt were to be made to invade Sweden, I knew the people would put up a stout resistance, with all the vitality they display by their Olympic Game prowess.

But until such an unhappy day chanced, they would go on living their accustomed lives as normally as possible with cool heads and clear consciences. Despite the ever-present danger of dwelling as near neighbor to the one enemy who would uproot the fine culture the Swedes had evolved—the people of the United States protected by Western Europe and the broad Atlantic can know nothing about such natural dread—they maintained a remarkable tranquillity while they sharpened their vigilance.

As we sped above Sweden's September-colored fields and forests, en route to Oslo, my thoughts turned away from the disturbing pictures of possible war to one happy aspect of Swedish civilization after another. High in the list of blessed achievements was the fact that Swedish capital and labor have both acquired consciences. Though the unions demand adequate compensations for their workers, the workers give steady, thorough, conscientious labor in return. While the Swedes have never been an emotional people in their religious life, Christian morality has, since the end of the Viking era, been accepted as a guide for action. And Sweden had put her house in such good order that Communism within is no more a danger today than unconscionable individualism was thirty years ago. Swedes of all classes seem to have learned the simple truth that true liberty can exist only with order and virtue.

Except for the intensification of the cold war between Russia and the United States, the year 1948 passed happily for Sweden with excellent crops, an expanded industrial output, and a much improved foreign trade balance. As a ship-building nation Sweden ranked second after Great Britain in 1948. The only event to cause national—and international—mourning was the assassination near Jerusalem of Count Folke Bernadotte, the United Nations' chosen mediator in Palestine and the person who had perhaps done more to relieve wartime and post-war sufferers than any other individual.

While Sweden increased production and went on arming herself for defense, she continued to make life less burdensome in little ways for her least fortunate people. By the end of the year the Government could announce that ninety per cent of all Swedish farms and country homes were electrified, and it reckoned that within a very few years Swedish homes and farms would be one hundred per cent electrified—this in a land so sparsely populated that many remote northern farms seem almost inaccessible.

When the Executive Council of the Swedish Federation of Labor met in Stockholm in November it supported the Government in its attempt to halt the wage-price spiral. In its statement the Federation emphasized that under present conditions a continued improvement in the living-standard of the workers in Sweden "cannot be achieved by means of wage increases, but only on the basis of an expanded production." "The Trade Union Movement," it announced, "is prepared to cooperate with other groups to restore the balance in Sweden's economy."

With all that Sweden does for the general welfare, the budget estimates for the fiscal year beginning July 1, 1949, showed a surplus of $200,000,000, while taxes remained unchanged. In asking for increased appropriations for the defense budget in these critical times, even the Defense Minister stressed the importance of proceeding with caution. "For in the long run," he said, "even the national defense is dependent on the success of Sweden's export program and the restoration of balance in the country's economy."

During the last month of 1948 and the first months of 1949 the leaders of the three Scandinavian countries met many times in an attempt to agree to a Scandinavian defense pact by which Norway, Denmark, and Sweden would stand together in defense against foreign attack. Since no one pretended it was meant as anything but a defense against Russia, and everyone agreed that material aid from the West was necessary, Russia immediately regarded the move as "a breach of neutrality and an insult to the Soviet Union."

The Danish as well as the Swedish premier made strong appeals to the Norwegians to stick with them as the best possible solution of a dangerous situation. But the Norwegians could not bring themselves to accept the condition that the Scandinavian pact would have to be free of other alliances. By Sweden's offering to form a defense alliance with her kin countries, Norway and Denmark, which would plunge her into war the moment either Norway or Denmark was attacked, the Swedish policy of neutrality was deeply revised.

"But," so the Government ministers reiterated, "the Swedish people do not feel inclined any more now than at an earlier period to take a stand in a front position in such a way that they thereby commit themselves to take part in the cold war that is now going on. The fact that Sweden has been able to maintain peace during the past 135 years undoubtedly has had a great effect, psychologically, on the attitude of the Swedish people toward its security problem. . . . The explanations why we have escaped may vary, but in any case our people cannot easily be persuaded that their security now demands that we throw away our policy of neutrality as mistaken and outmoded."

Much of the American press, while whole-heartedly believing in the Atlantic Pact, yet wondered if a Scandinavia united in a military alliance, with material and moral support from the Western Powers, would not be at least as strong militarily as if the three Scandinavian countries separately joined the Atlantic security system.

Mr. Walter Lippmann seemed to back up the Swedish viewpoint. In his syndicated column of January 18, he wrote:

Is it wise, desirable, and right to treat countries which border on the Soviet military orbit in the same way as countries which do not? . . . The obvious Soviet reply (if Sweden joined the North Atlantic Security Pact) would be to invoke her treaty with Finland, then to occupy Finland, and thus advance her military bases within striking distance of Sweden. When we realize that Sweden is much the strongest military nation in Scandinavia, that it has what many consider the third air force in Western Europe, a very considerable navy in the Baltic, and an armaments industry which is far from negligible, are we not bound to think twice before we take any steps to bring the Red Army right up to the frontiers of Sweden? *

But on February 21 the Norwegian Foreign Minister Halvard M. Lange announced that Norway had decided to pin her security to the Atlantic Pact, and that she had reached her decision despite Soviet warning.

Denmark, as well as Sweden, deplored this ending of the hope for a Scandinavian defense alliance. Her premier, Mr. Hedtoft, spoke of it as a tragedy. But then, feeling forced to lean towards the Atlantic Pact, Denmark shortly sent her own foreign minister for conferences in Washington. With Sweden isolated in northern Europe, Swedish Premier Tage Erlander admitted that while his country faced increased risk, nevertheless Sweden would stick to her traditional neutral policy.

By the great majority of Swedes the Government's alliance-free policy is not looked upon as an escape from realities. It is regarded as the best possible, though far from perfect, means of securing Sweden's existence as a free nation. The advantages seem greater than the disadvantages. And there is certainly no lack of courage involved in standing on their own feet however isolated.

Many of the Swedish premier's subsequent statements have been a rephrasing of the sentiment, "Any attack from the outside will make us defend our liberty with all of our resources."

* Copyright 1949 by the New York Herald-Tribune Inc. Used with permission of the author.

The resources of Sweden are by no means inconsiderable. Since the end of the war and by the New Year of 1949 almost $280,000,000 worth of war material had augmented Sweden's national defense, which was in good condition in 1945. In December, the Government announced that a number of new armored divisions were to be added. New super-rapid automatic guns, designed especially for defense against jet-propelled aircraft and guided missiles have been developed at the Bofors ordnance plant in Värmland. The Bofors automatic guns, which achieved fame in the last war, have been improved both as to firing speed and target sighting, horizontally, as well as vertically, and the new guns are capable of following a target four or five times faster than before.

In February, Allan Vougt, the defense minister, reported that since the cessation of European hostilities a thousand war planes had been added to the Air Corps. Sweden was the first country to buy in England the famous Vampire jet planes. The Swedish SAAB Aircraft Company in Linköping has developed a new war plane known as the J-29, which is expected to reach a speed of 600 miles an hour. As an added defense measure the training of conscripts begins now a year earlier than previously, in the year in which a conscript reaches the age of twenty instead of twenty-one.

The somewhat bitter first reaction from the failure of the Scandinavian defense discussions was shortly followed by calm and even optimistic reflections. As partners in the Atlantic Pact, Denmark and Norway would receive rearmament material which will undoubtedly benefit all Scandinavia, and United States help to them will relieve Sweden of much of the burden of defending the Scandinavian sector.

The unprecedented North Atlantic Treaty, proposing for the first time in peace to bind America in an alliance with European nations was made public on March 18. By its terms the United States and Canada and ten nations in Europe were pledged to resist automatically an armed attack against any one of them.

On March 19, alarmed Moscow shouted that the North Atlantic Treaty meant war with the Soviet Union. But what the treaty says is that it could mean war only in the case of aggression against an alliance member. Nations of the West chose to read the treaty as designed for world peace—and in any case it presents a rather formidable barrier against a nation with aggressive designs.

Sweden was faced with the choice of clinging to lone neutrality or joining the western security bloc. And, until Norway and Denmark were rearmed by the United States, the defensive power of Sweden continued to be a decisive factor in the prevention of a possible quick occupation of Scandinavia.

At the end of April when I asked the clear-sighted Mr. Lippmann permission to use his understanding paragraph quoted above, he cautioned me to consider at least two very important things that had happened since he wrote that January article. "One is," he said, "that owing to public criticism in this country and to some extent abroad, the original idea of creating bases in Norway was formally abandoned and assurances given to the Soviet Union, which they have accepted. The other important development is that the Soviet Union has quite obviously entered into a policy of appeasement in Europe, and therefore the threat to Scandinavia is not at the present time a real one."

An air mail letter from a friend in Finland dated June 6, 1949, bore cheering tidings from that valiant country, and further direct reassurance. "The situation here has changed considerably. Last year we had a Communist as our Minister of the Interior and other Communists in the cabinet; but now we have not a single one, and the influence of the Communist party has decreased very much. Economically our situation has improved more than we could imagine a year ago. Clothes, shoes, milk, tobacco, petrol and even chocolate are no longer rationed. In 1948 it was the fashion to say, perhaps we too are soon behind the iron curtain like Hungary, Czecho-Slovakia and the others. Now nobody believes that any more. When Norway joined the Atlantic naturally we were somewhat nervous, fearing Russia would demand some military bases in North Finland, but now that worry, too, seems to be over."

What blesses Finland blesses her next-door neighbor on the west. And all the omens in June in Sweden were auspicious. In buoyant spirit and tanned from his Riviera vacation, King Gustav, without any signs of fatigue, led the annual celebration of Swedish Flag Day on June 6. When he appeared at the Stadium, the sun was shining beneficently. The aged monarch, who was to be ninety-one on June 16, sat through the whole proceedings and at the end led the traditional four cheers for the Fatherland.

No one in or out of Sweden can be sure of what the nation's future course in the field of international relations will be. Only of one thing can everyone be certain: never will Sweden fight on the side of Soviet Russia. In the late tension the Swedes continued to maintain all the quietude and grace in daily living possible, though they knew well enough:

> In a world of fugitives
> The person taking the opposite direction
> Will appear to run away.*

It was typical of social democratic Sweden that the latest Nobel Award for Literature could go to the poet who wrote these lines, and who knew they applied to himself as one who quietly defended the culture of a society of clearly marked classes. It was further proof that in this nation unsurpassed in deliberate social planning, with a Labor Government in dominance for a quarter century, the salt of distinction still has savor.

In the words of the brief analysis of the writing of T. S. Eliot, as spoken by the Secretary of the Swedish Academy that made the award, the attitude and quality of the Swedes themselves seem reflected. Mr. Eliot's poetry, the analysis said, "is marked by a strict sense of responsibility and an extraordinary self-discipline. It is alien to all emotional clichés, completely stark, rugged, and unadorned, but now and then illuminated by a sudden ray from the timeless region of miracles and revelations."

The Swedes, as I have remarked before, are the most thoroughly self-disciplined people on the globe, and they possess a profound yet unstrained sense of responsibility. They are not to be swept off their feet either by their own emotions or by any emotional propaganda foreign or domestic. Though simple and uncluttered and without superfluous richness as their modern culture is, it is marked by grace and dignity. And Swedes have had uncommon gleams of inspiration and put into practice untried things which have worked to the gratification of all.

Swedes do not blame what troubles they may have on the Machine

---

* From *The Family Reunion* by T. S. Eliot.

Age in which we live. They do not delude themselves with the rationalization that modern man is the victim of science and cannot help getting into a mess. They are not fatalistic, nor do they believe national or personal faults lie in the stars. They believe remedies and the powers of betterment lie within the character of men themselves.

Sweden's noted cleanliness, her old-age pensions, politeness, control of alcoholic consumption, art galleries, parks, athletics, lyric poetry, seamanship, cinema stars, taste in color, love of flowers, ancient castles, standard stainless-steel kitchens, scientific achievements, respect for the individual, orderly farms, honest politicians, cordiality between capital and labor, bounteous contributions to charity, community singing, adult education, smörgåsbord, puctuality, pride in workmanship, obedience to law, and admiration for distinction, are all symbols and manifestations of Swedish thoughts and ideals. These things reveal the amenities and the virtues of the Swedish heart and the Swedish mind. They are what the Swedes have made of their life.

If a third world war should come and Sweden could remain materially neutral, she would be a bulwark of strength for the *non-aggressor*. If she should again miraculously escape, her democratic ways might prove a guide in starting the world anew. But the mere thought of Sweden or the other Scandinavian nations destroyed by atom bombs or by enforced Communism tempts one to cry out with Milton:

> If this should fail
> The pillar'd firmament is rottenness
> And earth's base is built on stubble.

In this time of stress and anxiety, however, it is better to recall Whitehead who declares, "Peace is not the negative conception of anesthesis. Peace is the intuition of permanence."

ACKNOWLEDGMENTS AND BIBLIOGRAPHY

Acknowledgments

WHEN MY WIFE and I first arrived in Scandinavia early in 1939 we did not know personally a single Dane, Norwegian, or Swede except those we had met aboard the *Drottningholm*. I bore only one letter of introduction. But from the moment our ship docked in Göteborg we knew a friendly hospitality and found persons in every position generous in their assistance. I am deeply indebted to scores of Swedes who gave graciously of their time in assisting me with factual material or who entertained us in their homes.

For receiving me and being most helpful in suggestions, as well as instrumental in the arranging of interviews with certain individuals, I express gratitude to H.R.H. Crown Prince Gustav Adolf. For advice and for introductions in south Sweden, for entertainment, and for permission to quote from his book *This Land of Sweden,* I am deeply grateful to H.R.H. Prince Wilhelm. For especially heart-warming hospitality I am indebted to Lennart Bernadotte and his lovely wife Karin. I am grateful to the late Prime Minister, Per Albin Hansson, for his frank conversations, and to the gracious Mrs. Hansson who received me at their home. For introductions into the Stockholm social and artistic circles I am indebted to Mr. Thorsten Laurin, the publisher and art collector, and Mrs. Laurin, a lady unsurpassed in charm in all Scandinavia. To August Lindberg and the late Gunnar Andersson, successive heads of the Federation of Labor, I am grateful for long talks on the history of the labor movement. It was the first interview with Mr. Lindberg in 1939 that made me wish a man of similar calibre and heart could be the head of every labor federation in the world.

Among the current and recent Social Democratic cabinet ministers to whom I am most obligated for their time are Gustav Möller, Ernst Wigforss, Osten Undén, and Gunnar Myrdal. Sven Dahlman, chief of the Foreign Office press bureau, was unusually helpful in numerous ways.

I want to thank Dr. Gustav Munthe, present head of the Swedish Tourist Traffic Association for putting at my disposal all the assistance I needed from that excellent organization. The two persons who were perhaps the most helpful of all in making appointments and assisting me with the problems of travel were Gertrud Jungbeck in 1939 and Gunnar Rosvall in 1946, both of the Swedish Tourist Traffic Association and both untiring in their good offices. Miss Jungbeck possessed an extraordinary gift for winning friends for Sweden. Mr. Rosvall is a remarkable young man, who at twenty-seven spoke seven languages, including Russian. With his amiable disposition, keen sense of humor, discrimination and efficiency he proved more than valuable to my post-war work.

For courtesies and statistical information I want to thank Tore Tallroth, assistant manager of the Swedish Institute, and his charming wife, and Mac Lindahl, chief of the American-Swedish News Exchange in Stockholm.

In the world of business and industry I am indebted for hospitality and assistance to Per Norlin, the dynamic young head of Scandinavian Airline System, to Martin Waldenström, head of the Kiruna Iron Mines, to Sigfrid Edström, former president of Swedish General Electric Company (ASEA), to Erik W. Forsberg, manager of the Sandviken Steelworks, and to the late Henning Beyer, owner of Orrefors Glassworks, who died in the fall of 1948.

A man who has aided almost every alien who has written on Sweden in the last twenty years is Nils Horney, foreign editor of the Social Democratic labor paper *Morgontidningen*. To him, I, too, owe much, for his store of information and his friendship. And to Folke Thunborg, one-time secretary of the Social Democratic Youth Movement, and son of a former labor agitator, I am grateful for enlightening conversations before and after the war.

For numerous courtesies to my wife and myself I wish to thank Dr. Börje H. Brilioth, for many years editor-in-chief of the Liberal Party paper, *Stockholms Tidningen*. To Professor Bertil Ohlin, the brilliant present leader of the Liberal Party, I am indebted for a memorable afternoon at his home on Norr Mälarstrand in Stockholm.

The list of all those who offered us hospitality or rendered assistance is too long to recite, but among those whose appreciative guests we were I must mention Mrs. Ambra Neiglick, Miss Britt Arpi of Siljansborg, Baron and Baroness Göran von Essen and Mr. Axel Jonsson of Göteborg, Mrs. Sigrid Arpi-Bertil of Stockholm, Captain and Mrs. Gyllensvan of Gränna, Olof Nobel of Båstad, Henry Odén of Karlstad, Professor Hans Nilsson-Ehle at Svalöv, Ernst Norlind of Borgeby Castle, and Lars Hökerberg, who published my *South by Thunderbird* in Swedish. To the late Elsbeth Funck we are indebted for a long week-end at her estate in Södermanland and to Elsa Gullberg, the noted designer, for entertainment at her summer home in the Stockholm archipelago, where she gave me a key to the understanding of the decorative arts of Sweden.

No one could have been more gracious in hospitality and in taking us on motor excursions and in helping us in innumerable ways than the retired architect and metaphysician Count Sigge Cronstedt. To him we owe very special thanks for his assistance and his heartwarming friendship.

To Carl Milles, the sculptor, and Erik Wettergren, director of the National Museum, and Gerda Boëthius, director of the Anders Zorn Museum in Mora I want to express thanks for entertainment and talks on Swedish art.

I want to thank, too, Miss Alma Hedin, the doer of good works, and her famous brother, the explorer Sven Hedin, for their kindness and hospitality to my wife and me in 1939.

To G. Hilmer Lundbeck, late long-time United States head of the Swedish American Line, and to his son and successor, G. Hilmer Lundbeck, Jr., I am grateful for special courtesies to my wife and me aboard their ships in 1939. To Stanley Robbins of the American Overseas Airlines I express warm thanks for securing me space on a plane, when none seemed available in the summer of 1946, and for numerous pleasant introductions in Scandinavia, especially the one in Oslo to Dick Bennett, who drove me up to Lillehammer to visit Sigrid Undset when there was no space to be had on Norwegian trains.

I am more than grateful to Captain Sigfrid Ericson, formerly of the *Drottningholm* and now of the *Gripsholm,* for numerous courtesies and for personal introductions in Sweden, and for his coaching of my wife and me in the art of skåling on the high seas. And to Skåne-born Madeleine Hamilton, writer and designer of ski costumes, whom we met aboard ship, and to her mother Countess Hedvig Hamilton, who made us feel at home on our first arrival in Stockholm, my wife and I shall ever be grateful.

In 1946 I was particularly fortunate in having Allan Kastrup, now director of the New York office of the American-Swedish News Exchange, as a traveling companion in Lapland and later in his own native southern province of Skåne. I am deeply indebted to Holger Lundbergh, of the same organization, for help with research. To Birger Nordholm and the Swedish Travel Information Bureau in New York and the Swedish Tourist Traffic Association in Stockholm am I indebted for most of the photographs that illustrate this volume.

My thanks to the editors of *Travel Magazine* and the *American Swedish Monthly* for permission to reprint chapters in this book which were used as articles in these magazines.

Most of all I wish to express thanks to Naboth Hedin for invaluable help and counsel during the writing of the book. I have not found a Swede in Sweden who is more knowledgeable in Swedish history and affairs than this American Swede from a farm in Småland, who, after a few years of country schooling, came to this country as an immigrant lad speaking no English, and who within seven years was graduated from Harvard *cum laude.*

As always, I am full of gratitude for my wife's unflagging assistance and indispensable criticism, as well as her many typings of the script.

BIBLIOGRAPHY

Before the summer of 1937 I had read little enough about Scandinavia and less about Sweden than Norway or Denmark. Except for the dramatist August Strindberg, the literature of Sweden is not as impressive in English translation as that of Norway or Denmark. Strindberg is in fact the only Swedish author to whom the word "great" may be applied. Sweden's two most famous literary sons before the nineteenth century, Swedenborg, the scientist-mystic, and Linnaeus, the botanist, were only incidentally men-of-letters. Sweden has never produced any novelist to approach Sigrid Undset or Knut Hamsun of Norway, which also gave the world Henrik Ibsen. Sweden has no present-day novelist the equal of Haldór Laxness, the Icelander. Nor has Sweden produced any writer as famous as Denmark's Hans Christian Andersen. And no Swedish fictionist translated into English in the past dozen years has equaled the contemporary Danish tale-teller Isak Dinesen in either distinction or popularity. (All four of her books—one under a nom de plume—have been Book-of-the-Month Club selections, a record achieved by no other foreign writer.)

Many years ago I had dipped into Ellen Key's works and read the three best of Selma Lagerlöf, almost all of Strindberg's plays and Longfellow's translations of Tegnér. And, of course, I had read with delight Axel Munthe's international best seller *The Story of San Michele,* which has several chapters on his native land. Marquis Childs' illuminating *Sweden: the Middle Way* was the first book about Sweden by an American that I read. Then in 1937, inspired by that charming Norwegian idyll *Northern Summer* by the Swedish-born Gösta af Geijerstam, I began to read extensively about Sweden—its history and its contemporary way of life and more of its literature.

A bulk of information about Swedish democracy and politics and economics is to be found in brochures and periodicals. It is impossible to list all the magazine articles I have read on Sweden after 1937. Since 1921 there have been twenty-two articles in American magazines on Carl Milles, the Swedish sculptor. The pamphlets, brochures and magazine articles on Social Security, Adult Education and Housing pass the hundred mark and are too numerous to list. I have read some twenty articles on Agriculture, over thirty on Swedish Architecture, and just less than thirty on Cooperatives.

While I have profited by reading widely in pamphlets and periodicals, as well as the books listed in the following bibliography, my judgments have been formed by looking into things for myself and talking with countless persons of diverse opinions, and then coming to the conclusions herein set down. The bibliography's divisions into classifications called General, Travel, Fiction, *et cetera,* are purely arbitrary, for the reader's convenience, as suggestions for further reading in Swedish subjects.

I have my own favorites in various categories and, of course, there may be better books on some subjects which I have not read, or which have not been translated. Of contemporary Swedish fiction since 1934, which has been published in the United States, I recommend particularly the proletarian novels of Gösta Larsson: *Fatherland, Farewell* and *Our Daily Bread;* Vilhelm Moberg's *Memory of Youth* and *This Earth Is Ours;* and Gösta Gustaf-Janson's *The Old Man's Coming.*

The finest book on Swedish travel by a Swede is *This Land of Sweden* by Prince Wilhelm. The most appreciative estimate of Swedish travel by a European is found in *Travels in the North* by Karel Čapek. The most pleasing book to come out of England is perhaps Maxwell Fraser's *In Praise of Sweden.* The best written book on Swedish travel by an American is Agnes Rothery's *Sweden: the Land and the People.*

Significant books on Swedish themes to appear in English since the last war are David Hinshaw's *Sweden: Champion of Peace;* Signe Toksvig's *Swedenborg: Scientist and Mystic;* the revised 1946 edition of Marquis Childs' *Sweden: the Middle Way;* Iona Plath's *The Decorative Arts in Sweden;* and Adolph B. Benson and Naboth Hedin's *Americans from Sweden.*

For three varying views on Swedish history one may read *A Short History of Sweden* by Ragnar Svanström and Carl Fredrik Palmstierna; *A History of Sweden* by Andrew A. Stomberg, and *A History of Sweden* by Carl Hallendorff and Adolf Schück. I have found the first one the most scholarly and the most helpful.

The best articles on Sweden by an Englishman living in Sweden are those of G. Howard Smith, and, to me, the most attractive articles on Sweden by a Swede living in the United States are by Madeleine Hamilton. Among the Swedish Americans who write about Sweden for the American magazines Naboth Hedin, Holger Lundbergh, and Alma Luise Olson have been the most prolific and varied. In editorial circles Dr. Henry Goddard Leach of the *Scandinavian-American Review* and formerly editor of the *Forum* has been, for some three decades, a champion spokesman for Sweden, as well as the other Scandinavian countries. As a contemporary translator of Swedish poetry, Charles Wharton Stork is unquestionably the most inspired.

GENERAL

Bjarne Braatoy. *The New Sweden.*

Anders Örne. *Cooperative Ideals and Problems.*

Axel Gjöres. *Cooperation in Sweden.*

Ulla Alm. *Cooperative Housing in Sweden.*

Eric Cyril Bellquist. *Recent Foreign Policy of Sweden.*

Adolph B. Benson and Naboth Hedin. *Swedes in America.*

Folke Bernadotte. *The Curtain Falls.*

Marquis W. Childs. *This Is Democracy.*

Marquis W. Childs. *Sweden: the Middle Way.*

David Hinshaw. *Sweden: Champion of Peace*

Henry Goddard Leach. *Scandinavia of the Scandinavians.*

Alma Luise Olson. *Scandinavia, the Background for Neutrality.*

E. Söderlund and Naboth Hedin. *Outlines of Sweden.*

General Survey of the Trend of Economic Development.

Social Work and Legislation in Sweden.

Sweden Speaks. A New York World's Fair Publication.

Sweden Past and Present. Published by the Swedish Tourist Traffic Association.

Sweden, A Wartime Survey. Edited and published in Sweden with the assistance of Public Authorities.

Sweden, Trade and Industry. The General Export Association of Sweden.

The Sweden Year Book. Edited and published with the assistance of Public Authorities.

Iona Plath. *The Decorative Arts of Sweden.*

Erik Wettergren. *The Modern Decorative Arts of Sweden.*

Nils G. Wollin. *Modern Swedish Arts and Crafts in Pictures.*

Laurin, Hannover, and Thiis. *Scandinavian Art.*

Hakon Ahlberg. *Swedish Architecture of the 20th Century.*

Karl Asplund. *Anders Zorn, His Life and Work.*

John Nilsen Laurvik. *Anders Zorn.*

Swedish Food. Edited by Sam Widenfelt.

HISTORY

Carl Hallendorf and Adolf Schück. *History of Sweden.*

Andrew A. Stomberg. *A History of Sweden.*

Ragnar Svanström and Carl Fredrik Palmstierna. *A Short History of Sweden.*

Carl Grimberg. *A History of Sweden.*

B. J. Hovde. *The Scandinavian Countries, 1720-1865.*

Hendrik Willem van Loon. *The Adventures and Escapes of Gustavus Vasa.*

George Munn. *Gustavus Adolphus, the Lion of the North.*

Nils Ahnlund. *Gustav Adolf, the Great.*

Francis William Bain. *Christina, Queen of Sweden.*

Francis Gribble. *The Court of Christina of Sweden and the Later Adventures of the Queen in Exile.*

Faith Compton Mackenzie. *Christina of Sweden, the Sibyl of the North.*

Robert Nisbet Bain. *Charles XII and the Collapse of the Swedish Empire.*

John A. Gade. *Charles the Twelfth, King of Sweden.*

Robert Nisbet Bain. *Gustavus III and His Contemporaries.*

Dunbar Barton. *The Amazing Career of Bernadotte, 1763-1844.*

Franklin D. Scott. *Bernadotte and the Fall of Napoleon.*

TRAVEL

Robert Medill. *Sweden and Its People.*

Jan and Cora Gordon. *Two Vagabonds in Sweden and Lapland.*

Dudley Heathcote. *Sweden.*

Harry A. Franck. *A Scandinavian Summer.*

Agnes Rothery. *Sweden, the Land and the People.*

Sydney A. Clark. *All the Best in Scandinavia.*

Clara E. Laughlin. *So You're Going to Scandinavia.*

Serge de Chessin. *The Key to Sweden.* Tr. from the French by Alice Stael von Holstein.

Cicely Hamilton. *Modern Sweden.*

Karel Čapek. *Travels in the North.*

Prince William of Sweden. *This Land of Sweden.*

Maxwell Fraser. *In Praise of Sweden.*

Carl G. Laurin. *Stockholm Through Artist Eyes.*

Erik Asklund and K. W. Gullers. *Stockholm: Summer City.*

Johan Olafsson and S. Olesson Turi. *Turi's Book of Lapland.*

Olive Murray Chapman. *Across Lapland with Sledge and Reindeer.*

Thora Thorsmark. *Children of Lapland.*

FICTION

Frans G. Bengtsson. *Red Orm.* Tr. by Barrows Mussey.

Hjalmar Bergman. *God's Orchid.* Tr. by E. Classen.

Gustaf av Geijerstam. *Woman Power.* Tr. by Esther Rapp.

Gustaf av Geijerstam. *The Book About Little Brother; A Story of Married Life.* Tr. by Edwin Björkman.

Gustaf av Geijerstam. *My Boys.* Tr. by Alfhild Huebsch.

Gösta Gustaf-Janson. *The Old Man's Coming.* Tr. by Claude Napier.

Verner von Heidenstam. *The Tree of the Folkungs.* Tr. by A. J. Chater.

Verner von Heidenstam. *The Charles Men.* Tr. by Charles Wharton Stork.

Gösta Larsson. *Our Daily Bread.*

Gösta Larsson. *Fatherland, Farewell.*

Gösta Larsson. *Ordeal of the Falcon.*

Vilhelm Moberg. *Memory of Youth.* Tr. by Edwin Björkman.

Vilhelm Moberg. *The Earth Is Ours.* Tr. by Edwin Björkman.

Vilhelm Moberg. *Ride This Night.* Tr. by Henry Alexander.

August Strindberg. *The Confessions of a Fool.* Tr. by Ellie Schleussner.

August Strindberg. *The Red Room.* Tr. by Ellie Schleussner.

Sweden's Best Stories. Edited by Hanna Astrup Larsen. Tr. by Charles Wharton Stork.

SELMA LAGERLÖF

Selma Lagerlöf. *The Story of Gösta Berling.* Tr. by Lillie Tudeer and Velma Swanston Howard.

Selma Lagerlöf. *The Story of Gösta Berling.* Tr. by Pauline Bancroft Flach.

Selma Lagerlöf. *The Wonderful Adventures of Nils.* Tr. by Velma Swanston Howard.

Selma Lagerlöf. *Jerusalem.* Tr. by Velma Swanston Howard. Introduction by Henry Goddard Leach.

Selma Lagerlöf. *The Holy City—Jerusalem II.* Tr. by Velma Swanston Howard.

Selma Lagerlöf. *Mårbacka.* Tr. by Velma Swanston Howard.

POETRY AND OTHER LITERATURE

Anthology of Swedish Lyrics, 1750-1925. Tr. by Charles Wharton Stork.

Johan Ludvig Runeberg. *The Tales of Ensign Stål.* Tr. by Charles Wharton Stork.

Erik Axel Karlfeldt. *Arcadia Borealis.* Tr. by Charles Wharton Stork.

Poems by Tegnér: The Children of the Lord's Supper, and Fritiof's Saga. Tr. by Henry Wadsworth Longfellow and W. Lewery Blackley.

Esias Tegnér. *Fritiof's Saga.* Tr. by C. D. Locock.

Sweden's Laureate: Selected Poems of Verner von Heidenstam. Tr. from the Swedish, with an Introduction, by Charles Wharton Stork.

H. G. Topsoe-Jensen. *Scandinavian Literature from Brandes to Our Day.*

Louise Nyström-Hamilton. *Ellen Key; Her Life and Work.* Tr. by A. E. B. Fries, with notes by Havelock Ellis.

Edward L. Greene. *Carolus Linnaeus.* Introduction by B. W. Evermann.

B. D. Jackson. *Linnaeus.* Adapted from the Swedish by Th. M. Fries.

STRINDBERG

August Strindberg. *Plays.* Tr. by Edwin Björkman. The Scribner's Edition (4 volumes).

Lizzy Lind af Hageby. *August Strindberg, the Spirit of Revolt.*

Gustaf Uddgren. *Strindberg the Man.* Tr. with Introduction and Bibliography by A. J. Uppvall.

V. J. McGill. *August Strindberg, the Bedeviled Viking.*
G. A. Campbell. *Strindberg.*

SWEDENBORG

J. G. Duffy. *Swedenborg, the Scientist.*
George Trobridge. *Life of Emanuel Swedenborg.*
Signe Toksvig. *Emanuel Swedenborg: Scientist and Mystic.*
Emanuel Swedenborg. *Heaven and Hell.*
Emanuel Swedenborg. *The Divine Love and Wisdom.*
Emanuel Swedenborg. *The Divine Providence.*
Emanuel Swedenborg. *The True Christian Religion.*

SPECIAL PAMPHLETS

Odhe Thorsten. *Consumer Co-operation in Sweden's Economic Life.*
Albin Lind. *Popular Movements in Sweden.*
Tage Lindbom. *The Swedish Labor Program.*
Konrad Persson. *Social Welfare in Sweden.*
Gunnar Rudstedt. *Sweden Tries New Penal Methods.*
Thorsten Sellin. *Recent Penal Legislation in Sweden.*
Gösta A. Hall. *Sweden's Forest Industry in Peace and War.*
Anders Hedberg. *Consumers Cooperation in Sweden.*
Naboth Hedin. *Guide to Information About Sweden.*
Arvid Mygård. *Sweden's Public Health System.*
Gunnar Hirdman. *Adult Education in Sweden.*
Naboth Hedin. *Main Facts About Sweden.*
Bertil Kugelberg. *The Saltsjöbaden Agreements Between the Federation of Swedish Employers and the Federation of Swedish Trade Unions.*
Arvid Wallgren, M.D. *Some Aspects of the Medical Profession in Sweden.*
A Country Setting for Industry. Supplement to June 1947 issue of *Industria.*
A Phase of Contemporary Art. Stockholm: Swedish Institute.
A Short Account of the Organization and the Propaganda for Thrift of the Savings Banks in Sweden.
A Survey of Social & Labor Conditions in Sweden. Swedish Employers Association.

"*H S B*," *Cooperative Housing.*

Key to Swedish Taxes. Stockholm: Swedish Taxpayers Association.

Kommunernas Skoluppgifter (Municipal School Tasks). Stockholm: Tidens forlag.

Kooperativa Förbundet. Stockholm: Co-operative Union and Wholesale Society.

Sweden, Ancient and Modern. Stockholm: The Swedish Tourist Association.

The Post War Program of Swedish Labor. Stockholm: The Swedish Trade Union Federation.